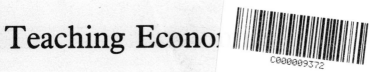

Teaching Econo...

Third Edition

Edited by
G. B. J. Atkinson, *senior lecturer in economics,*
Lancashire Polytechnic

Published on behalf of the Economics Association
Heinemann Educational Books

Heinemann Educational Books Ltd
22 Bedford Square, London WC1B 3HH

LONDON EDINBURGH MELBOURNE AUCKLAND
SINGAPORE KUALA LUMPUR NEW DELHI
IBADAN NAIROBI JOHANNESBURG
PORTSMOUTH (NH) KINGSTON

ISBN 0 435 33145 0

First published by the Economics Association 1967
Second edition first published by Heinemann Educational Books 1975
Reprinted 1980
Third edition 1985
Reprinted 1987

Typeset by Inforum Ltd, Portsmouth
Printed and bound in Great Britain by
Biddles Ltd, Guildford and King's Lynn

Contents

Part Four Methods and Techniques

Part Five Assessment

Contributors

Alain G. Anderton   Author and part-time teacher of economics, Codsall High School, Staffordshire.

Vivian Anthony   Headmaster of Colfe's School, London, and Awarder in economics, Oxford and Cambridge Board.

Brian Atkinson   Senior lecturer in economics at Lancashire Polytechnic, Preston.

Kenneth Brookes   Lecturer in education, Department of Educational Studies and Institute of Education, Hull University.

Willie Henderson   Lecturer in economics, Department of Extra Mural Studies, University of Birmingham.

Steve Hodkinson   Lecturer in education at Manchester University and deputy director of the Economics Education 14–16 Project.

Susan Holmes   Director of the Industry Project, 1981–4. Now Humanities Inspector, London Borough of Merton.

Steve Hurd   Senior lecturer in economics, North Staffordshire Polytechnic.

Daniel Jeffreys   Formerly Head of Department of Economics, Westminster School. Now senior economist, Economic Policy Department, CBI.

Barrie King   Head of School of Humanities and Business Studies, Barnfield College, Luton.

Thomas Linton   Lecturer in economics, Department of Economics and Business Studies, Moray House College of Education, Edinburgh.

Peter Maunder   Senior lecturer in economics, Loughborough University.

Richard A. Powell   Head of economics, Gaynes School, Upminster.

Keith Robinson   Director, Scottish Curriculum Development Service (Glasgow Centre).

Raymond Ryba   Senior lecturer in education, Manchester University, and director of the Economics Education 14–16 Project.

Simon Smith	Lecturer in economics and education, Brunel University.
Mike Tighe	Head of economics and business studies, Gateway VI Form College, Leicester.
Linda Thomas	Lecturer in economics education at the University of London Institute of Education and joint secretary of the Economics Research and Curriculum Unit.
Michael Webb	Lecturer in economics, Worcester College of Higher Education, and co-ordinator of the Hereford and Worcester Education and Industry Centre.
David Whitehead	Senior lecturer in education, University of London Institute of Education.
Roy Wilkinson	Reader in economics, Sheffield University and chairman and chief examiner for A-level economics, the Joint Matriculation Board.
Robert Wilson	Head of economics and business studies, Aberdeen College of Education.

Editorial Preface

In 1967 the Economics Association published *Teaching Economics* edited by Norman Lee. The primary purpose of this book was 'to take stock of the place of economics education in the wider context of education as a whole'. In 1975 a new edition was produced, again edited by Norman Lee but this time published by Heinemann Educational Books. In his foreword Norman Lee wrote, 'The purpose of the book is to review the place of economics education in the curriculum and to investigate the significance of developments in educational theory and practice for the teaching of economics. These developments are related to specific teaching situations and, wherever possible, include examples and information which will be of direct use to the teacher. Many of the contributions are liberally supplied with references so that the reader can follow up ideas and suggestions which, because of limited space, may have been briefly explained.'

That second edition had to be reprinted and the Economics Association felt that the time had come to produce a completely new edition which would reflect the developments that have taken place in the last decade. Although the editor and most of the contributors have changed, the essential purpose of the book remains as laid down in the second edition.

Teaching Economics is meant to be the standard work on the subject. While there are other excellent books covering particular aspects or giving helpful hints for teachers, *Teaching Economics* aims to analyse the underlying principles and concepts so that the teacher, an autonomous professional, can apply these generalizations to a specific situation. This situation may be an English secondary school, but the content of *Teaching Economics* is also useful for teachers in the rest of the UK, overseas, and those in further education.

Any undertaking such as this involves many people. Norman Lee gave me many helpful ideas. Pat Noble generously undertook to compose the index. A number of individuals, who must remain anonymous, made helpful comments on the first drafts of chapters. Laura Brown did much of the typing. Above all, I was helped by an editorial committee of Keith Robinson, Raymond Ryba, Linda Thomas and Robert Wilson who gave me invaluable advice. I am grateful to them all.

Happy teaching!

Brian Atkinson

Acknowledgements

The editor and publishers wish to thank all those mentioned in the sources for permission to reproduce copyright material, and The Controller of Her Majesty's Stationery Office, for permission to use Crown copyright material.

Thanks are also due to the following for permission to use questions from their examinations:

Joint Matriculation Board

Northern Ireland Schools Examinations Council

Oxford and Cambridge Schools Examination Board

Southern Regional Examinations Board

University of Cambridge Local Examinations Syndicate

University of London University Entrance and School Examinations Council

University of Oxford Delegacy of Local Examinations

Introduction

Growth and development

Over the last thirty years, the teaching of economics has shown a remarkable growth, though future prospects are full of uncertainties.

In the mid-1950s a sub-committee of the Economics Association wrote a small pamphlet on the teaching of economics and began by saying:

attempts to teach the subject of economics in some form are being made in many schools. Until recently, the subject was taught mainly under the guise of current affairs or citizenship and very little organised knowledge emerged. This may have led to more *mis*-understanding than understanding . . . often the subject is approached from the viewpoint of commerce. Since powers of deduction and abstract reasoning do not usually develop much before the age of 16, Economics teaching before this age must be largely descriptive. . . . Intensive economic analysis is not attempted until the VIth form.[1]

At that time only 1.2 per cent of boys and only 0.7 per cent of girls taking at least one O-level chose economics. The position was rather better at A-level, though it was still a minority subject chosen by only 5.0 per cent of boys and 1.3 per cent of girls taking at least one A-level.[2]

The Association's pamphlet both reflected the growing importance of economics as a school subject and was a cause of future growth. Economics – or political economy – has had some place in the school curriculum for a long period; for example, Malthus taught it to the cadets of the East India Company at Haileybury College,[3] but this was unusual. Until the 1930s the study of economics in schools was largely confined to the third-year sixth form where candidates for the Oxford and Cambridge Scholarship Examination took it in preparation for the General Paper.[4] In the 1930s university examination boards adopted a syllabus for the Higher School Certificate which included economics together with economic history, politics and British constitution in imitation of Oxford's PPE course (philosophy, politics and economics). However, these developments affected very few pupils and for some years after the Second World War economics as a subject was not to be found on the timetable of most schools.

To some extent, the rise of economics in schools was one aspect of an overall 'boom' in social science. In the 1950s and 1960s the world experienced considerable social and economic change and the universities responded by enlarging social science departments. New universities were founded and the first polytechnics designated; all of which gave some prominence to economics and the other social sciences. These developments fed down into the schools, particularly the sixth forms, where Say's Law, for once, had some validity as the increased supply of social science graduates moved into teaching and persuaded head teachers to introduce their subjects.[5]

Table 1.1   GCE and CSE entries in economics 1951–81, England and Wales

	GCE A-level		GCE O-level		CSE	
	Entries	Rank	Entries	Rank	Entries	Rank
1951	1,181	—	1,593	—	—	
1956	2,653	—	2,825	—	—	
1961	6,134	15/36	6,993	24/44	—	
1966	17,341	8/40	23,729	21/46	2,838	19/30
1971	26,454	7/38	26,871	12/46	17,450	18/38
1976	35,451	7/40	42,162	15/51	109,888	8/41
1981	42,596	5/40	43,321	17/50	18,995	15/38

Source: DES, Statistics of Education (HMSO).
Notes:
1. The figures for 1981 are for England (not England and Wales).
2. The figures for O-level for 1966 and 1971 include British constitution.
3. The figures for CSE in 1971 and 1976 are for economics and social studies; hence the apparent fall in 1981.
4. By 'rank' is meant the 'popularity' of the subject. Thus in 1981 out of forty subjects listed, economics was the fifth most popular at A-level.

The results can be seen in Table 1.1. Economics was seen as a subject for the clever child. At CSE it remained a very rare subject throughout the period. Even at GCE O-level it was a minority choice, and the figures in the table may give a misleading impression of the position of economics for children aged 16 or under, because many of the O-level candidates were actually to be found in sixth forms or in colleges of further education. Most pupils under 16 were not taught economics, though the position was a little brighter if a broad definition of the subject is adopted, for subjects such as commerce and social studies were rather more popular and included some aspects of the subject.

At GCE A-level, economics has shown enormous growth, though here again the figures may be misleading for the number of students taking business studies has also increased considerably. Some sixth forms learn elements of economics as part of general broadening courses or as part of general studies where questions such as What are the likely consequences of a continued high level of unemployment for Britain? What action is being taken to try to reduce unemployment at the present time and how effective is it? (JMB, 1979) illustrate the approach.

The growth has not been merely quantitative. The most notable development in recent years has been the Economics 14–16 Project, sponsored by the Economics Association after considerable effort. The first phase of the project was concerned with research to analyse the position with regard to the current teaching of economics and conducted surveys of teachers and children to ascertain present practice and possible future development.[6] This was funded by the Esmée Fairbairn Charitable Trust, and largely as a result of their continued support, a second phase based at Manchester University developed exemplar materials for use in schools and in 1983 was followed by a third phase concerned with dissemination. These activities should lead to an increase in the number of children of this age group learning economics; equally important, they should lead to an improvement in the *quality* of economics teaching. The opinion expressed in the 1950s suggesting that economics teaching before the age of 16 must be descriptive has been shown to be incorrect.

The large-scale project is not the only way in which economics teaching has developed. The second edition of *Teaching Economics* edited by Norman Lee[7] was followed by other publications that improved the way economics teachers thought about their subject. Thus *Extending Economics within the Curriculum*[8] was concerned with the teaching of economics to younger and less-able children and the *Handbook for Economics Teachers*[9] gave a mass of practical suggestions designed to help the teacher in the classroom. Numerous economics textbooks appeared that were vastly superior to their predecessors and the Association's journal *Economics*[10] continued to inform and educate its readers.

The improvements in teaching were reflected in, and encouraged by, changes in the assessment procedures adopted by the GCE boards. When the first edition of *Teaching Economics* was published in 1967, all the examination boards had a similar examination for A-level: two papers each of 2½ or 3 hours, both requiring essay-type answers. By the second edition in 1975 most boards had included multiple-choice questions and in turn this was followed by the inclusion of data-response questions. These changes discourage candidates from concentrating on one or two syllabus areas and regurgitating notes from textbooks. Data-type questions also encourage better methods of teaching. There is little doubt that A-level economics is a more formidable subject than it was twenty years ago.

So far this introduction has been concerned with the situation in England and Wales, though many of the developments in economics teaching either originated or were paralleled in Scotland where there have also been considerable changes. Until the late 1960s the economics content in terms of theory/analysis/policy was very limited, though there was some 'economic organization' and economic history. In 1969 a new Higher Grade syllabus in economics was introduced and this was followed in 1974 by a new, more satisfactory, syllabus at O-grade. In the same period new syllabuses were introduced in modern studies that included a significant element of economics. These developments no doubt influenced the Munn Report on the curriculum in Scottish secondary schools which recommended 'that all pupils undertake the study of one of the social subjects' and that 'all pupils in S3 or S4 should undertake the study of certain units of work which deal with the political, economic, industrial and environmental aspects of life in modern society'. The Report also placed economics as one of the subjects in the core area of the curriculum.[11]

The Scottish involvement in economics education was also to the fore in the work done at the Esmée Fairbairn Research Centre at Heriot-Watt University where a series of investigations into various aspects of the subject has led to a number of publications[12] and is influencing the teaching of economics throughout the UK.

Problems and uncertainties

Despite these encouraging developments, problems persist and the future looks far from untroubled. The growth of economics as a school subject tends to conceal a persisting lack of appeal to girls, as can be seen in Table I.2.

Table 1.2   Comparison of boys' and girls' entries and passes in economics, England 1981

		Entries	Passes as % of entries
A-level	Boys	27,464	62.8
	Girls	15,127	56.6
O-level	Boys	25,466	53.4
	Girls	17,855	48.5
CSE	Boys	9,426	12.9
	Girls	9,569	17.2

Source: DES, *Statistics of School Leavers* (HMSO, 1981).
Note: 'Pass' is defined as grades A–E at A-level, A–C at O-level and grade I at CSE.

Only at CSE do more girls than boys take economics and are more likely to obtain a grade I pass. However, the numbers involved are so small in comparison to the large numbers taking CSE that no reliable conclusions can be drawn from this tiny group. The overall situation is that girls are much less likely to take economics and that even when they do, they are likely to obtain poorer grades. There are several possible explanations for this. Most plausibly, this is a specific case of the general pattern that girls are less likely to take science and mathematical subjects; in other words, girls perceive economics as a 'boy's subject' and are therefore less likely to choose it or to do well at it than boys. This perception may be reinforced by the way economics is taught. First, most economics teachers are male – only about 15 per cent of members of the Economics Association are women. (The position in Scotland is rather different, as large numbers of women hold the Diploma in Commerce and teach economics alongside accounts and secretarial studies.) Textbooks are also frequently male orientated. Thus Stanlake's *Introductory Economics* – one of the most popular textbooks – contains sentences such as 'the individual is constantly confronted with this problem of choice. *He* has a limited income and must therefore choose between alternatives when *he* spends *his* income. *He* must decide' (my italics).[13]

There is no reason arising from the nature of the subject, nor from the nature of the sexes, why economics should not be as popular with girls as it is with boys. The problem is deep-seated and will doubtless persist, though teachers' understanding that a problem exists may ameliorate the position, and changes in society as a whole may cause more girls to take scientific subjects.

Further education is a second problem area. The FE sector grew considerably in the 1970s and, although separate figures are not available, it is probable that there was a continuous growth in the number of students taking O- and A-level economics in colleges. The FE sector also provides courses for professional examinations in sectors such as banking, and for occupations like company secretaries. Courses such as these include a good deal of economics. This area continued to grow. The real difficulties arose with the growth of the Business and Technician Education Council (BTEC, formed by amalgamations of the Business Education Council (BEC) and the Technical Education Council (TEC)) and its Scottish equivalent. This organization oversees and moderates courses at three levels, General, National and Higher. In 1981–2 some 54,000 students took BEC courses, of whom 58 per cent were female.[14] The main economics input into these courses is at National and Higher level; National is very roughly equivalent to GCE A-level, though much more business-oriented. With the growth of BEC, the role of economics has been downgraded; previously it had stood as a separate subject in its own right and as a compulsory subject in many business courses. Under BTEC the main economics input at National level is as part of a module 'the Organization in its Environment' where economics (mainly micro) is integrated with law and politics. At Higher level, colleges devise their own courses under advice from BTEC and there is no overall uniform pattern, though economics usually appears as an interdisciplinary part of a core module. Many BTEC courses are now taught in schools.

Thus economics has moved from being an independent compulsory subject in many courses to becoming part of a module. The change has caused considerable problems for economics teachers in FE, not least because of the difficulties inherent in an interdisciplinary approach. Moreover, the type of economics in BTEC is often unsatisfactory as it is tied too closely to a behavioural objectives approach which may well be inappropriate for the subject.

In recent years there has been a continuing debate about the kind of curriculum suitable for pupils in the years before the end of compulsory education. A number of official documents in this area have stressed the importance of children understanding 'industry'. For example, the DES consultative document *A Framework for the School Curriculum* emphasized that 'substantial attention should be given at the secondary stage to the relationship between school work and preparation for working life. Pupils need to acquire an understanding of the economic basis of society and how wealth is created.'[15] Properly interpreted this could lead to a development of courses that would enhance economic understanding among school leavers; what is quite probable is that a study of 'how wealth is created' will be taken to mean some generalized description of the importance of manufacturing industry.

A more direct threat to economics in schools arises from the twin phenomena of falling rolls and cuts in education spending. These cause schools to review their curricula. In many cases, faced with fewer teachers, they may choose to cut options such as economics. It may well be that economics as a separate subject on the school curriculum will cease to grow and perhaps decline for those aged 16 and under. Its future for this age level may lie as part of multidisciplinary courses. Properly constructed, such courses can provide valuable opportunities for learning economics.

The structure of this book
These possibilities and problems form the background to the rest of this book.

Part One   The Nature of Economics Education
Part One aims to analyse some of the basic theoretical issues that affect the teaching of economics. Chapter 1 is concerned with the essential nature of economic knowledge. This is intended to stimulate teachers to think about the subject itself, and its difficulty should not detract from the importance of the content. Chapter 2 discusses the purposes of teaching the subject and this leads in Chapter 3 to an analysis of the

psychological background of learning economics and its implications for teaching. These three chapters contain some original and controversial ideas and are meant to stimulate economics teachers into analysing the background to their pedagogy. To paraphrase Keynes, 'Practical men who believe themselves to be exempt from any intellectual influences are usually the slaves of some defunct pedagogue.'

The final chapter in Part One (Chapter 4) is concerned to help the teacher become more aware of the problem of values in economic education. All of us have political and ideological beliefs that may influence our teaching and pupils are often unaware of their own values. These can be clarified and examined in an economic context.

Part Two Teaching Economics in Specific Contexts
The chapters in this part of the book look at particular environments (such as the primary school), and the authors are concerned to answer the question: 'What are the problems and possibilities in this situation?' They are thus concerned not only with the nature of economics and the content required, but also with the context in which it is taught and with the methods that should be adopted to maximize the learning possibilities.

Part Three Economics Across the Curriculum
This part is largely concerned with the contribution that economics can make in a wider curriculum context. Chapter 9 sets the scene and analyses economics as part of an integrated approach while the remaining chapters are concerned with specific aspects – such as economics teaching and industry.

Part Four Methods and Techniques
The title of this part is fairly self-explanatory. However, while aiming to provide guidance in the use of techniques and methods, the emphasis is less on 'tips for teachers' than on the underlying rationale of the techniques and methods, so that teachers can apply the general points to their own specific circumstances.

Part Five Assessment
Chapter 19 in Part Five seeks to help teachers assess how well they are doing so that changes can be made where satisfactory learning does not seem to have taken place. Chapter 20 examines the problems and principles involved in the examination of economics at 16+ and concentrates on GCE O- and CSE-type examinations while Chapter 21 focuses on 18+ exams.

Conclusion

There is no single master blueprint for the teaching of economics. The editor, with the help of the editorial board, has sought to set out a structure for the book and has chosen topics that will be of help to the majority of teachers of economics. Inevitably though, some topics have had to be discussed only briefly or are not mentioned at all. Moreover, within the general constraints laid down, each chapter is the responsibility of the individual author and consequently some differences in treatment and judgement occur. As Lee pointed out in his foreword to the second edition, this 'places the responsibility for the *final* judgement on issues of economics teaching where it can only belong – with the individual teacher or lecturer'.

Notes and references

1. Edwards, G.J., Phillips, R.F.R., and Ryba, R.H., *The Teaching of Economics* (Economics Association undated, probably 1955).
2. Holley, B., and Skelton, V., *Economics Education 14 – 16* (NFER, 1980) p. 1.
3. James, P., *Population Malthus: His Life and Times* (Routledge & Kegan Paul, 1979).
4. Ciano, J.D.L., and Phillips, R.F.R., *The Economics Association and the Development of Economics* (Economics Association, 1977).
5. Szreter, R., 'The subject teaching periodical and curriculum innovation: the case of *Economics* and economics in English schools 1949–74', *Journal of Curriculum Studies*, vol. 13, no. 2, 1981, pp.103–11.
6. Holley and Skelton, op. cit.
7. Lee, N., *Teaching Economics*, 2nd edn (Heinemann Educational Books, 1975).
8. Robinson, T. K., and Wilson, R.D., *Extending Economics within the Curriculum* (Routledge & Kegan Paul, 1977).
9. Whitehead, D. (ed.), *Handbook for Economics Teachers* (Heinemann Educational Books, 1979).
10. *Economics* is published by the Economics Association, Temple Lodge, South Street, Ditchling, Sussex BN6 8UQ.
11. *The Structure of the Curriculum in the Third and Fourth Years of the Scottish Secondary School*, The Munn Report (HMSO, 1977).
12. For example, Lumsden, K.G., Attiyeh, R.E., and Scott, A., *Economics Education in the United Kingdom* (Heinemann Educational Books, 1980); and Lumsden, K.G., and Scott, A., 'The efficacy of innovative techniques in economics: the UK experience', *American Economic Review*, May 1983.
13. Stanlake, G.F., *Introductory Economics*, 2nd edn (Longman, 1971).
14. Business Education Council, *Annual Report, 1981–82*.
15. Department of Education and Science and Welsh Office, *A Framework for the School Curriculum* (HMSO, 1980) p. 33.

Part One
The Nature of Economics Education

1 The Nature of Economic Knowledge
Daniel Jeffreys

Introduction

When we teach economics we teach more than just another set of techniques. We teach a unique perspective, a way of thinking. If our teaching is to be effective this perspective must penetrate through particular detail with enough force to allow our students to emerge possessing that perspective. Before we can achieve this we must subject our discipline to close examination. This examination involves specifying to ourselves the elements of the economic perspective. But this cannot be achieved without establishing the nature of economic knowledge.

In line with these assumptions, this chapter will discuss the nature of economics, briefly analysing the significance of its roots and more substantially exploring its structure, language and mode of inquiry. The chapter will conclude with some comments upon the relationship between the nature of the discipline and the function of the economics educator; those who are already tempted to cry foul on the grounds of their belief that this relationship is all one way should hear the argument out – they may find some surprises in store!

However, before we can embark upon our exploration of economic knowledge we must make some preparations. We cannot hope to specify the nature of economic knowledge until we have developed some awareness of the nature of knowledge in general. This means developing an awareness of the function of disciplines as organizers of particular types of experience around distinctive concept groups.

The nature of knowledge

Few theories of knowledge now retain the belief that propositions describing human experience can be immutable. Instead, theories of knowledge currently tend to accept that experiences and the language used to describe those experiences are in two different categories. The difficult task is to build scientifically convincing relationships between the two. This is always seen as difficult because linguistic experience does not give direct access to 'raw' experience. Any experience will always be mediated through language, with the end result that a decisive empirical refutation of a proposition is always just out of reach. This led knowledge theorists to the belief that disciplines, and individual theories within those disciplines, are deductive rather than inductive structures.

To argue the case for deductive structures is to make two assumptions. The first is that a theory built inductively would be deceptive because the 'raw' experiences that provided the material for the induction would not be 'raw' at all. In order to get access to those experiences, a linguistic structure would have to be imposed upon the data and this structure would contain many implicit assumptions drawn from existing theoretical presuppositions.

Second, given that the data will be absorbed through a linguistic structure, with its implicit assumptions, it is better to make this 'drawback' explicit by starting from assumptions. In effect, by starting with a world vision or a paradigm or a hard core, these assumptions would permit the deduction of hypotheses that could be tested against the various interpretations of received data. This allows for two forms of appraisal: an internal one expressed in terms of the degree of logical consistency between the elements of the theory, and an external one expressed in terms of the success with which the theory can accommodate agreed counter-instances from experience without disturbing the logical consistency of the theory or producing tautologies.[1]

The literature assessing the methodology of economics is dominated by the methodology of scientific research programmes (MSRP) technique developed by Imre Lakatos.[2] In the MSRP, knowledge is regarded as a function of the accuracy of the language through which we interpret reality. However, that language never interprets reality with complete success: thus the need for abstraction and generalization. Reasoning from this assumption concerning the descriptive failure of language, MSRP assumes that the core of theories will be removed as far from reality as possible. Indeed, in most cases the core will be a set of *a priori* propositions. The clear implication here is that it would be fatal for the core of a theory to attempt to be descriptive because this would leave it directly open to test; whereas the whole point of the core is to protect the overall perspective of the theory because direct empirical confrontation is not the perspective's function.

The structure of the core is determined by the attempt to assess what the world would look like if it perfectly conformed to the objective of the theory.[3] For example, an objective of economic theory is to describe the conditions for the optimal allocation of resources. Rather than devising a theory inductively from experience to describe these conditions, neoclassical economics builds an *a priori* model – perfect competition – which would generate the optimal allocation in a frictionless world. Reality is then analysed in terms of its degree of conformity with this limiting case. As will be seen presently, it is both a strength and weakness of this procedure for economic theorists that it does not require abandoning the core of the theory if an empirical counter-instance occurs. In effect, the core carries with it the characteristics of the discipline. Specify the contents of the core and the theories deriv-able from the core, and you have partly specified the characteristics of a particular form of knowledge.[4]

Knowledge and the nature of economic knowledge

Two conclusions follow from this discussion of the knowledge process that are important for our quest. First, a necessary condition for any knowledge of empirical reality is the development of a core of assump-tions established prior to experience to guide our research. This condition carries the requirement that the core be conceptual. The core must be a set of concepts defining a perspective that in combination generate, as a matter of logic, statements that will in turn function as testable propositions.[5] Determining the nature of a particular form of knowledge is partly to determine the assumptions that define that form's core. This in turn amounts to determining the form's key concepts. Thus to specify the nature of economic knowledge is partly to specify its core or its key concepts.

Second, a further necessary condition for knowledge is that we have some programme that will allow us to suggest how we can travel from the core vision to the complex and confusing events of the real world. This is essentially the method used to convert the core assumptions. These start off as deterministic truths of logic and they need to be converted into more open-ended hypotheses concerning tangible events. This conversion process is the methodology of the discipline. However, because this methodology determines the field of contact between the theory and those aspects of reality it seeks to describe, it also helps to decide what will be 'known' at the end of the process. Not all methodologies are the same, either in terms of particular theories or whole disciplines, and the nature of the methodology chosen will help determine the nature of the knowledge produced by the discipline. It is partly because both the core and the methodology of economic science are highly deductive that it is so difficult to produce decisive refutations of either individual propositions or whole theories. Evidence for this argument is widespread and no more so than in the parallel develop-ment of sophisticated econometric theories and evidence in both Keynesian and monetarist macroeconomics.

Thus, we have seen that to specify the characteristics[6] of the dis-cipline and hence its nature, is partly to specify its methodology. Given that the key concepts and the methodology both partly determine the nature of the discipline, if we take the two together we should be as close as we need to be to a complete statement of a discipline's nature. That economics might be fruitfully analysed in this way can be demonstrated through this statement from Keynes:

It seems to me that economics is a branch of logic, a way of thinking . . . one can make some quite worthwhile progress merely by using the axioms and maxims. But one cannot get very far except by devising new and improved models. . . . But it is the essence of a model that one does not fill in the real values for the variable functions. To do so would make it useless as a model. For as soon as this is done, the model loses its generality and its value as a mode of thought.[7]

Keynes has summarized here the elements of the argument as it has now been presented and as it will be pursued in the particular field of economics. Disciplines are specialized forms of linguistic structure. These structures produce distinct ways of thinking. These distinct modes of thought are embodied in the discipline's models and in the way in which these models are compared with those elements of reality that the methodology of the discipline can adequately identify. We begin our application of these observations to economics through a cursory examination of the discipline's roots.

The historical basis of the deductive approach:
(i) Smith and Ricardo

There are two points in the development of economics where the discipline shunned induction as the basis of its approach and opted instead for deductive procedures. Both occurred as the discipline was laying down roots and hence dictated the pattern for later growth. One occurred at the root of classical theory, one at the root of neoclassical theory. In the latter case, induction was finally cast off as an engine for the production of theory. As Katouzian puts it: 'the progress of economic ideas was accompanied by a gradual evolution in the methods of economic analysis, broadly speaking, from a partial concrete and causally empirical, to a general abstract and deductive approach.'[8] Adam Smith (1723–90) is acclaimed as the author of the first serious work of political economy, but his successor, David Ricardo (1772–1823), was the more influential in terms of the development of the essential characteristics of economic science. Adam Smith was pragmatic in his outlook and this is reflected in the fact that all his work constantly repudiates the claim that he was a 'pure speculator'. In the *Wealth of Nations* Smith constructed a system that was partly logical and partly empirical. Katouzian has said of him that, 'He was content to face a conflict between fact and theory and leave it at that, without suppressing either.'[9] It is because Ricardo believed that one had to be suppressed that a crucial methodological break occurs where Ricardo takes over the work of Smith.

The problem that most concerned the classical economists was the theory of value or, more explicitly, the problem of how value was distributed to the factors of production. Smith's resolution of the problem is essentially inductive, in that it rests upon observations made of what would be a reasonable distribution from the perspective of experience of the state of nature. However, there is an inconsistency between the logically inducible position that in the state of nature, goods are exchanged according to the ratio of their labour content, and the need to account for the private ownership of land and capital in a developing industrial economy. Smith settled the problem for himself by retaining his labour theory while associating it with a raw descriptive statement that the value of product was divided between rent, profit and wages. This settlement is a good example of the tensions that exist between any theory attempting to characterize some essential aspects of behaviour with the use of *ceteris paribus* conditions, and the need to give determinate values to variables that constantly change the nature of the behaviour that is being described. In short, if one makes a decision, for example about the range of interest rate movements, this can help decide what actual movements occur. Ricardo looked at these kinds of tensions and decided that they were unacceptable. Ricardo argued that the tension could be resolved by the promotion of a purely speculative method. His work relies upon the laying down of general assumptions from which are derived 'sets' of laws determining the likely sequence of behaviour. As Katouzian has argued:

[Ricardo] . . . was the founder of 'pure economic theory' as an almost autonomous exercise in pure logic. All that was needed was a few assumptions and the rest would follow. If the resulting theories were logically consistent they would be true and acceptable; if not, they would be false and should be rejected. This became the sole criteria of success for a theory.[10]

Thus, at this crucial point in the development of economic theory and methodology the discipline received a decisive jolt towards deductive technique. The significance of this is greater than appears at first sight. A deductive system requires certain pure universals at its heart; that is, concepts that are self-defining and that apply in any contexts where they or their derivatives are represented. In addition, when all values of the concepts in the system are specified, the system must be in logical equilibrium, that is, there must be no inconsistencies.

An obvious 'universal' candidate for Ricardo was the 'rationality' that led to a uniform ratio of values in general equilibrium. What is important here is that a chosen method has specified an outlook regarded as optimal for the problems presented by reality, for example, general equilibrium as a solution to the need for efficient resource allocation in a constrained environment. This outlook has in turn required a concept that would be consistent with the method, that is, rational maximization. Ricardo's retreat from the problems of matching fact and theory led to the first formulation of a version of economics that was essentially a linguistic structure with internal criteria of meaningfulness; that is, the grammar and the syntax of the structure were defined by an assumed perspective.[11] Given that Ricardo's formulation provides part of the bedrock of contemporary economic knowledge, this is a development of fundamental importance.

The historical basis of the deductive approach: (ii) Psychology repulsed

The second development occurred as neoclassical economics was attempting to settle an issue at the root of its system of appraisal.[12] This was the issue of how best to handle the concept of 'utility'. In pursuit of a solution, a fierce battle was fought between those who believed that 'utility' should be given an empirical meaning grounded in psychology, and those who believed that the discipline would fall to the charge of psychologism unless it developed a theory of utility that was neutral with regard to any particular experience of satisfaction.

It is not the function of this chapter to discuss the battle in detail,[13] rather to report its resolution. The development of the Slutzky–Hicks–Allen techniques of indifference analysis in the 1920s and 1930s killed off the idea that psychology could contribute to utility theory. One result of the development of indifference theory was to make such a contribution seem superfluous. What is important to us are the arguments used against the protagonists of a psychological contribution and the effects of the triumph of those arguments on traditional theory.

The views of Knight are representative of the reaction to the use of psychology in economic models. As Coats has reported, Knight argued that: 'the basis of a *science* of conduct must be fixed principles of action, enduring and stable motives. It is doubtful, however, if this is fundamentally the character of human life.'[14] In a later work Knight claims: 'there are no laws regarding the *content* of economic behaviour, but there are laws universally valid as to its *form*'.[15]

The emphasis here is upon seeing economic knowledge as distanced from its subject-matter, experience of which is viewed as explicitly subjective. The only way enough critical distance can be established to allow the discipline its claims to scientific objectivity is through making statements of a logical nature about the *form* of behaviour, not its content. Thus an indifference map makes reference to the form of behaviour, that is, the constraint of a general maximizing law, through the use of ordinal as opposed to cardinal measures. As evidence of the methodological continuity of this view, compare the second of the two quotations from Knight with the earlier quotation from Keynes. Their implications are identical.

The implications for traditional theory of its victory over the psychologists are important, because the core of the discipline was not merely preserved intact. As Coats puts it:

the hard core of economic theory was . . . reinforced, as its key terms were more carefully specified . . . the fundamental assumption, which had earlier been identified with the popular notion of the economic man, was reformulated in less objectionable terms as the abstract concept of rationality, or the logic of choice.[16]

Thus the result of this successful defence was a reinforcement of the earlier victory of deductive *a priori* logic in the battle for the direction of economic methodology. By the end of the 1920s the essential components of microeconomic theory had been established.[17] They amounted to the belief that basic economic theory is necessarily abstract, static and general in form. This implies that the fundamental assumptions of economic theory must be simple, uniform and constant; they can be neither too 'realistic' nor directly subject to falsification.

We are now in a position to claim that whatever the core of economic science, its methodology is essentially a matter of deductive analysis. As economic educators, we must realize the important implications of this. We have to find ways of showing our students how the manifestly practical reality of economic life can be analysed meaningfully via a structure that deliberately distances itself from that reality – the familiar 'what's-the-point-of-perfect-competition?' problem! Before we can undertake this task we must see how the economic perspective is formed from the combination of the key concepts of economics with an *a priori* methodology. The key to this is the phrase 'the logic of choice', because in some form this idea functions both as a methodological principle and a key concept. In short it is the most promising candidate to represent the 'economic perspective'.

The economic perspective

The characteristics of the structure of deductive logic are the same as the characteristics of a linguistic structure. The important point about such structures is that the internal characteristics of a language can be successful in performing some tasks without describing anything external to the language. This also applies to disciplines. If we determine certain definitions for given concepts we also determine what subordinate concepts will follow from the original set of superordinate concepts. In economics we can deduce from the definition of the superordinate concept of a competitively efficient market certain subordinate concepts. These subordinate concepts must not create friction between any variables involved in determining competitive equilibrium, that is, their qualities must be peerless: perfect information, perfect mobility, etc.

These deductive linguistic structures can have two functions. They can either be wholly formal, in that all the values of the system can be found within the system, whatever the nature of external reality, for example, pure mathematics. Alternatively, they can be 'transcendental'. This is to say that the definition of the superordinate concepts will be determined by the need to be consistent with what the world must be like, if it is to be a world we can function in and understand.[18]

If we accept that economics is characteristic of a deductive science we need to know which one of these categories it fits. Given its orientation towards a determinate reality specific to a fixed problem, that is, scarcity of resources, then it is clearly the second. This means that it is a *determinate deductive science* – as opposed to the wholly formal option that is indeterminate. In essence, economics has a discipline structure formed by logic and shaped by a determinate reality.

Having developed the nature of the deductive logic that provides the characteristic methodology of economics, we can now begin to see how economics comes to possess its unique mode of inquiry. Each determinate deductive science will have chosen those elements of reality it will accept as determining its field of inquiry. The different elements chosen produce different discipline languages. The choice in economics of constrained choice as a key determinant has given the subject just such a distinctive discipline language. This is so because once you have scarcity the only way this situation can be made compatible with a world we could understand is through the medium of rational choices in a constrained environment. This provides two fundamental elements: one from human action, the other from external reality. Rationality provides the element of human action; constrained choice provides the element of external reality. Both of these taken together allow the discipline to develop the epistemological perspective[19] that is vital to its adequate functioning. The function of a determinate deductive logic is to provide just such a specific medium for comprehension. The concept of 'rational economic man' is not accidentally chosen, it is a necessary conclusion from economics' chosen field of inquiry. What this means is that economics is in some sense a behaviour science (not behavioural). In analysing behaviour we are essentially analysing choices in the face of some specific set of problems. Each and every economic problem entails options that are viable and options that are not. We need to be able to say what determinants of behaviour make some options viable. In every case the viable options will be those that are consistent with a rational act. This functions at two levels. In terms of pure theory, the concept of rational maximization of profits, utility, welfare, etc. determines just one possible outcome in each situation.[20] For example, in perfect competition, equilibrium, and hence the point at which an economic agent's act is rational, is unique. In practice, where there is some real-world friction the possibilities are more open-ended. In such cases we insert *ceteris paribus* clauses to allow us to say which options are more attractive, given the value of certain variables. The technique of determining the value of these variables may be inductive but the theory structure, once the *ceteris paribus* clauses have been specified, is purely deductive. That is, given certain premises (fixed variables and *ceteris paribus* clauses) a conclusion (a policy recommendation) must follow deductively. Whether the deduction is valid or not depends partly on the laws of logic and partly on the laws of the particular brand of rationality employed in economics. It is this latter item that we must now go on to specify.[21]

The economic perspective and the logic of choice

We have now established that the methodology of economics is deductive and that a determinant of the success of the deductions made is the laws of rationality. This gives a fuller meaning to the phrase 'the logic of choice'. In economics we have a logic where deductions are partly determined by formal *a priori* statements concerning the nature of rational choice. The important implication of this is that some ability to get inside this logic is a precondition of economic literacy.

Thus we have a logic based upon laws of rationality which itself produces a logic of choice. To make the logic function, we require certain key concepts that are up to the task of determining the field of economic rationality *and* of allowing that field to function adequately in analysing choice behaviour. These concepts must have one very important characteristic: to justify their position they must be representative of all the essential operations required of economists. In practical terms this entails the following. If a student has managed to get inside the key concepts, then he or she should have at least a theoretical capacity to understand all the other elements of the discipline; although in practice, *ad hoc* elements – such as an absence of mathematical ability – might prevent this understanding.

The ability to achieve this stems directly from the place of logic within the discipline. Because the logic of a discipline and the perspective of that discipline produce a discipline language, the ability to understand is placed in a similar functional relationship to the discipline language as the ability to use words is placed in ordinary language. Words are defined in terms of other words. This means that the economist will have a consistently different approach to problems experienced by all. An example will make this point more effectively.

Should water be provided free? A non-economist would probably approach the issue in terms of total provision. Most debates will involve basic value judgements expressed in terms of private v. public provision. The dispute normally revolves around the belief that water is so much a necessary part of human needs that the ability to pay should not be an issue. What very few debates involving exclusively non-economists will refer to, except by accident, is the kind of marginal question that would be a vital characteristic of an economist's approach.

An economist would be happy to go along with a water service structure provided free but would probably be less pleased with a service that operated without *any* charges. The argument would normally run along these lines: what benefits will have to be forgone to provide an *entirely* free service compared with the benefits forgone by charging for marginal consumption beyond a certain point? In other words, the economist would try to get the consumer to focus on the real costs of the service under conditions of relative scarcity.

It would be this combination of opportunity cost analysis and marginal thinking that would make the economist's approach distinctive. For instance, somebody with complete antipathy to water charges might not realize that, for example, a junior school or a sports centre cannot be provided because of the funds needed to provide very high-quality water, whether it is to be used for drinking or one of the other many uses – ranging from dish-washing through to toilet flushing to washing the car. Thus, an economist might accept the case for a free basic service, but would probably argue qua economist in favour of marginal charges for additional consumption beyond the basic provision if the benefits forgone by completely free water were outweighed by the marginal benefits of the charge.[22] The question to be answered now is how does the economist come by this characteristic approach?

The approach can be analysed back to the perspective that determines the nature of economic knowledge. The process of this analysis demonstrates that even at the most applied level an economist has as part of his conceptual framework a perspective that goes directly back to the purest theoretical vision in the 'core'.

To demonstrate this is not difficult. We merely need to understand why the issue is seen in a marginal way and why questions are asked concerning benefits forgone. We have thought of the economic perspective in terms of the conceptual framework required to operate within the context of scarce resources. The key element of this framework is that acts of economic agents are rational. This assumption operates at two levels to determine both the 'pure' logic of the situation and the 'practical' logic of the agent's decision. To allow the assumption to function in an explanatory way we need to discover which concepts would most adequately represent rational maximization in a constrained environment. Mathematically speaking, maximization is unusable unless we operate with marginality. Logically speaking, where there is a constrained environment a given use of scarce resources must entail an opportunity cost.

Thus the value of these concepts is only guaranteed (they could be accidentally valuable in other frameworks) if they have the relationship described here to the concept of rationality. This is why the *frequent* distinction between an economist's approach and that of the non-economist is not accidental. It is because the former operates within a particular conceptual framework that generates a distinctive linguistic structure.

The role of key concepts

These remarks allow us to fit economics into two key observations made above. It has already been stated that any discipline, and hence economics, requires certain key universals at its heart. These must be self-defining and must apply in all contexts where they or their derivatives are represented. The concept of rationality in economics implies the law that individuals always choose that option that is the best, given the available knowledge: 'It is the assumption that any individual, in his economic life, will never undertake an action that adds more to his losses than his gains, and will always undertake an action which adds more to his gains than to his losses.'[23]

This view of the concept of rationality allows it to be both self-defining, in that the law is an *a priori* truth, and also applicable in all contexts where the derivatives from the central concept are represented. In short, there are *two* constraints at work behind the assumption that choice behaviour is characteristic of economic man. The first constraint is the obvious one, that is, scarcity. The second is a less obvious constraint, yet the imperative to act rationally is just as much an essential component of the analytical qualities found in models based on choice behaviour.

These remarks affect those key concepts that we have said will be involved in the task of determining the field of economic rationality. If we accept for the moment that the concept of rationality is the pure universal of the discipline, then it follows that it will be present in some form in the key concepts. More explicitly, it will help decide which candidates are accepted as key concepts.

The second key observation is that disciplines have distinctive modes of thinking and these distinctive modes are embodied in the discipline's models. We can now see that economic models will be produced deductively with the deductions evaluated through the logic of rationality. The evaluation here is an appraisal in the internal sense discussed above. If this is the characteristic of the models it must also be the characteristic of the mode of thinking.[24] This can now be specified as deductive rationality in constrained environments – the logic of choice behaviour. On the basis of this specification we can state that each key concept must contain some element of the perspective of deductive rationality in constrained environments. We now turn to the list of concepts that satisfy this specification; we will also be looking to them to be representative of all the essential operations required of economists.

The key concepts of economics

We will limit the list of key concepts to three: opportunity cost, efficiency and marginality. The importance of limiting the group is to establish the principle that such a group must not be exceeded in any area of the discipline, that is, no further concepts must be added that cannot in some way be shown to be logically related to the core concepts.

Opportunity cost is a prime example of a deductive concept that organizes other concepts. In this role it helps determine the set of subordinate concepts in the test ground of the discipline that are acceptable derivatives of the superordinate core concepts. In effect it adjudicates over which interpretations of data are consistent with either the perspective in the core or those theoretical models that represent the perspective. For example, it would render inadmissible the suggestion that unemployment could be correctly conceptualized as a voluntary act in a context where leisure has a disutility and subsistence welfare benefits are unavailable.

The central assumption of opportunity cost is that each act excludes other possible acts at any given moment of action. The strictness of this assumption makes it logically identical to a fundamental law of geometry, that is, only one object can occupy any given point in three-dimensional space at any given time, with the result that other objects are logically forbidden to occupy that space. This has important implications. Given the way we interpret space through our formal and intuitive knowledge of geometry, we could no more imagine two objects occupying the same space as we could a square circle. But once an individual interprets production and consumption space through the formal and intuitive knowledge of scarcity, their inability to imagine an act of production or consumption with no opportunity cost is of the same order.

In addition, opportunity cost is a necessary condition of the concept of economic rationality as well as a derivative of it. In order for there to be the necessity that each act be an act for the best, there must be alternatives that are determinate, that is, if they were chosen they would exclude the optimal act. This is the sense in which many people nominate opportunity cost as the best representative of the way in which economists look at the world. There is no economic problem that does not involve the perspective that each alternative has a cost and that one of these alternatives will have the least cost. The search method for the least-cost alternative is essentially deductive. Combine this method with the agent-specific concept of rationality and the act-specific concept of opportunity cost, and you have the 'economic perspective', arguably a synonym for the nature of economic knowledge. Technically, this point is made most forcibly when all the elements of microeconomics are synthesized into welfare optima. The top-level optima requires:

$$MRTxy = \frac{MCx}{MCy} = \frac{Px}{Py} = MRSxy, \text{ yielding } n$$

which shows the tightest connection of interlocking opportunity costs. The mathematical implications of disturbing this optimum underlines this point. All clearing values of any individual component of the equation that does not satisfy the general equilibrium will yield welfare values that lie in a 'numerical range' below n. It should be clear from these remarks that the two remaining superordinate concepts are slightly less fundamental than opportunity cost.

Marginality derives its importance from the fact that the appropriate unit of appraisal in relation to maximizing economic behaviour is that of the *increment*. Individual economic agents are persistently involved in economic activity and rarely ask questions of whether to produce or consume in absolute terms – thus the difficulty of teaching first-year economics students the paradox of value! This argument is supported by the observation that the mathematics of maximization are a question of marginal analysis; total revenue can be equal to or exceed total costs without profits being maximized. The other important aspect of the concept of marginality is the way it allows the concept of rationality to function dynamically in models. Rational appraisal has to occur continuously, not intermittently. This is a condition of its producing maximizing results, for example, the strings of simultaneous equations in general equilibrium analysis. The only way that this appraisal can be continuous is if it is marginal. Thus marginal thinking characterizes the psychology of a rational maximizing agent.

Efficiency functions as a limiting concept.[25] It is a way of assessing the operation of the other key concepts; marginal decisions must produce efficient results, the cost of different opportunities is assessed through relative efficiencies. The concept is also directive and it is this quality that allows it to be used as more than just a synonym for rationality. Decisions can be rational but inefficient. The concept of efficiency allows us to compare optimal general rationality, which is not specific to any given economic agent, with agent-specific rationality; Pareto-preferred and non-Pareto-preferred positions in welfare economics could be a good example of this use of efficiency. The most efficient economic agent would be the one with perfect information and perfect mobility. That agent's behaviour could be explained entirely in terms of his orientation towards a Pareto optimum. But we need to allow, *pace* Hicks, for the subjectivity and imperfection of individual economic agents. The concept of efficiency allows the standard concept of rationality to be represented at both levels.[26] In effect, both efficient and inefficient choices are rational acts, but only one of the options expresses general rationality. It is this distinction that partly explains the failure of the general equilibrium model, as opposed to the general equilibrium perspective. If act-specific and agent-specific rationality produced the same results then all markets would clear on the standard competitive assumptions. However, as with theories such as the liquidity trap and money-illusion, individual agents have an agent-specific desire to act rationally that can take them off in an entirely different direction to the option suggested by the criteria of act-specific rationality:

we need to know whether the individual can list all the possible alternative 'states of the world' that he feels may occur . . . or whether he feels that there may be some residual, 'totally unknown', state of the world that could possibly occur. . . . Furthermore, we need to know whether the individual feels able to attach *probabilities* to these various possible states . . . and, of course, to take decisions accordingly.[27]

This point can be made even more precisely in terms of marginal efficiency by placing emphasis on the different subjective valuations of risk: 'if one individual's utility function can be shown to be a concave transformation of another individual's utility function, then the former individual is more risk-averse than the latter'.[28] What this entails is that there is a specifiable difference between individual perceptions of a rational act, but this can only be incorporated by dropping numerical assessments in favour of a vector or a scalar. This is essentially an information problem and an individual's failure to re-evaluate his version of risk in line with the conditions derived from general rationality will stem from his own interpretation of the marginal efficiency of information gathering.

Efficiency has a further function. It provides a criteria by which we can judge the success of each change in the value of a set of variables. Just as every act has an opportunity cost so, given standard equilibrium/disequilibrium conditions, every act must have an efficiency condition. Any act will change the value of variables such that efficiency retains the same value, falls or rises. This is not a contingent matter; defining an economic act as a choice with a cost *entails* an attendant efficiency condition. This enables a clear distinction to be made. Rationality and opportunity cost are the key philosophical concepts with the greatest power in defining the economic perspective. Marginality and efficiency are the key operational concepts[29] with the greatest power in permitting the perspective to function predicatively. Taken together, marginality and efficiency supply the cutting edge of the discipline. Thus we see the world through the perspective concepts while we perform and create in the world through the operational concepts.

One question remains: what of macroeconomics? Readers could be forgiven for thinking that the argument presented here is derived entirely from microeconomics. However, there is no *a priori* case to be made against applying the remarks made in this chapter to the economic analysis of aggregates. This claim rests on the belief that the analytical core of macroeconomics is the same as microeconomics:

An important element of the common 'vision' of Keynesians and monetarists is the assumption that the supply side of the economy is perfectly competitive. The perfect competition approach suggests a harmonious equilibrium outcome in which the interests of various groups in society are reconciled. It also suggests that observed outcomes result from the *choices* made by the people involved.[30]

The major difference between microeconomic and macroeconomic approaches lies in the empirical techniques developed to cope with the behaviour of aggregates and the development of particular aspects of the microeconomic model to characterize both the economic and institutional structure of the economy as a whole: 'The Kaleckian approach . . . starts from an oligopolistic view of the world . . . the oligopolistic approach brings conflict between groups to the fore, particularly between capital and labour.'[31]

This point can be made more forcibly by showing how the four concepts cited above fit the standard interpretations of the three major macroeconomic positions. Sawyer has argued that the Keynesian, monetarist and Kaleckian positions can be distinguished through their different approaches to the causes of unemployment:

In the monetarist view, unemployment hovers around the 'natural' rate of unemployment and is . . . voluntary. In the Keynesian view, unemployment arises from a malfunctioning of the system, mainly a lack of aggregate demand, which can be corrected by appropriate government action. In contrast, in the Kaleckian approach, unemployment serves to rein back the demands of labour for higher real wages to a level which is compatible with the profit demands of oligopolists.[32]

In each of these cases the determinant in the final analysis is derived from marginal choices made by rational agents seeking to achieve a more efficient allocation of their own resources. The resulting distributions will in turn be analysed, through the act-specific concept of rationality, in terms of the contribution of individual decisions to the efficiency of the whole.

In the monetarist model the focus falls on workers' interpretations of available information, for example, the problem of 'money illusion', and the resulting decisions they make in maximizing their gains from the work/leisure trade-off. In the Keynesian approach we require a similar explanation of choice behaviour, this time the analysis needs to account for the behaviour that leads to the downward inflexibility of wage rates. In suggesting that workers would accept a decline in the real wages associated with a rise in prices but not a fall in money wages, Keynes said: 'Whether logical or illogical, experience shows this is how labour in fact behaves.'[33] At another level Keynes offered a less inductive explanation when he explained 'money illusion' as a function of the belief that a reduction in money wages entails a relative reduction in the distribution of income for those who consent. Whether inductively or deductively derived, the implication is the same – the worker makes a rational marginal choice concerning the efficiency, in personal maximizing terms, of the available options. The Kaleckian view is even simpler to reconcile with the key concepts as it requires a straightforward version of risk-aversion in the face of an absolute choice between income and unemployment. The major difficulty here would lie in expressing the acceptance of lower wages in marginal terms.

The remaining issue in this part of the argument is the 'aggregation problem', that is, does the behaviour of aggregates produce problems of a different *kind*, as opposed to a different degree, of complexity? It would seem not, the aggregation of individual choices doesn't produce the need for an analytical system outside of choice behaviour. Rather, it requires a technique that can account for the indeterminate results that occur at the aggregate level on the basis of clearly determinate micro results: but this is an issue of methodology, not perspective. It was Keynes's distinctive way of dealing with the disequilibria derived from the aggregation process that made his work unique, not any fundamental change in the economic perspective.

Conclusion

In conclusion, we can say that the nature of economic knowledge is determined by the economic perspective, which is itself determined by the use of deductive analysis combined with an agent-specific concept of rationality and an act-specific concept of opportunity cost. This allows us to see what makes economics special. The purpose of analysing economics through the philosophy of science was to establish that the procedures of economics could be seen in a way similar to other sciences. To establish this was to demonstrate two important aspects of economic knowledge. First, economics has the structure and potential of an objective discipline. Secondly, economics is a unique form of inquiry. This second aspect rests on the fact that each discipline language contains a unique perspective because of its particular choice of core vision and methodology. This perspective is inherent in all the concerns of the economist through the two operational concepts of efficiency and marginality.

Where economics will travel in the future is not easy to predict, but as long as the perspective defined here continues to prevail, we can expect increasing formalization and increasingly sophisticated deductive methods in empirical analysis via the agency of econometrics. This direction of development increases the challenge for economics educators. We can no longer encourage our students to describe passively economic phenomena. Instead, we should wish them to be inside the discipline operating, in however limited a sense, as economists. Given this objective, we cannot dodge the necessity to direct our teaching towards an understanding of the deductive use of key concepts. In one sense this simply means that we should encourage our students to take material dealing with economic behaviour and reason through their own analyses. This would entail reasoning through what they see as the connections between the concepts they have experienced and the behaviour under examination. The pedagogic emphasis should be upon discouraging moves in the analysis that would break the natural chain of economic reasoning. The more successful and automatic this becomes, the more the student will be 'inside the discipline'. This last phrase is, I think, the key to what will be considered progressive for economics education in the future. However, substantial research needs to be done before we really have an easy operational understanding of what 'inside the discipline' means.[34]

Notes and references

1. It is important to be clear about this distinction because it will crop up throughout what follows. The internal form of appraisal is concerned with the conceptual outlook of the discipline. The process of internal appraisal is the thought process of any particular discipline and will not be found in the same form in other disciplines. The external form is more open-ended and conditional, containing elements of both common sense and perspectives essential to the discipline.

2. Almost every recent work employs some version of Lakatos in discussing methodological issues in economics. See: Latsis, S. (ed.), *Method and Appraisal in Economics* (Cambridge University Press, 1981); Katouzian, H., *Ideology and Method in Economics* (Macmillan, 1980); Blaug, M., *The Methodology of Economics* (Cambridge University Press, 1980); and, Jeffreys, D., 'Economics and methodology', *Economics*, vol. 19, pt 4, no. 84, winter 1983.

   All of these four works contain a list of books for those wishing to pursue

Lakatos's work further. The last two of the four contain book lists specifically designed for economists looking for an introduction to methodology relevant to their particular needs. For those who do not wish to go further than one original source, the classic work is Imre Lakatos, 'Falsification and the methodology of scientific research programmes', in Lakatos, I., and Musgrave, A., *Criticism and the Growth of Knowledge* (Cambridge University Press, 1970) pp. 91–195.

3. This is fundamental. The core of a theory is based upon an assumption about some aspect of behaviour. The core purifies this assumption discarding all conditional characteristics and ending up with a model of what the world would look like if that assumption were true and if no barriers existed to prevent its operation in all contexts. If we assume that economic agents are rational, the purest form of that rationality would occur where there were no barriers to rational functioning. Such an occurrence would require perfect competition. Perfectly competitive outcomes can only be compared with their imperfect counterparts if the core of the theory offers the basis for comparison.

4. Questions have been raised over this argument concerning the relationship between the core, theories and the discipline. It has been suggested that the theory must be subordinate to the discipline but this does not mean that they cannot both be seen in terms of a core vision and a protective belt of testable propositions. Theories may be part of the protective belt surrounding the perspective of the discipline but each theory must have a core composed of concepts from the perspective protected by more open-ended hypotheses.

5. Before we proceed we need to obtain a concrete grasp of the concept of a 'core' and its relationship to the derived testable propositions. Imagine a traffic policeman. His faith in motor cars and contempt for drivers is such that he believes all accidents are caused by driver error. This is not something he tries to prove; it is his assumption about his immediate field of action. If an accident does occur he does not try to prove it was driver error – for him this is what is meant by the phrase 'road traffic accident'. Rather, he looks for evidence to decide what kind of driver error has occurred. His 'testable propositions' are a list of do's and don't's for making this decision. If he comes across 'pure' mechanical failure he saves his theory by, for example, arguing that this was caused by a 'factory accident' which itself relied upon human agency.

6. Whenever the phrase 'characteristic' is used in this context from now on it means 'some element of economic theory or methodology which could be accommodated within the framework of the core or the methodology'.

7. Keynes, J.M., *The Collected Writings of John Maynard Keynes*, vol. XIV: *The General Theory and After* (Macmillan, 1973) pp. 296–7.

8. Katouzian, op. cit., p. 18.

9. Ibid., p. 22.

10. Ibid., p.24.

11. At one level abstract disciplines are self-contained languages with their own descriptive form and syntax. As with any distinct language the criteria of meaning are internal; words are defined in terms of each other and only partially in terms of their success in describing things outside the language.

12. The system of appraisal involved here is of the internal sort defined above.

13. For an excellent account, see Coats, A.W., 'Economics and psychology – the death and resurrection of a research programme', in Latsis, op. cit., pp. 52–76.

14. Knight, F.A., *Risk, Uncertainty and Profit* (Cambridge University Press, 1943) p. 14.

15. Knight, F.A., 'The relations of utility theory to economic method in the work of Jevons', in Rice, S. (ed.), *Methods in Social Science* (Cambridge University Press, 1970) p. 67.

16. Coats, op. cit., p. 53.

17. The relationship between microeconomics and macroeconomics is discussed in detail below where it will be argued that the core perspective is the same, notwithstanding the implications of Arrow's Theorem.

18. A little more could be said about this. A transcendental approach, derived from Kant, makes an assumption about human consciousness. It then takes any given concept and specifies what connections between the assumption and the concept are logically permissible. The logically permissible connections tell us what the world must look like if it is to be one our assumed consciousness could function within. In economic terms, we assume that human consciousness is rational and utility-maximizing. If we then take the concept of 'consumption' some definitions of this concept will be consistent with our assumption, others not. The consistent definitions will tell us what economic reality must look like given our initial assumption. Astute readers will see that this description is very similar to more general descriptions of model building.

19. This simply means that it can develop a view of the kind of knowledge that can be obtained within its particular field.

20. Some say that this means that economic theory is *overdetermined*, resulting in an inability consistently to maintain intermediate cases, for example, oligopoly in the theory of the firm. For a valuable discussion of this, see Latsis, S., 'A research programme in economics', in Latsis, op. cit.

21. As the science develops, handling data to support particular hypotheses will make inductive methods more important. Inductive methods become more important because as the formal conditions of the assumptions in the core of the model are relaxed it may be necessary to derive explanations and predictions from trends. For instance, in perfect competition the firm is assumed to be a profit-maximizer. Part of this explanation is based upon the concept of normal profit, given that normal profit is viewed as a cost. For this concept to work there needs to be identifiable entrepreneurs assessing opportunity costs. In a large-scale joint stock company, where ownership is divorced from control, the explanations developed cannot rely upon the notion of normal profit. Explanations of profit seeking in this type of firm may depend as much upon discerning trends, such as sales/income-maximization, as developing general assumptions to provide a basis for deductions.

    Similarly, we may know that the money supply affects the price level given the deductive structure of the equation $MV=PQ$. However, it may require an inductive analysis of the variety of monetary aggregates in order to determine which particular monetary aggregate can take the place of M. In short, this means that induction is a tool that can be used to support, expand or strengthen the deductive analysis of the relationship between concepts and assumptions.

22. This point can be supported by looking at problems that are paragons of the economic approach and considering the difficulties that arise in teaching these problems. While my evidence is personal and impressionistic, I believe there is some significance in the fact that first-year A-level students find the paradox of value so difficult, yet the same students tend to find much less difficulty with the marginal work/leisure trade-off when they come up against it in their second year.

23. Robinson, J., *The Economics of Imperfect Competition* (Macmillan, 1969) p. 6.

24. Both uses of the term 'characteristic' here are in the special sense defined earlier; see note 6 above.

25. Some have argued that efficiency and marginality should be the only two concepts accepted as key concepts. It has been suggested that 'efficiency' and 'opportunity cost' are mutually exclusive on the grounds that the existence of opportunity costs is constant evidence of an inefficient world. This seems unacceptable. Opportunity cost is the force that creates the need for efficiency because the existence of scarcity and its attendant opportunity costs creates the context in which the law of rational maximization forces minimum subjective opportunity cost. The two *can* be mutually exclusive in practice, because of imperfections in the information possessed by individuals. However, this is a different issue, which is discussed in detail below.

26. It is important that we can see the concept of rationality operating for both the high theorist and the applied economist. An applied economist sees himself working with imperfect options that he will assess largely through the procedures stemming from opportunity cost. However, ask him why he has this approach rather than the techniques available to, for example, the sociologist. His answer will eventually lead you back to the economic perspective; the way one looks at behaviour if you think of rational maximizing agents operating through efficiency and marginality. A reproduction of this process is a good way of getting students to appreciate and understand the economic perspective. Take any *Financial Times* article; ask your students to make predictions about possible options implied by the article; take each option and analyse it back to its roots; determine which are consistent with the economic perspective and which are not; explain why the non-economic perspective should be discarded.

27. Hey, J.D., *Uncertainty in Microeconomics* (Martin Robertson, 1979) p. 11.

28. Ibid., p. 50.

29. The distinction between philosophical and operational concepts is a useful one. It allows us to distinguish between those concepts that set the epistemology (the boundary of knowledge) and the ontology (what exists within the boundary) of a discipline and those concepts that allow the discipline to probe, explore and explain.

30. Sawyer, M.C., *Macroeconomics in Question* (Wheatsheaf, 1982) p.4.

31. Ibid.

32. Ibid.

33. Keynes, J.M., *The General Theory of Employment, Interest and Money* (Macmillan, 1936) p. 9.

34. My thanks must go to Linda Thomas, David Whitehead, Bill Baird and

Mark Blaug for invaluable comments on various drafts of this chapter. Of course, none of them is responsible for the result.

2 The Objectives of Economics Education
Willie Henderson

This chapter deals with the analysis of statements made about the overall objectives of economics education. Consequently, it deals with different interpretations about 'economics' as a subject, the particular justification being offered, and the content and approach to an overall curriculum that the set objectives suggest. The chapter examines, primarily, the help available in clarifying purposes from the discipline itself.[1]

The chapter is divided into three main sections. The first part looks at some recent (and not so recent) statements about the nature and purpose of economics education. A sample of such statements is examined and most are shown to be either partial or misleading when evaluated in terms of economics as a social science.[2] The second part offers an alternative way of looking at problems in economics teaching. The third part consists of a brief conclusion and some suggestions of ways of avoiding major pitfalls.

Literature on the objective of economics education

Literature on the purposes of economics education exists at different levels and consists of a number of contrasting views. Part of the literature is highly specific and discusses the objectives of teaching particular groups, for example, academically able sixth-form students,[3] or primary school children at the pre-operational level of age-related development.[4] Given that 'economics education' can span the whole age range of formal schooling plus a variety of adult educational activities, the task of looking for overall objectives may not be a particularly helpful way to proceed. For educational purposes there may be no concept of either an 'educational aggregate' or a single 'educational problem' equivalent to the single 'economic problem' with which elementary principles courses tend to begin. The educational problem is bound to vary with the age–stage structure of learning, the resources available, the characteristics of adults or children – either in terms of inherent abilities or social expectations and/or conditioning – the aims of the institution, etc.

Nevertheless, a number of attempts have been made to state either overall objectives for education in economics or for broadly defined groups, for example, primary school children, 11–16-year-olds, and so on. The attempts reviewed here can be summarized as:

A   economics education as economics socialization;
B   objectives by consensus;
C   objectives set by the needs of 'economics understanding' which has latterly been replaced by the needs of 'economic literacy'.

As will be shown, from the point of view of formal economic analysis, some of these notions share certain misunderstandings.

A   Economic education as economics socialization

Socialization is the process of preparing for life in a given society. The socialization process takes place both implicitly (in the home, wider family, street) and explicitly (in schools, church or other associations). In economics education the theme of economics socialization arises in a number of different contexts. Sometimes economics education is seen as being capable of making an important contribution to citizenship education or to workers' education; sometimes it refers to increasing personal ability to operate as an economic agent in a given economy. Examples of the kinds of statements are provided below:

The American version of citizenship education (Joint Council for Economic Education):

We take the objectives of economic education to be responsible citizenship and effective decision making.

While this is undoubtedly an accurate description of the aims of the Joint Council (see the criticisms made by Boyer below),[5] are they the objectives of education in economics? Are they consistent with the assumptions of formal economics and, as a set of objectives, are they clear? Effective decision-making by whom: citizens, governments or markets? And on whose terms? What does economic analysis itself tell us about 'responsible' citizenship – does it tell us to seek out self-interest and thus, inadvertently, provide the social good? Does it tell us to be suspicious of government intervention in markets or to promote government involvement in order that private costs reflect social costs? To tax avoid but never to tax evade or to do neither? Smuggling and corruption may both be economically legitimate responses to an economic system in which a state intervenes beyond its capacity to sustain that intervention despite any other notions of behaviour that 'good' citizenship might suggest.[6]

An example of a confusion that economics for 'responsible citizen-ship' can get into at the interface between objective and the handling of content comes from a classroom event observed in Ghana. The teacher was dealing with the idea of the entrepreneur seeking out the most profitable market. In the course of the lesson, one student asked about the profit-seeking activities of those near the Ghana–Togo border who smuggled cocoa out of Ghana to earn higher prices in Togo. Here was an excellent opportunity to explore the economic dimensions of a legal problem. The teacher, in the interests of promoting 'good' citizenship and in line with the (then) military government's campaign, chose to respond to the question by saying, 'If you know of such activities, you should report them to the police.' The opportunities to discuss the problem as one for economic analysis, for example, a response that tries to predict the kind of price differentials, risk and transportation costs that give rise to such behaviour being profitable; a response that explores the policy alternatives and the procedures concerning the taxation of cocoa and the level of government expenditure in cocoa and non-cocoa regions, were both avoided and the standard 'legal' argument applied.

The point is that economics for responsible citizenship must have (if it is to be true to economics) a critical component. Such a critical component might not suit the establishment view of what constitutes 'good' citizenship. In this respect, the last word should perhaps be left to Alfred Marshall who said, 'It is almost impossible for a student [of economics] to be a true patriot and to have the reputation of being one in his own time.'[7]

Perhaps a clearer statement of economic education's possible contribution to social and personal decisions is supplied by Horton and Weidenaar (whose work is more fully examined below):

Economics also provides frameworks and tools for rational, individual discrimination among social alternatives in the light of one's values. 'Better' social decisions will result.[8]

While this is a hopeful view of the possible contribution of economics education to policy formation (if policy formation is the sense in which social decisions/alternatives is to be understood), it is somewhat naïve. Economic analysis might help suggest what policy ought to be. It might also help tell us why policy is what it is (e.g. because organized self-interest groups have more influence than unorganized groups). Because such knowledge exists, does not mean that it 'will' lead to 'better' (presumably in this context 'rational', even-handed) social decisions. There are other motives. Analytically, the statement ignores the following points:

1   Rationality is an assumption made in economic analysis to facilitate the building of predictive models.
2   While individuals with an economics training may be prepared to use rational analysis to understand economic behaviour, in their personal life

and actions each starts with their own pattern of resource endowments and priority rankings that will suggest, in turn, different views as to what constitutes either a correct personal choice or 'good' policy. Economists, for example, will be as anxious as any other members of society to off-load some of their costs on to others. A nation of economists would still face economic and policy problems.

3 That it is conceptually possible to have the best economists in the world and the worst economic policy.

Although the factual and analytical objectives raised above do not entirely negate the points being made by Horton and Weidenaar, they clearly show their limitations. It is only by testing such statements from the economics standpoint that some clear indication of their strengths and weaknesses be gained and hence the implications for the objectives– content interface be evaluated.

The British version of this kind of thinking is as follows:

First, a school ought to consider why anyone needs to enjoy economic competence these days. The term means, broadly speaking, the presence of certain factual knowledge about the national economy; certain specific skills which enable a citizen and 'worker' to operate within it, and certain concepts which enable us to form balanced and informed judgements about economic matters.[9]

The statement is not without interest. There is every reason to increase the economic competence of individuals but in what sense or senses is economic competence being used in the passage? Indeed, is the explanation of the meaning of economic competence credible?

(a) Factual knowledge about the national economy It is reasonable to suppose that economics can supply factual knowledge about the national economy. But for what purpose? What is 'national' to be taken to mean – aggregate economics or the structure of production? Why national rather than local or international?

(b) Certain specific skills that enable a citizen or worker to operate within it What are these skills – and are they specific to economics?

(c) Certain concepts that enable us to form balanced and informed judgements about economic matters What are the economic concepts that enable us to form balanced judgements about 'economic matters' and what are these 'economic matters'? Does it mean judgements about the causes and consequences of price changes in particular markets or does it mean 'balanced judgement' on aspects of macroeconomic policy? Is there, for example, any simple conceptual basis for making balanced judgement about monetarist economic policy? Is the notion of balanced and informed judgement a loose way of indicating if/then statements (e.g. if you believe that inflation is a greater evil then such and such follows)? In which case the balanced and informed judgements of Keynes, Friedman, Galbraith or Marx would certainly be different.

Policy issues at this level are areas of lively economic controversy[10] in terms of the relevant concepts, of the nature of the empirical evidence, and the value judgements involved.

It is hard to approve of this kind of muddle as a clear and useful set of objectives for economics education. If they were to constitute a starting point, all of the statements in this section would require rigorous analysis to prevent us from falling into the trap of teaching either rationality (a job for the psychologists?) or conformity to an existing order (ideology disguised as 'good' citizenship) or notions of 'good' economic policy and behaviour not founded on (say) welfare economics.

Statements seem to be primarily concerned with a particular educational philosophy that aims at fitting people better for operating in a given society rather than for people thinking about the sort of society they want and of being capable of working towards it.

B Objectives by consensus

Another example of an attempt to arrive at a set of objectives that gets some of it correct and some of it wildly wrong is the objectives by consensus approach. This approach is set out by Horton and Weidenaar who, in an attempt to clarify the purpose of economics education, undertook to gather information on the views of 200 experienced people who teach economics. The aim of the research was to negotiate an agreed set of objectives. The starting point was the observation that no consistent set of generalizations about objectives directed the efforts of economics teachers. The aim of the project was 'goal concentration'. In consulting the 200 experts individuals were given the chance to select 'best' and 'worst' objectives.

The result of the first round of negotiations was three goals supported by different categories of respondent to different degrees. These were:

1 To help us to be more capable as direct participants in the economy – as consumers, workers, businessmen or investors.
2 To 'improve' decisions when we act in our society as citizens.
3 To improve our understanding of the world in which we live.

Horton and Weidenaar report that the first goal is not acceptable in itself because economics is not the most efficient way of 'improving' participation (business studies, trade union studies, the study of consumer rights under the law or old-fashioned civics might in educational terms perform just as well). Even this argument is not primarily concerned with 'improving' participation unless the educational system itself is effectively reorganizing an individual's human capital in ways that increase actual participation (the ability to earn and to spend).

The second goal is seen as possible and useful but partial, and the third one is seen as broad enough to include the others. The authors add that this third goal necessarily encompasses the goal of understanding better the market or free enterprise system, albeit independently of whatever one's own evaluation of it may be.

The next stage was to achieve a consensus goal that, with some technical assumptions of considerable importance, emerged as:

The aim of economic education is to improve our understanding of the world in which we live. Without this understanding we are frequently confused and unable to identify, analyse and interpret successfully the economic aspects inherent in so much about us. The goal reflects our conviction that comprehension of the economic realities of one's world enhances self-confidence and self-esteem. Accordingly both intellectual and emotional barriers are lowered for the making of rational individual decisions, in the light of one's values, in both personal and social matters. Economics also provides frameworks and tools for rational individual discrimination among social alternatives, in the light of one's values. Hopefully, better social decisions will result.[11]

Where is the economics content of this final goal? It has valid content in the sense that it points us in the direction of the 'real world', it reminds us that the recipient of economics courses ought to benefit in some way (being able to understand that world) as a result of the learning. If, however, we were to substitute the terms 'education in politics' or 'sociological education' and 'politics' and 'sociology' for economic[12] education and economics in the above passage the end result would still be a statement that made some kind of educational sense. We could substitute 'geography' and 'history' and it would still be educationally 'acceptable'. This, despite the fact that there exists an intellectual tension between economics and some of the other disciplines.

While this similarity of objectives could be taken to mean that the objectives of economics education are in part similar to the objectives of other disciplines, economics teachers ought to be prepared to make an economic argument for the existence of economics in the curriculum.

Any statement about the objectives of economics education must be more than a statement about a series of (expected) outcomes that will result from learning a wide range of social sciences subjects. *None of the above comes to terms with the fact that the distinguishing feature of economics as a subject is that it has a formal analytical structure.*

C Economic literacy as an objective

There are another two ideas that have been used to suggest an overall set of objectives for economics teaching – the idea of economics understanding and the later notion of economics literacy. Thus W. Lee Hansen uses the idea of economics literacy as partly a substitute for, and improvement upon, economics understanding. Hansen, despite a lengthy paper on the idea, does not provide a clear definition of economic literacy. For example:

There is a need for an operational definition of economic literacy with which it would be possible at a reasonably low cost, to determine the extent of individuals' economic literacy. We would not expect, desirable though it would be, to have an exact measure of literacy. Nor would we want a definition of economic literacy to depend on substantial amounts of formal instruction in economics. However, we would like a measure which indicates that the level of economic literacy has observable consequences in people's behaviour and in their beliefs about the economic system.[13]

This at first sight seems to be suggesting some kind of diagnostic test for economic literacy of the same sort that language experts can apply to determine the reading ages of students. If this is so, it might then be presumed that 'economic literacy' has something to do with an ability to manipulate the formal vocabulary and models of elementary economics. The passage later specifically excludes a definition that depends on 'substantial amounts of formal instruction in economics'. Rather, the aim is to find a *measure* that has observable consequences in 'behaviour'.

Here we are back to the old confusion between 'everyday' life and the study of everyday life that has caused trouble before. Obviously, if students have no experience of everyday life then the study of economics is going to prove difficult. If students have experience of getting and spending then an awareness of that experience and an involvement of it in the education will be essential to the successful development of formal understanding.

However, to put aside formal economics and to try and measure economic literacy in terms of 'observable consequences in people's behaviour' is a nonsense. When trade unionists demand wage settlements aimed at maintaining a given real income net of tax they will ask for a percentage increase greater than the expected rise in the price level. This understanding that real purchasing power has got something to do with the relationship beween money-in-the-pocket and prices in the shops is an expression of an intuitive understanding (or is it based on bitter experience?) that sometimes escapes those responsible for the formation of government policy. Both intuition and experience are what makes everyday economic life possible, that is, economics as a substantive activity.[14] But everyday life does not necessarily present formal tools required to analyse events in the world. Economic theory has a system of understanding based on ideas such as economic man (a logical fiction), market equilibrium (the result of a consistent set of assumptions) or indifference curve analysis (a technique to demonstrate income and substitution effects). These devices are used to promote reasoning. Formal reasoning, about the changes in economic life, is the hallmark of mainstream economics. One of the purposes of reason is the construction of predictive economic models. We assume the existence of economic man as a (rational) economic maximizer in order to obtain strong predictions. As economists we neither say that such a person actually exists nor do we necessarily imply that it would be a 'good thing' if people were actually economic men in this sense. 'Economic man' is a fiction, but a fiction that helps us predict the likely direction of change in a market. It is also possible to act rationally and be mistaken (decisions require information and the 'correct' amount of information may not be available).

Rationality in economic analysis is not an individual state of psychological grace. It refers to ends/means relationships and does not tell us anything in itself about the validity of those ends. Nor does it tell us that the ends will be achieved for the reason just given. In other words, rationality is a technical device used to establish a strong prediction.[15] How people actually behave in markets is essentially what we are trying to predict. In the analysis of market changes, economic literacy is of no practical use.

Others have made rigorous attempts to deal with the notion of literacy in economics. Daniel Jeffreys, in an unpublished paper, analyses the notion of economic literacy by way of a philosophical analysis of the term literacy.

Jeffreys sees the analogy of literacy and economic literacy as valid when economic literacy is taken to mean (if I understand him correctly) assisting students to understand the nature and purpose of economics discourse. To find educational objectives, any questioning of what it means to be economically literate must then become a questioning of the purpose and structure (both superficial and deep) of economics discourse. In Chapter 1, Jeffreys outlines what he sees as the core concepts of economics ('the use of deductive analysis combined with an agent-specific concept of rationality and an act-specific concept of opportunity cost'). These are what I regard as necessary spectacles for viewing the world through economic 'eyes'. The educational task as I see it is not to start with these spectacles as given and to trace out logical consequences (the old-fashioned method of teaching Euclidean geometry), but to assist students to put on the spectacles and appreciate the consequences.

A possible way forward

It is possible to take either a narrow or broad view of what constitutes economics discourse. In the narrower view, the discourse would simply be economics texts. Economics textbooks (i.e. the kind of writing normally looked at by students on introductory courses) have a set of characteristics that make them different from politics or sociology texts. They look more like science texts than other social science texts.[16] They are highly linear (the student must refer back and look forward sometimes over many chapters to build on or develop specific points). They contain many examples of principle first, application second (i.e. the rule-example sequence) and the logical status of the examples (i.e. fact or fiction) is often unclear to the uninitiated. Also, as in science texts, there are numerous counter-factuals in evidence.

Introductory texts tend to present the *product* of economic investigation and principle formation rather than *either* the practice of economics *or* historical, as well as logical, stages in the construction of models and principles. Even so, the discourse is highly organized in terms of the presuppositions of the discipline and substantially different from the kind of writing that students on introductory courses have to read in other subjects to pose them particular problems. One of the implications of being concerned with the development of economic literacy is to be concerned with the development of the kinds of reading and thinking skills students must have if they are to understand economics texts: the skill of distinguishing positive from normative statements, of distinguishing empirical statements from predictive statements, of going from a text to a diagram and vice versa, of seeing the relevance of a hypothetical example. Another implication of a narrow view of economic literacy would be to reconsider the established structure and sequencing that is in evidence in economics textbooks, that is, reconsideration of principle first, application second.[17]

A wider notion of economics literacy can also be based on a wider sense of economic discourse. The wider view of discourse would look at problem forming, problem setting, the questioning process, problem refining, analysis and solution, as it takes place in different 'levels' of economic discussion and at different stages (e.g. before and after the event of the construction of a working model). Such discourse could be located anywhere economics is purposefully used to clarify questions and construct a correctly argued economic solution, for example, in the classroom and lecture room, in draft research papers and policy memoranda, that is, in the context of economic ideas in action. This wider view of discourse means moving away from economics as a ready-made subject with a predetermined product and simple, ends-dominated purposes and a move towards it as something with which both students and teachers are more speculatively involved. While economics has moved a long way since Marshall, his idea of economics not as a 'body of concrete truth, but an engine for the discovering of concrete truth' might be one that is educationally productive and worthy of exploration.[18]

The view of the objective of economics education as being to understand the evolution and purpose of economics discourse is novel. There does not exist as yet, in either the study of economics method (a study that tends to deal with questions of scientific-testing) or in the study of economics teaching, any considerable body of direct research into the nature of such discourse and problems pupils have in coping with it.[19] Nevertheless, if the key to economics education does lie in the formal contribution economics can make to an individual student's ability to reason about social problems, then further research into the difficulties that the highly idiosyncratic way of thinking that economics poses for new learners is also essential if realistic objectives for economics teaching are to be formulated and met.

If the process of economic analysis is to be the starting point for thinking about the objectives of teaching (and hence the objectives–content interface) then we may have to recognize that:

1 Some of the processes may be beyond very young children.
2 Working on process might need to start on a formulation of real-world experiences. In the Third World production and consumption is at an elementary level, much more visible than it is in the UK. On the other hand, in the UK, economic problems are much more accurately and openly reported upon in the press and on television. If students do not have real-world experiences to build upon, then such experiences might have to be provided via some kind of economic agent approach directed not at making them either 'better' or 'specific' economics agents or 'good' citizens but to give them contrasting experiences of instituted economic activity. Consideration of such experiences may help them to see the need for theory and so help them put on 'economic spectacles'.
3 If insight into, and activities for, economics education as understanding the process and relevance of economic argument is to be the focus then some attention might have to be paid to the problems that confronted earlier economic doctrines. This might be particularly so with respect to value theory and to notions of economic protectionism.
4 For sources of ideas about process we might have to consider what economists actually do and effectively use. (Such an approach could lead to a revaluation of microeconomics.)
5 In any reconsideration of objectives, it may no longer be appropriate on the basis of process to think either in terms of looking for statements that are beyond economics itself nor of discrete ends to be achieved. The first part of this chapter showed how difficult it is in terms of overall objectives to make unambiguous statements and to match these up with ways of handling concepts in the classroom.
6 Teaching for product usually fails to integrate the real world to be

analysed, students' experiences of that world and the development of, and purposeful use of, tools for analysis. Thus the considerable difficulties that students experience in recognizing the whole range of different kinds of allocation problems that can be explored by simple supply and demand analysis. As economic techniques become more complex, this problem of recognizing the economic dimension to a problem is likely to become more acute, not less so. At the introductory level the problem is complicated by the long-established principles of textbook writing in which principles are developed first and application or exemplification (often fictional) comes second. This way of working is inherent in the discipline because of the existence of logical fictions and such counter factional statements needed for the building of formal models. This pattern is hereafter referred to as the 'rule e.g.' mould.

7   Looking at the implications of process might mean, in the schools, a more Marshallian approach – constantly deriving questions from, and relating back, with analysis as an intermediary, to the real world. Not only would this mean breaking the 'rule e.g.' mould wherever possible but the changes of focus – from the concrete to the abstract; from the specific to the general – is likely to enhance learning anyway.[20]

8   Engaging in thinking about process will ultimately involve students in identifying and grappling with the kinds of problems posed in economics rather than in learning the 'stories' of economics as told in the textbooks.

9   Thinking about the process of economic argument would also mean having a subject-based reason for thinking about the learning process and hence the possibility of a genuine 'negotiation' between valid subject-related objectives and valid learning objectives.

I have elsewhere attempted to work out a teaching strategy based on a simple understanding of economics as a model-building science. The basic objectives of such a course I took to be to seek 'to provide the student with the opportunity of becoming familiar with the way in which economics handles simple, real-world problems' (i.e. the objectives of economics education is to learn economics). Reality is the starting point and located in a strategically simple real-world question. The model becomes a way of simplifying and translating reality that can assist in predicting associations in the real world.

An illustration will help to show the part understanding process might help in organizing the teaching and the learning. Take a standard lesson on the factors of production. This could be taught as a simple lesson in labelling. A definition would be provided, learned and applied. But such treatment would *not* satisfy the idea of trying to replicate a process of economic argument. The teacher could begin by playing around with a series of questions for him or herself. For example: Why do we need a definition? How is a definition arrived at? Are the definitions unambiguous? Can they be used to reorganize reality as we know it? How can we use the definition to extend our experience? Having understood that there is a narrower and wider aspect to the definitions, the process-oriented teacher will look for ways of replicating the questions in classroom work to assist students discover the need for definition and hence the definitions themselves (subject to guidance through exemplification) within the context of (say) comparing two simple production processes.[21]

An approach to objectives for economics teaching along such lines would (I think) satisfy ideas of achieving economics literacy. Curriculum development along such lines would only be fully possible with an increase in resources devoted to spelling out educational implications of this way of thinking. The aim of this approach would be the learning of economics by finding a basis in each lesson for 'doing economics'. As in other areas of economic and education life, compromise would have to be found but this approach to objectives avoids claiming the impossible for the consequences of increased economics understanding.

Conclusions

That there exists a confusion about the objectives of economics education in the literature cannot be denied. Part of the problem seems to stem from a lack of negotiation between the presuppositions of economic theory and specific educational goals. The notion of liberal education carries with it the ideas of rationality, balanced judgement, the even-handed consideration of values and evidence in exploring the world. This might account for the confusion between rationality as a technical device for furthering economic knowledge and rationality as a state of educational/psychological grace. The latter may or may not be shared by those willing to make use of the former but even if it is, there are enough areas of controversy – about values, about the relationship between theoretical concepts and empirical evidence and about the limitations of economic knowledge (i.e. the limitations imposed by the illuminating power of the spectacles) – to ensure that those who have economics understanding realize both the power and the limitations of analysis.

There is also in the literature a lack of clarity as between the formal demands of economics as a thought process, participation in 'the economy' as a substantive activity and the status of the knowledge and experience gained from that participation. The latter may be valuable but it is not economics. The core concepts of economics are essential to the illumination of instances but the instances themselves will not give rise to the core concepts. In this narrow technical sense economics does not have an experiential basis. (Appeals to experience sometimes made in arguments about methodology are made within the context of fairly refined economic reasoning.)

However, in a wider sense, experience is not unimportant. Those who participate in economic life can, normally, be expected to think about it and to construct theories (e.g. price as exploitation, price as cost-of-production, value as the value of labour), some of which have an important niche[22] in the respectable history of economic thought. Experience can both help and hinder the development of economics thinking, but either way the learner's experience has to be engaged. Real-world experience (either actual or simulated) might help to set up problem framing and setting, for example, choice as a fact. It might then help the process of question formation, and hence stimulate inquiry into (say) the kinds of questions that can be asked about prices and hence (eventually) the development of a theory of price. (Supply and demand analysis is not the only theory available.) A questioning of experience might question the need for theory and hence assist in the putting on of the spectacles in a self-aware sense.[23]

It is in this wider, suggestive sense that there may be scope for the economic agent approach – not designed for normative purpose but to put down an experiential basis for asking questions about economic life. This will not in itself lead to formal economics because formal economics makes use of assumptions and techniques that do not literally exist. The consistent textbook pattern – rule followed by application, definition followed by example – is the textbook manifestation of this fact. It is precisely because of this that there will exist an intellectual tension in the consideration of reality.

Although this chapter has used some of the presuppositions of economic theory as a basis from which to evaluate statements made about fundamental objectives of economics education, this is not to be taken to mean that educational activities in economics must only be organized on a full-bodied discipline basis. In any negotiation between wider educational goals and economics teaching, the discipline ought not to be expected to make a contribution that it can itself sustain. On this basis we cannot, as economists, teach people directly to be 'better' consumers, citizens or workers. Nor can we teach people to be rational, though we can help them to see that formal analysis, founded on the technical notion of rationality, can assist in the clarification of ideas about the functioning of markets or the causes and consequences of government policy. The result of such activity may well have beneficial effects at some stage on resource allocation but only as a consequence of individuals having understood the nature of economic argument and of being able to recognize a context within which economic thinking is relevant. Whether it has any directly observable consequences in society will depend partly on the individual and collective willingness to trust economic analysis (not high among the general public) and on the individual's ability to influence others. This is not 'understanding the world in which we live': understanding the world in which we live is a life-long activity (with numerous false starts) but it is understanding the strengths and weakness of the consequences of seeing the world in terms of choice, rationality, opportunity cost.

Notes and references

1. It does not deal with the problem of setting objectives at the level of the individual lesson for a specific group of students. The interaction between overall and specific objectives in chs 1 and 2 of Willie Henderson, *Teaching Economics in African Secondary Schools* (Heinemann Educational Books, 1980) is relevant.
2. This chapter has not been conceived as a review of existing literature and therefore makes only a highly selective reference to established literature.
3. Joint Committee, *The Teaching of Economics in Schools* (Macmillan, 1973).
4. Fox, K.A., 'What children bring to school: the beginnings of economic education', *Social Education*, vol. 42, no. 6, 1978, pp. 478–81.
5. Boyer, W.H., 'Economic miseducation', *Education Perspectives*, vol. 17, no.2, 1978, pp. 30–2. Boyer makes the point that the Joint Council calls for 'objectivity' and a 'rational, unemotional approach' to economics teaching but points out that the philosophy of the Joint Council directs students towards 'liberal and conservative ideologies' by the kind of revealing omissions it makes in its publications. In other words, the Joint Council is concerned as much with economics socialization as it is with economic argument. Whether we agree or not with Boyer's argument and evidence, it is clear that we must, as educators, be quite certain that we understand the formal meaning of 'understanding', 'rationality' and the nature of 'prediction'.
6. Many branches of economic analysis are more concerned with the development of criteria for 'good' state behaviour rather than 'good' citizen behaviour, for example, the rules for a 'good' system of taxation.
7. From an unpublished paper by Marshall and quoted by Pigou in *Memorials of Alfred Marshall* (Macmillan, 1925) p. 89.
8. Horton, R.V., and Weidenaar, D.J., 'Wherefore economic education?' *Journal of Economic Education*, vol. 7, no. 1, 1975, pp. 40–4.
9. DES, *Curriculum 11–16 Working Papers by HM Inspectorate: A Contribution to the Current Debate* (HMSO, December 1977).
10. In the past, controversy of this sort has been virtually removed from elementary texts; see Cameron, J., Cole, K., and Edwards, C., 'Teaching economics principles as part of development studies', *Institute of Development Studies Bulletin*, vol. 2, no. 3, July 1980, pp. 4–13 (section headed 'Avoiding the issue in standard textbooks and blaming politicians').
11. Horton and Weidenaar, op. cit.
12. The American usage is without the 's'.
13. Hansen, W. Lee, 'The state of economic literacy', in Wentworth, D.R., *et*

al., *Perspectives on Economic Education* (New York Joint Council for Economic Education).

14. On page 14 of the *General Theory of Employment, Interest and Money*, (Macmillan, 1936), Keynes has the following to say about workers' behaviour:

> Thus it is fortunate that the workers, though unconsciously, are instinctively more reasonable economists than the classical school, in as much as they resist reductions of money-wages, which are seldom or never of an all-round character, even though the existing real equivalent of these wages exceeds the marginal disutility of the existing employment, whereas they do not resist reductions of real wages, which are associated with increases in aggregate employment and leave relative money-wages unchanged, unless the reduction proceeds so far as to threaten a reduction of the real wage below the marginal disutility of the existing volume of employment.

15. See Jeffreys's section on the key concepts of economics (Chapter 1 above).

16. Evidence of unwillingness to face controversy in some texts has already been presented. This is a difference between introductory economic texts and introductory scientific texts. They are similar to, but not the same as, science texts.

17. Tadros, A., 'Linguistic production in economics text', unpublished PhD thesis, University of Birmingham, 1981, is an attempt to use English as a key to unlock the structure of an economics text. Henderson, W., 'Metaphor in economics', *Economics*, vol. 18, part 4, no. 80, winter 1982, is also an attempt to think out thought process/language process issues. Mead, R., and Henderson, W., 'Conditional form and meaning in economics text', *English for Special Purposes Journal*, vol. 2, no. 2, July 1983, try to look at 'if/then' language in Lipsey to see what kind of statements are signalled by 'if/then' constructs. At a simpler level, students frequently find it difficult to go from written statements to diagrams and from diagrams to written statements (and hence to distinguish between illustration and prediction).

18. From Keynes, J.M., *Alfred Marshall* (Macmillan, 1956) p. 70.

19. There is some; for example, Linda Thomas's work on the psychology of understanding economic concepts. See Chapter 3.

20. If students are not simply to learn a principle and then apply the principle in a given context then they need to be faced with the question 'what kind of ideas do we need to explore this problem'. This is what I mean by 'before the event' unfolding this content. Henderson's 'Metaphor in economics', op. cit., is an example of the kind of thinking that we would have to do, as economics educators, to explore for ourselves problems created by before the event approaches to economics teaching.

21. Henderson, *Teaching Economics in African Secondary Schools*, op. cit., chs 1 and 2.

22. And some of which are still being actively explored by economists who belong to a different intellectual tradition from that which forms the basis of Chapter 1.

23. That is, in the sense of being aware that the spectacles help us to focus on events but accepting that a different kind of 'seeing' aid would focus in a different way.

3 The Core of Economics – A Psychological Viewpoint
Linda Thomas

Introduction

In the early 1970s J.M. Oliver wrote:

> There has been an embarrassing difference between the rigour and elegance with which economists have thought and written about economics and that with which they have thought and written about the teaching of economics.[1]

> There is much to be proud of in modern economics but, I fear, much less in what is known about the teaching of economics.[2]

Since that time, partly because of the explosive growth of the subject at A-level and partly in response to government statements such as the Green Paper, *Education in Schools: A Consultative Document* (1977) and reports by the DES[3] and Schools Council,[4] economics education has been the focus of more searching attention.

Significant advances have occurred in our knowledge. First, we know more about the nature of economics knowledge and its significance for economics education. Second, the objectives of economics education have been clarified. Third, we now appreciate more thoroughly the kind of economics understanding that is achieved by our students. Our ability to educate in economics is influenced by each of these areas: by the demands of the discipline; by educational ideas; by our knowledge about learning. Chapters 1 and 2 deal with the first two areas. The first part of this chapter is concerned with the psychological aspects of economics education and it describes some of the advances that have occurred in our knowledge of psychological aspects of economics understanding.

It is true that a great deal of work remains to be done. For example, it is not yet possible to provide a definitive account of the process that enables a student to 'get on the inside' of the discipline. Both Jeffreys and Henderson demonstrate that further research is needed.

Teachers may therefore not be convinced of the importance of the advances that have occurred since they cannot easily be represented in the form of practical prescriptions. But even if we cannot yet use the knowledge gained in the last few years in a practical way, some progress has been made, as is shown in these three chapters. Indeed it is possible to argue that enough progress has been made to form a sound basis for critical analysis and evaluation by teachers of the effects of changes in education, of developments in the curriculum and, in particular, of statements emanating from the debate about economics education.

In other words, although we cannot say 'do these things and your students will understand economics', we *can* say such things as 'that is unrealistic' or 'this is based on a discredited theory' or 'these are the assumptions underlying the statements' or 'if you do that, your students are unlikely to understand economics', etc. The second part of this chapter attempts to conduct this kind of analysis by evaluating some of the recent statements made about various aspects of economics education against the views contained in Chapters 1 and 2 and the first part of this chapter.

Economics education and economics understanding: a psychological account

Theories of instruction are traditionally used to produce a practical interpretation of particular learning theories. They are generally concerned to identify the implications of a particular learning theory stance for the construction of efficient learning environments. Two approaches in particular, one associated with Bruner[5] the other with Gagné[6] and Bloom,[7] have had some influence on the way in which teachers approach their task.

The learning experiences model

The chief features of the 'learning experiences' model, which owes much to the work of Gagné and Bloom, are detailed task analysis, the setting up of operational statements of the desired pupil behaviour, and the identification of efficient sequencing of subject matter. In this model, the teacher begins by identifying desired outcomes and setting objectives. By asking 'what would the individual have to be able to do in order to attain successful performance on this task?' and repeating the procedure for each prerequisite[8] mentioned, the teacher develops learning hierarchies that identify all the elements of the total performance. These elements are then restated in the form of precise objectives. Learning is seen purely as a function of the mastery of a particular objective.

This model is not at present particularly helpful to the economics teacher because it is impossible to answer the question 'what would the individual have to be able to do in order to know economics?' Indeed, it may never be possible to specify, in behavioural terms, the meaning of being on the inside of economics, in the same way as it is possible to specify what it means to be able to cook or to drive a car or to be a banker! And we may never even be able to specify, in behavioural terms, what it means to understand specific economics concepts. For example, consider the use of the learning experiences model to analyse the task of understanding the concept of elasticity. It may be possible to produce a learning hierarchy to identify all the elements of a successful 'elasticity' performance. But where would the students' understanding of the appropriateness of its use as a tool in certain situations appear in such a specification of performance? And how could this understanding be resolved in any sensible way into prerequisite parts? Yet the kind of understanding that informs the student when to use and when not to use a concept and that eventually develops into an appreciation of the kind of analysis that is appropriate in different circumstances is crucial in economics.

The learning experiences model may therefore never be particularly useful. But it is our duty as economics teachers to attempt to specify as clearly as possible what we mean by understanding a concept and therefore to find alternative ways of doing so.

The structure of the disciplines model
One possibility exists in the totally different approach to classroom learning that emphasizes the importance of the structure of the disciplines.

This work is inspired by the arguments of Bruner, who suggested that: 'any idea or problem or body of knowledge can be presented in a form simple enough so that any particular learner can understand it in a recognizable form'.[9] In a later work, Bruner reconstructs the events that provided the impetus and inspiration for *The Process of Education*. The late 1950s and 1960s: 'was a time of great concern over the intellectual aimlessness of our schools. Great strides had been made in many fields of knowledge and these advances were not being reflected in what was taught in our schools.'[10]

So in order to bridge the gap between the disciplines and the curriculum and in order to afford access, for pupils, to the knowledge that they require in a modern society, Bruner, among others, emphasizes the importance of the structure of knowledge, and of the disciplines:

The prevailing notion was that if you understood the structure of knowledge, that understanding would then permit you to go ahead on your own; you did not need to encounter everything in nature in order to know nature, but by understanding some deep principles you could extrapolate to the particular as needed.[11]

The structure of knowledge
Bruner is a developmentalist who, heavily influenced by Piaget, believes that cognitive development is the result of interaction between individuals and the environment with which they come to terms via language. Unlike Piaget who is concerned with organizational structure

or the operational characteristics of the processes that allow us to 'code' our experiences and form internal representations, Bruner[12] is more interested in the processes themselves. He proposes that Piaget's stages[13] should be reinterpreted in terms of representational process, the process used to represent experience. He describes three stages: the enactive, in which the child represents by means of systems of action appropriate for achieving a certain result; the iconic, in which the child represents by means of perception and imagery; and the symbolic, which allows coding to be in terms of a set of symbolic or logical propositions drawn from a symbolic system. The system, like any language, is governed by rules or laws for forming and transforming propositions. It operates as an explanation of the development of intellect, it functions at the same level of generality and it works in much the same way as Piaget's concept of formal operations. First, it is actualized in all uses of language or symbols or tools, in sequential behaviour and in the organization of experience. Second, once it is available, the individual has the potential to know everything, that is, to re-create all knowledge.

A theory of learning cannot stop at this point, since a general theory of intellectual development is not a complete explanation of the way in which the individual is empowered to learn or to construct the systems of knowledge. Bruner suggests that symbolic representation, especially language, allows the individual to organize experiences into more generalized forms, that is, to conceptualize. The process of conceptualizing implies the development of a knowledge of coding systems, that is, the rules that allow concepts to be formed. These may then be utilized to create order by allowing the connections between concepts or categories to be systematically explored. The order that is imposed on particular categories takes the form of general categories or coding systems; when these are totally abstracted from experience they take the form of generic coding systems.

Bruner perceives the disciplines as possessing their own means of imposing order on the conceptual world. He uses the word structure to denote this ability. It consists of a set of underlying principles that set out the legitimate connections between, and the legitimate definitions of, the discipline's categories. In other words, it describes the organizing principles that apply to the body of knowledge represented by the discipline. Bruner's message, as is illustrated above, is that in order to make the disciplines and the results of the knowledge explosion accessible to pupils, 'the curriculum of a subject should be determined by the most fundamental understanding that can be achieved by the underlying principles that give structure to that subject'.[14]

The use of logical structures in economics

Many economics educators, convinced by the argument that emphasizes the need to simplify, suggest that the proper starting point in the design of economics courses is a conceptual analysis of economics as a discipline. A number of attempts to identify the subject's underlying principles have been made; for example by the Joint Council,[15] Senesh,[16] Wiggins,[17] Lumsden and Attiyeh,[18] the Joint Committee,[19] Holley,[20] and the Manchester Economics Project.[21]

Some of these attempt not only to specify the 'core' of the discipline but also to specify the logical connections between content elements and core principles. (*Our Working World*[22] and the Manchester Economics Project[23] – the practical schemes that are the results of attempts to implement Senesh's[24] ideas – are also spiral curricula since the logical connections between elements and core principles are arranged in a spiral pattern.) One factor that is common to them all is the fact that the existence of scarcity and unlimited wants is designated as the core and the remainder of economics is derived from it.[25] Whether or not the resulting format is accepted as a valid specification of economics depends to a certain extent on the outcome of the debate about the nature of economics knowledge.[26] But some of the implications of this view of economics understanding deserve immediate attention. One of these concerns the status of students' real-life economic experiences.

The problem of experience

Senesh, for example, is convinced, 'that children's experiences are potentially so meaningful that the fundamental ideas of economics can be related to youth experience, at first-grade level'.[27] Wilkinson also argues that, 'the principle of developing an awareness from the pupils' experience would seem to be generally applicable at any stage'.[28]

It may, indeed, be possible to teach economics in an intellectually honest form to very young children. But the results of my own work[29] cast doubt on the suggestion that students' experiences necessarily or even normally form a sound basis for economics education.

A third approach – psychological structures

The research study into adolescent pupils' understanding of some economic concepts that I conducted in 1979–83 was not initially set up to investigate pupils' economic misconceptions. It was designed to explore various aspects of economics understanding and, if possible, to identify their characteristics. First, it was concerned with the circumstances in which the word 'comprehension' might be legitimately applied with regard to individual concepts. For the purposes of the research, the concepts chosen were wealth/income, money, shops, costs, the dynamics of industrial change, price, standard of living, the law of diminishing returns, *ceteris paribus*, opportunity cost, elasticity and average cost. Second, it was concerned with more general differences in ways of understanding economics, for example, the characteristics of and differences between understanding terms, understanding concepts and understanding the economics approach. Eventually it became impossible to ignore a third area – the implications of the study for the existence of economics misconceptions.

The underlying assumption was that understanding in economics cannot be identified simply by examining the logical structure of the subject (the method used by Senesh, for example, and advocated by Bruner), or by analysing a given concept in terms of prerequisite skills and concepts (the method advocated by Gagné, for example). What was also required was a close analysis of student performance in order to expose the distinctive features of and indispensable conditions for comprehension – the psychological structure of the concepts.[30]

In order to do this as objectively as possible, tests were constructed.[31] Two hundred and thirty-seven 12- to 19-year-old pupils were given twenty-nine tests in 1-hour individual interviews conducted during ordinary school days. The answers they gave to each individual task were recorded, transcribed and scored by referring to the detailed descriptions of performance provided by Elkind, Piaget and Shayer.[32]

Individual concepts
For each individual concept, the answers awarded the same score were grouped and the different groups were scrutinized to identify the similarities and differences between them in terms of understanding economics. Finally, these relationships were analysed in order to obtain some, at least, of the distinctive features of and indispensable conditions for comprehension of each individual concept. Appendix 3.1, for example, illustrates the use of this procedure to obtain distinctive features of comprehension of the concepts of money, price and standard of living.

Three ways of understanding
On the basis of this research, it is possible to make three general and tentative statements about economics understanding. First, comprehension of such concepts as money, wealth/income, and shops in economic terms is dependent on students' willingness to reassess terms whose meanings have, hitherto, been formed as a result of their previous experiences.

Second, comprehension of such concepts as costs, price, standard of living and the law of diminishing returns, in economic terms, is dependent on students' ability to perceive them as operational systems,[33] rather than as a means of classifying experience. This may have some teaching implications. For example, the results of the costs items suggest that pupils may have to perceive cost as a system of interrelated variables – factor inputs and outputs – which specifies the effect of changes in any factor on the interrelationships, in order to be able to comprehend the concept in economic terms. The implication for learning is that it may be more important for pupils to explore the system and its interrelationships, for example, the alternative adjustments available to the system to enable it to absorb, counteract or nullify the effect of changes in wages, rent and interest, than to quantify and describe its components, for example, fixed costs, variable costs, rates, salaries, wages and raw material costs. Another implication of the results of items on costs is that teachers should be aware of the strength of the 'costs equal price' myth.

The results of the item on price suggest that pupils may have to perceive price as a mechanism that eliminates excess supply or demand in order to comprehend it. The implication for learning is that it may be more important to concentrate on the instrumentality of price – price as a mechanism – rather than to follow the normal instructional sequences – the demand curve as the relationship between demand and price and the supply curve as the relationship between costs and price – which emphasize the identity between price and costs or price and demand.

The results of the item on the law of diminishing returns suggest that pupils may have to be aware of the constant factor assumption in order to comprehend the law of diminishing returns. The implication for learning is that the normal instruction method, in which the short-run situation is treated separately from the long-run, may exacerbate the problem and that it may be important to consider the effects of varying all factors of production in order to emphasize the effect of keeping one or more factors constant.

The results of the item on standard of living suggest that pupils may have to be capable of applying rather than merely articulating a rule linking proportional changes in two variables in order to comprehend standard of living. The implication for learning is that the provision of situations that require application of the rule may be essential if full understanding is to be achieved.

Third, comprehension of the nature of economic explanation and the use made by economists of *ceteris paribus* clauses and of the notion of opportunity cost is dependent on students' ability to disassociate themselves from the task and to adopt an objective, scientific approach. This may imply the need for teachers who wish pupils to tackle problems of an economics nature in an economics way to present the problems so as to encourage as full an analysis as possible and to discourage any tendency to personalize the problems. It may even be necessary to avoid problems that tempt pupils to provide solutions that are based on an appeal to individual or mass opinion. These implications are fully explored in the last section of this chapter.

Economics misconceptions
My research also unexpectedly provides evidence about the nature of the link between pupils' experiences of the economic world, the kind of order they impose on these experiences, and economics understanding. For example, answers to the costs tasks that I used demonstrate the existence of the belief that costs and price are identities and that all wage rises must inevitably lead to an increase in price; answers to the supply and demand task show that many students see price as a means of exploitation; answers to the standard of living task show that it is often perceived as an entity that must be protected or defended; answers to the money task show that it is often seen purely in terms of its physical representation (see Appendix 3.1). Clearly, these preconceptions are formed on the basis of past experiences; they are well established and useful ones since they allow students to make some sense of the real world; but they do not necessarily match an economics understanding in the sense that the term is used here. Paradoxically, the fact that our students do create an order out of and impose some sort of sense on their experiences may prove to be the greatest challenge for economics teachers.[34] It is certainly possible to predict that economics understanding will never be easily achieved since, at the very least, it requires some redefinition of terminology, a realignment of attitudes towards the nature of economic argument and a reformulation of concepts in operational terms.

It is possible to argue that the data that are produced as a result of experience of the physical world incorporate that form of understanding that is labelled scientific understanding. It is *not* valid to argue that the data that are produced as a result of experience of the economic system necessarily incorporate that form of understanding that is called economics understanding.

This may imply that economics teachers who want their students to develop *economics* understanding cannot afford to assume that experience of what Henderson calls 'economics as a substantive activity' (p. 38) will suffice. Instead they must either create imaginative experiences that incorporate, in the data, the intended form of understanding – economics understanding – or, by selecting from the range of experience of the economic system available to the pupil, impose a structure on that experience which would achieve the same result.

As has been previously argued, we are not yet in a position to say precisely what should be done to achieve this. But by examining the implication of this work, it is now possible to conduct some evaluation of existing courses and statements and also to provide some general, non-prescriptive guidance. This is attempted in the next section.

Sense or nonsense in economics education

The role of description
The following statements were made (i) by a teacher of economics who wanted to point out the implications of integrating economics within social studies courses below the age of 16 (ii) by the DES, and (iii) by the Social Sciences Working Party Report.

(i) 'You will need to produce material for non-specialist teachers and non-specializing pupils of a multinational firm, of a trade union, the economy of a town, the decision-making process in local government over rates and expenditure.'

(ii) 'There are certain economic facts that the curriculum ought to impart to pupils. For example, the nature of the "world of work" implies that pupils should know what we mean by industry or commerce. Actual examples of these things need to be given. The position of Great Britain as a trading and manufacturing nation with a growing service sector requires a description of industrial morphology, regional patterns of industry and work and communications. Pupils ought to have an accurate grasp of the extent and nature of the work force, the changing nature of British industry, the size of imports and exports, and of rates of exchange between the main international currencies and the pound sterling.'[35]

(iii) '*Content*
4.1   By the end of a social science course at 16+ students should have some understanding of:
4.1.5   the processes of decision making, formal and informal, at national, local and individual levels;
4.2   Any syllabus with the title Economics should include . . . 4.1.5'.[36]

In educational terms, these suggestions may make sense, but it is difficult to avoid the implication that since economic phenomena exist, pupils ought to know about them. The immediate problem with this view is a logistics one; since all economics phenomena that exist would have a valid claim for inclusion in such a course, how can an excessive amount of content be reduced to manageable proportions? What criteria are available in order to create an order of merit of economics facts and institutions? Who decides whether or not information about the market in pawpaws in Peru should be included in an economics course in Putney? Are textbook content, the interests of teachers and students or examination syllabuses the only guides?

The next problem that must be faced by this view of economics is that it is not consistent with the analysis of economics education contained in these chapters. First, it does not share the discipline's purpose – the

search for general principles of behaviour – or its deductive methodology, since it implies that if enough information is provided about an
economics phenomenon, its explanation will become self-evident.
Second, it does not share the discipline's perspective, it has no theory
base, no view of the world beyond the exposition of mere information
about how things are. Third, by implication, it makes no contribution
to an economics education that seeks to make the economics way of
looking at things accessible to pupils. Lastly, it ignores the problem of
describing the link between experience or information about economics
phenomena and economics understanding.

Economics teachers are well aware of the importance of the existence
of the institutions, habits and mechanisms that form the economic
system, and of the need to promote understanding of the functions of
institutions. But they regard them as part of the product of an
economics education, and would argue that the description of institutions and the provision of information, as ends in themselves, are a
waste of time. If they are to be included in the curriculum they must be
justified by some other means.

What are economics problems?

The Economics Association's submission to the GCE and CSE boards'
joint council for 16+ national criteria included this statement:

*Aims for an Economics Course for a target group consisting of the most able 60% of
the age group*
a. To develop a knowledge and understanding of the basic economic problem
    of allocating scarce resources among competing groups in society.

The ultimate aim of a course in economics at this level should be to develop in
pupils a capacity to analyse and discuss problems of an economic nature at
various levels in the community.[37]

Unfortunately, this multipurpose use of the word 'problem' creates
some confusion. Economic *problems* are the reason for the existence of
economics because they give rise to attempts to solve them – the
techniques, behaviours, institutions, constraints, mechanisms, policies, motivation, habits of economics systems. The economists' *problem*
is to find a way of analysing and explaining how the system works. The
discipline of economics encapsulates the economists' way of approaching the task, that is, by analysing choice behaviour. This uniquely
economics way of doing things may be described as a common purpose,
methodology and perspective; it is shared by all mainstream economists. The *problem* for the economics teacher is to facilitate the process
by which students develop an appreciation of and an ability to participate in the economics way of working.

It is necessary to note with respect to the first part of the statement that while a proper understanding of the rationale for economics is probably a prerequisite of the process of initiation into the discipline's way of working, it is difficult to see why it is elevated to the status of an aim.

In addition, the second part of the above statement requires redefinition if it is to conform to the analysis conducted here. There are many ways to analyse and discuss problems of an economics nature; the engineer, sociologist and economist will approach the same problem very differently. What is crucial in economics education is that pupils are expected to analyse and discuss problems of an economics nature *in an economics way*.

What does the phrase 'in an economics way' mean at A-level?

At A-level, the phrase probably implies at least some appreciation of the use of the notion of rationality to develop models of constrained maximization. But it is also important to ensure that students understand why economics exists and that they appreciate the purpose, procedures and rules of economics discourse – the economics perspective and methodology – so that they are able to participate in it even if their contribution is an unsophisticated one.

Examination syllabuses at A-level tend to support this view. The Southern Board's syllabus, for example, states that the purpose is 'to test a candidate's grasp of a framework of elementary analytical techniques which can be applied to a wide range of problems in the fields of both micro and macro economics in a market economy' (p. 50). The London Board's syllabus stresses that economics understanding means more than reproduction – it means also the ability to apply. The move towards the introduction of data-response papers, initiated by the JMB, is a reflection of this view.

The literature is not over-endowed with examples of practical teaching situations illustrating this approach. At this stage it is not easy to provide useful prescriptions. But some progress has been made. Daniel Jeffreys in a footnote provides one example; David Whitehead's chapter contains another. Papps,[38] in an account of the Sussex University problem-oriented approach, showed how the students were encouraged to use their economics. For example, discussion of the question 'Should the miners be paid the increased wage which they are demanding?' was channelled into three avenues: (i) discussion of the economic analysis appropriate for this question and the economic implications of this analysis (e.g. would you expect an increase in miners' wages to affect the demand for coal?), (ii) discussion of the facts involved (e.g. what is the elasticity of the demand for coal?), (iii) discussion of value judgements about the objectives of policy and conflicts between different objectives (e.g. is the question concerned about the distribution of income, inflation or the supply of fuel? Or all three?).

What does the phrase 'in an economics way' mean below A-level?
Surveys of the non-A-level sector of school and further education curricula by King,[39] Holley and Skelton,[40] Besley[41] and Cressey[42] reveal that the numbers of non-A-level students studying economics is small and that economics courses are mainly descriptive and institutional. However, these surveys also reveal the large variety of courses in which economics plays a part, for example, commerce, social economics, understanding British industry, family economics, money management, economics and public affairs, social education, world of work, skills for living and integrated social studies courses.

If the problem facing economics teachers below A-level is to find ways in which they can make an economics education contribution to skills for living, world of work, descriptive courses, etc., it is important to translate the notion of economics understanding that is contained in this and the previous chapters into a form – a working definition – that is acceptable at this level. The following checklist is an attempt to do this (i.e. to define the meaning at this level of the phrase 'in an economics way') in a non-prescriptive way.[43]

CHECKLIST – A WORKING DEFINITION OF ECONOMICS UNDERSTANDING

Economics teachers will enable students to achieve the realism and objectivity that are essential features of economics understanding if they insist that courses to which they contribute encourage students to respond to situations and experiences that necessitate choice in an economics rather than a personal or intuitive way, to examine those situations by means of an economics rather than a descriptive approach, and thereby encourage them to develop an economics perspective *because they will then*
(1) be in a position to correct any misconceptions formed as a result of early economics experiences;
(2) be able to combat the effects of a too enthusiastic initiation into 'rules' of consumer and producer behaviour;
(3) be able to begin to appreciate the use of economic power and the potential for exploitation;
(4) be able to identify when value judgements are being made and the difference between facts and values;
(5) have got a feel of the method – analysis of choice behaviour – economists employ to understand, predict and explain the behaviour of the economic system.

**Examples of the
economics approach**
The use of the concept of opportunity cost as a means of analysis –
to determine the relevant variables for analysis and to gather and
evaluate information.[44]

Economics teachers will directly improve the level of economics
understanding if they make sure that courses to which they contribute
allow students to conceptualize – that is, to appreciate the economics
characteristics of the institutions and variables and to explore relationships and interconnections – *because they will then*
(1) be able to use the concepts[45] that are used by economists to classify and to
describe relationships;
(2) have gained some idea of how the economic system works, not only how
institutions work;
(3) be able to tell the difference between the way an institution views the
world and describes its functions and the way an economist would do so.

**Examples of concepts
and relationships**
Money, price, standard of living, costs, etc.; the role and importance of industry and institutions; the meaning and implications
of economic growth; the difference between income, value added
and wealth; the effect of government; the relationship of the parts
to the whole.

Economics teachers will be able to prepare the ground on which to
build economics understanding if the courses to which they contribute
give their students an adequate information base *because students will
then, for example, be able to identify the terms that are used in newspaper
and television reports.*

Examples of information
The meaning of terms such as banks, balance of payments,
exports, etc.; the characteristics and functions of institutions
such as trade unions, VAT, etc.

Economics teachers will be able to lay a sound foundation for
developing economics understanding if they use the courses to which
they contribute to provide their students with opportunities to develop

and practise intellectual, procedural and practical skills *because they will be able to act confidently in the complex modern world not only as informed but also as competent consumers and producers.*

Examples of skills
The ability to handle simple data and statistics; knowing where to go for information; practising decision-making skills; getting into the habit of respecting evidence.

Conclusions

The report of the Joint Committee on the teaching of economics in schools lists the qualities that it considers a student of economics would be encouraged to develop. These include:

a capacity to understand the mutual interrelations and interdependencies of the various elements in an economic system and to take account of them in handling economic problems; a capacity to apply to an economic problem the models of economics analysis that are most appropriate to it; a capacity to follow and sustain an economic argument and to make logical inferences from given information.[46]

During the past ten years, considerable efforts have been made to translate this into more concrete course structures and prescriptions, especially at A-level. But a great deal of the economics that features in many courses that purport to provide economics education bears little or no resemblance to the above description. Therefore there is a need to review progress and to examine the present situation in the debate.

The burden of the argument presented here is that economics education must, first and foremost, be true to the discipline itself and help pupils to develop an economics perspective since this must be the only way to develop students' understanding of economic processes and systems. Other educational objectives will automatically be achieved as a result; in particular, an opportunity will be provided to dislodge the preconceptions formed on the basis of experience.

Appendix 3.1

Psychological structures

The distinctive features and indispensable conditions for comprehension of the concepts of money, price, standard of living
MONEY
Question (Money I)
Can you tell me what money is?

Score = 0
Criteria
A score of 0 was awarded for definitions in terms of the physical characteristics of money, or for definitions with moral overtones.
Examples
'Things that are worth something because they're made of valuable metal'
'It's small, hard, round coins made of metal'
'To me it doesn't mean anything'
'Some people think it's important'
'The thing people get for working'
'It's a way of saying you've got something in coins and notes'
'It's round and shiny and makes a noise when it's dropped'
'Green paper'

Score = 1
Criteria
A score of 1 was awarded for definitions in terms of the function of money as a medium of exchange.
Examples
'Do you mean what you use it for?'
'What you use to buy things'
'When you work you earn money and you can buy things'
'Something you spend'
'A thing you can exchange for goods'
'Saves you going out and taking things'
'Form of trading, instead of trading with corn as they did long ago'
'Metal and paper circulated to buy things'
'It's not so much what it is, as what it's used for'
'Just bits of paper – used for swopping'

Question (Money II)
There are two shops in Paris and London selling identical pens. In the first money pile there are four fifty-pence pieces and in the second pile there are four five-franc pieces. Each franc is worth about 10p. How much is 5 francs? What can you tell me about this amount of English money and this amount of French money? If you went into this shop in London you could buy the four pens by using your £2.00. How much does each pen cost? If you went into this Paris shop you could buy these four pens with your 20 francs. How much does each pen cost? The pens are identical aren't they?

Now let's repeat the experiment but on a different day. If you go into the same London shop you find you can still buy four pens with £2.00. But when you look at the price of the French pens in the Paris shop you find that you can only buy three pens for 20 francs.
(i)   Is £2.00 now worth more than 20 francs, the same as, or less than 20 francs?
(ii) Have you still got the same French money now?

Score = 0
Criteria
A score of 0 was awarded if answers showed that the subjects perceived money as possessing an unchanging value.
Examples
   (i) *PB* 'The same as'

(ii) *PB* 'Yes, it's the same.'
   I 'But you can only buy three pens now.'
   PB 'Yes'
   I 'What's happened?'
   PB 'Price has gone up'
   I 'Have you still got the same French money then?'
   PB 'Yes'
(i) *LB* 'The same as; the value of pens has gone up'
(ii) *LB* 'Yes, it's the same'
   I 'But they won't buy as many pens'
   LB 'I know'
(i) *DC* 'The same as that'
(ii) *DC* 'Yes'
   I 'But you can only buy three pens now'
   DC 'It's worth less. Oh! no, the price has gone up'
   I 'So it's worth less?'
   DC 'Yes'
   I 'So what about that money? Have you got the same?'
   DC 'Yes'
   I 'But it's worth less?'
   DC 'No, worth the same'

Score = 1
Criteria
A score of 1 was awarded to answers that perceived that the value of money changed under certain circumstances but that explained this in terms of price rises and therefore frequently got the direction of change wrong.
Examples
(i) *NA* 'More than that'
(ii) *NA* 'No'
   I 'Why not?'
   NA 'Because they're worth more'
   I 'But have you got the same money?'
   NA 'Yes, you've got the same amount'
   I 'But you can only buy three pens now'
   NA 'You get one of the coins back'
   I 'No'
   NA 'Oh! they've gone up'
   I 'But you've got the same money?'
   NA 'Yes'

Score = 2
Criteria
A score of 2 was awarded for answers that agreed, either with or without guidance, that the value of money was changed as a result of the transformation.
Examples
(i) *DW* 'More than'
(ii) *DW* 'No, it's lost its value'
Discussion
Answers to the first of the money questions showed that 179 pupils, the vast majority of pupils in the sample, when asked to define money, gave a functional

rather than a perceptual definition. But only 80 of them also responded to the second money question in a way that showed that they were prepared to separate completely the idea of money and its physical representation, and gave answers that were called level A answers. Two other kinds of responses were made to the transformation which was performed in the question and these illustrated two different interpretations of the concept of money. One set of answers, called level C answers, showed that pupils, despite the definitions given in response to the first money question, believed that money was represented by its physical characteristics. In fact, twenty-seven pupils who had *defined* money in functional terms showed by their reaction to the transformation task in the second money question that they *understood* money to be something that was unaffected by its usefulness in terms of the degree of purchasing power it conferred – all that was important was its physical characteristics, that is, the figures printed on it. The other set of answers, called level B answers, also showed that pupils did not believe that the transformation had made any significant difference to the money; what had changed were such things as prices or the relative values of the French and English money, but the money itself had remained the same since its physical characteristics had not altered.

The preliminary explanation and description of the questions were used to check pupils' ability to deal with the computations involved. Only four failed to do so.

PRICE

Question

Study this apparatus. You may undo the clamps and move the arms if you wish. When the arms are clamped in this position we can allow this arm to represent the demand, for, say, ice-cream, that is, the number of ice-creams which, at the end of school for 10 minutes, pupils want to buy from the ice-cream seller outside the gate. This arm we can call supply, that is, the number of ice-creams which during the same time, the ice-cream seller is willing to sell. The level of coloured water in the supply arm we can call the price of ice-cream. If it's a very warm day then you'd expect the demand for ice-cream at any time during the day to be higher than it would be if it were a very cold wet day. So we would expect to raise the demand tube.

(i)   What happens to the price of ice-cream when I raise demand?

(ii)   Can you tell me what to do to the apparatus to lower the water level?

(iii) What should I do if I want to reduce price to its original level?

Score = 0

A score of 0 was awarded for answers that could not be objective about manipulating demand and supply.[47]

Examples

(iii) *GB* 'Supply more ice-creams'
        I 'Or what do I do to demand?'
        GB 'Put the price down'
        I 'That's what I want to do'
        GB 'Sell less ice-creams'
        I 'I thought you said more?'
        GB 'I mean sell more'
        I 'What about wanting ice-creams? Should you stop them wanting?'

> *GB* 'No, make some people have them'
> *I* 'But watch. What happens?'
> *GB* 'Price goes up'
> *I* 'So what do I do?'
> *GB* 'Bring price down'
> *I* 'How?'
> *GB* 'Sell less ice-creams'
> *I* 'But if I stop the number of people wanting ice-creams what would happen to price?'
> *GB* 'Go up. Oh! no, down'

Score = 1
Criteria
A score of 1 was awarded for answers that showed some perception of the need to manipulate the variables involved but without reference to the system.[48]
Examples

> (iii) *PA* 'That goes down'
> *I* 'Meaning?'
> *PA* 'Less boys wanting ice-cream'
> *I* 'Or that side?'
> *PA* 'Up'
> *I* 'Meaning?'
> *PA* 'The number of ice-creams go down'
> *I* 'No, this apparatus predicts it should go up. Does that make sense?'
> *PA* 'Yes, because he'll make more profit the more people buy if price is lower'

Score = 2
Criteria
A score of 2 was awarded for answers that showed the effects of variables on the system but that gave no explanation of the system's operation.[49]
Examples

> (iii) *CA* 'That goes down'
> *I* 'Meaning?'
> *CA* 'Less girls want ice-creams'
> *I* 'Or?'
> *CA* 'This side up'
> *I* 'Meaning'
> *CA* 'Prices will go up and there won't be enough ice-cream'
> *I* 'No, if it is put up, price goes down. Does that make sense?'
> *CA* 'Oh! yes, I see. If he brings more he can put it down because he'll have the same money as he had before'

Score = 3
Criteria
A score of 3 was awarded for answers giving partial explanations co-ordinating the effect of variables and forces within the system but unable to generalize.[50]
Examples

> (iii) *PB* 'Bring price down'
> *I* 'How?'
> *PB* 'More ice-creams'
> *I* 'Does that make sense?'
> *PB* 'If it was a nasty day it would be because he'd want to get rid of them'

(iii) *AB* 'Raise supply tube'
I 'Does that make sense? If supply rises does price fall?'
AB 'No, not really. Um. If he's got more in his van, demand won't be as much because he's got more than he can sell. No, price'll have to come down'

Score = 4
Criteria
A score of 4 was awarded for answers that generalized to cover the case where demand did not necessarily decrease or remain constant, thus giving a full explanation of the equilibrium of the system.[51]
Examples
(iii) *GH* 'More ice-creams to sell'
I 'Does that make sense?'
GH 'Yes, if he's got more to sell more people will want to buy if price is lower'
(iii) *RT* 'Number of ice-creams goes up'
I 'Does that make sense?'
RT 'Yes, with all those boys wanting them, if he brings more ice-creams it's cheaper at the same time'
Discussion
This item provides evidence of the psychological structure of the concept of price. The answers given in response to the question were grouped according to Piagetian criteria and scrutiny of the groups revealed different concepts of price. The level of understanding of the concept of price that was revealed by one set of answers, called level A answers, was a sophisticated one. Price was conceptualized as the mechanism that could eliminate excess supply or excess demand. Some of the other answers seemed to be extremely varied in character but, in fact, they all conceptualized price in the same way, as an instrument under the control of the suppliers of goods which was used by them to protect or improve present levels of income; they were therefore called level B answers. This conceptualization allowed pupils to support a variety of arguments such as the following: an increase in supply could lead to a reduction in price because the supplier's income would remain constant; an increase in supply could result in bulk buying and a reduction in costs and therefore a reduction in price would not endanger the supplier's income level; an increase in demand would allow an improvement in the supplier's income level; an increase in supply could result in increased costs and therefore an increase in price would be necessary to protect the supplier's income level.

The answers that also conceptualized price as an instrument under the control of suppliers but in which the concept reflected an ethical stance were called level C answers. Price was perceived as a means of exploitation.

These categories represent different levels of meaning of the concept of price. They are derived from the groups formed on the basis of the Piagetian criteria but it can also be argued that they are qualitatively different in economic terms. A fully articulated economic conceptualization of the concept of price is able to trace the effect of changes in demand and supply. An increase in demand leads to an excess of demand over supply at the original price. This may lead to a rise in price which will cause some degree of contraction in the original increase in demand and to which suppliers will respond by raising supply. These responses to the price rise, whether in the form of a fall in demand or a rise in supply, will not, of course, cause a change in the new price level. An excessive rise in supply, or one not caused by a change in price, leads to an excess of supply over demand at that price with corresponding effects. None of the answers to this item achieved this level of articulation but an examination of the relationship between the three levels of answers reveals that a distinctive feature of comprehension of the concept of price is its perception as a mechanism.

In other words, level A answers make more economic sense than level B or level C answers and the major difference between the three types of answers is that level A answers indicate a willingness to regard price as a mechanism rather than a way of classifying experience.

STANDARD OF LIVING

Question

When we talk about how well off we are, we are really trying to give some idea of the kind of things we can afford to buy. So what do you think would be the effect of your getting a wage rise one week? Would you be better off (would you be able to buy more things)? What would happen if you did some extra work for a mate of yours during the weekend? Would you be better off (would you be able to buy more things)? What would happen if suddenly the price of clothes fell by half? Would you be better off (would you be able to buy more clothes or more of other things)?

Mr Jones is an ordinary working man whose one idea is to make sure that he stays as well off as he is now. He doesn't want to be better off and he doesn't want to be worse off either.

I want you to tell me what you think has happened or what you think is going to happen in Mr Jones's life if these three events occur:

(i)   One Friday Mr Jones opened his wage packet and immediately went to ask his foreman if he could work overtime next week;

(ii)   Mr Jones usually shopped in the local hypermarket once a week. One week the prices of all the goods which Mr Jones normally bought rose.

(iii) Mr Jones's wage rise was paid on the same day as his train fares to and from work were raised.

Score = 0

A score of 0 was awarded for answers which were unable to manipulate the system with any objectivity.

Examples

(i)   *AB* 'He's trying to get more money'
      I 'But does he want more money?'
      AB 'Yes, he's changed his mind'
      I 'No, he doesn't want to be better off. So what's happened?'
      AB 'He's short'

(ii)   *AB* 'Buy somewhere else'
      I 'No, everywhere is more expensive. So is he worse off?'
      AB 'Yes'
      I 'Does he want that?'
      AB 'No'
      I 'So?'
      AB 'He'll buy general things he needs'

(iii) *AB* 'He'll be worse off'
      I 'So what will he do?'
      AB 'Don't know'

Score = 1
Criteria
A score of 1 was awarded for answers in which variables were seen to require manipulation but in which wages, for example, were not perceived as part of the system.
Examples
(iii) *TA* 'He wasn't as well off as he thought he was going to be'
   I 'What would he do?'
   TA 'Ask for another pay rise?'
   I 'Would the extra fares take up all his pay rise?'
   TA 'No, but he's got to pay his rates and his food and his taxes and look after his wife'
 (i) *AB* 'He's been working harder – or he's been working the same for more money'
   I 'Why should he do that?'
   AB 'To be better off'
   I 'But he doesn't want that, does he? So what's happened?'
   AB 'His demand for something has increased so he wants more money to buy it'
 (ii) *AB* 'He must buy less things'
(iii) *AB* 'He'll want more money to get on the trains'
   I 'But he's had a wage rise. Does he still want more money?'
   AB 'I think he would. He'll want more work because everything's increasing all the time'

Score = 2
Criteria
A score of 2 was awarded for answers that correctly predicted the effects of changes in variables on the system but that could not explain the equilibrium in the system because they chose to disregard the effect of increasing wages.
Examples
 (i) *RB* 'He's lost money'
 (ii) *RB* 'He's got to get a wage rise'
(iii) *RB* 'He'll have to ask for a rise'
   I 'He's already had one. Why does he need another one?'
   RB 'He's got to pay his train fare, get his food and his living'

Score = 3
Criteria
A score of 3 was awarded for answers that could explain the relationships involved in the system in the form of a law but which did not use the law to generalize.
Examples
(iii) *DJ* 'He'd need another increase except their prices could go up again'
   I 'But he's had a wage rise. Isn't that enough?'
   DJ 'Only just'
   I 'Would he need another rise?'
   DJ 'If he wanted to be better off. Otherwise, no'

Score = 4
Criteria
A score of 4 was awarded for answers that were capable of applying the law in general.
Examples
   (i) *IT* 'Inflation, goods have gone up. He needs more money'
  (ii) *IT* 'Ask for more money or overtime'
 (iii) *IT* 'It depends if it balances or not'

Discussion
This item provides evidence of pupils' understanding of the concept of standard of living. The answers given in response to the questions were grouped according to Piagetian criteria and they revealed different ideas about standard of living. The conception of standard of living that was illustrated by one group of answers, called level A answers (scoring 3 or 4), was framed in terms of the relationship between proportionate increases in wages and prices; in the third part of the item, comparisons were made between the effect of disproportionate changes in wages and train fares.

Answers, labelled level B, were unexpected because they demonstrated quite clearly that the effects of increases in wages on the standard of living were disregarded not because they were misunderstood but because they were considered to be in some way outside the jurisdiction of the rule that was discussed and accepted during the preliminary explanation and that was applied to the standard of living of the person in the item.

Answers that conceptualized standard of living in terms of a predetermined and subjectively formulated notion of an acceptable level of 'well-offness' were called level C answers. Changes in the variables were always considered in relation to this standard and were judged accordingly.

These categories, representing different levels of meaning of the concept of standard of living, are derived from the groups formed by applying the Piagetian criteria. It is possible to argue that they are qualitatively different in terms of their economics content and that they show that one of the distinctive features of comprehension of the concept is an awareness of the objective nature of its structure and its place in an ordered system of variables. Another distinctive feature of comprehension is a grasp of the concept as depicting relative changes in such variables as prices and incomes. That is, pupils must be capable of applying rather than merely articulating a rule linking proportional changes in two variables in order to comprehend standard of living.

Notes and references

1. Oliver, J.M., *The Principles of Teaching Economics* (Heinemann Educational Books, 1973) p. 13.
2. Oliver, J.M., 'The educational value of economics: some practical implications', in Whitehead, D.J. (ed.), *Curriculum Development in Economics* (Heinemann Educational Books, 1974) p. 137.
3. DES, *Curriculum 11–16 Working Papers by HM Inspectorate: A Contribution to the Current Debate* (HMSO, 1977); DES, *A Framework for the School Curriculum* (HMSO, 1980).
4. Schools Council, *Schools Council Principles and Programmes* (Schools

Council, 1979); Schools Council, *The Practical Curriculum* (Methuen, 1981).

5. Bruner, J.S., *Towards a Theory of Instruction* (Harvard University Press, 1966).

6. Gagné, R.M., *The Condition of Learning* (Holt, Rinehart & Winston, 1977).

7. Bloom, R.S., *Human Characteristics and School Learning* (McGraw-Hill, 1976).

8. 'Prerequisite' is the term used to describe the actions identified as necessary for successful performance.

9. Bruner, op. cit., p. 44.

10. Bruner, J.S., 'The process of education revisited', *Phi Delta Kappan*, vol. 53, 1971, pp. 18–21.

11. Ibid., p. 18.

12. Bruner, J.S., 'The course of cognitive growth', *American Psychologist*, vol. 18, 1964, pp. 1–5.

13. Inhelder, B., and Piaget, J., *The Growth of Logical Thinking from Childhood to Adolescence* (Routledge & Kegan Paul, 1958).

14. Bruner, J.S., *The Process of Education* (Harvard University Press, 1961) p. 31.

15. JCEE, *Master Curriculum Guide in Economics for the Nation's Schools. Part 1. A Framework for Teaching Economics Basic Concepts* (Joint Council on Economic Education, 1977).

16. Senesh, L., *Our Working World* (Science Research Associates, 1963); Senesh, L., 'Organising a curriculum around social concepts', in Morrisett, I. (ed.), *Concepts and Structure in the New Social Science Curriculum* (Social Science Consortium, 1966).

17. Wiggins, S., *et al.*, *Econ 12. Instructor's Guide Test Edition*, spring 1967, p. 8 (Pleasant Hill, California: Centre Costa Department of Education, 1971).

18. Lumsden, K., and Attiyeh, R., 'The core of basic economics', *Economics*, vol. 9, pt 1, no. 37, summer 1971.

19. Joint Committee on Economic Education, *The Teaching of Economics in Schools* (Macmillan, 1973).

20. Holley, B.J., 'Economics education 14–16, some basic principles', unpublished paper, 1978.

21. Manchester Economics Project, *Understanding Economics* (Ginn, 1976).

22. Senesh, *Our Working World*, op. cit.

23. Manchester Economics Project, op. cit.

24. Senesh, L., 'The organic curriculum', *The Counselor*, 21 March 1960.

25. It is interesting to note that not one of the schemes that include such ideas as the margin and opportunity cost in their sets of core principles attempts to specify a logical unfolding of economics content.

26. It is, however, interesting to note the cautionary tone of more recent pronouncements. Senesh himself in 1978 (see note 27) admits that his programme 'failed professionally' (p.4). He is dissatisfied with the situation and, in seeking to find reasons, places some blame on teachers who are unable to relate economic concepts to children's experiences or, as he says, 'in using these experiences as take offs to help children become airborne' (p. 4).

The implication is that teachers do not find the task of teaching the

Senesh view of the conceptual structure of economics as easy as he is inclined to believe.

Even Bruner in a review of his earlier work (see note 10) is compelled to state: 'I believe I would be quite satisfied to declare, if not a moratorium, then something of a de-emphasis on matters that have to do with the structure of history, the structure of physics, the nature of mathematical consistency' (p. 21).

27. Senesh, L., 'Educational experiences of an economics educator', *Journal of Economics Education*, 1978, vol. 10, no. 1, p. 3.
28. Wilkinson, R., 'An approach to the teaching of economics in schools', in Whitehead, D.J. (ed.), *Curriculum Development in Economics* (Heinemann Educational Books, 1974) p. 175.
29. Thomas, L.M., '12–16-year-old pupils' understanding of economics', unpublished PhD thesis, University of London, 1983.
30. Psychological structure is used here to describe the conditions that are necessary for understanding, in a logical sense, to occur. It is an orientation to a problem, a perspective, rather than a behavioural prescription. It has implications both for the learner and the teaching situation.
31. It was important to achieve as objective a classification of performance as possible and to reduce contamination from my own subjective perception of the meaning of economics understanding. There was little point in using a subjective interpretation of what it means to comprehend a concept if the intention was to expose that meaning.

Therefore, since the study was required to produce an objective representation of students' economics understanding, it had to find some externally validated yardstick. No other available construct has been as fully developed and validated as the Piagetian one. The original model has attracted a great deal of attention and has not survived intact. But the utility of some parts of the model is accepted even by the full-blown model's sternest critics. For example, the classification scheme developed by Piaget as a means of imposing order on descriptions of behaviour across a range of tasks has been developed by Shayer (Shayer M., 'A test of the validity of Piaget's construct of formal operational thinking', unpublished PhD thesis, University of London, 1978, and 'Has Piaget's construct of formal operational thinking any utility?' *British Journal of Educational Psychology*, vol. 49, 1979, pp. 265–76) and by the *Concepts in Secondary Mathematics and Science* project teams into an extremely useful tool for investigating scientific understanding. On the assumption that these tasks, adapted and developed by Shayer and Elkind (Elkind, D., 'Concept formation', in Elkind, D., and Flavell, J.H. (eds), *Studies in Cognitive Development* (Oxford University Press, 1969)) from the original Piagetian tasks (Inhelder and Piaget, op. cit.), could also be legitimately used to expose students' understanding of economics material, they were given an economics format. In other words, the reformulated Piagetian model was used merely as a tool – an objective measure. None of the other implications of the full-blown Piagetian model applied.

A random sample was drawn from all 12–16-year-old pupils attending the five middle and three high schools in one area in a south London borough. Two hundred and thirty-seven students were individually interviewed. The use of the interview meant that some flexibility in interpreting responses was required and therefore some subjectivity was unavoidable. It was kept to a minimum by cross-referencing to the original descriptions.

The study did not pretend to do more than tentatively suggest some of the things that are involved in the term 'understanding' when it is applied to economics material. But the use of an objective instrument meant that the results obtained did not initially depend on my interpretation of economics and its logical structure. The psychological structures were not a property of the material or of the discipline, alone, but of students' interaction with the experiences provided in the tasks.

32. See references within note 31.
33. The term operational systems is used to describe those concepts that define the relationships or interconnections that economists impose on experience. In a more sophisticated form operational systems and models are synonymous (see Appendix 3.1).
34. Hodges, J.D., in 'Responses to "needed materials in pre-college economic education" ', in Wentworth, D.R., Hansen, W.L., and Hawke, S.H. (eds), *Perspectives on Economics Education* (JCEE, 1977) makes the same point when he suggests that pupils' experience of the economics world 'contribute to the development of both economic conceptions and misconceptions' (p. 184).
35. DES, *Curriculum 11–16 Working Papers*, op. cit., p. 54.
36. Social Sciences Working Party Report, *Draft National Criteria for the Social Sciences* (16+ GCE and CSE Boards' Joint Committee for 16+ and National Criteria, 1982) pp. 2–3.
37. Economics Association, *Criteria for an Economics Course Assessed at 16+* (Economics Association, 1982) p. 3.
38. Papps, I., 'Teaching or learning economics: a conflict of objectives', *Economics*, vol. 13, pt 3, no. 59, autumn 1977.
39. King, B.L., 'Economic understanding and BEC National Level Students', MA dissertation, University of London, 1982.
40. Holley, B.J., and Skelton, V., *Economics Education 14–16* (NFER, 1981).
41. Besley, J., 'An investigation into the introduction of economics into the curriculum for pupils aged 12–14 years in secondary schools in London and S E England', unpublished MA dissertation, Monash University, 1981.
42. Cressey, D., 'The provision of economics education in the UK', MA dissertation, University of London, 1982.
43. For reasons given earlier, it is not yet possible to provide concrete or prescriptive suggestions, but it is possible to be more precise than some 16+ and 17+ statements.
44. Economists rely extensively on the notion of rationality which allows them to develop the model of constrained maximization. Below 16, a case may be made for using opportunity cost as an adequate way of representing the economics perspective (see Chapter 1).
45. And later, the models.
46. Joint Committee, op. cit., p. 23.
47. See Inhelder and Piaget, op. cit., pp. 135 and 150.
48. Ibid., pp. 136 and 153.
49. Ibid., pp. 139 and 156.
50. Ibid., p. 141.
51. Ibid., pp. 164 and 160.

4 Values in Economics Teaching
David J. Whitehead

Introduction

It is not the purpose of this chapter to discuss the academic controversy about objectivity, the status of positive economics, or whether economics is a science.[1] Given constrained space and the ready accessibility of the values literature, it is intended to describe some practical techniques for dealing with the relationship between 'ought' and 'is' in the economics classroom. Teachers interested in the debate on value-free social science will find it is summarized and reaches its apogee in chapter 5 of *The Methodology of Economics*,[2] in which Professor Blaug argues that:

We have overstated the case in suggesting that normative judgments are the sort of judgments that are never amenable to rational discussion designed to reconcile whatever differences there are between people. Even if Hume is right in denying that 'ought' can be logically deduced from 'is', and of course 'is' from 'ought', there is no denying that 'oughts' are powerfully influenced by 'ises' and that the values we hold almost always depend on a whole series of factual beliefs. This indicates how a rational debate on a disputed value judgment can proceed: we pose alternative factual circumstances and ask, should these circumstances prevail, would you be willing to abandon your judgment? A famous and obvious example is the widespread value judgment that economic growth, as measured by real national income, is always desirable; but is it, we might ask, even if it made the bottom quartile, decile, quintile of the size distribution of personal incomes absolutely worse off?

It is the scientism of much of modern economics that makes it dismal. As Professor Pearce argues: 'the positivist teaching of economics is one of the dominant factors explaining the widespread image of economics as an arid and dull subject'.[3] The acceptance of a value dimension might help teachers communicate with their students. Values, in the Blaugian sense, are infused in both teachers' and students' mental make-up. Further, no one denies that the choice of theories and topics bespeaks values, as do the methods of teaching deployed. Again, how teachers' attitudes and values are reflected in their choice of economics topics is considered elsewhere, and is not debated here.[4] Teaching methods indicate attitudes towards the nature and purpose of learning, but are not specifically related to the subject of economics (except in so far as learning economics does not involve 'doing' economics).[5]

Thus the ground is cleared for an attack on the question of students' attitudes and values. It is a commonplace that students have a more or less coherent set of values, which they may apply to the economic analysis they are taught. Is it possible to develop in students a more articulate awareness of their value positions, a clearer distinction between what is uninformed prejudice and what is fundamental, and a more tolerant sensitivity to the views of others? This chapter is written for those teachers who think that such objectives may be feasible, and that an attempt to achieve them is worth undertaking. But before proceeding to some practical approaches to teaching about values, it might be helpful to analyse what is already known about economics students' attitudes.

Research on values

Shortage of space precludes a thorough survey of the literature on the attitudes of economics students. By 1981, there had been some seventeen investigations on the subject of attitude change in economics students at secondary schools.[6] The main impression obtained from these studies is the extreme complexity of measuring changes in the attitudes of economics students. Most of the questionnaires used in the research on the subject assumed unidimensionality (that attitudes varied uniformly across a conservative–radical spectrum) when attitudes might more plausibly be thought to display a number of different dimensions. Many of the empirical studies were unsatisfactory in their research design. Non-random samples were selected, no control groups were set up, and results could not be generalized. The typical experiment involved the 'treatment' of a one-term (American semester) economics principles course, but rarely was any information provided about the content or objectives of such a course. It must be doubted whether significant attitude change could be observable after such a short period of time. Moreover, no attempts were made to assess whether any measured attitude changes persisted over time, for example over the six months following the end of the economics course. After a thorough review of the literature, it is difficult to avoid the conclusion that after almost twenty years of research in this field, it is impossible to make any authoritative statements about the various hypotheses concerning attitudes of economics students. Nevertheless, to encourage wider debate and experiment, a list of typical hypotheses emerging from these studies is as follows:

1 Attitudes to economic issues change as a result of exposure to an economics course.
2 Increased understanding of economics is associated with a more conservative attitude to economic issues.

3   'Conservative' students increase their understanding of economic principles more than 'liberal–radical' students.

4   Economics teachers influence their students' attitudes.

5   Female students show greater attitudinal change after an economics course than do male students.

6   Male students register more extreme responses to statements on economic issues than do female students.

7   Students who have been taught an economics course become more/less dogmatic depending on whether it is micro/macro in emphasis.

8   The older the student, the more conservative his/her attitudes to economic issues are likely to be.

In a large-scale longitudinal study conducted in 1982–4, measuring the change in attitudes to economic issues of a random sample of A-level economics students, the pre-test results provided some statistics that bore upon some of the above hypotheses.[7] In their responses to an economics attitude scale, students embarking on an A-level course in economics in independent schools registered significantly more 'conservative' scores than did students in maintained schools. However, no significant differences in scores were found between those students who had studied O-level economics and those who had not, or indeed between those students who were starting an A-level economics course and a control group who were not. Nor was gender a significant predictor of attitudes. It appeared that students studying 'arts' A-level subjects in combination with economics scored significantly less conservatively than those studying only science or a mixed combination of subjects with economics. Neither age, nor score on a personality test measuring open-mindedness, nor initial understanding of economics as measured by an objective test, appeared to be related to students' attitudes. Teachers' responses to a scale of economics attitude statements were also measured, and it emerged that students started their economics A-level course with views on economic issues considerably to the 'right' of those of their teachers.

Unfortunately, this chapter was written before the above study was complete, and definitive empirical findings must await the post-test results and final publication of the research.

Academic discussion and investigation are important in guiding and informing teachers, but there are practical problems of classroom procedure. Just as most research on value questions has taken place in the USA, so also has that country been the testing ground for the development of exercises seeking to clarify values issues in the classroom. The aim of the remainder of this chapter is to describe some of these activities.

Values clarification exercises

A Openers

One technique for eliciting information about students' attitudes is the 'opener'. This is a diagnostic activity for sampling students' attitudes prior to teaching a topic.

1 Use of survey

One way of doing this is to use a survey, which may be repeated at the end of the unit of study, to see if attitudes have changed at all. In subjects where beliefs are strongly held, knowledge may change attitudes. Below is an example of a Likert-type attitude scale to survey attitudes towards trade unions. The collected data may be summarized in a separate table.

For each statement, circle the number in the column that best describes your reaction.

What are your opinions about trade unions?

	Strongly agree	Agree more than disagree	Disagree more than agree	Strongly disagree
1 I am in favour of strong unions.	1	2	3	4
2 Public employees (teachers, refuse collectors etc.) should be able to belong to unions and have the right to strike.	1	2	3	4
3 Doctors, lawyers and dentists should have the right to strike.	1	2	3	4
4 Most unions are democratically governed.	1	2	3	4
5 The government restricts unions too much.	1	2	3	4
6 Students should be required to join unions even if they are only working part time.	1	2	3	4
7 Unions should participate in local and national politics.	1	2	3	4

	Strongly agree	Agree more than disagree	Disagree more than agree	Strongly disagree
8 Unions increase efficiency and motivate workers to want to do a good job.	1	2	3	4
9 Every person who has a job should have to join a trade union.	1	2	3	4
10 Unions' right to free collective bargaining should not be limited.	1	2	3	4

Scoring procedure: add up the numbers you circled and divide by ten to get your average score. However, inconsistencies in responses may be as interesting as a student's average score.

Survey of attitudes about trade unions

Numbers of responses

	Strongly agree	Agree	Disagree	Strongly disagree
Statement				
1				
2				
etc.				
– – – – –				
Totals				

Source: Adapted from Helburn, S.W., and Davis, J.E., *Preparing to Teach Economics: Approaches and Resources* (Social Science Education Consortium, 1982).

2   *Brainstorming*

Another way to sample students' attitudes prior to starting a topic is to use the brainstorming technique. This activity has a number of uses, for example as a diagnostic strategy in an opener, but the spontaneity that it encourages is particularly helpful for eliciting fundamental value positions.[8]

In a brainstorming session, the class is asked to react to a question or problem by writing down or calling out any association that comes to mind. These ideas are then collected or grouped in some way. The rules of brainstorming must be clarified with the class at the outset. It helps to post them on an overhead projector transparency. They are as follows.

1 Say anything that comes to mind.
2 Discussion of statements is not allowed.
3 Evaluation or criticism of statements is ruled out.
4 Ideas may be repeated or developed by another student.
5 Even if you think you have exhausted your ideas, still go on.
6 Silence is all right.

Usually about ten minutes suffices for a brainstorming session. Afterwards, the ideas should be processed. This is one of the most valuable aspects of the activity, for students often fail to grasp concepts, distinguish ideas or make generalizations. One approach is to ask the class to suggest which reactions, ideas or feelings seem to be similar. The various responses may then be grouped into clusters, and the teacher can discuss with students the problems of classifying particular ideas. Alternatively, students may be asked to search through the ideas for the good or promising ones.

Whether the exercise is done orally or in writing, the students' responses are likely to be much livelier than in normal class discussions. Oral brainstorming involves whole group work while the written variety is normally individual. Written brainstorming may precede or take the place of oral brainstorming. It is often useful to ring the changes to add interest.

The technique places the teacher in a less dominating role than usual, and students will tend to be more forthcoming. If the students write down their brainstorming ideas, it prevents 'piggy-backing' or building on others' ideas, which is a pity, but it does have the advantage that the teacher will be able to elicit responses from *all* group members during the processing stage, and the fact that even the shyer students have something written down in front of them will help them not to dry up when asked to contribute.

The technique also leaves most of the group wanting to say or write more, rather than wishing that the activity had finished much sooner. Because the students have not had to edit out possibly irrelevant remarks, their flow of ideas has not been interrupted, and the mental liveliness induced by the technique tends to transfer with benefit when more traditional methods are again employed.

As an example of the use of the technique, a class of fourth-year students were asked (in 1979) to note down very quickly the ideas that came into their heads when 'trade unions' were mentioned. This was *before* the class had started the topic in their economics lessons. Sample individual responses were as follows:

Individual 1
Labour Party, shop stewards, strikes, NUPE, protecting the workers, pickets, Tolpuddle martyrs, too much power, control of the government, Leylands – more pay, lock-outs, against industrialists, against 'secret ballot', use of 'show of hands' method of voting, general strike.

Individual 2
Parasites of the economy, all they do is cause trouble, they ruin governments, their strikes affect a lot of people, they take the incentive to work out of the workers, semi-communists.

Individual 3
Strikes, workers, tea, power (too much).

Individual 4
Mean trouble, cause strikes, put the economy in disarray, negotiate on behalf of the worker, think only of themselves, fight for rights, money grabbers, picket, I think their leaders should study aspects of economics, should link unemployment with inflation, always think they're a special case involving pay settlements.

Individual 5
Workers' solidarity, equality among workers, the growth of socialism, protection of the proletariat against the bourgeoisie, the furtherance of socialism, social democracy, the gradual abolition of private enterprise as a ruling factor.

Individual 6
Go slow, strikes, closed shop, white-collar worker, blue-collar worker, picket lines, lock-outs, blackleg, scabs, Arthur Scargill, miners, TGWU, Lenin, Karl Marx, NUPE, sit-in, work-to-rule, secret ballot, Gestapo.

The use of brainstorming often provokes just such a jumble of knowledge, error, prejudice and value statements. It illustrates that beginning students of economics are not *tabulae rasae*; they have already acquired, mainly through their upbringing, but also perhaps through history lessons, the tabloid press and television, an assortment of ideas, and the teacher is able to make some initial judgement on the sorts of bias and misconception that he or she will need to sort out, and the kinds of myth that need dispelling (though it would be wrong to imply that this is a simple task).

The next exercise, while not especially innovative, has some stimulating suggestions in sections 5(c) and 5(d). The analysis involves five steps, which are listed below. After each phase, some appropriate questions are suggested.

B   Teaching activity involving analysis of issues
1   Identify and clarify the value question:

'Incomes ought to be distributed more equally'.

2   Assemble alleged facts:
Help students to gather and organize facts relevant to making a value judgement by ensuring that (i) value assertions are not mistakenly collected as part of the group of relevant facts, (ii) a fairly wide range of facts relevant to judging the value statement is assembled, (iii) fact-gathering is carried out in such a way as not to overwhelm students with the complexity of factual material.

Why ought they to be? How much more equally? Who are the poor? What sort of income do they get? From whom? What effects might a more equal distribution have? What is the relevance of the MPC (marginal propensity to consume)? What measures might be used? What effects might greater progressivity in our tax system have? Are you considering pre- or post-tax incomes? What is the concept of relative poverty? How poor are 'the poor' in the UK today compared with the UK 100 years ago or India today? etc. etc.

3   Assess the truth of alleged facts:
Encourage the students to find supporting evidence, and to assess the source of the alleged fact.

Where did you get your statistics? What are the margins of error? Who compiled the figures? Why should we believe what this person or institution says? For what purpose were they collected? Do different sources present different statistics in line with their political position?

4   Clarify the relevance of facts:
Are the facts about the value statement under consideration? Do the facts cast a desirable or an undesirable light from the point of view of the value judgement being made?
From the mass of evidence obtained, what is relevant in deciding whether incomes ought to be more equally distributed? Have you selected statistics that support your own point of view? Are the policies you are suggesting likely to have the effects that you desire?

5   Arrive at a tentative value decision:
(a) Formulate the value principle explicitly, imagine other situations in which it would logically apply, and decide if one can accept its application in these situations.
(b) Assemble facts that show that the value principle is a case of some more general value principle.
(c) Exchange roles with someone else affected by the application of the value principle and consider whether he or she can still accept the principle as it applies to him or her in this role.
(d) Imagine what the consequences would be if everyone in similar

circumstances were to engage in the action being evaluated, and consider whether one can accept these consequences.[9]

(*a*) *Do you now wish to state the value proposition differently? How would implementation of this policy objective affect you personally? How would it affect your household income? Should this value principle be adopted by other countries? Would it affect very poor and very rich countries equally?*

(*b*) *What underlying principle makes you want to enforce this particular value?*

(*c*) *Imagine you are a self-made businessman who has developed a profitable firm, created a lot of employment and produced a new product much in demand. You now face much higher taxes, so that some of your income may be transferred to the poor. What is your attitude now to this change in policy? etc., etc. Other role cases.*

(*d*) *Could this policy be carried out even if the richer in society were opposed to it? What is the evidence that such redistribution has taken place in the past?*

The largest contribution to classroom activities for values clarification has been made by Professor Helburn. Several of her original learning strategies are reproduced below.

C   Clarifying values through productive discussion

The class is arranged in small groups, to discuss two or more opposing positions on a value issue. This may be based on reading done for homework, for example the students may be given a collection of letters to newspapers about the right to strike in 'essential' industries such as gas, electricity and water. The teacher then presents short statements to the groups about the issues involved. Such small-group work provides more opportunity for all the class to be involved in discussion, and group solidarity buttresses the morale of the presenter in putting forward the group point of view.[10]

Procedure

1   Before the lesson, carefully construct the statements that you want students to react to and discuss. They should be general statements like: 'The right to strike should be banned'; 'Strikes in nationalized industries should be made illegal'; 'When the two sides in a trade dispute in a nationalized industry cannot agree, arbitration should be compulsory'; 'The costs of a strike in an essential industry far outweigh the benefits, even to the striking workers.' If possible, devise four value statements on the same broad theme, and make them sufficiently controversial for wide differences of viewpoint to emerge.

2   Ask the class to decide on their own position with respect to each statement (strongly agree, agree, disagree, strongly disagree), and vote

on it by a show of hands. Do this for each statement. The aim here is to find a 'good' distribution, that is, one in which about half the class is on the 'agree' side and the other half on the 'disagree' side. Testing each statement in this way helps to eliminate weak statements as well as uncovering the one or two that most divide the students. Use the statement with the most even distribution for this exercise. If two have a 'good' distribution, let the class choose which they would like to discuss.

3   Divide the class into groups of four to six, with an equal number of 'agrees' and 'disagrees' in each group. The idea is to set up groups with conflicting opinions so as to generate value discussion. Allow the students to choose their own groups if possible.

Ask the groups to discuss the value statement. When they have finished, they are asked to write a statement reflecting the group's position. The students should try to strike a balance between listening to opponents' views and presenting their own. It is important that each student should regard it as his duty to participate in this way.

This is not an exercise in reaching agreement in the group, so more than one statement from each group is permissible. It is an exercise in values clarification: each student should be more aware of his/her own position on the statement by the end of the exercise and should better understand others' positions. In particular, students will become aware of the questions of definition that often cause confusion or disagreement. Some students may change their views as a result of the exercise, but this is not an essential objective.

4   (optional). If the teacher wishes to emphasize listening and persuading skills, a 'stop session' may be used as a check on the interactions and communications in the small groups. After the small-group discussion has been going on for some time, ask the groups to stop for a few minutes to allow each person in the group to evaluate his or her and others' participation in the group. These personal reactions or evaluations are shared among group members. If there are improvements that could be made in individual or group behaviour, these may be discussed briefly before the group resumes its work. The teacher suggests (on a handout or overhead projector) to group participants that they may like to consider the following questions:

(a) How well was I listened to? How well did I listen to others? What evidence am I using to back up these conclusions? How can I improve my participation in the group?
(b) How did I contribute to or make more difficult the discussion or group work?
(c) Identify those students in the group who were helping to accomplish the group work: (i) the risk takers (ii) the listeners, (iii) those who

helped others to express themselves, (iv) the people with ideas, (v) the articulate people, (vi) the group leaders.

(d) What improvements can be made to increase the effectiveness of the group in accomplishing its task?

Participants in each group should be asked to think about or write down their reactions to these questions. Students should share their reactions with the group. If a group has had problems, concrete suggestions for change should be made, and the group should then resume its discussion using the new methods.

5   After twenty or twenty-five minutes of discussion, ask the groups to read out their agreed statements. Find out if anyone in the groups changed his or her position. Ask why. Develop a discussion on the nature of value disagreements: why do people disagree, what keeps people from listening to each other, and how are conflicts resolved? Ask the students to draw conclusions from the experience.[11]

D   Discussion of public policy issues
Another variant of this method has been suggested by Helburn. The procedure to adopt is as follows:

1   Select a newspaper article.
2   Go through it with the class, getting them to suggest what value issues are involved.
3   Ask the students to consider what public policy issues are implied by the article, and what policy alternatives exist.
4   See if the students can think what concepts in economic theory might be useful in sorting out the problem.
5   The teacher collects the information generated by the class discussion on the board or overhead projector.
6   The teacher presents the class with a series of statements about the article. The objective is to find a statement that splits the class fairly evenly from 'strongly agree' through 'agree' and 'disagree' to 'strongly disagree'. The statements need to be contentious and a little ambiguous. The students respond to the statements by putting their hands up for 'strongly agree', etc., and the responses are classified on the board by the teacher.
7   Having chosen an appropriate statement, the class is then divided into four groups, and each group moves to a corner of the room in accordance with their views, that is, 'strongly agree' in one corner, 'disagree' in another, etc. Each student then relates to others in his group why he thinks as he does about the statement at issue. As students are with like-minded individuals, they will be more confident in explaining their point of view.

8   In the final phase, students are divided up into groups of four, one from each 'camp'. They have twenty minutes to talk to each other and come back with a statement about the article with which they all agree. An important instruction to the students is to listen carefully and actively to the 'opposition', asking for clarification when needed.[12]

A similar activity involves presenting the class with two newspaper articles on the same topic, but which report it in different ways and with contrasting headlines. Students are presented with a copy of each article and asked to read both of them. Next they summarize each article, indicating what information appears in both pieces, and where the two reports differ. The class is then divided into groups, and they are asked to discuss and report on the similarities and differences between the two articles. They must also analyse the content to separate out fact and opinion. In the final stage, students are asked to form a hypothesis on the possible reasons for the selection of the headline in each case; to assess how valid each headline is in relation to the content of each article; and to propose an alternative headline which, in their opinion, accurately reflects the content of the articles.[13]

E   Analysis of conflict

Another technique, which combines inductive and deductive inquiry, may be used to study policy issues – for example, on the redistribution of income, policy towards multinational companies, or the control of pollution. Students learn to discuss rationally, and discover that many of their disagreements on policy issues can be resolved by such processes.

As Blaug suggests, it is possible to distinguish between 'pure' and 'impure' value judgements. So long as a value judgement is impure, a debate can be held on the facts of the case, which is satisfactory because there is a firmer tradition for settling disputes about facts than for settling disputes about values. 'It is only when we finally distil a pure value judgement – think of a strict pacifist opposition to any and all wars, or the assertion that "I value this for its own end" – that we have exhausted the possibilities of rational analysis and discussion. There is hardly any doubt that most value judgements that are expressed on social questions are highly impure and hence perfectly amenable to the attempt to influence values by persuading the parties holding them that the facts are other than what they believe them to be.'[14]

With this method of analysing conflicts, students learn to identify and distinguish the following.

(a) *Issues of definition.* These involve the clarification of the meaning of the issue to others and the meaning of terms or words. For example, what does 'excess profits' mean in relation to a monopoly in the public or private sectors? In economics, many terms have more than one meaning: for example, 'capital', 'money', 'investment', 'full employment'.

(b) *Issues of fact.* These relate to the actual realities of a particular situation.

(c) *Issues of prediction.* These involve people's interpretation of the possible consequences of a given situation or set of facts. A person's interpretation of the facts is sometimes difficult to separate from the actual facts themselves. For example, two people may agree that traffic congestion in towns has increased in recent years, but disagree about the possible effects of the increase. One might argue that it has led to an increase in road accidents and pollution, while the other might consider that other facts account for these changes. The argument may be essentially one of interpretation of facts.

(d) *Issues of value.* These involve people's perception of the relative goodness or rightness of a particular situation. In most economic arguments, the main issues usually involve people's beliefs or things that they want. Such arguments are conflicts over goals and the way to allocate scarce resources. People involved in such a disagreement believe that their own well-being or some of the things they value highly are at stake. In analysing most serious economic disagreements, it is essential to uncover the main value conflicts.

Sometimes issues concerning values are related directly to the personal wishes of the people involved in the dispute. For instance, in union–management disputes, the issue involves the costs of running the business on the one hand, and wages and working conditions on the other. Similar kinds of issues are involved in certain political decisions; for example, where to locate a new motorway, or a new prison or mental hospital. Such decisions concern 'who gets what' very directly.

Other sets of choices concern national priorities. Disagreements about whether more should be spent on education or defence are value questions. Such questions involve beliefs about the best form of social organisation, the role in society of government, firms, trade unions and families. The individual's position on these kinds of issues finally depends upon his general set of values or world-view.

Often a person's values may be discovered by noting the facts, interpretations and definitions he uses to support his case: normally he will choose those that best fit his argument. By identifying the issues of fact, interpretation and definition in a controversy about values, the observer can usually identify a person's value position, even if he does not state it.[15]

F   Socratic dialogue

Another approach, which is more traditionally teacher-centred, is to adopt the so-called 'Socratic dialogue' (a misnomer, since Socrates, like most teachers, did most of the talking). Here, the teacher chooses a controversial issue, and asks the student to take a position on the issue, state that position, and defend it. The emphasis is not only on the knowledge provided by the teacher, but on the process by which the student arrives at a decision on the topic, on the careful consideration of alternative decisions, and on the utilization of analytical concepts and strategies, regardless of the position that is finally reached.[16]

The following is an example using this technique to discuss the national debt issue.[17]

1   Ask students to develop a policy statement about the national debt. What should be done about it?

2   Ask students to read their statements aloud.

3   Select one statement and ask for a justification. Usually the response will be a mixture of analysis based on information, and values based on the student's own personal position. For example, a student might respond that all deficit financing should be curtailed because the level of interest paid is becoming too high and because future generations will have to pay off the national debt. The statement clearly has an anti-debt bias.

4   The teacher may wish to persuade the class to agree, if he or she accepts the student's position as sound.

5   The teacher provides an analogy that illustrates the value conflicts in the student statement. For example, one might use the analogy of a large company selling debentures to finance expansion. The idea here is to present the analogy in such a way that the value bias is in the opposite direction to the student statement.

6   Now ask the student if he wishes to reconsider the original statement. If he does, point out a conflict that he may not have thought of. For example, isn't it possible that deficit financing will cause the value of the pound to decrease? The point here is to focus on the student's thinking on the nature of the policy dilemma.

7   When several conflicting value issues have been raised, ask the students to develop policy statements that consider the value conflicts. This makes students think more analytically. For this learning activity, the teacher often plays devil's advocate, trying to suggest alternatives and objections. The mode is adversarial, and the objective is to get the students to think and to articulate their viewpoint.

G   Learning skills of advocacy

Another strategy may be deployed when students are studying strongly

held positions (e.g. monetarism/Keynesianism, underlying which
there *may* be different value positions), and where there is considerable
disagreement among them about which is the *right* point of view.[18] The
purpose of the activity is to help students gain skill in advocating a
position they agree with in such a way as to persuade others to change
their position. The activity involves students reading or hearing three
or four different positions on a particular issue that interests them. It
requires students to analyse the positions, look for valid points in the
argument, take a moderate stand, and present the original position in a
more moderate or convincing way to the disbelievers.

1   Have students read or listen to three or four different positions on
a particular issue, for example, the Conservative, Liberal/SDP, and
Labour points of view on government spending. Students should note
down their 'gut' reactions to each statement.
2   Ask students for a show of hands about their reactions to each
statement. Note these on the board or overhead projector as shown
below, on the first assessment row.

Positions	Very positive	Positive	Negative	Very negative
1st position				
1st assessment	3	6	8	4
2nd assessment				
2nd position				
1st assessment				
2nd assessment				
3rd etc.				

(Students will be asked their opinions again, at the end of the activity.)
    Now divide the class into groups to work on each position. Groups
should comprise students who are very positive or positive about a
general position.
3   Ask each group to write a statement defending and advocating the
position they support. The group should choose a presenter whose aim
will be to convince the 'unbelievers', in a three- to four-minute speech.
4   Bring the class back together and ask each group presenter to make
a statement. Allow a few minutes for questions and answers.
5   Ask the students to re-examine their value positions. Ask each
group to consider whether points have been made by other groups that
it had not considered, and whether there are positions that anyone
wishes to learn more about. Then ask students to react to each position
again as at the start of the activity. See if there has been a shift in

positions and, if so, explore the reasons for the shifts.

A simpler approach, also suggested by Helburn, involves selecting two contrasting newspaper articles on the same topic, say from *The Financial Times* and the *Guardian*, or the *Daily Express* and the *Daily Mirror*. Editorials are probably more useful than straight news stories, since the former contain more controversial statements.

Ask the class to jot down the arguments that they think are important in the articles, and then to work out what value assumptions are involved. Next, ask them to summarize the extracts, listing the issues involved. The students then break up into groups and compare their summaries with each other. Finally, the full class participates in a debriefing session, sharing their insights about the main issues that arose from the articles.

H   Other techniques for exposing and clarifying values

Many role-play exercises and simulations enable students to empathize with particular individuals and social groups, or to feel the effects of performing some economic activity. Others, such as the income distribution simulation, and assembly line, may be found in the *Handbook for Economics Teachers*.[19]

Alternative strategies might include the framing of questionnaires for students to use with their friends, family or in the neighbourhood, to enable them to construct profiles of a variety of viewpoints and evidence about particular issues. Debates tend to place a premium on being extrovert and opinionated, unless sensitively handled, but might be used sparingly. Visiting speakers may provide new perspectives, especially if it is possible to challenge students with less mainstream philosophies and lifestyles such as those suggested by Wright,[20] which is essential reading for economics teachers anxious to think about how they should deal with this question.

Less orthodox reading might be suggested to enable students to appreciate the diversity of viewpoints among economists.[21] However, a problem with some materials that find their way into educational institutions is that their lack of objectivity is not explicit.[22] Many ephemeral pamphlets are produced and distributed with the support of some organization that wishes to disseminate its message. Four types of bias identified by Helburn and Davis are:[23]

1   Undue reverence for market solutions to both economic and social problems (several states in the USA mandate the teaching of 'free enterprise economics' in schools. In 1982, the Premier of Queensland, Australia, stated that secondary school students would be taught the theories of private enterprise to protect the Queensland way of life).[24]

2　Focus on some institutions (banks, insurance companies) to the exclusion of others (unions, co-operatives).
3　Insufficient attention to current social problems.
4　Lack of opportunity for students to consider value questions.

It is important then for the teacher to be aware of potential biases when selecting materials for personal or student use. Helburn and Davis suggest five categories of questions that might be asked initially by anyone selecting curriculum resources:

1　*Publisher.* Who is the publisher?[25] Does the publisher normally produce educational materials for use with students? Can a point of view be detected in the publisher's literature?
2　*Balance.* Are the materials balanced in terms of rationale or philosophy? Is the value position underlying the resources made explicit? What is the relative emphasis on the free-market mechanism as the major economic problem-solving mechanism in society?
3　*Student opportunity.* What opportunities are presented in the materials for students to clarify their own values, analyse the values of others, and make and defend decisions?
4　*Problems.* Do the materials address such social issues as education, housing, health, employment? How are students asked to approach such problems, if they are presented?
5　*Perspective.* Are the resources concerned with local, national or international issues? Are the interrelationships shown between the three perspectives? Such preliminary questions can help teachers to decide whether a given set of materials appears to be congruent with their general teaching philosophy and view of the role of economics education, after which a more penetrating analysis may be undertaken.

Problems in using values exercises

Some teachers may consider that the elucidation of values is not their concern. It is unlikely that their students will be given the opportunity to examine their own and others' values. Even those who would like to experiment with some techniques may encounter difficulties. For teachers who normally employ highly orthodox methods, it is not a simple matter to change gear for values clarification activities. Students who are not used to discussing issues, nor even to listening to and valuing others' opinions, will not automatically acquire skills that require patience and practice. Teachers need to be sensitive to relationships within the group, and should not impose one point of view, even inadvertently, simply by virtue of their authoritative role. Such exercises will flow much more easily in an open classroom atmosphere where freedom of expression is encouraged, where student-initiated questions are frequent, and where respect for others' viewpoints is tolerated.

Economics teachers may hold strong value positions themselves, but they need to ensure as objectively as possible that all major points of view are adequately represented. 'An unending search for objectivity must be as much a part of the good teacher as is his ability to communicate an excitement about his area of work. But objective teaching still leaves ample room for provoking students into recognising their value judgements. And it leaves room for demonstrating to them the critical lesson that those value judgements sometimes colour the facts of the world around them.'[26] A similar exhortation is voiced by Leamer: 'I have noted that many social scientists who are the most aggressive verbal advocates of objectivity, especially for others with whom they disagree, are most likely to present their values as facts and to select carefully facts in support of their own values. I suppose one of the highest tributes that could be paid to a teacher would be that he so adequately prepared his students to evaluate the opinions of others, that in spite of their admiration for him they could and did subject his most inspired arguments to the same scrutiny he had taught them to subject the opinions of others.'[27]

Most alternative teaching strategies are quite time-consuming, but this is an argument for a reasonable rather than a zero time allocation. More serious is the sacrifice of classroom time that could have been used to develop knowledge of the economics on the syllabus. Gradually, however, statements about values education are being introduced into economics syllabuses. For example, a 1982 report stated that by the end of a social science course at 16+, students should have some understanding of 'the ways in which ideas and values are generated in social life, the nature and role of these ideas and values in their changing social, economic and political context'.[28] Another example appeared in the draft objectives of a unit of exemplar material produced by the Economics Association 14–16 Project. In a section on consumers, it is stated that an objective is to influence attitudes towards stereotyped and prejudiced views about the causes of inequalities in consumption levels both within an economy and between economies.[29]

Another stumbling block may be parental opposition. Parents in British Columbia, Canada, were encouraged to write in a circular letter to the Minister of Education: 'You are hereby notified that . . . is not allowed by the undersigned to participate in, or be subject to instruction in humanistic attitudinal development (. . .), values clarification, decision-making techniques (. . .), etc. etc. without the consent of the undersigned by express written permission.' Rather like religion and sex education, values clarification may be either banned or compulsory!

An additional problem was highlighted by an observed lesson involving values clarification. Each group had to consider a particular viewpoint, and then present their agreed view to the rest of the class. Although most of the groups contained male and female students, in every case it was a male student who emerged as presenter. In the only group consisting of female students only, none wished to act as presenter, and the teacher took over the role for them. Sub-groups conditioned to be less assertive may require particularly sensitive treatment to encourage confident responses.

The liveliness induced by such activities was amply illustrated by this lesson. Not only did the class continue for ten minutes after the end of the school day, but when the teacher formally finished the lesson, students continued to argue among themselves for some considerable time. Students whose thinking has been 'released' or 'wound up' in this way may well bring a more critical awareness to conventional lessons, stimulating the teacher as well as each other. Whether this should be regarded as a problem depends on the teacher's value set!

As with the work of Raths *et al.* on moral development strategies,[30] value clarification has had a major impact in the USA though it is equally controversial, especially regarding the role of the teacher. It is important to ensure that if the Humanities Curriculum Project tactic of substantive neutrality is adopted,[31] the students do not assume that particular value positions are implicitly accepted by the teacher. Also, it would be wrong for students to be coerced by teacher or class pressure into discussing beliefs or values that they or their parents would prefer to be kept private.

Lawrence Senesh, one of the great economics educators of this century, stated that 'it is my conviction that value neutrality destroys a free society (. . .). The tragedy of social science, particularly of economic education, is that we separate true and false from good and evil. Smith divided his lectures in Glasgow into four parts: natural theology, ethics, justice, and expediency (wealth and power). He elaborated on ethics in his book *The Theory of Moral Sentiments*. He elaborated on expediency in *The Wealth of Nations*. The two volumes together represent the two components of our value system . . . you have to introduce Adam Smith not only as a scientist, but also as a professor of moral philosophy.'[32]

Similarly, economics is not just a set of theories. We are unjust to our students if we do not expose and examine with them the underlying value structures in the society that those theories attempt to explain.[33]

Notes and references

1. For sources related to the teaching of economics in schools, the following articles are recommended:

Szreter, R., 'The teacher of economics and the problem of political bias', *Economics*, vol. 9, pt 6, no. 42, pp. 353–7, winter 1972–3; Helm, R., 'Values in economics', *Economics*, vol. 15, pt 1, no. 65, spring 1979, pp. 11–15; Lee, N., 'A note on bias in economics education', *Economics*, vol. 15, pt 1, no. 65, spring 1979, pp. 16–17; and Dawson, G., 'The objectivity of economics', *Economics*, vol. 16, pt 1, no. 69, spring 1980, pp. 24–7. See also Papps, I., and Henderson, W., *Models and Economic Theory* (W.B. Saunders, 1977) pp. 28ff. for a useful discussion of the positive/normative distinction.

2. Blaug, M., *The Methodology of Economics* (Cambridge University Press, 1980) pp. 133ff.

3. Hardwick, P. *et al.*, *An Introduction to Modern Economics*, foreword by Professor D. Pearce (Longman, 1982).

4. See especially Helm, op. cit.; Lee, op. cit.; and Dawson, op. cit. Allen, D.I., 'Learning models and teaching strategies in commercial and economic education', in Gregory, A., *Directions in Commercial, Economic and Legal Education in Australia* (Victorian Commercial Teachers Association, 1979), and Bell, G., and Gregory, A., *Sources for Courses. A Handbook for Teachers of Economics* (VCTA, 1980) ch. 5, provide other cognate teaching strategies.

5. Drake, K., 'Economics: cracks in a monolithic curriculum', *Educational Studies*, vol. 3, 1977, and Jackson, D., *Introduction to Economics. Theory and Data* (Macmillan, 1982) provide contrasting viewpoints.

6. For an exhaustive survey, see Whitehead, D.J., 'An investigation of some aspects of attitude change in economics students', unpublished PhD thesis, University of London, 1984. A typical study is that by Wood, S.W., 'A study of the association between economic understanding, dogmatism, liberalism/conservatism and other affective elements for economics students in the Amarillo public schools', unpublished PhD thesis, Texas Tech University, 1972.

7. See Whitehead, op. cit.

8. Helburn, S.W. *et al.*, *Economics in Society. Strategies and Methods* (Addison-Wesley, 1974).

9. Superka, D.P. *et al.*, *Values Education Sourcebook* (Social Science Education Consortium, ERIC Clearinghouse for Social Studies/Social Science Education, Boulder, Colorado Co. 80302, USA 1976) p. 56.

10. Helburn, op. cit., pp. 71–2.

11. Helburn, op. cit., p. 67.

12. Helburn, S.W., 'Discussion of public policy issues' (personal communication to the author, 1979).

13. Bell and Gregory, op. cit.

14. Blaug, op. cit., p. 133.

15. Helburn, S.W. *et al.*, *Teachers' Guide to 'Economics in Society'* (Addison-Wesley, 1973) p. 31.

16. Oliver, D.W., and Shaver, J.P., *Teaching Public Issues in the High School* (Logan, Utah, Utah State University Press, 1974; first published Houghton Mifflin, 1966) pp. 126–30.

17. Helburn, *Economics in Society*, op. cit., pp. 56–7.

18. Ibid., pp. 72–4.

19. Whitehead, D.J. (ed.), *Handbook For Economics Teachers* (Heinemann Educational Books, 1979).

20. Wright, N., 'Values', in ibid., pp. 256–61.
21. A fresh perspective is offered by Coleman, J.R., *Comparative Economic Systems – An Enquiry Approach* (Holt, Rinehart & Winston, 1968). See also Whitehead, *Handbook for Economics Teachers*, op. cit., p. 279, for an unorthodox reading list.
22. Webster, A., 'Ideology and "A"-level economics textbooks', *Economics*, vol. 14, pt 3, no. 63, autumn 1978, pp. 85–7.
23. Helburn, S.W., and Davis, J.E., Preparing to Teach Economics: Approaches and Resources (Social Science Education Consortium, 1982).
24. Skelton, R., 'Bjelke plans private enterprise course for high schools', *The Age*, 6 November 1980, p. 3.
25. An interesting critique of company-sponsored resources produced in collaboration with a professional economics teachers' association is given in Williamson, J., 'Educational materials and the corporate sector; some ideological implications', unpublished mimeo, University of Queensland, 1983.
26. Coleman, J.R., 'A new chance for economic literacy', in Warmke, R.F., and Draayer, G.F. (eds), *Select Readings in Economic Education* (Division of Research, College of Business Administration, Ohio University, 1969) p. 26.
27. Leamer, L., *The Economist as Teacher* (South Western Publishing, 1975).
28. *Recommended 16+ National Criteria for Social Sciences* (GCE and CSE Boards' Joint Council, 1983).
29. Economics Association 14–16 Project, *An Introduction to the Project's Work on Exemplar Materials* (University of Manchester, 1983) p. 12.
30. Raths, L.E., *et al.*, *Values and Teaching*, 2nd edn (Columbus, Ohio, Merrill, 1978).
31. *The Humanities Project. An Introduction*, Schools Council/Nuffield Foundation (Heinemann Educational Books, 1972) pp. 16–29.
32. Senesh, L., 'Hopes and frustrations of an economics educator', address to the Joint Council on Economic Education, 8 October 1978; reprinted in *Journal of Economic Education*, 1978.
33. I am obliged to the following for permission to use copyright material: Addison Wesley Publishing Company Inc., Utah State University Press, Social Science Education Consortium Inc., Houghton Mifflin. This chapter has been immeasurably improved by comments on earlier drafts by David Butler, Richard Dunnill, Alan Gregory, Suzie Helburn, Linda Thomas and Ron Wilkes.

Part Two
Teaching Economics in Specific Contexts

5 Economics in the Early Years of School
T. M. Linton

If one studies the two previous editions of *Teaching Economics* for guidance and advice on the teaching of economics in primary schools, one is struck by the slow rate of educational progress over the two decades these editions cover. Lawrence Senesh's 'Organic Curriculum' in the 1960s edition, outlining fundamental economic concepts (see Appendix 5.1), remains as educationally prophetic in the UK today as it was then. While Senesh himself is disappointed that things have not developed more rapidly, substantial advances have been made in economic education in American elementary-school curricula. In the 1970s edition the only contributor on pre-secondary school economic education was Hazel Sumner and her chapter on economics in the context of social studies[1] outlines the problems of introducing economic concepts into primary-school curricula. Changes in educational content and practice are notoriously slow but this rate of educational development appears particularly laggard.

One part of the explanation seems to lie in the failure to demonstrate the utility of its inclusion into the primary-school curriculum. This difficulty appears to have been overcome in the majority of American states where detailed curricula in economic ideas have been produced for primary teachers.[2] No such educational responses have been forth-coming in the UK and this chapter attempts to analyse the causes of this educational inertia and at the same time offers a programme of curricular change designed to meet this need.

It is not difficult to marshal the formidable array of arguments that might be advanced against economic education in the primary school. There is not enough time to teach economics. Teachers may not use the concept of opportunity cost explicitly but they certainly appreciate its relevance in curricular planning; if a new subject comes into the curriculum another goes out. Also, a new subject entails extra preparation and few teachers of younger children have qualifications in economics. Its educational value may not be thought commensurate with the expenditure of time and effort required of the teacher.

Another deterrent may be the financial stringencies now being practised in educational finance. Costs of new materials may be felt prohibitive.

Formidable though these arguments are, there are signs that times are changing and the case for economic education is becoming more pressing than ever before. Economic decision-making for the average citizen has now reached a point where economic knowledge is essential. As a parent, a worker, a trade unionist, and an elector, he or she has to make economic choices that may fundamentally affect his or her life. For the majority of adults these decisions are often made on pragmatic, even whimsical, grounds, for few have the opportunity to develop the tools of economic understanding in any systematic way. The need for general economic education, especially in countries priding themselves on their democratic processes, appears to be overwhelming.

This clearly demonstrable need for economic education for all must also be taken in conjunction with the profound changes in developmental theories of learning. The work of Piaget[3] and Bruner[4] has revolutionized educational thinking on academic disciplines. Building upon Piagetian theory on children's development, Bruner advanced his singularly important hypothesis that has radically influenced teaching since the 1960s: 'We begin with the hypothesis that any subject can be taught effectively in some intellectually honest form at any stage of development.'

The effect of this educational revolution in the USA has been for economic education to make substantial inroads into social-studies curricula in elementary schools. Central to these schemes of work has been Bruner's 'spiral curriculum' which has been used to identify fundamental economic ideas which are reinforced through the pupils' school career. In this way economic education has become embedded into social-studies curricula in the majority of American states, and is often taught to quite young children.

A curriculum for economic education

The remainder of this chapter draws substantially on the outcome of an experimental course piloted in Scottish primary schools.

Aims of teaching economics to young children

1   To create an awareness, through situational involvement, of an expanding spiral of basic economic concepts, including needs, satisfaction (consumption); resources, scarcity, work (production and distribution); specialization, interdependence, co-operation (exchange).
2   To enable pupils to appreciate an ever-widening range of adult problems, whenever possible, in real, as distinct from theoretical, terms, and so promote and enrich social maturation.

3 To encourage and assist pupils in making simple judgements and to
   inculcate habits of systematic investigation.
4 To achieve economic literacy and numeracy.

Course content

Course content requires coherent and unifying themes and the relationships between these should be explicit and meaningful. The framework
in Figure 5.1 was designed to provide that rationale for the economic
programme. It draws upon American examples, notably that devised
by Professor L. Senesh, formerly of the University of Colorado. The
numbers indicate a progression linking the major economic concepts,
outlined below.

Such a curriculum would of course take up a substantial amount of
time and in many schools this may not be available. Where time is
limited there is no necessity to cover the entire area; it is much better to
remember that content should depend on the nature of economics, the
age and ability of the child and the constraints of the context in which it
is taught. The emphasis should be on the child understanding some of
the most important economic concepts and starting to think *like* an
economist. This can be achieved in a relatively brief time and can fit
into a wide variety of courses where the economics element is just part
of an integrated course.

Standard of living (1–4)

As all children are consumers, before they are producers of goods and
services this theme provides a useful starting point for involving
children in economic concepts and concerns. A whole range of
economic ideas, including consumption, scarcity arising from the
conflict between unlimited wants and limited means, have a practical
application to a child's daily living. The economic choices he or she
makes daily provide homely and topical examples for discussion and
analysis. Where better than in spending of his limited pocket money is
opportunity cost better illustrated? The family budget also provides an
excellent vehicle for exemplifying economic terms, for example by
pupils analysing spending patterns on food, clothing, shelter and
leisure. By working out the costs of a number of separate meals, pupils
can estimate the cost of feeding a boy or girl for one week. Calculations
can be extended to include the distribution of money on other items
such as clothing, housing and leisure.

Money and its use (5–7)

Pupil interest in money is not difficult to arouse and this can be
canalized into investigating how money functions within the economic
system. The physical difficulties barter presents are best demonstrated

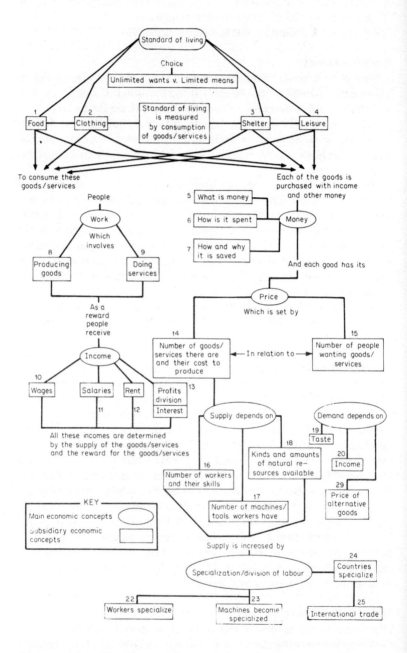

Fig. 5.1 Teachers' guide: economic concepts in the primary school.

by practical examples. Children can be encouraged to bring items into the school that they value at, say, 50p and they should then be allowed to try to trade these in the classroom with a record being made of the successful transactions. The problems of matching values, divisibility, etc. are therefore highlighted and the need for a medium of exchange can be practically demonstrated. Money's other properties as a store of value and a standard of value can then be developed using similar techniques.

Pupils can then be introduced to the different forms of money that are used in commercial activities, with the teacher creating situations where children can make financial decisions for themselves.

Earning a living (8–13)

Easy economic linkages are possible between this section and the preceding one on money. The general objective is to analyse why different income earners receive different returns for their provision of goods and services. Pupils can examine a variety of occupations in terms of the different skills, experience, training, responsibility, danger, etc. entailed in the performance of these jobs. Concepts such as wages, salaries and fees are of central importance.

Finally, consideration is given to money payments made by government in cases where the individual is unable to work through illness, disability or unemployment.

The market and prices (14–15)

An understanding of how the market operates in allowing buyers and sellers to come into contact with each other is essential to economic awareness. Because of the abstract value of the market concept, pupils should be introduced to it whenever possible in a practical way. The job centre and the local supermarket provide examples of the labour and consumer goods markets. By drawing upon examples from local towns and cities, teachers can demonstrate how these markets are required to meet not only local but also national and international needs of consumers. Historical examples of the medieval fair and market, and geographical examples of wheat, sugar and oil selling, can be used to give a real-life perspective to the section, particularly where economics forms part of an integrated course.

The concept of price is a difficult one for pupils to grasp as it is the end product of a number of interacting forces involving demand and supply. It is essential that carefully chosen practical experiences are used so that the child learns the concepts involved.

By doing this, pupils may be able to appreciate the importance of prices in allocating resources in the British economy by giving information to consumers, producers, workers and savers.

Pupils should also understand how prices are a way of rationing goods and services among consumers and productive resources among producers. Pupils can search for examples where the prices of certain commodities have increased substantially because shortages have occurred, for example, oil, potatoes. The higher prices will ensure that only a small number of consumers will be able to purchase certain goods.

Supply and demand (16–21)

In order to exemplify how demand or supply factors operate in the economy, teachers should select some good that pupils or their parents are likely to buy. A number of commodities such as bicycles, crisps, records or games will provide a useful launching pad for consideration of supply. Pupils should try to list the different resources required in the production of a bicycle, with the teacher organizing them under the headings of natural, human and capital resources. The pupils will then be able to see how the bicycle manufacturer has to use his skill and ability to bring these various factors together in an efficient manner if he is to sell his bicycles successfully to the consumer in the market-place. With this exemplar pupils can then study local businesses, using photographs, and similar headings to those in the bicycle investigation.

Demand patterns for a particular product such as bicycles should also be investigated with children's tastes and buying capacity being considered. Advertisements might provide a starting point and pupils' likes and dislikes can be analysed. Similar studies of pupils' tastes can be conducted to indicate how manufacturers respond to consumer wants.

Specialization (22–25)

Although children have not yet adopted the specialist roles of their parents, they are very aware of how specialization increases output and efficiency in production, resulting in more satisfaction of consumer wants. Pupils can examine specialization in a variety of ways; for example, they can examine how and why different countries have specialized in the production of goods, for example, French wines, Swiss cheese, Japanese motor vehicles, etc., and they can provide and discuss examples of technical specialization such as the use of robots in car manufacture.

The economic glossary in Appendix 5.2 lists the main economic terms that pupils should have understood on completion of the course. This is in no way definitive, but should provide teachers with a fairly comprehensive coverage of the terminology needed for economic comprehension for this age group.

Before consideration is given to the approaches and methods used to teach the course outlined above, a few observations need to be made. There is no rigid time scale against which the material should be taught. It has been used as a one- or a two-year teaching syllabus and teachers have found both approaches have their educational advantages and disadvantages. It should be noted that, while the objectives and structure are economically oriented, there is considerable flexibility in the content, which is in no way economically prescriptive.

Teachers should amplify and articulate economic concepts through historical, geographical and arithmetical examples, as appropriate.

Approaches to economic education

Successful subject presentation requires varied and interesting approaches and economic education is no exception. While it is as yet in its educational infancy, it has developed a number of techniques that should assist intending teachers in making it meaningful to pupils. It is essential that these should present economics in concrete rather than abstract terms. This means that the pupils' direct experiences with school, home, parental activities and the market-place are actively exploited and developed by the teacher. The multidimensional nature of the subject is clearly exemplified below in the various approaches that teachers have already used in teaching the discipline.

Visual dimension

The most effective teachers value visual presentation as an important adjunct to pupil comprehension and many of the concepts of economics lend themselves to pictorial representation. The concept of circular flow of money takes on a new dimension when it is exemplified through the analogy of a pocket-money flow. One primary school in a mining area built up an elaborate flow chart. Starting with the coal-mine manager paying the coal-miner his wage, the chart next depicted the child receiving his pocket money from the father. This pocket-money then flowed on into the local sweet shop, whose owner then transferred it to the warehouse selling confectionery goods. This company then paid taxes to the government which, in turn, advanced money for the mine's upkeep. Different environmental conditions produce different flow charts. Other money flows can be used to establish linkages between customers and bankers, and employees and businesses.

Factors of production also lend themselves readily to pictorial display. As often as possible, local conditions should be used as the springboard for action and homely examples have much to commend them. A brick wall, which was in the process of being built outside the classroom window, produced an extremely effective exemplar to highlight the importance of the different factors of production. Under natural resources pupils grouped sand, cement, water, stone etc.

Labour was subdivided into different specialists such as architects, surveyors, clerk of works, bricklayers and lorry drivers. Under capital resources appeared lorries, cement mixers, earth movers and cranes. Colour codings were used to identify the different factors. Innumerable industrial products as diverse as oil, crisps, carrots or cars can be analysed using this visual technique.

Written material

Written exercises can be devised to test pupil comprehension of the new economic vocabulary, involving definitions of terms and economic relationships. A number of economic essays such as 'The job I should like to do when I grow up', 'The story of a cheque', 'An oilspill at sea', 'The Ten Commandments of pollution' might form the basis of written assignments. Another method of initiating written work might be to use a 'What if?' approach. Triggers for this might be: 'What happens if the price of petrol doubles?' 'What happens if British people buy more and more foreign cars?' 'What happens if people begin to save more of their money?' 'What happens if fewer children are born?' These questions prompt pupils to think of causal connections occurring in the economy and ensure that their economic understanding has a practical application. Note that careful preparation (such as class discussion) is needed before young children can write meaningfully on such topics. Pupils can also make lists of spending priorities in relation to limited money supplies. This can be done at the level of buying a birthday present for, say, £10 from a list of alternative goods and evaluating these goods against certain criteria.

Numerical material

The course outlined above allows considerable scope for the development of arithmetical skills and expression.

In the standard of living section, work with numbers is important in the calculation of costs and prices. Ability to calculate percentage changes over a time scale of weeks and months is required for effective comparisons to be made regarding cost of living movements. Money-related topics also afford pupils opportunities for numerical manipulation, involving the calculation of interest, the production of pie charts of pocket-money spending habits, and weekly family expenditure. Parental occupations can be represented on frequency diagrams. Sets and subsets, covering the various factors that determine differential incomes, also provide interesting visual displays. Among these variables can be included, responsibility, danger, training and education. Various diagrams can also be used to differentiate between necessities and luxuries in family budgets. Bar charts and block graphs are easily constructed from data on shop distribution, job rating or crisp popularity.

Practical work

As economic concepts have an everyday focus in the pupils' lives they lend themselves readily to practical activities. The importance of assembly-line procedures can be demonstrated in the production of various commodities made within the classroom. Schools have produced puppets comparing the specialization of the assembly line with that of individual production. Pupils can then discuss the merits and demerits of assembly-line methods. Numerous other goods, such as Christmas cards, miniature rocking chairs made from clothes pegs, and chocolate fondants can be produced with pupils costing raw materials, labour and other expenses involved in their production and calculating profit margins.

Consumer choice is a pertinent and relevant concern for all pupils and surveys can be conducted into consumption patterns for a variety of commodities. Pupils can analyse class demand schedules for different brands of crisps. Similar investigations can be carried out into consumption of other goods such as sweets, cereals and jeans.

Barter transactions give an excellent vehicle for pupil activities. The difficulties of achieving a double coincidence of exchange can be clearly demonstrated as pupils attempt to exchange different commodities. Pupils can also attempt to develop a medium of exchange using such articles as marbles, comics or counters.

Role playing, drama and discussion

Economic concepts lend themselves to role-playing situations and some of the following simulations may assist teachers to create a high level of pupil involvement. Opportunity cost might be exemplified by simulating a class auction with all pupils having a sum of money, say £100, to spend, and a number of items for which they can bid. Choices have to be made and criteria of value of the different alternative choices can be considered in the debriefing session. A number of other roles might also be assumed such as the farmer, the shopkeeper and the housewife, and the opportunity cost of a decision for each might be imagined and analysed.

A variety of roles can be assumed by pupils where important economic decisions have to be made. Pupils might imagine themselves as managers of companies selling jeans, bicycles, skateboards, toys, etc. These situations will help pupils to understand something of the suppliers' concerns as he or she takes account of taste, incomes and alternatives.

A number of occupational simulations also have educational possibilities. A Job Centre with its different jobs provides pupils with the chance to assume occupational roles, involving both professional and manual workers. Discussions too can develop out of headings such as

'I'd rather be a diver than a banker' or 'a pop singer rather than a car mechanic', with pupils weighing up the economic pros and cons of the different occupations. Additional discussions can arise after pupil investigation into occupational qualifications. Using this information pupils can argue the case for differential incomes among different employees.

Conclusions

Conclusions must be of a tentative nature bearing in mind the limited teaching of economics that has been attempted in primary schools, but the following findings might be advanced as meriting attention.

First, there is clear evidence that children in the upper primary school can understand basic economic ideas. The statistical evidence of tests of economic comprehension (see Appendix 5.3)[5] support this assertion. Significant gains were made by pupils on pre- and post-tests. Teacher impressions too substantiate the statistical findings. As measured by the aims outlined in the economics curriculum (see above), pupils increased their economic awareness in terms of effective use of economic terminology and made economic judgements involving real-life situations. In short, there was substantial evidence of heightened economic numeracy and literacy. These findings are not dissimilar to other research in Scotland[6] that demonstrated that basic economic ideas could be taught effectively in the first two years of the secondary school.[7]

Secondly, there was general agreement that the economic approach to environmental studies added a different and more meaningful dimension to its teaching. The economic rationale gave greater cohesion and continuity to the subject than had previously been the case, and it was felt that it became more relevant to real-life situations. Any subject content changes were more than compensated for by a more practical approach than that previously adopted.

As can be seen from examples already quoted, there was a high level of pupil involvement in all parts of the course and their interest in it was extended far outside the classroom setting. All teachers remarked on the pupils' heightened awareness of everyday economic events and felt that this was a direct consequence of their exposure to economic ideas within the curriculum.

Finally, some observations must be made on the potential difficulties of developing such economics-based courses in primary schools as outlined above. Teaching qualifications and competency are essential prerequisites of a successful teaching programme and this course is no exception. Formal economics teaching qualifications are obviously singularly rare in the primary sector and a considerable element of school-based in-service training had to be introduced into experimental schools. All teachers felt that this provided them with a basic repertoire of teaching content and method, and their involvement in the course increased their competency with the materials. Pre-service courses would obviously be needed if primary teachers were expected to introduce a core of economic ideas into the primary curriculum and these would only become educationally prescriptive if the opportunity cost of the inclusion of economic concepts was demonstrably higher than that of some other social studies element in the primary curriculum. As yet, few primary teachers have ever considered their curricula in terms of this educational calculus!

Curricular changes are rarely made as a result of frontal assault, but usually occur gradually in response to mounting environmental and educational pressures. There are signs that today's adult requires a much greater economic awareness in his daily life than did his or her predecessors. It is hoped that the educational system is flexible enough to make a response that will provide its future citizens with an economic curriculum relevant to that challenge and that these pioneering efforts may encourage more primary teachers to introduce a wider economic perspective into their teaching.

Appendix 5.1

Fig. 5.2 The fundamental idea relationships of economic knowledge.

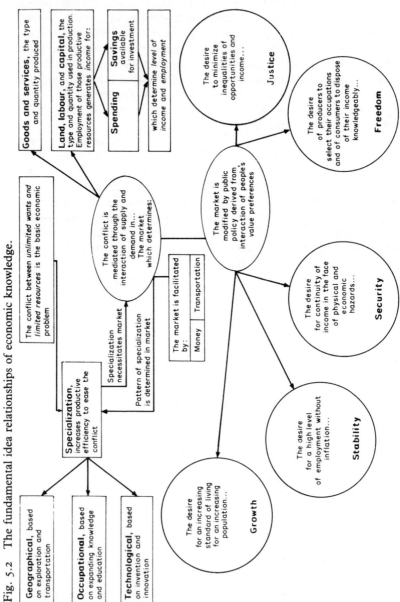

Source: Senesh, L., 'Teaching economic concepts in primary grades', in Lee,

Appendix 5.2   Economic Glossary

Borrow
Business firms
Capital resource
Cheque
Coin
Communicate
Consume
Consumer
Cost
Currency
Customer
Deposit
Dependent
Dividend
Division of labour
Earn
Efficient
Exchange
Export
Factory
Free
Goods
Government

Hire
Human resource
Import
Income
Increase
Input
Interdependent
Interest
International trade
Invention
Labour
Lend
Limited
Loan
Loss
Manager
Market
Mill
Money
Output
Produce
Producer
Production

Profit
Natural resource
Primary industry
Productive resources
Resource
Rent
Responsibility
Risk
Salary
Save
Secondary industry
Services
Skills
Specialization
Spend
Taxes
Trade
Unlimited
Value
Wages
Wants
Warehouse
Withdrew

Appendix 5.3

The Primary Test of Economic Understanding was not devised primarily to suit the experimental economics material used by the teachers. It was designed to evaluate pupils' comprehension of five economic generalizations that could be said to form the core concepts within most economics courses:

1   Because of limited income, consuming units must choose which of their many wants for goods and services they will satisfy through purchases in the market-place.
2   Scarce resources are required for the production of goods and services.
3   Households earn money income by selling the services of their productive resources to businesses and, in turn, use household income to purchase goods and services from businesses.
4   Some of the people's wants for goods and services are satisfied through governments.
5   Households may save part of their money income.

The test consists of sixty-four questions involving either a 'yes' or 'no' response but the test items are paired in such a way that only thirty-two marks can be scored. The items are matched in the following manner: 1–33, 2–34 etc. . . . 32–64. Only if the pupil answers both paired items does he or she score one mark.

Below is an example of how questions are asked twice to ensure that the pupil has grasped the economic concept:

Q.11   Goods provided by government are limited because resources are
limited   YES : NO

Q.43   Government has enough resources to produce all the goods
and services people want   YES : NO

The test has been extensively piloted in American elementary schools and has
been widely used in Scottish primary schools where statistically favourable
results have demonstrated its reliability. As it was not designed specifically to
test the Scottish economics course, it was felt that it could provide a reliable
external assessment for measuring the effectiveness of the teaching scheme.

Pupil attainment on pre- and post-tests
Maximum score = 32

School	Pre-test	s.d.	Post-test	s.d.	t	% gain
A	15.6	4.72	20.3	5.01	.001	30.1
B	20.3	3.41	25.5	2.19	.001	25.6
C_1	15.6	3.95	20.7	5.02	.001	32.7
C_2	18.9	5.30	20.9	4.62	.01	10.6
D	17.1	5.63	21.8	4.89	.001	27.5
E	14.9	5.57	18.3	8.16	.001	24.2
5 schools 6 classes	17.1	4.76	21.3	5.56		

Only in two schools, A and B, were control classes available and their results
were recorded as follows:

	Pre-test	Post-test	%
School A			
Control	14.9	15.3	2.7
Experimental	15.6	20.3	30.1
School B			
Control	17.9	18.6	3.9
Experimental	20.3	25.5	25.6

The significant increase in mean scores on the post-test recorded by the
experimental classes in both schools were in no way matched by the mean scores
of the control classes. Previous errors appeared to recur in the post-test in both
control groups, and their exposure to the normal environmental studies course
in primary seven did not assist them in answering the post-test.

Notes and references

1. Sumner, H., 'Integration and sequence in economics for 8–13-year-olds', in Lee, N. (ed.), *Teaching Economics*, 1st edn (Economics Association, 1967).
2. There is a national centre for research in elementary economic education at Lesley College, Massachusetts, which circulates teaching materials.
3. Piaget, J., 'Piaget's theory', in Carmichael, L. (Ed.), revised by Mussen, P.H. (ed.), *Manual of Child Psychology* (New York, John Wiley, 1970).
4. Bruner, J.S., *The Process of Education* (Harvard University Press, 1960) pp. 30–40 *passim*.
5. Davidson, E.G., and Kilgore, J.M., *Primary Test of Economic Understanding* (Joint Council for Economic Education, University of Iowa, 1971).
6. Scottish Central Committee on Social Subjects, Bulletin 3, *Economics in S1 and S2. A Feasibility Study* (Scottish Education Dept, HMSO, Edinburgh, n.d.).
7. Ibid.

Two other sources from which material has been drawn in the compilation of this chapter:

Scottish Money Management Association, *The Primary Pupil and Money Management* (available from Moray House College of Education, Holyrood Road, Edinburgh).

Linton, T.M., 'Scottish primary pupil and economic understanding', unpublished MEd thesis, University of Edinburgh, 1979.

Two recent publications by the Scottish Money Management Association have been produced to assist primary teachers in teaching economic concepts within environmental studies:

An Economic Approach to Environmental Studies (1983)
Environmental Studies in Practice (1983)

Both are obtainable from Moray House College of Education.

6 Economics for the 14–16-Year-Old
Raymond Ryba and Steve Hodkinson

If some people think that schools are not appropriate places for instructing young people in economic competence, then two questions arise: Where else can this task be undertaken methodically for all citizens? In an industrial democracy, can we leave this task to mere chance, probably depriving vast numbers of people of an understanding of the very processes and issues which affect their lives as citizens and workers?

Introduction

The telling quotation with which we have chosen to begin this chapter is taken from Her Majesty's Inspectors of Schools' important 1977 report on *Curriculum 11–16*.[1] It highlights particularly clearly the great change in thinking that has taken place about the role of economics in the curriculum below sixth-form level since the last edition of *Teaching Economics* was published.

At that time, the teaching of economics below the sixth form still appeared of little significance. Only a minority of schools had developed any economics teaching below the age level of 16; and most of these concentrated on GCE O-level option courses, mainly for boys. A little economics was also beginning to be taught within CSE courses, but this was mainly within the framework of 'social studies' syllabuses; and, even so, the numbers involved were small. Despite signs of change – reflected in the beginnings of the growth of GCE and CSE entrant statistics for economics – only a very small minority of pupils studied economics below the age of 16 as an examination subject. And, although some economics was being introduced to a wide band of youngsters in Scotland, within the context of modern studies, only a handful of enterprising schools in England and Wales offered it to their pre-sixth-form pupils within a non-examination context.

Today, as we write, despite a rapid increase in economics teaching below the sixth form, both within public examination courses and outside them, economics still remains very much a minority subject in the pre-sixth-form curriculum of most schools.[2] Yet numbers choosing to study economics as an O-level or CSE examination subject continue to grow and there are rapidly mounting pressures in favour of introducing at least an element of economics into the education of every young pupil within the context of compulsory schooling. These trends are likely to lead to an explosion of economics teaching in the 14–16 age range during the next decade.

Let us nail our colours to the mast. We welcome this possibility and believe it to be right. We also think that those who do not yet believe that essential elements of economic understanding *can* be taught meaningfully to this age range can be shown to be wrong by reference to the splendid economics teaching already going on in some schools. And we should not like to see this unique opportunity to bring the general curriculum of schools more up to date mishandled through half-hearted or uninformed management. We therefore believe it to be vitally important that economics teachers be fully consulted and involved in the process of extending economics in this context in their own schools.

The case for economics at 14–16

The first task facing most teachers who wish to teach economics at this level will be to convince their head teachers and colleagues of the importance of the case for doing so. It therefore seems appropriate to indicate the strength of support that now exists for the inclusion of some economics in every pupil's schooling. This support, coming both from specialists in economics education and from HM Inspectorate and the Department of Education and Science, is increasingly unanimous about the impossibility of envisaging general education to be complete without at least a minimum element of schooling contributing directly to economic literacy.

Some economics teachers have of course pressed this view for more than a century,[3] but with little effect on what has actually been taught in schools. The great change that has taken place over the past two decades is that, following the raising of the school leaving age to 16 in 1967, there has at last been official support. Already in 1965, the Schools Council, in anticipation of the raising of the school leaving age, had stated that 'everyone, these days, needs some contact with the language and ideas of elementary economics'.[4] In the late 1960s and early 1970s, important articles appeared in *Economics*, not only pressing for the development of an economics component in general education but also sketching out its possible dimensions.[5] In 1975 the Economics Association organized a major research seminar on 'extending economics within the curriculum', and its outcomes were published in 1977.[6] Also in 1975, the Association formulated proposals for a three-year project concerned with curriculum development related to economics in the 14–16 age range. Funded by the Esmée Fairbairn Trust in 1976, this was to become the first phase of the Association-sponsored Economics Education 14–16 Project.[7]

The year 1977 saw the first official support for economics education at government level. In that year, the Green Paper *Education in Schools: A Consultative Document* proposed that one of eight major educational aims should be: 'to help children to appreciate how a nation earns and maintains its standard of living, and properly to estimate the essential role of industry and commerce in this process'.[8]

The year 1977 was also the year in which HM Inspectorate published their important first *Red Book*,[9] and, again in that year, the Economics Association published its influential report, *The Contribution of Economics to General Education*.[10] Both these documents argued strongly for an economics component in general education and set out guidance on the objectives to be sought and the appropriate content to be included.

Since then a number of further pronouncements, culminating in those contained in the DES document, *The School Curriculum*, have continued to develop and strengthen the case for economics in the curriculum.[11] There has also been further support from HM Inspectorate; and politicians of all parties have added their voices in favour, as have leading industrialists and trade unionists. In 1983 this rising tide of support was further strengthened by an unequivocal ministerial statement by Sir Keith Joseph, Secretary of State for Education, to the effect that 'Economics or the economic "facts of life" should be taught to school children'.[12] He has returned to this theme several times since.

The most important of all these pronouncements, in terms of the future place of economics within the 14–16 curriculum, are those contained in *The School Curriculum*. This is because, following its publication, DES Circular 6/81 enjoined each local education authority to:

(a) review its policy for the school curriculum in its area and arrangements for making its policy known;
(b) review the extent to which current provision in the schools is consistent with that policy;
(c) plan future developments accordingly.

It indicated that the Secretary of State expected schools to set out their aims in writing and develop their curricula in the light of what is said in *The School Curriculum*. As this volume goes to press, local authorities and their schools are faced with having to meet these requirements. There could therefore be no better time to press the case at school level for the development of courses that can meet those needs related to economics set out in *The School Curriculum*. The most important of these are that:

. . . pupils need to be given a better understanding of the economic base of our society and the importance to Britain of the wealth creating process (para 53(a)).

and:

An increasing number of local authorities and schools have recognised the importance of establishing links between the education service and industry; each side has much to contribute to the other (para 53(c)).

Even more important for the future development of economics education at this level has been the work of the Economics Education 14–16 Project. Following its first research-oriented phase, its second phase concentrated on the development of appropriate exemplar teaching materials and associated teacher guidance. It was also concerned with the piloting of pre-service and in-service teacher-training approaches based on these.[13] Publications based upon this work are now beginning to be available and a number of local authorities and training institutions are already co-operating with the project to offer in-service opportunities to teachers to develop their knowledge and skills in relation to 14–16 economics teaching.

In these circumstances the following key sentence from the Economics Association's report on *The Contribution of Economics to General Education* remains as valid as when it was written:

If education is to fully prepare school leavers for their future roles in society, provision must be made in the curriculum for all pupils to have an opportunity to develop a basic level of competence in economics and to acquire at least the socially necessary standard of economic literacy.[14]

It is in this spirit that the remainder of this chapter has been written.

Economic competence at 16: the notion of economic literacy

For those pupils who choose economics as a GCE or CSE option, or who go on to study economics in the sixth form, the syllabuses of the examinations for which they are being prepared, as interpreted by their teachers, obviously constitute an unavoidable indicator of the notion of economic competence as the examination boards see it. We shall come back to this point later in the chapter. For others – for those whose abilities do not match the bookish requirements of some of these syllabuses, for those who will leave school at 16, and for those who will go on to study other subjects after 16 – these syllabuses are generally over-demanding in some directions and inappropriate in others. What then is required, as a starting base for all pupils, is a notion of what minimum level of economic competence should be aimed for.

Given the pressures on the curriculum, and the limitations on what can be attempted with the least-able pupils, that minimum can only be related to the provision of access for all youngsters to a 'starter kit' of knowledge, skills and attitudes, from which later development, whether in more advanced courses or in the 'school of life', can develop safely.

That minimum level is what is meant by economic literacy. Of what does it consist? Obviously there are many different views. But the findings of the Economics Association's ad hoc committee on *The Contribution of Economics to General Education* offers a carefully considered starting point.[15] First, it saw 'three overriding purposes for which some economics education for all pupils of secondary age is essential'. These were:

1   To provide school leavers, within their varying intellectual capacities, with that economic knowledge and those economic skills and concepts which will enable them to better understand the world in which they live, and the sophisticated workings of their own economy.
2   To develop an understanding of the more important economic forces and institutions with which they will come into contact as producers and consumers, and of the crucial interdependence of economic actions.
3   To ensure that all pupils acquire sufficient knowledge of economics and the methods of the social sciences to enable them to participate fully in the decision-making processes of a modern industrial democracy.

Its justification for this view was not simply that the level of economics understanding implied would constitute a degree of economic competence. It also felt that it would contribute to general education by bringing pupils into contact 'with kinds of knowledge and ways of thinking which would be of undoubted value to them in their future lives and of benefit to the society of which they will be members'.

Within this framework, it believed that the main contribution of economics to general education lay in the social and political area of the pupils' preparation for life. In particular, it stressed the importance of understanding something of the economic basis that underlies most major social and political issues, and the mutual economic interdependence of all the constituent parts of modern society. It also underlined the potential contribution of economics to pupils' linguistic development, to the development of a range of basic general techniques of analysis and evaluation, to the experience offered in logical thinking and the generation and testing of hypotheses related to social affairs, and to the introduction offered to clear thinking about important moral issues such as equality, equity and the nature of business ethics.

In the committee's view, these purposes could be met by the development through economics teaching of a range of skills, of appropriate conceptual knowledge, of appropriate content and of sensible attitudes and notions of value. It divided skills into 'over-arching' and 'specific' ones, and stressed the importance of developing these through the study of economics as well as in other subjects. In terms of 'over-arching' skills it was concerned with those skills, like the development of logical thought processes, which, while taught through economics, 'may be generally applied to a variety of situations'. More specific skills that it stressed included the ability to:

(a) identify the economic aspects of particular issues, and correctly apply relevant economic concepts and principles;
(b) distinguish between statements of facts and expressions of opinions;
(c) organize and present economic ideas in an accurate, reasoned, and relevant way;
(d) evaluate decisions, arguments and reliability of information in terms of economic criteria;
(e) process data related to economics, including the collection and collation of data and their use and presentation to support arguments and points of view;
(f) present and discuss ideas, concepts, and arguments in a clear and accurate manner and with reference to appropriate supporting data.

For the committee, it was clear that economics was of such relevance to current events and to the future life of pupils that it afforded a valuable means of developing these skills.

As regards the *development of conceptual knowledge*, the committee particularly stressed the importance of 'teaching economic concepts, rather than only economic facts'. It saw these as ranging from very general concepts through to very specific ones. At the general level it identified those not specific to economics – for example, statistical and visual concepts such as real versus nominal rates, averages, index numbers, graphs and diagrams, and those that were much more specific – for example, core economic concepts such as scarcity and choice, resource allocation, income distribution and economic efficiency. At a more specific level, it drew attention to the need to develop some understanding of such things as opportunity cost, income and wealth, production, specialization, exchange, inflation, economic growth and imports and exports. More specific still, the following concepts were suggested as examples of what should be known, at least at an elementary level, in relation to specific problems: consumers, producers, industry, the firm, imports, exports, investments, savings, effective demand, market supply, types of costs and revenue and of equilibrium. Obviously, how far such concepts can be developed depends on the time available, the objectives aimed at, and the ability of the youngsters. Nevertheless, the committee was in no doubt that an appropriate selection could and should be made.

In terms of minimizing content of a more factual kind, the

committee's view was that much of the choice would be determined in the first instance by the skills and concepts that the teacher sought to develop. In this belief, it knowingly (and rightly) *reversed* the order of selection of so many examination boards whose syllabuses tend to concentrate on the facts. It stressed the importance of relating taught factual knowledge to the achievement by all school leavers of an understanding of the simple processes of resource allocation in a particular market situation and something of the workings of the macroeconomy. It also suggested that economic content best suited to helping pupils to understand the world around them and their place in it should include some knowledge of the main differences between economic systems and conditions in different parts of the world, the patterns of international trade between them and those things that will most help them in adult and working life. Included in these it particularly noted:

(a) the role of money and the working of various financial and commercial institutions;
(b) how prices are arrived at;
(c) how wages and other factor prices are determined;
(d) the consequences of changing prices for firms, industries and employment;
(e) the economic role of government and its part in allocating the resources available to society;
(f) the means used to raise government revenue;
(g) the changing pattern of government spending with respect to publicly provided services and government economic policies.

Summing up its views on content, it felt it important to ensure that: 'pupils do not leave school wholly ignorant of the economic facts of life and incapable of exercising the powers of discrimination which are necessary in their roles as consumers, producers and citizens'.

Turning finally to the question of attitudes, the committee warned of the importance of avoiding an approach that sought directly to persuade pupils that certain economic actions or consequences were right or wrong, good or bad. It stressed, on the contrary, the role that economics should play in helping young people to distinguish between positive analysis and normative judgements. It held the view that pupils could be helped, through economics, to 'develop, refine and articulate their *own* personal values which then condition the judgements they make on the different economic issues confronting them'. To do this, it set out four ways in which economics at this level might usefully contribute:

1 By developing a clearer understanding of the distinction between facts and values in economic issues and thereby facilitating their more reasoned examination.

2 By developing a clearer understanding of the different basic values held by individuals in society and of the different government policy objectives to which they give rise (e.g. higher material standards of living, reductions in income, inequities, broader social objectives) so that pupils may develop their own personal attitudes to such values and policy objectives.

3 By developing a clearer factual understanding of the nature and operations of major economic institutions, so that pupils' attitudes towards such institutions are not ill-informed or prejudiced through possessing incomplete or biased knowledge.

4 By developing a clearer appreciation of the need to examine the costs (in terms of the alternatives foregone) as well as the benefits of proposed economic actions in order to promote a more 'balanced' attitude in economic decision-making by consumers, workers and the electorate.

Obviously, the views summarized above are only one interpretation of what should be aimed for in order to achieve economic literacy. They also leave much work for individual teachers to do in formulating their own individual schemes of work in relation to the needs and possibilities within their own schools and in deciding to what depth to go. That is as it should be. But the committee's work does provide a useful and carefully considered starting point.

Placing economics in the curriculum 14–16

In introducing this chapter we forecast an explosion of economics teaching in the 14–16 age range during the next decade. Such a development was foreseen by head teachers in England and Wales in the mid-1970s when Holley asked them to gaze into the crystal ball.[16] Of those asked, almost half considered it 'likely' or 'very likely' that economics would become available as an optional subject in their school's curriculum by the late 1970s, and just over one-third saw it as contributing to an integrated (social studies) option. Relatively few head teachers, on the other hand, saw a role for economics within the 'common core' of the curriculum either as a separate subject or as part of an integrated course.

Had these expectations been fulfilled, and even the most cursory glance at published examination statistics will demonstrate that they have not, a dramatic expansion of separate subject economics would have occurred.[17] As it is, however, once head teachers and colleagues have been convinced of the need to include economics in the general curriculum, the second major task to be faced will be to negotiate an appropriate curriculum slot.

In Scotland, experiences with O-grade economics have been similar to those elsewhere. Introduced in 1974, it has failed to reach the status of a major teaching subject. In 1982, for example, only 4.2 per cent of O-grade candidates were entered for economics and a proportion of these were post-16 entrants. However, as a result of the acceptance of the reports of the Munn and Dunning committees, by 1986 economics will have a place in the recommended 'core' curriculum for all 15–16 year olds.[18] In the new structure pupils will choose one subject from economics, geography, history and modern studies. Whatever that choice, at least one element of the course must be concerned with the political, economic, industrial and environmental aspects of life.[19]

In Scotland the curriculum debate at all levels in the educational system has resulted in the decision that economics should be taught and assessed as part of the 'core' curriculum, both as an optional separate subject within that 'core' and also as an element within other subjects.

In England, Wales and Northern Ireland the future is less certain. Despite the increased involvement of central government in curricular matters, national implementation of a single framework is unlikely and the autonomy of head teachers and their teaching staffs in framing school curricula will remain large. Such arrangements have inevitably led, and will continue to lead, to a rich variety of contexts in which aspects of economics are offered to young people. Table 6.1 gives an insight into this variety. Even within a very small sample of schools, economics is to be found as a separate subject, as part of social science courses, as part of courses leading to an understanding of industrial society and within many general courses designed for all or restricted-ability bands of pupils.

As a result of the recent government decision to support the development of GCSE and the work of the GCE and CSE Boards' Joint Council for 16+ National Criteria, those teachers who negotiate a role for economics within the elective area of a school's curriculum seem likely to have a range of options open to them.[20] The reports of the 16+ National Criteria working parties in business studies, economics and social sciences appear to be leading to syllabuses in which aspects of economics can be studied within a single-subject economics framework, as part of a business studies 'core plus options' approach or as integrated social science.[21] Moreover, the criteria proposed for the aims and objectives of such syllabuses seem to envisage a broader and more worthwhile view of economics education than the factual knowledge-loaded syllabuses that are current and which we have commented upon earlier.

However, a decision to take the opportunity afforded by the continued existence of separate-subject economics syllabuses will not be an easy one for schools to make and, indeed, many may decide that this

Table 6.1 Details of courses, ability groups and teachers in a number of Economics Education 14–16 Project pilot schools*

School	O-level	CSE	Other examination	Non-examination	Above average	Average	Below average	Economics	Others
1		Commerce			✓	✓	✓	2	
2		Social Economics	Social and Community Studies	Money Matters		✓	✓	2	1
3		Commerce		Careers/Social Education	✓	✓	✓	1	8
4		Office Practice/Social Economics				✓			2
5	Government/Economics/Commerce			Common Studies	✓	✓	✓	1	1
6				Local Studies	✓	✓	✓	1	
7	Economics	Commerce		General Studies	✓	✓	✓		1
8		Social Economics						1	
9				Economics		✓		1	1
10				Personal and Social Education		✓		1	1
11		Commerce				✓	✓	1	
12		Commerce	Commerce 16+			✓	✓	2	1
13	Understanding Industrial Society				✓			1	1
14	British Industrial Society	Social Economics				✓	✓		1
15	Economics/Social Economics			Integrated Studies	✓	✓	✓	1	2
16	Social Economics			Social Science	✓	✓	✓	1	4

* During the period from autumn 1981 to December 1983 the Economics Education 14–16 Project worked with some fifty schools in England, Wales and Northern Ireland to pilot exemplar teaching materials developed during the period by the Project.

framework is neither appropriate nor possible given both the resource constraints and the pressures on them to provide some economics education for all pupils. For the minority of schools who currently offer economics to GCE O and CSE levels, a decision to continue it in that form may be at the expense of some education in economics for their pupils in general. Moreover, such an arrangement will inevitably re-inforce the current provision of economics which is geared towards the higher-ability pupil in schools.[22] On the other hand, it is bold indeed to move away from such provision when examination status, and especially O-level status, traditionally enhances its importance in the eyes of pupils, parents, teachers and timetablers alike. It is of course quite conceivable for economics as a separate 'option' subject to exist along-side 'core' courses that have elements or modules of economics in them. The illustrations from the 14–16 Project trial schools network shown in Table 6.1 illustrate this well. However, arrangements such as these imply an ability on the part of curriculum planners to devise schemes of work in which 'option' courses extend and enrich the 'core' course rather than repeat it. Moreover (as is shown in Table 6.1) they may involve considerable numbers of non-specialists in the teaching of economics. The success of such schemes may well depend therefore upon the willingness of economics teachers to support and encourage the involvement and professional development of their non-specialist colleagues.

In some areas of the UK, and especially in urban areas, school reorganizations designed to overcome the problem of falling pupil rolls and to accommodate changing attitudes towards educational provision for 16–19-year-olds pose particular difficulties for those planning to incorporate economics into the general curriculum. Not only are such reorganizations leading to smaller-sized schools with fewer teachers and therefore less flexibility in the elective area of the curriculum, but they are also taking specialist economics teachers out of those schools that deal specifically with young people aged 14–16 years and placing them in the sixth-form college/tertiary sector.

In such constrained circumstances the future pattern of economics in the elective area might well be within integrated social science/business studies 'options' rather than in single-subject courses, supported by 'core' general courses that include an element of economics. On the other hand, it might well be that many schools find no place for economics in the elective area, choosing to develop aspects of it within contemporary studies, personal and social development, or community studies 'core' courses. The success of schemes such as these will un-doubtedly depend greatly upon real co-operation between teachers in schools and on the level of support given to them by their local authori-ties. Our experience in working with teachers and local education authorities on the Economics Education 14–16 Project has given us hope that they are becoming increasingly prepared to face such challenges.

Choosing materials and methods

The teaching resources used in any particular lesson or sequence of lessons are key elements in the learning process. How they are perceived by teacher and learner both contributes to learning and helps to shape relationships in the classroom. Chosen carefully, with due attention to the particular characteristics of the students and schemes of work concerned, they can motivate the learner, helping to bring within his or her experience the abstract realities of the world outside of that experience or alternatively placing past experiences in a new framework.[23] Chosen haphazardly or with a narrow unimaginative view of resources and methods, and indeed of economics education as a whole, they can act as a block to the development of economics understanding.

Almost all teachers use a blend of resources developed by themselves and by others; but, for most, the many pressures of teaching usually mean a heavy reliance on published materials. Collecting, evaluating and finally selecting from an array of course texts, topic books, workbooks, tapes, slide sets and others is no easy task.

For those mainly concerned with traditional courses leading to examinations at 16+, the difficulty, at least superficially, is the least. Thus the conventional GCE O-level syllabus, relying heavily on the acquisition and recall of factual knowledge about the UK economy and institutions,[24] and intended for the top 20 per cent of the ability range, is now served by a growing number of well-tried books. At the time of writing, few school economics cupboards are without their copies of *Descriptive Economics*, *Elementary Economics*, *Social Economics* and *Introductory Economics*.[25] These and similar books written by a first generation of O-level textbook writers provide detailed and uniform descriptive accounts which successfully meet the narrow needs of the examiners.

In recent years, the revision of a number of O-level syllabuses, the emergence of new economics-related syllabuses and the plethora of Mode 3 CSE syllabuses have both broadened the scope of economics 14–16 and extended it down the ability range of students. Alongside such developments, a second generation of authors has emerged providing a greater variety of approaches and material for both teacher and student. It is well worth contrasting the breadth of stimulus resource material and student exercises in *Economics in Action* and *An Introduction to Social Economics* with some of the earlier texts.[26]

In a similar way the emergence of objective test items and data-response questions in O-level and CSE examinations has led to the development of workbooks both to complement texts and to stand in their own right. *Basic Economics: Workbook* is typical of the former and *Data Response Questions in 'O' Level Economics* typical of the latter.[27]

There has thus been a slow but steady development in the textbook/workbook field, with authors and their publishers showing a heightened awareness of the needs of a broader band of student users. Institutions such as the Life Offices' Association, the Banking Information Service and others, as well as individual building societies and banks, have also played a part in this development, providing resource materials in the field of personal money management and the financial sector of the economy.[28] Industry too has sponsored initiatives like the *Foundations of Wealth* series of films.[29]

And yet real deficiencies in available published resources still exist. Television and radio programmers, for instance, mindful of the relatively small (if growing) market for economics broadcasts at the pre-A-level stage, have planned little for 14–16-year-olds. It was not until 1983, for example, that BBC Schools Radio ventured into O-level economics with a series called *Economics: Supply and Demand*.[30] The deficiencies do, however, go deeper than this. If economics teaching for this age group in the 1980s and 1990s is to take on the emphases described in this chapter, then there is a need for resource materials (published or self-initiated) that allow students rather than teachers to grasp the nettle, and to develop strategies for approaching problems and issues with an economics dimension.

As regards published work, the Economics Education 14–16 Project has surveyed and reviewed a very wide range of material available to the economics teacher. The outcomes of that review have been brought together in the form of two annotated resource lists. *An Annotated Bibliography of Pupil Books* provides author, publisher, price, format and content details for a selection of some 130 texts, topic books, workbooks and dictionaries.[31] Its sister volume, *An Annotated List of Non-Textbook Resources*, provides similar details for some 300 tapes, slide sets, simulations, booklets, films, case studies and more.[32] Together they provide a first approximation of available published resource materials. Given their standardized format, they also provide some guidance and initial assistance to teachers in the selection process.

Other sources also exist that help teachers to evaluate the usefulness of resource materials. Not least among them is the Economics Association's quarterly journal *Economics*.[33] Its reviews section regularly provides space for new textbooks and resources materials, the reviews being written mainly by practising economics teachers. Moreover, from time to time the economics education section of *Economics* provides review articles on resource materials. One such article, 'An evaluation of classroom materials in economics', by Linda Thomas, provides a clear framework for use by teachers when evaluating the usefulness of classroom materials, together with an example of the framework in use.[34] Among other sources, *The Times Educational Supplement* devotes annually a number of its pages to a review of books and resources for teaching economics; and, in *Money Management Review*, produced termly by the Life Offices' Association, economics materials loom large.[35] The *Handbook for Economics Teachers*[36] edited by David Whitehead, provides an Aladdin's cave of teaching ideas written and tried out by individual teachers (many suitable for economics 14–16). It also offers address lists for a range of other resources.

But useful as are such guides and sources, there still remains much for the individual teacher to do in order to devise appropriate resource-based learner-oriented teaching materials and approaches to meet the needs of pupils across the whole ability range. To help teachers in this task has been the objective of the Economics Education 14–16 Project.

This project, set up by the Economics Association, was specifically concerned during its second phase (1980–3) with the development of exemplar curriculum materials, containing teacher guidance and pupil materials. The project team, in co-operation with many schools and teachers, has created and piloted a set of resource-based teaching units relating to three areas of economic experience – the young person as consumer, as producer and as citizen.[37] These units are designed not only to stand in their own right as teaching materials, but also (and most importantly) to serve as a stimulus to teachers to adapt and supplement to suit their own particular circumstances. Hopefully, as a result of their use, teachers will approach the development of their own schemes of work and resource materials with increased confidence and expertise.

Figure 6.1 illustrates the approach that the project has adopted for its exemplar units. Objectives are listed in each unit as *key ideas* (concepts, relationships and areas of knowledge in economics), *skills* (intellectual, data processing, communication, etc.) and *attitudes* (awareness of values, distinction between facts and values, etc.) and are intended to contribute towards the achievement of economic competence in young people. Embodied in the *learning styles*, techniques of *classroom organization* and *pupil materials* in the units is a belief that the structuring of situations which engage pupils in the learning process, which stimulate and maintain their interest, and which involve their active participation, can lead to the achievement of the broad objectives referred to here and earlier in this chapter. Taken together, these four aspects of the project's approach to the development of its exemplar teaching materials provide a framework for others to use in the creation of their own materials and one that teachers in various parts of the UK are now actively using.

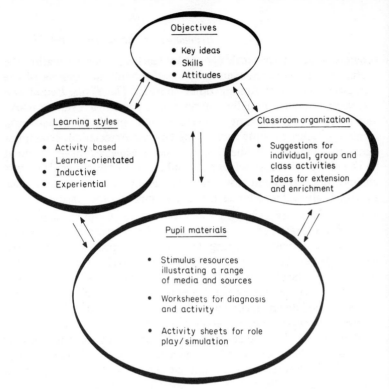

Fig. 6.1 The Economics Education 14–16 Project: an exemplar materials approach.

Source: Economics Education 14–16 Project.

Some units are *diagnostic* in that they are intended to draw out from pupils what they already know so that it can be restructured or added to in group discussion. To achieve this, open-ended situations are created in which pupils respond in their own way to stimulus (photographic, statistical, written, etc.). Such an approach often helps to bring out pupils' misconceptions about matters economic and thus provides a useful beginning to a lesson or sequence of lessons.

Both *deductive* and *inductive* inquiry-based approaches are frequently involved within the same unit. Both approaches are important in the teaching of economics but all too often the inductive approach is given a low priority since it involves considerable structuring and preparation on the part of the teacher and its outcomes are less predictable.

Role-playing and *simulation* are illustrated in a number of units. They usually involve small groups or teams of pupils and therefore impose a form of classroom organization on the teacher that is not without its hazards but that considerably opens up the learning context. In one unit, for example, the factory production of a good is simulated using both individual working and specialization by process.[38] In this way the essence of a simulation is exemplified through the isolation of one aspect of the processes involved (in this case the method of organizing the work-force) thus allowing the teacher to draw out particular teaching points from the simulation exercise. Role-playing exercises, possibly more than other techniques, provide a forum for pupil attitudes to be revealed and thus the debriefing period that follows such an activity takes on added importance, for it must take participants 'out of the role' so that they can analyse objectively what they have been engaged in doing.

The case-study approach to teaching economics is exemplified in a number of units with real-life cases being presented in different ways (for example in the form of a cartoon strip or as a set of documents).[39] Moreover, while a number of case studies include worksheets designed to draw out aspects from each case, they do so in contrasting ways. One worksheet, for example, adopts a methodical, step-by-step approach to a limited number of concepts, while another uses the case study to raise a broader range of issues.

The learning styles and teaching approaches adopted do, moreover, provide examples of ways of varying the size of the learning group as well as organizational techniques that make active and continuous pupil involvement possible. Some units involve pupils working in *groups* or *teams*, and most provide opportunities for *individual study* or for the *class* to interact as a full group. The variety of resource materials selected for the exemplar units – photographs, slides, case studies, role sheets, questionnaires, surveys, video, cartoon strips, audio tape, statistical data and others – not only provide working examples of the use of such resources but also collectively provide for a learning situation that is both purposeful and rich in variety.

In outlining part of our work on the Economics Education 14–16 Project, we have aimed to give insights into the types of resource materials that will remedy the deficiencies referred to earlier in this section. In our view, the development of materials that help teachers to think about the possibilities for opening up the learning situation, which lead them to set problems to their students rather than simply to provide ready-made answers, and which help them to shift the balance in the classroom in a variety of ways from teacher to learner, are those most likely to meet the requirements of economics education for all 14–16-year-olds.

Conclusion

Although we have not ignored in this chapter the problems faced in teaching those option groups in the fourth and fifth forms studying economics for the GCE O-level or the CSE, we hope we may be forgiven for not giving pride of place to these areas of 14–16 work. In our view, the major challenge is that of extending economics in the general curriculum to meet *every* pupil's 'entitlement'.

Our intention, has thus been to offer help, at a more general level, with regard to four key questions related to the teaching of economics across the whole ability range at 14–16. These questions, as we see them, are:

1 Why should economics be taught to this age range?
2 What constitutes an appropriate level of economic competence at 16?
3 Where in the curriculum can economics teaching be inserted?
4 How, in this age range, can economics best be taught?

We do not pretend to give complete answers to any of these questions. Those are the prerogative of each teacher in the light of the particular context in which he or she works. We hope nevertheless that what we have said, taken together with the copious references to further sources we have offered, will provide a sound base of support from which individual readers can take matters further as appropriate.

For those already teaching economics across the whole of the 14–16 age cohort, we hope that at least our final two sections will be of particular use. The questions they confront are those about which, according to Holley, teachers are most anxious to have help and guidance. Obviously, in the space available, we have been unable to do more than raise the main issues and offer guidance as to sources where they can be followed up more exhaustively.

For others, we suspect that those sections that deal with the first two of our four questions will be just as important, if not even more so. The fact remains that, for most schools, and for most children in them, particularly girls, the less able and those leaving at 16, the teaching of economics in any form is still largely absent. Good intentions alone will not change this picture. If things are to change – and they surely must – battles remain to be fought and won by economics teachers. There will be a need to establish a dialogue with head teachers and colleagues who may not be easily convinced by what is now a formidably supported case.

We hope, therefore, that those few economics teachers more fortunately placed in this respect will recognize that the earlier sections of the chapter which might at first appear superfluous to them are not really so; that, to the majority of our readers they may be of considerable value in negotiating recognition and a proper place for the development of at least a minimum level of economic understanding for all young people by the age of 16.

Certainly, if that goal is to be reached, this is the right time to engage in its pursuit. To quote again from the final paragraph of the Economics Association's statement on *The Contribution of Economics to General Education*:

At this time of fundamental reconsideration of the shape of the curriculum for general secondary education, the opportunity should not be missed to ensure that the development of economic competence is given a fuller place in general education. Accepting the challenge will not be without difficulty. . . . However . . . if education is to fully prepare school leavers for their future roles in society, provision must be made in the curriculum for all pupils to have the opportunity to develop a basic level of competence in economics and to acquire at least the socially necessary standard of economic literacy.[40]

Notes and references

1. DES, *Curriculum 11–16: Working Papers by HM Inspectorate: A Contribution to the Current Debate* (DES, December 1977).
2. See Holley, B., and Skelton, V., *Economics Education 14–16, Phase I: Final Report* (Economics Association, September 1978, and NFER, 1980).
3. Thus, Millicent Fawcett's *Political Economy for Beginners*, published by Macmillan in eight editions from 1870 to 1896, was specifically written to 'help to make Political Economy a more popular study in boys' and girls' schools'.
4. *Raising the School Leaving Age*, Schools Council Working Paper no. 2 (HMSO, 1965).
5. For example, Lee, N., 'Economics education for the Newsom child', *Economics*, vol. 8, pt 1, no. 31, 1969; and Robinson, T.K., 'Extending the contribution of economics to the curriculum', *Economics*, vol. 9, pt 2, no. 38, 1971.
6. Robinson, T.K., and Wilson, R. (eds), *Extending Economics within the Curriculum* (Routledge & Kegan Paul, 1977).
7. The possibility of an Association-sponsored project in this age range was first discussed in the early 1970s and the Economics Education 14–16 Project itself was first conceived in 1974.
8. *Education in Schools: A Consultative Document*, Cmnd. 6869 (HMSO, 1977).
9. DES, op. cit.
10. Economics Association, *The Contribution of Economics to General Education* (report of an *ad hoc* committee of the Association, 1977).
11. Department of Education and Science and Welsh Office, *The School Curriculum* (HMSO, 1981).
12. Sir Keith Joseph as reported in *The Times*, 11 August 1983.
13. For an account of the Economics Project's remit and outcomes, see Ryba, R., Hodkinson, S., *et al.*, *Understanding Economics* (Economics Education 14–16 Project, Manchester University, 1983); also, other Project publications and papers by Robinson, T.K., Holley, B.J., and Ryba, R., *Economics*, vol. 16, pt 3, no. 71, autumn 1980.
14. *The Contribution of Economics to General Education*, op. cit., para. 8.

15. Ibid.
16. Holley and Skelton, op. cit., ch. 3.
17. In 1980, for example, O-level economics entries had only reached 43,000 compared with 130,000 for history, 170,000 for physics, etc.
18. The Munn Report, *The Structure of the Curriculum in the Third and Fourth Years of the Scottish Curriculum* (HMSO, 1977); The Dunning Report, *Assessment for All* (HMSO, 1977).
19. For a summary of economics in the Scottish school curriculum, see Robinson, T.K., 'Economics in the secondary school curriculum in Scotland', *Economics*, vol. 19, pt 4, winter 1983.
20. The Joint Council of GCE and CSE Boards for 16+ National Criteria was established by the boards in response to a government invitation for them to work nationally and jointly to prepare draft general and subject-specific criteria for the proposed 16+ examination system.
21. GCE and CSE Boards' Joint Council for 16+ National Criteria, *Report of the Working Party for Economics* (September 1983); GCE and CSE Boards' Joint Council for 16+ National Criteria, *Report of the Working Party for Business Studies* (1983); GCE and CSE Boards' Joint Council for 16+ National Criteria, *Report of the Social Sciences Working Party* (1983).
22. See, for example, the evidence presented in Holley and Skelton, op. cit., ch. 3.
23. See Chapter 13 for a fuller exemplification of this point.
24. See, for example, the Associated Examining Board's Economics Syllabus 1, Economic Principles.
25. Harbury, C.D., *Descriptive Economics*, 6th edn (Pitman, 1981); Harvey, J., *Elementary Economics*, 5th edn (Macmillan, 1983); Nobbs, J., *Social Economics*, 3rd edn (McGraw-Hill, 1981); Stanlake, G.F., *Introductory Economics*, 4th edn (Longman, 1983).
26. Christie, D., and Scott, A., *Economics in Action* (Heinemann Educational Books, 1977); Anderton, A.G., *An Introduction to Social Economics*, 2nd edn (Heinemann Educational Books, 1984).
27. Harvey, J., *Basic Economics: Workbook* (Macmillan, 1981); Baron, D., and Connor, J., *Data Response Questions in 'O' Level Economics* (Heinemann Educational Books, 1979).
28. See, among many others, *Spending and Saving*, Life Offices' Association/Associated Scottish Life Offices, Buckingham House, 62/63 Queen Street, London EC4R 1AD (a teaching pack on money education containing graded worksheets, teacher's notes, etc.); *Understanding Banking*, Banking Information Service, 10 Lombard Street, London EC3V 9AT (a series of booklets on banks and their services).
29. Sponsored by Esso, ICI and Unilever, the *Foundations of Wealth* series of seven ten-minute films on video cassette are available from Unilever Education Section, PO Box 68, Unilever House, London EC4P 4BQ.
30. This series of five, twenty-minute programmes was broadcast in spring 1983 with an accompanying text, *The Potherbridge Challenge*, written by Linda Thomas.
31. Economics Education 14–16 Project, *An Annotated Bibliography of Pupil Books* (Economics Association, 1981).
32. Economics Education 14–16 Project, *An Annotated List of Non-Textbook Resources* (Economics Association, 1984).

33. *Economics*, journal of the Economics Association, Economics Association, Temple Lodge, South Street, Ditchling, Sussex BN6 8UQ.
34. Thomas, L., 'An evaluation of classroom materials in economics – a case study', *Economics*, vol. 19, pt 3, no. 83, autumn 1983.
35. *Money Management Review*, Life Offices' Association/Associated Scottish Life Offices, Buckingham House, 62/63 Queen Street, London EC4R 1AD.
36. Whitehead, D.J. (ed.), *Handbook for Economics Teachers* (Heinemann Educational Books, 1979).
37. Phase 2 of the Economics Education 14–16 Project (1980–3) was based at Manchester University and sponsored by the Economics Association. It was particularly concerned with the development of exemplar curriculum materials aimed at providing a basis for the extension of economics education across the whole ability range of the 14–16 age group. Full details of the project can be obtained from the Economics Education 14–16 Project, Department of Education, University of Manchester, Manchester M13 9PL.
38. This unit, *Production Record Sheets*, is illustrated in 'Understanding economics: an introduction to the project's work on exemplar materials', *Economics Education 14–16 Project*, 1983 (available free from the Project Office, Department of Education, University of Manchester, M13 9PL).
39. Ibid. See, for example, *Budgeting* and *Price of a Perm*.
40. *The Contribution of Economics to General Education*, op. cit., para. 38.

7 Economics for the GCE A-Level Student
M.J. Tighe

The nature of the sixth-form student

In a study by the Schools Council of the general curriculum in the sixth form in 1972, the changing nature of the sixth-form student was emphasized.[1] The Council reported an enormous increase in the number of pupils pursuing A-level courses. Between 1962 and 1970 the numbers virtually doubled. Because of population trends, the numbers entering the sixth form to follow A-level courses have not continued to grow so rapidly in the 1980s. However, two other important facts emerged from the Schools Council report. The first was that 31 per cent of all sixth formers left after only one year of their course. The second was that of 'the most academic group of sixth formers, no less than 64 per cent are unlikely to take any degree course in the University or Polytechnic'.[2]

It is clearly important to recognize the nature of the sixth-form student in designing an appropriate A-level course. The evidence produced by such bodies as the Schools Council would suggest that the traditional A-level course, largely influenced by university requirements, is no longer appropriate to the majority of sixth-form students. There has been considerable discussion in recent years over the emergence of a so-called 'new sixth' which is not necessarily academically oriented but merely seeking vocational qualifications or a consolidation of the work done in the first five years of secondary education which may have produced a limited number of recognizable examination results either in GCE O-level or CSE. Although this chapter concentrates on the sixth-form student, many of the comments are applicable to further education where there is considerable overlap with A-level on BTEC and CEE courses.

The new entrant to the sixth form may therefore be broadly classified in one of the following groups. These are not mutually exclusive and students may be wrongly classified for a variety of reasons. For example, some students, for social, cultural or linguistic reasons, may appear in a lower category despite an above-average intelligence. Moreover, students must not be seen or treated as 'types', if only because stereotyping may result in low expectations and achievement.

1   *The academically gifted student.* Such students are likely to have a strong O-level background with high-grade passes in a range of subjects. They will be capable of handling abstract concepts and the processes of deductive and inductive logic. They are also likely to have well-developed oral and verbal skills. These are clear candidates for some form of higher education but although they may provide an academic challenge for the economics teacher, probably only a small proportion will take their studies of the subject into university or polytechnic. Very few will emerge as professional economists but others may incorporate economics as part of a more general course.

2   *The honest plodder.* These students will have a more limited ability to appreciate abstract concepts and are likely to be better at deductive rather than inductive logic. They will have acquired certain basic skills and will be capable of intelligent oral discussion but will be more limited in expressing themselves on paper. This is likely to be reflected in their examination results, which may still be impressive in terms of numbers of passes but liable to be mostly GCE O-level C grade. Many of these students will be quite capable of passing A-level but may then proceed no further because of limited academic ambition or family commitments that encourage early employment. Some will attempt higher education courses but only a few will survive through sheer determination and hard work.

3   *The non-academic student.* Such students may have acquired one or two passes at grade C but have taken mainly CSE examinations and achieved grades 2 or 3. These students will have very limited powers of logic and are unlikely to have the verbal skills necessary to succeed in traditional examinations. They may also have learning difficulties and be unable to retain large quantities of factual knowledge. Many of these students will spend one year in the sixth form extending and improving their O-level achievements, and a few may go further. Some may mix a mainly O-level course with the study of one A-level in a subject where they have demonstrated above-average ability. A student may study A-level mathematics, for example, after passing at O-level with an A or B grade but continue O-level work in English and science and start a new course in economics or sociology where there will be no previous record of failure. Such students may have an extended sixth-form life and a few may spend as many as four years in the sixth, eventually obtaining one or two A-level passes and a small collection of O-level passes achieved over a number of years. Some of these students may apply for vocationally based courses at polytechnics.

4   *The foundation student.* These students will have a very weak academic background. They will have achieved no O-level passes or CSE equivalents but may have CSE grades 4 and 5 or even be unclassified. Many of these students will never reach O-level standard but need

some basic skills in order to survive in society. Some may remain unemployed for most of their lives or perhaps will manage menial or part-time employment. The economics teacher will be closely involved with such students in association with colleagues concerned with communication and numeracy skills. Such students will need to appreciate the problem of choice with very limited resources, how to manage money effectively, how to borrow, and to see the relevance of problems such as inflation and unemployment. Much work is being done to provide effective and meaningful courses for such students.

Economics in the sixth-form curriculum

Those students falling into category 3 or 4 above would normally require an elementary course in economics that would emphasize practical, experiential learning.

It is students in categories 1 and 2 that are the main concern of this chapter, that is, the more academic, average or above-average-ability sixth-form student. It must be recognized, however, that such students are not seen in isolation but are often taught in very mixed ability groups.

A-level courses in economics appeal to students for a variety of reasons. For the more able student there is intellectual stimulus. For those seeking careers in banking, accounting, insurance or business management, the vocational element is attractive. For others, the element of citizenship is valued. Moreover, it can form a useful companion to a wide variety of other subjects.

The approach to teaching economics at A-level is largely a matter of individual choice. Many teachers feel that a spiral technique is essential in conveying the meaning and significance of economics. It is desirable to move from what the student already knows or can easily imagine to more complex abstract analysis. The difficulty at all levels is how far to take an explanation without involving numerous other concepts, each of which requires explanation. The spiral technique enables topics to be briefly examined as and when necessary and reconsidered in greater depth when the appropriate moment arrives. It is possible that certain topics will be revisited several times throughout an A-level course. It is possible to use an inductive approach where students derive economic theories from their attempts to solve basic economic problems. The use of case studies or economic models in computer programs can be useful in this respect. Games and simulations can also bring out many important economic concepts but the teacher may find that presenting the theory first makes the simulation more useful as a revision technique. Many students can appreciate the importance of the profit motive in business behaviour but cannot see why profits should be maximized when resources are not used to full capacity. The link between cost and revenue is not always made clear in this analysis and the concept of optimum output is frequently misunderstood as being the most profitable output. The computer program 'Maxpro'[3] is quite helpful in this respect. Students may also better appreciate the difficulties faced by businessmen in seeking profitability by visits to local firms. Comparisons can also be made between small and large firms. Theories of credit creation and the relevance of the financial institutions to both government and consumer can also be made clearer by visits to banks, building societies and insurance companies.

The relevance of mathematics to economics

Many students (and their teachers) have been concerned about the increasing mathematical presentation of economics at university level. It is important, however, for schools and colleges to provide an opportunity to study statistical source material in order to extend their students' limited experience of macroeconomic variables. This may also enable certain mathematical or statistical skills to be developed. These have become increasingly necessary with the changing nature of the A-level examination, which contains data-response and numerically based objective questions. The case for the acquisition of mathematical and statistical skills has been strongly argued in *The Teaching of Economics in Schools*,[4] which states that 'for specialisation in economics at degree level an ability to understand and deploy certain mathematical and statistical techniques as well nigh essential'.

The less numerate student (and teacher) may well be put off by such trends, particularly if the student does not intend to pursue this subject beyond A-level, but certain basic skills are essential and well within the grasp of most sixth formers. Students should be able to use and interpret graphs, two-dimensional diagrams, statistical tables, bar charts and pie charts. In discussing inflation, for example, it is essential to understand the basis on which the index of retail prices is calculated and the importance of weighting this index. Questions requiring some calculation of such an index are frequently set at A-level. The concept of elasticity requires an understanding of proportion or even calculus. Many examination questions on supply and demand analysis involve simultaneous equations. The analysis of national income determination uses linear equations and a graphical presentation.

Many official publications that are relevant and readily accessible to the A-level student also contain information in statistical form – such as bar charts and histograms, graphs and various indices of prices, trade and employment trends. One such example is the *Treasury Economic Progress Report*, published monthly. Students of economics should be familiar with such devices in order to understand the factual background to the theories studied on the A-level syllabus. It should not be necessary, however, to undertake a full-scale explanation of the more complex mathematical concepts, which may well be beyond the capacity of the average student. An elementary survey of the mathematical devices used in the presentation of statistical material is all that is really necessary. Increasingly, however, students of A-level economics are also studying pure mathematics with statistics, or even economics with a double A-level mathematics component. These students should have no difficulty with the mathematical concepts involved in economics and some may even go on to study econometrics at university. It should be pointed out, however, that these students form a fairly small proportion of the total A-level entry. At the other extreme will be students who are barely numerate and who need a great deal of help in coping with the more mathematical objective questions and statistical data-response questions.

The use of computers in teaching economics at A-level

More detailed comments on the use of computers may be found elsewhere in this book but the following remarks relate specifically to the A-level syllabus. The increasing ownership and familiarity with computers has already had a great impact on the sixth-form curriculum. Computer studies itself has enjoyed a growth rate unprecedented in recent years, and given the rapid changes in technology that have lowered the cost of hardware, many more students have been able to gain access to computer keyboards. Some subjects lend themselves to explanation by means of computer programs and certainly economics is very suitable in this respect.

Much of the early software development was completed by the Schools Council Project Team in 1978,[5] but these early programs lacked visual impact in the form of graphic displays and tended to concentrate on macroeconomic simulations where students could assume the role of Chancellor of the Exchequer and attempt to control the economy by manipulating just two variables, taxation and government expenditure. Such simulations have proved to be extremely valuable in stimulating student interest and understanding of the problems faced by governments in managing the economy. There is still very little software in the area of microeconomics but this is perhaps understandable given the attraction of 'real-life' macroeconomic simulations and the difficulty of constructing meaningful programs in microeconomic theory. Phase II of the project has gone some way towards meeting this deficiency.

As more A-level students combine the study of economics with that of computer studies, more programs may be devised that can be relevant to the A-level syllabus. A number of useful programs have been produced by my own students as part of the practical work involved in

A-level computer studies. Concepts such as price elasticity of demand and supply and a simulation of the working of the Stock Exchange have worked well in programs that can be tailored by the teacher to the needs of a particular group of students. Programs can be designed to reduce tedious mathematical calculations to a minimum so that the consequences of a particular economic policy prescription can be seen in a matter of seconds. Balance of payments statistics or unemployment trends can be displayed more effectively and respond more quickly to changing policies introduced by the student running the program.

The widespread adoption of micro computers in schools and colleges has greatly increased the opportunities for computer aided learning (CAL) and computer aided teaching (CAT) in economics. Economic statistics need no longer remain a mystery to the less numerate student because calculations can be completed quickly and easily and data presented in a visual form so that basic principles can be more easily assimilated. At the more mundane level, programs can be devised to mark objective test questions and thus reduce this tedious burden for the teacher. With the production of more relevant software, many more teachers can use the computer as an additional teaching aid. Teaching with the help of a computer can assist economics understanding for both the less numerate and less literate student. The student may be guided in the comprehension of economic principles without the worry of complex calculations and the poor essay writer is helped to grasp essential concepts with a more visual approach. The problems of government decision-making in areas such as fiscal policy may be readily appreciated by the student using an appropriate program. Such skills are vitally important not only in essay-type examinations but also in comprehension tests increasingly used by the A-level boards. Teachers must help their students develop an understanding of economic statistics not only for the short-term purpose of passing examinations, but also to assist them in understanding economic decision-making in the society to which they belong.

The A-level syllabus

The syllabus taught at this level has changed quite considerably over the years. There are some minor differences between the examination boards in terms of content and style of examination papers, but the major topics and the kinds of skills expected of students are common to all boards. The major change in content has been away from what might be called 'descriptive economics', involving the detailed study of particular industries or financial institutions, towards a more analytical study of economic theory and economic policy-making. To some extent, content has been influenced by trends in university teaching that have been reflected in the examination questions set. There are now fewer essay-type questions in microeconomic theory and many more in macroeconomics. Questions dealing with economic decision-making at both national and international level are much more common, from policies to control inflation and unemployment to the problems of underdeveloped countries. Objective test and data-response questions are frequently based on official economic statistics of the balance of payments, unemployment, industrial disputes, national income and retail prices.

Examination boards also set out the skills that will be tested such as factual recall, analysis and evaluation, comprehension and application. In the setting of objective test questions, for example, these skills are clearly identified before such questions are pre-tested prior to use in the actual examination. In the past the boards did not specify these skills in their outline of the A-level syllabus in economics.

Methods of assessment have also changed over the years. The syllabus is no longer tested solely by means of essay questions in two three-hour papers, but increasingly the boards have devoted a large proportion of examination time to objective test and data-response questions which can more effectively test some of the skills outlined above. Although knowledge still accounts for the largest element of most syllabuses in economics, there has been a move towards the testing of higher skills, such as evaluation and application.

The syllabus produced by the examination board is usually fairly broad in coverage and will give no guidance on the most appropriate order to follow in the teacher's own scheme of work. The ultimate decision will be that of individual teachers in line with their own aims and objectives for the course. Some topics, for example, may be considered too difficult to be approached in the early weeks of an A-level course. The theory of income determination and economic growth may be considered too difficult for any but second-year students. It is often the approach rather than the topic that matters in the end and more teachers now introduce the more difficult topics – such as income determination, inflation and unemployment – much earlier in the course.

Aims and objectives of an A-level course

The following guidelines are set out not in any prescriptive sense but as a summary of my own views:

1   *A developmental approach.* The economics teacher will constantly be faced with the problem of having to put the cart before the horse in order to explain adequately a particular economic concept. Ideally, simple concepts will be introduced first in order to establish a firm foundation on which to build more complex structures. Student ques-

tions, however, often demand a cursory visit to more complex questions before basic concepts have really been established. Although there is the danger of excessive distraction from the central issues, a well-structured approach will enable a solid bedrock of understanding to be established without avoiding important issues until some indefinite future lesson. The spiral approach is useful here so that concepts already established or only briefly introduced may be revisited as necessary.

2 *Economic theory and economic reality.* Whenever possible, economic theories are explained in a realistic context. Students often find abstract economic analysis difficult and welcome the use of real-life illustrations or the case-study approach. Conversely, whenever descriptive topics are introduced, students can be reminded of the underlying economic theory so that the student does not automatically separate theory from practice.

3 *Using the students' own experience of economics.* It is important to identify the nature of the economic experiences of a particular age group so that appropriate references can be made to these when economic theory is explained. Younger students can readily appreciate the principles of opportunity cost when choosing how to spend their limited pocket-money. Older students may prefer to consider how to spend the earnings from part-time employment on clothing, entertainment or holidays. Some aspects of monetary theory and credit creation can also be linked to students' daily experiences. These can be reinforced by visits to local banks, building societies and insurance companies. Most regions of the country have local examples of specialization, economies of scale, structural unemployment and the problems of import penetration.

4 *Familiarization with economic data.* It is important to familiarize the student with economic statistics, the raw material for the economic theorist and the economic policy-maker. Economic statistics can be related to publications such as the *Monthly Digest of Statistics*,[6] *National Income Blue Book*[7] or the *Balance of Payments Pink Book*.[8] Where limited finance precludes the regular purchase of such official publications, many statistics can be obtained from bank reviews, *Treasury Economic Progress Reports* and the statistical summaries based on the *Bank of England Quarterly Bulletin*, all of which can be obtained free of charge. The Banking Information Service[9] is also a useful free source of economic developments in money and banking and international trade. Very few A-level textbooks integrate economic data with theoretical discussion but more recent publications have adopted this approach.[10] Many teachers have found the 'schools briefs' published by *The Economist* useful sources of quantitative data for the A-level student. Useful articles may also be found in the quality newspapers.

The content and order of an A-level course

The final decision on content and order must remain with the individual economics teacher. Many teachers have tended to cover microeconomics in the first year and left macroeconomics until the second year. Very often, however, student interest in the subject has been initiated by exposure to economic issues in the media. The topics with which students have become most familiar and curious about are those making the newspaper headlines and dominating news bulletins on radio and television. Problems such as unemployment, the rate of inflation, the balance of payments and government policy on taxation and the money supply are mentioned almost daily in the media. Such topics can be introduced at a much earlier stage and the more technical intricacies of microeconomic theory can be postponed until the latter part of the course.

The sequence of topic presentation in my own establishment is something of a compromise but students are given a taste of what economics is about as early as possible and fundamental problems are considered along with the methodology used by the economist. Lack of space precludes a detailed analysis of our scheme of work but the following outline should provide some guide as to order and depth of approach.

A course outline in A-level economics

1   *The economic resources.* The dependence of the subject on the fact of scarcity and the need for choice is emphasized. Some of the specialized vocabulary of economics is introduced and the circular flow of resources stressed. This can also be an opportunity to introduce national income concepts.

2   *An introduction to comparative economics.* The nature of the economic problem can now be considered in different economic systems. Some elements of economic development can be mentioned at this stage but the main objective is to answer student questions on how the UK compares with other economies and to stress that whereas political systems may differ, the basic economic problem remains the same. Source material for this section is fairly scarce but *An Introduction to Comparative Economics* by Marsden *et al.*[11] is useful.

3   *Economic methodology.* The techniques used by the economist may be considered in isolation and this can be helpful in defining the role of the economist; but in practice economic methodology is better explained as part of the analysis of a particular topic. Methodology may therefore appear several times during the course. For example, it may be involved in explaining the concept of elasticity and, more commonly, the theory of the firm. Part one of Professor R.G. Lipsey's *Introduction to Positive Economics*[12] is an invaluable aid in teaching

economic methodology. The sixth edition has a new introductory chapter including elementary linear algebra along with the verbal and diagrammatic exposition in order to improve the presentation of the models.

4 *Production.* The purpose of production is to satisfy consumer wants. The factors of production are examined in some detail so that some important economic concepts – such as the law of diminishing returns – may be explained. It is also possible to indicate some elementary theory of distribution.

5 *Specialization and division of labour.* This topic will have been briefly mentioned in section 1 but can now be explained in more detail linking back to the factor of production capital described in the previous section. Students may now more easily grasp the idea of internal and external economies of scale and some local examples can be used. Reasons for and types of industrial merger will now appear relevant to the student.

6 *Population.* This important topic may be taught as an entirely separate unit or be merged into section 4 as background to the factor of production labour. The topic is analysed in some depth including world population trends, factors affecting population growth, the Malthusian theory of population, the idea of optimum population and the main features of the UK population including age, sex and occupational distribution. The significance of population trends for the UK and the world will be stressed and current problems in developing countries explained.

7 *Location of industry.* This topic can stimulate student interest in their own locality as well as indicate regional problems in Europe and the world as a whole. The changing motives for industrial location over the years are explained and some analysis of government regional policy provided. There is now an early opportunity to examine the problem of regional unemployment and use some comparative regional statistics.

8 *Types of business units.* Not a very stimulating topic when taken in isolation, but with surveys of and visits to a variety of local businesses it is possible to cover most of the types from sole proprietor to public corporations.

9 *Company finance.* The main methods of raising business capital are explained and again local examples may be relevant as well as the share issues published in the national press. This topic also provides an opportunity to introduce stock market investment. Students may participate in local and national investment competitions as well as within the classroom. For a faster response to stock exchange investment, a locally produced computer program can simulate actual decisions using the daily share quotations in *The Financial Times*.

10 *The price mechanism.* An elementary explanation of the working of

the price mechanism will have been given in the analysis of different economic systems, but now it is possible to examine demand and supply functions and the concept of equilibrium price. Marginal utility theory is used to explain the shape of the demand curve, but indifference curve analysis and revealed preference theory are better left until later in the course. Price elasticity of demand and supply, income and cross-elasticity of demand can be made more palatable with real-life illustrations of pricing policies in both the public and private sectors. There will also be local examples within the students' experience.

11   *National income.* The national income flow diagram may now be reintroduced from section 1 and using this as a base, the complications involved in attempting to measure national income can be explained. It is useful to have some up-to-date income statistics available so that the steps involved in calculating by any of the three methods can be made clear. UK statistics can be obtained from the *National Income Blue Book* and some international comparisons appear from time to time in the *Treasury Economic Progress Reports*. The pitfalls involved in using national income statistics both domestically and internationally will be explained, and finally the students will make their own calculation of real national income per head for the UK using the most recent statistics available.

12   *The determination of national income equilibrium.* The complexities of this topic necessitate the spending of some considerable teaching time and the use of as many visual aids as possible. Again, the basic income flow diagram will be used and made more complex with overlays to cover the various injections and leakages. The Keynesian national income formula may then be established. Some time will also be spent carefully explaining the multiplier and accelerator principles and the diagrammatic presentation of the consumption function.

13   *Unemployment and inflation.* These topics are closely involved with the previous analysis and help place it in context. Some reference will be made to the economic conditions of the 1930s and some comparison made with the present day. Again the explanation of these topics is likely to be quite time-consuming in discussing the nature of unemployment and inflation, the likely causes of these problems and possible policy prescriptions. The changing perception of the Phillips curve analysis will also be examined. Students are introduced to the retail price index and calculate rates of inflation from recent statistics.

14   *Money and banking.* Again there is a clear link with the previous section. The nature and functions of money and the current measures of the money supply are explained. The quantity theory can be used as the basis for the later discussion of monetarism. Credit creation and the functions of the commercial banks and the Bank of England may be

more acceptable with visits and some comparisons can be made with other financial institutions.

15 *Monetary and fiscal policy*. Some aspects will have been introduced in section 13 but this is an opportunity to look at demand management policies in the postwar period and the rise of monetarism. The details of government expenditure, types of taxes and the changing importance of direct and indirect taxes are discussed. Current UK statistics will be used for illustration, including the PSBR and the national debt.

16 *The theory of international trade*. The theory of comparative advantage draws on the work done on opportunity cost in section 1 and specialization in section 5. Students find this topic quite difficult and need many examples to work through before understanding is achieved.

17 *The balance of payments*. The structure of the balance of payments account is explained and recent statistics used to illustrate visible and invisible trade, the current and capital accounts and official financing. Some indication is given of changes in product composition and area destination of UK visible trade in recent years. Explanation and calculation of recent terms of trade figures are provided and trading areas such as the EEC examined in some detail.

18 *International finance*. This topic covers fixed and floating exchange rates and their respective merits and demerits, the problem of international liquidity and the role of the IMF. The impact of devaluation/depreciation or revaluation/appreciation of the currency on the balance of payments and the economy in general can be considered in terms of elasticity. Some current international financial problems can be examined as part of a general north/south debate.

19 *The theory of the firm*. This topic brings together many elements of microeconomic analysis and serves as a useful illustration of economic methodology. The full range of possible models from perfect competition to pure monopoly will be examined. The analysis can be intellectually stimulating and students enjoy challenging the relevance of these models to the real world. The degree of monopoly in the UK economy and the government's attempts to control it are considered in some depth.

20 *The trade unions and employers' associations*. Trade unions can be introduced as an example of monopoly. The aims and functions of trade unions and employers' associations as well as their role in the economy are examined. After commenting on their structure, organization and membership, some indication of their influence can be given by reference to numbers of industrial disputes and their relationship with the government. Only a brief historical survey is provided but recent legislation will be covered in some detail. Students' attention will be drawn to union activities reported in the newspapers and local factory

visits can be very helpful. There is an interesting contrast in Leicester-shire between the non-unionized Pedigree Petfoods and the strongly unionized engineering establishments. A detailed look at their role in wage determination is left until the following section.

21   *The theory of distribution.* This topic is introduced with a link back to national income and its distribution between wages, interest, profit and rent. It is interesting to contrast this with wealth distribution and recent statistics may be found in *Social Trends*.[13] The theoretical analysis of the determination of each form of income makes use of supply and demand, perfect competition and elements of monopoly. Students become closely involved when discussing problems such as equal pay for women and the element of economic rent involved in payments to pop stars, film and television actors. The investigation of interest rate theory can be linked back to international capital movements in section 18.

22   *Economic growth.* The study of economic growth provides the opportunity to revise many topics covered earlier in the course. The growth prospects of the UK and the factors affecting growth are examined. A brief survey of growth theories is provided, including their possible application to various economies – particularly the less-developed economies. Students are encouraged to consider other possible economic strategies than pursuing a faster rate of growth. As a useful revision exercise, students are able to simulate government decision-making in Cabinet groups. Each group member is required to consider the importance of their own area of responsibility for achieving faster growth. Alternatively, students may use a computer simulation such as 'Fiscal'[14] where the impact of changes in government expenditure and taxation on economic growth may be examined. The simulation is given greater realism by the effect of policy changes on the government's prospects of re-election which are reflected in an opinion poll.

The final stage of the course will tie together various loose ends. Items omitted earlier for reasons of clarity can now be more effectively explained. Ideas such as indifference curve analysis and revealed preference theory can now be used as alternative explanations for the shape of a demand curve. If time permits, price and income consumption curves may be derived from indifference curve analysis.

Teaching method

The brief outline above is based on the sequence followed at Gateway VI Form College. The content and order used in other institutions will largely be determined by their respective staff. Other factors will be the skills, knowledge and qualifications of the teacher as well as the size and composition of individual teaching groups. Small-group work is often desirable and in larger institutions with more than one economics teacher, some specialization may be possible. Staff may be happy to concentrate on teaching topics in which they have a particular interest. This might be difficult where teaching groups are large, not only because of timetabling problems but more importantly because of the reduced student contact time with a particular group. One solution can be lecture-type lessons, perhaps to a year group with tutorial sessions for smaller group sizes. Again, student subject choice and timetabling problems may prevent this approach.

There is still considerable room for experiment in teaching method to small and large groups so that both the more-able and less-able students can benefit from a sixth-form course in economics. Every opportunity should be seized to use new techniques and reduce the dependence on traditional 'chalk and talk'. Many suggestions for the use of audio-visual aids, computer programs, games and simulations and field trips may be found elsewhere in this book.

Notes and references

1. Schools Council Working Paper no. 45, *16–19: Growth and Response* (Evans/Methuen, 1972),
2. Ibid., p. 20.
3. Schools Council Computers in the Curriculum Project: Economics Topic 4, *The Theory of the Firm* (Longman, 1983).
4. Joint Committee of the Royal Economic Society, the Association of University Teachers of Economics and the Economics Association, *The Teaching of Economics in Schools* (Macmillan, 1973).
5. Schools Council Computers in the Curriculum Project, *Economics* (Edward Arnold, 1978).
6. *Monthly Digest of Statistics* (HMSO).
7. *National Income and Expenditure* (HMSO, annually).
8. *United Kingdom Balance of Payments* (HMSO, annually).
9. Banking Information Service (BIS), 10 Lombard Street, London EC3V 9AT.
10. Livesey, F., *A Textbook of Economics*, 2nd edn (Polytech, 1982).
11. Marsden, C., Adams, S., and Crewdson, J., *An Introduction to Comparative Economics* (Heinemann Educational Books, 1980).
12. Lipsey, R.G., *An Introduction to Positive Economics*, 6th edn (Weidenfeld & Nicolson, 1983).
13. *Social Trends* (HMSO, annually).
14. Schools Council Computers in the Curriculum Project, *Economics: Topic 6 Fiscal Policy* (Longman, 1983).

8 Economics in Further Education
Barrie King

Further education is, by virtue of its complex and diverse provision, closely associated with industry, commerce and the public sector. Its membership is, as a result, arguably more aware than those in other sectors of the education service of the importance of vocational relevance for its curriculum. The growth and development of economics within that curriculum has not unnaturally therefore been influenced by both internally and externally held views of what, in fact, constitutes an appropriate vocational relevance.

Throughout the 1950s and 1960s economics flourished in the further-education environment. Students of the subject were thought to acquire not only basic institutional and quantitative aspects of economic reality, but also to develop a rational and economic way of thinking about a problem. It was seen as a vocationally useful subject and found its way into a vast array of courses, often assuming a major role within them. Economics was to act as an educational linchpin in such courses as the Ordinary National Certificate in business studies, drawing together component functional specialisms.

In more recent years, however, the value of abstraction and theory in economics in courses designed to aid the development of the young employee has been called into question. Criticisms of the traditional approach have been articulated in demands for a greater practical business orientation and reflect a belief that a study of economics should have as a general aim the engendering of an understanding of the environment and operations of business, and not be an end in itself.[1]

Some economics educators have responded to this challenge with accusations of basic ignorance or misunderstanding on the part of the critics. They claim that such views expose a lack of understanding of the nature and purposes of an economics education, which may suggest a confusion between the subject and the way it is sometimes taught and examined. Such protestations have, however, had little, if any, influence on the curriculum planners. Pressures have certainly been brought to bear on the nature of the economics provision within the further-education sector in the quest for vocational relevance, and this has led to a reappraisal of both course content and the teaching strategies to be deployed in its promotion. The outcome of these developments is difficult to quantify, but that the role of economics within the overall provision has changed is beyond question.

Recent developments make it imperative that we attempt to assess the value of economics within the curriculum. Fersh[2] adopts a direct approach with his contention that 'there has been a need for economics understanding throughout all of history because man has always faced the economic problem'. He continues: 'clearly individuals, firms and governments are involved in this economic environment and it is therefore appropriate that the vocationally orientated provision of courses in business studies should incorporate a promotion of economic understanding among participating students'. Mace[3] develops the point further with his assertion that 'to argue that economics is not related to business is to ignore the fundamental concepts around which business and economics revolve'.

The claims made for an economics education do not however rest entirely on the basic concepts of scarcity, choice and opportunity cost; indeed, certain skills may be acquired in addition. Economics may be regarded as aiding the development of language in certain specific ways, thereby assisting in the important acquisition of the basic tool of communication. The subject has its own terms that are increasingly playing a part in the citizens' and employees' everyday vocabulary and the required precision in the use of language is very important, especially in business. Economics may also be seen to aid the development of appropriate numeracy skills in so far as it conveys an ability to construct and use simple graphs in addition to the development of elementary statistical techniques.

Furthermore, we may remind ourselves of the traditional postwar viewpoint by recalling Robbins's apparent belief that a study of economics may assist in the development of desirable skills for individuals in a complex society.[4] Dunning has claimed that a person who possesses the information embodied in economic concepts is capable of conceptual thinking in the economic domain and that to teach a person economics is therefore to equip him with a skill that has obvious implications for vocational education.[5]

Economics may then be seen as an instrument of intellectual training involving the development of occupationally desirable capacities of logical thought, discussion, communication, and numeracy. If it does no more than provide a realization that organizations cannot be truly independent in that they rely on a complex web of relations and that market forces are not the only criteria on which to decide issues of resource allocation and relative efficiency, however, then it must aid the personal development of the young employee and must as a result be vocationally useful.

A pertinent question on the topic of the significance of an economics education and one that has been raised by a number of commentators including Whitehead,[6] is, are the skills of evaluation and logical thought generated by a study of economics unique to economics students or may they be developed by alternative means? As Whitehead points out, such competences may of course be taught and learned in many curricula contexts and not just economics. However, as he also observes, this in no way dilutes the validity of a study of economics and the subject has the added advantage of allowing the development of such skills via content which is of great relevance to an understanding of both the business environment and business operations.

It is, however, important to design the syllabus with care and with particular relevance to the aims and objectives of the course as a whole. This may indeed have been a serious weakness in the past. If a study of economics is to result in the development of the skills and abilities previously outlined, it is desirable to develop the understanding of a basic structure, however limited, in order that the subject is not presented in a descriptive, superficial way that is likely to encourage an emphasis on memory and provide an inadequate basis for further study. Economics is capable, when presented in a thoughtful and professional manner, of making a valuable contribution to the curriculum of a vocational course, and if as a result economics educators are encouraged to evaluate the contribution of their subject to the curriculum then this must be of benefit.

None the less, there is little room for complacency in so far as the critics of the traditional role of economics in vocational education now appear to occupy a very important and influential role in respect of the curriculum development processes of a number of validating bodies. Economics as a separate subject has, for example, disappeared from certain courses certificated by the Business and Technician Education Council (BTEC), the Association of Accounting Technicians and the Rating and Valuation Association. In each case the move has been towards the introduction of an integrated module entitled the 'organization in its environment', involving the disciplines of economics, government and law.

A basic core of economics

Regardless of the circumstances of the economics provision within further education colleges, it behoves an economics lecturer to consider what constitutes the basic structure or core of economics in regard to the aims of those courses on which he is to teach.

Exactly what concepts should constitute that core is of course the important question to be answered, but in so far as economics appears in different guises within the wide range of courses there can be no easy or glib response given. It is possible, however, to identify a basic structure of economics understanding and knowledge that may enable the young employee to bring an economics perspective to bear on any problem-solving or decision-taking task with which he is confronted in the working environment.

Gowland[7] has appropriately identified economics as the analysis of choice. In his analysis economics is seen to provide the tools with which to analyse those situations that necessitate choice and thereby to bring about this perspective. The basic concepts to be identified are simply scarce resources/unlimited wants which lead to the need for choice at the margin resulting in opportunity cost and efficiency in minimizing that opportunity cost. The learning of these basic concepts is regarded as a prerequisite to the successful acquisition of basic economic principles and problem-solving skills.

An ability to identify the particular variables involved in a problem and to make predictions as regards the relationship between those variables in situations that result from decision-taking, is seen as the end product of a study of economics. This does, of course, require that the student be introduced to the techniques and methods that economists use to analyse the variables influencing any choice situation. It is relevant to note, given that every individual situation in reality differs from the next, that model building and theories may in this context be seen as having much to offer despite the persistent modern criticism of 'lack of relevance'.

The matter of relevance in economics education is, as one would expect, one of great importance and is examined in the debate concerning the validity of the positive/normative dichotomy. If the goal of economics is prediction and explanation then the achievement of determined outcomes via orthodox positive economics is of value. The inevitable loss of realism has led to belief that the subject is naïve, in error and has little to offer.[8] A less extreme view is held by Blaug[9] who, in claiming that the traditional distinction between positive and normative economics is acceptable, observes that it is the scientific method of economists that has been sadly lacking. According to Blaug, this weakness has resulted in an overemphasis on both unrealistic and relatively unimportant areas within economics such as growth theory and marginal productivity theory.

The expansion of the basic core or structure should then depend upon the individual course aims and objectives and pay regard to the time available and prior knowledge of the student intake. 'To do the job well', as Dunning[10] once reminded us, 'takes time' and if learning the nature of the relationships between economic concepts is thought to be appropriate in a course of study then time should be found. Many courses in further education are based on a part-time day or evening mode of attendance and, as a result, time is much restricted. Also, external constraints and practical difficulties may seriously limit the time available. It is surely preferable that a restricted number of concepts be added to our basic structure in a meaningful and efficient manner rather than the simple generation of a superficial knowledge – albeit of a wider array of concepts – the attendant danger of which is the development of a body of generalizations that have only technical significance – what has been referred to as 'to masquerade as economics'.[11]

Recent developments

Two important developments in recent years, within the further-education environment, have been the introduction of an objectives-based approach, such as that illustrated by the economics syllabuses of the Royal Society of Arts, and the apparently growing popularity among validating bodies for the previously mentioned integrated modular approach. There are courses, such as the BTEC National Certificate in Business Studies, which are both integrated and objectives-based and seek ultimately to be genuinely interdisciplinary, as opposed to the traditional multidisciplinary design.

Deciding upon desirable objectives for economics education is another complex and difficult task and understandably is open to much debate and disagreement.[12] There are many criticisms that may be levelled at the principles of an objectives-based approach in economics. The BTEC National Level courses, for example, are often accused of an overemphasis on description and low-level cognitive skill development with a resultant inadequate emphasis on economic concepts. Difficulties are thought to exist in respect of the interpretation and achievement of the vast number of learning objectives so painstakingly outlined in the guide syllabus of the organization in its environment module.

Irrespective of these and other perceived difficulties, objectives are playing an important part in the economics education provision in further education. What is more, their use may be credited with forcing a consideration of the balance of an economics course, or element, and the weight to put on various activities within it. Objectives may also be seen to offer a yardstick against which an examiner/assessor can measure the effect of teaching in order to evaluate attainment and to see how a student has changed as a result of his exposure to economics.

On the issue of integration, it has been a long-standing and often voiced complaint that many subjects, including economics, seek to cocoon themselves in an artificial isolation away from other, often related, disciplines.[13] It is not altogether surprising that this should be the case given the existence of an element of professional rivalry and the potential for inextricable confusion of the curriculum given a zeal for excessive integration. Critics of the integrated approach may find the

Australian term 'fused' a more apt description. Subject-based teaching is after all much 'neater' than that involving an integrated or inter-disciplinary approach.

BTEC's view on the matter, however, is that few problems or decisions to which an employee may be required to attend are uni-disciplinary in nature and that the traditional watertight compart-mentalized approach to relevant subject matter acts as a barrier to informed judgement.

The implementation of an integrated approach does inevitably have implications for the economics teacher. The effect may differ between colleges and between departments within a college. Lecturers may be required to cope with an entire module for a particular group of students and must therefore acquire teaching skills in associated disciplines, for example in law and government, if they do not possess them already. Alternatively, some college departments remain loyal to the notion of individual specialisms, in which case economics lecturers will contribute directly to only a part of the module and will therefore be required to work closely with other lecturers in a course or module team.

Both possibilities may present practical difficulties that should not be underestimated. In respect of the latter scenario, it should be noted that even the most conscientious and aware members of a course team may focus their efforts and limited time on syllabus planning and not on developing appropriate and successful teaching strategies. An account of the experience of lecturers in New College Durham, and their attempt to implement an integrated approach to the teaching of the organization in its environment module at the BTEC National Level, is worthy of attention.[14]

The successful implementation of such a module by a team of lecturers will inevitably involve both the preparation of integrated programmes and collaborative thinking. The minimum expectation of those involved would be that they come to understand at least the scope of disciplines other than their own and acquire, as a result, a feel for integrative possibilities. These developments require the sacrifice of much independence. Within the course or module team decisions must be taken explicitly. Co-operative planning is essential and lecturers must have a specified role at any one time. They must also do what colleagues expect, otherwise chaos ensues. Perhaps one should also raise the possibility of conflict arising out of issues concerning role allocation or differing educational attitudes and goals – a not un-common feature of life in a college of further education. This could be a potentially difficult situation for a newly appointed economics lecturer.

Teaching strategies

In considering the teaching strategies that may be adopted in the promotion of economics education, one could no doubt cover a whole range of possibilities. Economics lecturers are of course aware of the opportunities available to them, ranging from formal exposition to role-play simulations. It is likely to be the case, however, that for the majority of lecturers traditional pedagogy will be the order of the day, involving a combination of didactic and diagnostic approaches.

Although it is highly desirable that economics lecturers adopt a well-balanced mix of approaches, further education does appear to encourage and promote this traditional strategy. The very term 'lecturer' may indeed be indicative of it. Lecturers are timetabled on the basis of class contact hours, and a department's finances, not to mention the number and grades of posts, may be influenced by the record of actual student hours. In consequence, lecturers are usually allocated to a particular class, in a given room, issued with a register and expected to perform. If the situation is typical, in that the student group is large in number, and the lecturer will see them for a limited time each week, then anything other than a traditional approach may be considered a luxury and out of reach.

An emphasis on a didactic approach may, as a result, be a tempting prospect given the circumstances a lecturer finds himself in. He may, by controlling the environment to a significant degree, be able to regulate the pace of learning and provide a quick way of presenting students with a structure to which new principles may be added.

Many students in colleges of further education may be classified as adult and their attitudes are not only important but are often freely articulated. The less able of them or those who feel under the greatest pressure will often demand the 'security' of a traditional approach from which they are able to secure a 'prop' of notes which, if committed to memory, will, hopefully, see them successfully through an examination. Clearly, such circumstances are not necessarily conducive to the development of a worthwhile understanding and knowledge of economic concepts.

A traditional approach may indeed be little more than information processing and may leave the student with only one meaningful decision to make, namely, whether to participate in the learning experience or not. Student motivation, even with an adult group, may not always be sufficiently positive to avoid problems in this area. Mature students may actually respond in a negative manner, thus denying any hope of an advancement in their understanding. The situation may be alleviated and genuinely improved by the inclusion of a significant diagnostic element in which the lecturer creates an encounter with the students consisting of a sequence of questions. The purpose of questioning may therefore be seen as a method of reducing the problems of motivation as well as means of probing and restructuring student knowledge.

Those economics lecturers who hold strong views on the value of a more clearly defined and more substantial basic structure of economics than that outlined earlier, may suggest that a clearly defined sequence is also a priority. In such a context the traditional pedagogy may both allow and support such a view. It may well be a satisfying exercise for a subject specialist to sit down and map out the order of presentation of the various elements of the syllabus from the standpoint of a clear logical sequence. The results of such a labour may have to be modified only to take into account the age or maturity of the students, their mode of attendance and any personal characteristics that they may bring to the course.

Any attempt to deny the sequencing of content and the lecturer's carefully arranged materials may be seen as certain to result in a patchy and superficial knowledge of economics. Objections would certainly be expected if they are faced with the introduction of a more random approach to economics teaching that denies this sequence and therefore the presentation of materials in a particular order. To such objectors it may appear that the attainment of the projected benefits of studying economics must depend upon the subject being taught '*en passant*' while working out a series of problems, thus tempting providence by way of leaving gaps in the students' knowledge. Certain branches or aspects of economics might never be introduced to the student at all.

The interdisciplinary, thematic style of BTEC courses in business education does, of course, pose a challenge to traditional thinking in respect of economics education. It is quite possible, however, that the sequencing of content in an integrated approach could in itself be extremely limiting, but as such courses are intended to be based on a problem-solving strategy it may not in practice be quite the same thing.

The acquisition of problem-solving skills may well accommodate Gowland's previously noted views on the nature of an economics education. Choice and decision-taking are, after all, essential features of such activities. Problem-solving techniques involve the identification and analysis of the problem, the devising of a number of possible solutions, the evaluation of those solutions and the selection or recommendation of what is seen as the most appropriate solution. Part-time students may additionally gain the benefit of analysis based upon their own experience and workplace.

In specifying a sequence in which all students should learn, the lecturer is, in any case, forced to overlook the possibility that there may be alternative routes to the attainment of a particular objective, especially when the skills of analysis and synthesis are required. The structured approach may be seen to limit the possibility of discovery and the satisfaction that may accompany it.

There are, indeed, practising economics lecturers in further-education establishments who are not fully convinced by the need for a detailed structure and well-regulated sequence. These lecturers believe that the logical arrangement and systematic view of economics is something that should be aimed for rather than started with. The logical conception of the subject as a whole may in fact be unsuited to many of their students' minds until sufficient material has been acquired.

If there is such a divide of opinion, surely the lecturer's well-ordered 'tidy mind' approach must give way to the interests and needs of the students, however disjointed and messy the practice may be. Gaps in a student's education and economic knowledge may, after all, be filled at a later stage, if indeed they are found to be important enough to need filling. They may also be filled more readily and easily given the successful acquisition of a limited basic structure in the first instance.

Even allowing for the previously expressed misgivings and apprehension about the implementation of BTEC courses, their introduction may be considered to have afforded encouragement and an opportunity for experiment with alternative teaching strategies and approaches in economics. The development of these alternative strategies has not, as was hoped, however, resulted from the system of BTEC moderation. This was launched with a remit that included the motivation and encouragement of course teams and individuals in the development of new teaching approaches. None the less, the system as a whole is flexible, although it is not always perceived as such, and the enthusiastic and innovative lecturer is able to influence the actual practice if not the principle of the BTEC experience. Perhaps the greatest benefit of the introduction of these courses is that they have encouraged a break with traditional administrative and pedagogic practices and have forced a consideration of activity-centred learning.

One important question that should be continually put in respect of these and other courses is: 'Does the course material have sufficient relevance to the observed needs of the students?' The desire for relevance has led to a vast growth in the use of case studies and simulations that are thought to be effective in respect of development, analysis and problem-solving skills. Simulations may also be considered appropriate in terms of attitude and value formation – a long-neglected area of the subject given our traditional emphasis on positive economics – and in the development of social skills. The experience to be gained by participating in these less formal teaching strategies may well be of significant benefit to an economics lecturer planning his approach to the whole of his teaching.

A variety of approaches is probably essential in a consistently successful learning environment, if such a thing is possible. This mix may be thought to be desirable not only as a means of creating and maintaining interest in economics but also in the development of an appropriate operating framework for the student in his employment. In recent years there has been witnessed, in addition, an increasing attention paid to experiential learning, that is learning acquired from work and other experiences. The participation of a student from a working environment, be it as part of a work placement scheme or a full-time job, is not new to the teacher of economics but it is a challenging prospect that could possibly be further developed. One technique employed in some colleges is the development of business simulations via hypothetical firms or organizations. These firms may be used to form the integrating link between the separate disciplines involved in a single module or in the course as a whole. Business games – which may also be thought appropriate in this context – and, simulated organizations may be implemented with the aid of the colleges computing facilities.

It is important that whatever teaching strategies are used by economics lecturers, the emphasis should be on learning and not on teaching. There may in practice, however, be a very restricted range of choices open to the lecturer. Those already employed in colleges of further education will need no telling about underprovision which, when manifested in the form of a lack of suitable accommodation, visual aids, reprographic facilities and the like, may mitigate against the efforts of even the most determined supporter of a student-centred approach.

Assessment and evaluation

Changes in the further-education curriculum in respect of the aims and objectives, content and method of an economics education have generated a movement within colleges to revise traditional thinking about methods of evaluation. Examinations are now seen in many courses, particularly BTECs, as forming only a part of an assessment programme. As it is the programme as a whole that is required to be both balanced and integrated, it is not necessary to examine on the total economics specification or even to seek a balanced examination coverage of the subject-matter.

Assessment in the BTEC courses involving economics instruction comprises a combination of individual module assignments and cross-modular assignments in which it is hoped that the interdisciplinary approach will be given practical significance. There are no precise rules but clearly the economics content and its assessment must be related to the course aims. The BTEC view is that assessment should seek to measure the student performance of the activities in a task. It is based on a belief that learning occurs by doing, that doing requires in-course, task-oriented assignments, and that each task is comprised of a number of activities.

Economics understanding, where appropriate, is as a result likely to be assessed by means of student attainment in the writing of a report or memorandum or in the performance of some role-play exercise and not in the traditional essay-writing medium. The task is required to be vocationally relevant and should seek to test the skills of argument, evaluation, analysis and problem-solving.

This approach does generate, as a logical consequence, a need to develop an explicit approach to assessment in order to ensure an adequate coverage of the objectives and an appropriate emphasis on each relevant type and level of knowledge, understanding and skill required of the students. Additionally, it should identify the overall type of performance and achievement appropriate to each graded level of attainment recognized. It must specify minimum performance on any objectives that are crucial in securing a satisfactory, or pass, standard. Assessment criteria should be clearly specified and may differ for different student groups given alternative modes of attendance. They should be closely related to the assignment function and objective, be adequately explained to the student and applied in a manner that is consistent both internally and with the course requirements. An adequate explanation of the assessment procedure to the student may encourage economics lecturers to be more precise in their own understanding and interpretation of the subject, and just what it is that their teaching is intended to achieve.

These developments clearly indicate a move towards a criterion-referenced system of assessment. There exists in further education a departure, at least in part, from the emphasis on relative performance embodied in normed-referenced assessments in favour of an evaluation of student attainment relative to an established criterion of performance. Any attempt to implement a criterion-referenced assessment of economics understanding must, however, rely on the ability of an economics lecturer to identify clearly the appropriate behavioural objectives involved. It is therefore important, initially, to establish just what 'to know economics' actually is and then to specify the abilities or skills required in its application in behavioural terms. Beyond this, the lecturer must determine the minimum criteria that must be achieved for each assessment grade.[15] The use of criterion-referenced techniques may then assist in indicating the level of a student's mastery of given objectives and the success of a particular piece of instruction. It may identify specific problems requiring remedial action and may indicate the speed at which an individual might progress through a series of objectives, particularly if they are organized hierarchically.

Changes in administrative practices, including timetabling and the development of distant learning, when accompanied by a greater attention to criterion-referenced assessment techniques, may allow and encourage economics lecturers to cater for and provide individualized instruction more readily than is now possible. It is, in fact, likely that alternative part-time study routes involving flexible patterns of attendance will become an increasing part of the further-education provision of the future.

In a more cautionary vein, however, it might be appropriate to again consider the question of the validity of the behavioural objectives approach. A host of additional issues are raised including: What is mastery? Is there a hierarchy within economics? And are criterion-referenced tests reliable? None of these concerns should be disregarded without careful consideration of the issues involved. Satterly[16] has much to say on the matter and his work, albeit directed towards a school-based curriculum, provides an important contribution to the debate.

A significant development in further education, as elsewhere, has been the introduction of the student profile. Its use is seen by the Further Education Curriculum Review and Development Unit (FEU)[17] as a response to the perceived weaknesses of existing forms of assessment and although they are as yet, by and large, restricted to a variety of vocational and pre-vocational preparation courses, it is possible that they will become a more common feature of further-education provision in the future. The recruitment of Manpower Service Commission-sponsored youth training scheme students into established courses that incorporate an economics component is likely to be followed by the introduction of some form of student profile in order to satisfy the requirements of the sponsoring agents.

Student profiles often mean different things to different people. The FEU approach is complex in that it involves the use of profiles both as a formative process before certification and as a summative process as a means of certification. BTEC anticipate that colleges will aim at using assessment procedures for course work that will build up a profile of each student's performance. They ask simply that such profiles do not depend exclusively on the summation of grades by some mechanical and predetermined formula.

The introduction of profiling into economics education may provide an opportunity to broaden the scope of the testing of economic understanding. Economics lecturers may be able to devote more attention to normative economics and the question of values within the subject. In addition to providing a means of generating new curricula ideas, the use of profiles may also generate advantages such as greater teacher/student interaction with an enforced feedback to learners, offer an opportunity for assessment to become an integral part of the learning process and provide an option to modify the learning programme as it occurs.

Huge practical difficulties do, of course, exist regarding their implementation. Individual consultation with large numbers of students is very time-consuming and any full-scale implementation can only be initiated at the expense of teaching time, a fact that may make their introduction a daunting prospect to both lecturers and administrators alike.

A little developed, although potentially useful, aspect of the move towards profiling is the emergence of the exit profile. Here the certificating bodies prepare profiles of what has been attained by students, not individually but collectively in achieving a particular grade or qualification. These profiles identify the general educational competences and specific knowledge skills attested to by a qualification. They would appear to be useful in clarifying suitability for admission to subsequent courses and in promoting a guide to the development of appropriate conversion and bridging courses. Both the Associated Examining Board and the City and Guilds London Institute have experience in this type of profile.[18]

Assessment is, however, only one part of the evaluation process, albeit an important one. Evaluation is a feedback mechanism or 'loop' as it is referred to in the 'Economics in society' materials of Suzanne Helburn and others,[19] allowing for the revision of any, or all of, the stages of curriculum development. Some of the validating bodies for courses with an economics component involve themselves, usually through participating colleges, in a process of course evaluation. The BTEC system of annual reviews is, by now, a well-known example of this practice. Individual lecturers are afforded the opportunity of commenting upon the course and its operation. College departments need not, however, await the prompting of an external agency to involve themselves in the evaluation process in which economics lecturers have an important contribution to make.

Individual lecturers may independently, or in association with other members of a course or module team, involve themselves in evaluation. The assessment and return of students' course work, in its various forms, does of course provide feedback to the student and this practice is in itself of great importance in guiding the student and possibly in influencing motivation. A careful analysis of the marks or grades awarded to student work may, however, provide the lecturer with an important insight into the effectiveness of particular teaching strategies or into the realism of certain course objectives. Relevant information may also be elicited from the use of carefully constructed student questionnaires and interviews.[20]

Although the practical importance of a realistic evaluation of objectives, content and method appears to be obvious in any curricula setting, it would seem to be even more so given recent developments in economics education. The integration of economics with other disciplines in a common module in certain courses and the emphasis on the use of alternative teaching strategies has led to experiment and in some cases uncertainty. This is a situation that must inevitably necessitate continual evaluation of all aspects of the curriculum.

Conclusion

The intention of this chapter has been to outline some of the major developments in further education and to consider their relevance to economics education. Such a task is difficult to complete adequately in a single chapter and it is inevitable that little more than a superficial treatment of a range of issues has been possible – certainly more questions have been put than answered. However, given that changes are taking place, the knowledge that economics lecturers are responding in a thoughtful and positive way does indicate a not too unhealthy environment.

The nature of the economics provision will, in the foreseeable future, no doubt be heavily biased in respect of vocational relevance. That it will also remain easily recognizable as economics is not so certain. An active involvement on the part of economics lecturers in the process of curriculum development within the further-education sector, particularly in the evaluation of the economics provision on offer, is therefore essential.

Notes and references

1. Froggatt, D., 'Survey on the suitability of the ONC economics syllabus', *Political and Economic Planning Paper*, 1973, p. 27.
2. Fersh, G.L., 'The need for economics understanding' in *Economics and the Business Curriculum* (Joint Council for Economics Education, 1972) p. 7.
3. Mace, G.R., 'The role of economics in the BEC National Curriculum', *Journal of Further and Higher Education*, vol. 4, no. 3, autumn 1980, p. 63.
4. Robbins, L., *An Essay on the Nature and Significance of Economic Science*, 2nd edn (Macmillan, 1949).
5. Dunning, K., 'To know economics', *Economics*, vol. 9, pt 4, no. 41, summer 1972, p. 230.
6. Whitehead, D.J., 'Should economics be taught to all secondary pupils', in Robinson, T.K., and Wilson, R., *Extending Economics Within The Curriculum* (Routledge & Kegan Paul, 1977) pp. 45–67.
7. Gowland, D.H., *Modern Economic Analysis* (Butterworth, 1979) p. vi.
8. Ward, B., *What's Wrong With Economics* (Macmillan, 1972).
9. Blaug, M., *The Methodology of Economics* (Cambridge University Press, 1980).
10. Dunning, op. cit., p. 229.

11. Robbins, L.C., *The Nature and Significance of Economic Science* (Macmillan, 1935) footnote, p. 42.
12. See Drake, K., and Ryba, R., 'Educational objectives in economics education', in Lee, N. (ed.), *Teaching Economics*, 2nd edn (Heinemann Educational Books, 1975) pp. 61–73.
13. Pring, R., 'Curriculum integration', in Hooper, R. (ed.), *The Curriculum: Context, Design and Development* (Heinemann Educational Books, 1977) pp. 226–7.
14. Bodingfield, J., Callaghan, P.M., Ellison, T., and Todd, I.A., 'An integrated and student centred approach to the teaching of the organisation in the environment at BEC National Level: one college's experience', *Business Education*, spring 1982, pp. 16–28.
15. See MacIver, L., 'Theory of objectives applied to the teaching of economics', and Ryba, R., and Drake, K., 'Towards a taxonomy of educational objectives', in Whitehead, D.J. (ed.), *Curriculum Development in Economics* (Heinemann Educational Books, 1974).
16. Satterly, D., *Assessment in Schools* (Basil Blackwell, 1981).
17. FEU, *Profiles*, September 1982.
18. See 'Profile and profile reporting', *Coombe Lodge Report*, vol. 14, no. 13, The FE Staff College, 1982.
19. Helburn, S., Sperling, J., Evans, R., and Davis, J., *Economics in Society: Strategy and Methods* (Addison-Wesley, 1974).
20. Wilhelm, F.T., 'Evaluation as feedback', in Hooper (ed.), op. cit., pp. 320–35.

Part Three
Economics Across the Curriculum

Curriculum Integration and
Disciplines in the Social Sciences – A
Case Study
T.K. Robinson

Introduction

The issue of integration within the social science area of the curriculum
has already been explored in earlier editions of *Teaching Economics*. In
their chapter on 'Economics education and educational theory', which
appeared in both previous editions, Lee and Entwistle posed some
fundamental questions about the relationship between economics and
other social sciences, especially from the standpoint of how far the
assumptions drawn from disciplines such as psychology, ethics and
sociology should be 'taken as given' or examined carefully by the
economist and the teacher and made quite explicit to the learner. In this
context, they considered an approach to a study of society through an
integrated course of social studies which would focus on issues such as
housing, crime, poverty and transport, rather than through separate
courses in the individual disciplines.[1]

The second edition also contained a chapter by Lawton entitled
'Economics in relation to other subjects within the curriculum', in
which he argued that a curriculum has to be seen as a selection from the
culture of society and that the case for the inclusion of economics and
other social sciences in a common curriculum for pupils in primary and
secondary schools should be based upon the 'situations' pupils are
likely to find themselves in when they leave school. Since so many of the
activities of adults have social, political and economic dimensions, he
believed that the social sciences score very highly on a list of priorities
derived from a situational analysis. Lawton therefore proposed a social-
science programme for pupils in the 8–13 age range which would
investigate a variety of human groups through projects, beginning with
those groups in which the pupils are participant members (e.g. family,
school), or can easily observe though not having membership (e.g. local
firms), and moving on to groups that are separate from pupils in time
and space, or may be created in their imagination and simulated in the
classroom. This would lead into a consideration of certain basic ideas
about the nature of society such as evolution, civilization and community. Throughout this period there would be no attempt to

introduce separate disciplines but in the third year of the secondary
school there would be six half-term modules in history, geography,
sociology, anthropology, politics and economics, and, in the fourth and
fifth years, the final stage of the common curriculum would be a multidisciplinary approach overlapping with the single-discipline stage, each
discipline enriching the others by interaction.[2]

As a contrast to the approach adopted in the earlier editions of
Teaching Economics, the long-standing and often vexed issue of disciplines and integration within the social-science area of the curriculum
will be considered in this edition from a different perspective – namely,
how a policy has been evolved within one education system and how
that policy is being gradually translated into practice at different stages
of the secondary school. The experience to be drawn on is that in
Scotland in the past decade.

Some features of the Scottish secondary school curriculum

Public-sector education in Scotland is a partnership between central
and local government. The Secretary of State for Scotland is responsible to Parliament for the overall supervision and development of the
education service through the Scottish Education Department (SED).
The provision of education is one of the duties of the nine regional
councils and three islands councils, which are known as education
authorities. Responsibility for the content and management of the
school curriculum rests with education authorities and head teachers,
but the Consultative Committee on the Curriculum (CCC), first established in 1965, is the main advisory body on the curriculum to the
Secretary of State. The CCC is responsible for a number of curriculum
committees and for the Scottish Curriculum Development Service
Centres, which promote development in particular subjects and areas
of education. Together with HM Inspectors of Schools, the CCC is the
main source of the curricular guidance issued by the Secretary of State
to education authorities. CCC members are appointed by the Secretary
of State in their personal capacity; the majority are educationists from a
wide variety of backgrounds, including universities, colleges, schools
and education authorities, and a small number represent parents,
industry and commerce.

Pupils transfer from primary to secondary education at the age of 12
and a large proportion attend education authority secondary schools
with a comprehensive intake. There are 444 secondary schools maintained by education authorities, and fifty-three independent schools.
The first two years of secondary schooling (S1/S2) are regarded as an
exploratory period during which the progress of pupils is observed and
they are given experience of a wide variety of subjects so that they can
find out where their particular aptitudes, abilities and interests lie:

most are educated in mixed-ability classes for the whole of this period. At the end of the second year, a preliminary decision is taken with regard to those subjects that pupils will attempt in Scottish Certificate of Education (SCE) examinations: these are conducted by the Scottish Examination Board (SEB), a statutory body set up in 1965. Some pupils combine certificate courses in some subjects with non-certificate courses in other areas of the curriculum.

Candidates are normally presented for the SCE Ordinary Grade examinations at the end of the fourth year, and almost half remain at school voluntarily beyond the statutory leaving age. These pupils are presented in a number of subjects at the higher grade in the fifth or sixth year: the more able candidates take four or five subjects and preserve a balanced curriculum, though obviously with less specialization than is possible at A-level. The Certificate of Sixth Year Studies is open to pupils who have normally taken sufficient Highers at the end of the fifth year and are contemplating further or higher education. In this course these pupils have to demonstrate ability to pursue independent study, in most cases by completing a piece of research as a test not only of intellectual ability but also of capacity for personal study.

The social subjects in the secondary school

The Scottish Central Committee on Social Subjects (SCCSS) was established under the CCC to review the teaching of social subjects in secondary schools, to consider the relations between them and to promote their development. In Curriculum Paper 15 published in 1976, it defined the social subjects as 'those subjects which are particularly concerned with the study of society, and of the individual's relation to society and to his environment, whether or not those subjects are included in the curriculum of the secondary school in Scotland'.[3] The term thus refers collectively to subjects such as economics, geography, history, modern studies, politics and sociology.[4] Modern studies is of particular importance in regard to integration within the social sciences as it is defined as a multidisciplinary study of contemporary society, deploying skills, concepts and knowledge drawn selectively from the social subject disciplines to focus on social, economic and political issues of concern to individuals and groups at local, national and international levels. In the Curriculum Paper, the Committee argued that a basic aim of the social subjects should be to open the fields of skills, knowledge and understanding to pupils so that they can develop their potentialities to the full both as individuals and as members of society. It believed that the following cognitive aims apply to the social subjects generally:

1   To extend pupils' knowledge and understanding of their own

society and their relationship to it.
2 To increase their knowledge and understanding of the world in which they live.
3 To promote a knowledge and understanding of the dynamics of social and environmental change.
4 To develop learning skills, problem-solving skills and methods of study.

In the affective domain the social subjects should aim to foster the following qualities in pupils:

(a) an inquiring attitude;
(b) a willingness to consider different viewpoints and ways of life;
(c) an appreciation of human values;
(d) a concern for the needs of society and of the environment;
(e) a respect for evidence as a basis for forming judgements and drawing conclusions.

Social subjects courses in S1/S2 have traditionally contained compulsory and separate courses in geography and history. As early as 1947, the influential Advisory Council on Education in Scotland recommended a combined social studies approach, but this was resisted by the Scottish Education Department (SED) although it was 'prepared to consider schemes of work which proposed to attempt the unification in a well-planned way'.[5] Almost twenty years later, Curriculum Paper 3[6] confirmed that all pupils in S1/S2 ought to take geography and history but added that the main purpose of these courses should be to contribute to general education rather than specifically to prepare for any subject or course that follows. Significantly, this paper referred to the argument that more attention might be paid to education in economics at this stage, and also that the teaching of geography and history might be more closely co-ordinated.

By the time Curriculum Paper 15 appeared, a feasibility study in economics, involving the piloting and evaluating of a two-year course, had been undertaken, and a small but growing number of schools had already introduced courses in modern studies at the S1/S2 stage. In addition, a considerable number of schools had embarked on programmes of social education containing elements of civic and political education and sociology.

At S3 and above, certificate courses at Ordinary and Higher grades were available in economics, economic history, geography, history, and modern studies, and in the previous decade there had been a progressive development of non-certificate courses in the social subjects in S3 and S4. For these courses, SCCSS had recommended the adoption of a multidisciplinary approach to matters of immediate relevance for the pupils concerned, and had defined this aproach as 'one which involves the study of situations, problems or areas, using two or more of the social subjects disciplines'.[7]

The question of balance

SCCSS regarded the attainment of balance within the curriculum as a whole, and also within the area concerned with the social subjects, as an important general aim. It believed that while the overall aims of the various social subjects might be broadly similar, there were important differences in content and approach, sufficiently substantial to suggest that every effort should be made to ensure a spread of experience over the field. It suggested that this increased breadth of study within the social subjects might be achieved in a number of ways:

(a) through integrated studies;
(b) by broadening the approach of existing school subjects;
(c) by increasing the number of social subjects within the curriculum with a reduced time allocation for each;
(d) by a combination of such approaches.

In considering the relative merits of these approaches, the Committee had to consider in some detail the arguments for and against both a discipline-based and an integrated curriculum structure, and it made use of a diagram (Figure 9.1) as a means of clarifying its own thinking and conducting the discussion on the basis of clear definitions of terms such as multidisciplinary, interdisciplinary and cross-disciplinary.

It will be seen that the figure makes some fundamental distinctions and confines the term 'integration' to single courses drawn from more than one discipline and based at least on linked subject units. These units may be taught by subject specialists, but the more developed forms of integration would employ team-teaching methods, and the fullest form would be an entirely fused or synthesized course taught by a single teacher. A multidisciplinary approach is here defined as one involving a considerable variety of forms of collaboration between subject departments and, as a result, a much more limited definition is given to the term 'interdisciplinary'.

Integration and the disciplines

The argument of those who favour curriculum integration normally begins with a critique of the disciplines on the grounds that the division of knowledge into separate compartments is artificial and arbitrary and limits the development of pupils' understanding. Because of pressure on the timetable, a curriculum based on disciplines inevitably leads to some forms of knowledge being underrepresented and this becomes even more apparent with the exponential increase in knowledge. In

Fig. 9.1

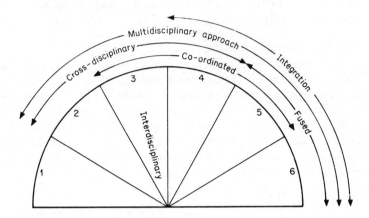

1 Pure subject-teaching without any deliberate attempt to use contributions from other disciplines.
2 Outward-looking subject-teaching seeking and emphasizing links with other subjects whenever the possibilities occur, but still carried out by subject specialists with no attempt at co-operation with other subject specialists.
3 Outward-looking subject-teaching with co-operation between different subject departments regarding sequence of study and structure of syllabus; still a separate subject-course taught by subject specialists.
4 Course based on linked subject units; a single course, drawing in this way from more than one discipline; subject units taught by subject specialists.
5 Single, fused or synthesized course drawing from more than one discipline; team-teaching methods employed.
6 Single, fused or synthesized course taught by a single teacher.

Source: Scottish Central Committee on Social Subjects, *The Social Subjects in Secondary Schools*, Curriculum Paper 15 (HMSO, 1976) appendix B, p.74.

addition, such a curriculum ignores the interests and activities of the learner, and because disciplines are the creation of adult minds and are normally imposed upon pupils, they do not necessarily reflect their mode and level of understanding. If one of the major aims of education is to enable pupils to gain a better understanding of society, it is doubtful if this can be achieved through discipline-based study as the processes and problems of society are larger than the scope of any single discipline, however important. It has also been argued that a discipline-centred curriculum incorporates inefficient methods of teaching and learning, depending too much on memorization and repetition, and makes use of theories and concepts that are too difficult for many pupils to understand. By contrast, integration fosters the natural inquiry of pupils which does not appreciate or respect the division between disciplines, and it enables them to gain a deeper and more realistic understanding of the multi-faceted nature of contemporary society.

Counter-arguments favouring a discipline basis for the curriculum rest on a belief in the existence of certain 'realms of meaning'[8] or 'forms of knowledge'[9] which should provide a balanced curriculum and help to develop habits of rational thought. Disciplines, it is contended, are based on key concepts and ideas, and the process of learning consists of visiting and revisiting these concepts using examples and illustrations appropriate to the level of understanding of the pupils. This undoubtedly presents challenges for the teacher in a single discipline and would probably prove too daunting if subjects were merged together in some form of integrated course. In addition, it may not be valid to assume that studies organized on a thematic basis will necessarily produce a unity of knowledge in the minds of pupils. If disciplines are a convenient and efficient way of classifying knowledge, they should help pupils to find answers to their questions and so aid their process of learning. These considerations suggest that an adequate introduction to distinctive disciplines is essential before topic work of any intellectual quality is practicable; hence integrated studies become a stage of generalization following the precise learning of individual subjects.

SCCSS regarded the debate on the disciplines and integration as fundamental to any decision on the overall structure of courses within the social-subjects area of the curriculum, but it did not find it possible to subscribe entirely or without reservation to either set of arguments because of a belief that some at least of the advocacy from each side consisted of criticism of the worst that might be discerned in the other. The Committee believed that it would be preferable to base a judgement on the positive potential of each approach.

Curriculum implications at different stages of the secondary school

So Curriculum Paper 15 set out a basic philosophy for the social subjects in the secondary school in Scotland and considered some of its implications for courses at different stages. Inevitably, since the arguments over the relative merits of a discipline-based and an integrated curriculum are contentious, the views of the Committee did not go unchallenged. Because of this, and also because of significant new general influences on the curriculum that have inevitable consequences for social subjects, there have been a number of important reflections on, and developments of, the thinking of the Curriculum Paper since 1976.

S1/S2

The broad conclusion of the Paper was that for S1 and S2 there should be a foundation of discipline-based studies and that a single integrated course at this stage, either in place of or in addition to the existing disciplines, was not favoured. Geography and history would continue to form the basis of social-subjects courses for every pupil at this stage but some broadening of this area of the curriculum was nevertheless favoured. One means of achieving this might be by recommending the adoption of an experimental two-year course in economics which had been devised by a national working party, piloted and evaluated in a number of schools in the period 1974–6:[10] an alternative means would be through some form of integrated study in the final term of S2, building on the foundation of earlier discipline-based studies. On the basis of its philosophical position, the Committee did not feel able to recommend multidisciplinary or integrated courses in modern studies or of a modern studies-type in S1/S2. This proved to be a controversial decision and critics of the Committee contended that it was based on inadequate knowledge and understanding of courses being developed in an increasing number of schools. Accordingly, it was decided to conduct an inquiry into the teaching of modern studies in S1/S2 to obtain more information on the types of courses being developed in terms of content, methodology and assessment, and their relationship with other social subjects elements in the curriculum.[11] A further working party was established to consider possible forms of integration in the third term of S2, building on earlier discipline-based courses,[12] and in 1980 SCCSS was invited by the Committee on Secondary Education (COSE) to set up a study group on the whole S1/S2 social-subjects curriculum with the following remit:[13]

1 To undertake a summative review of the work carried out in S1/S2 by the SCCSS and its predecessors.
2 To review the structure and organization of the social subjects in S1/S2 and, taking into account the types of courses which are already in existence in the schools, to make recommendations to COSE on possible alternative forms of course organization in the social subjects in S1/S2.

In carrying out the above remit, this Committee was conscious of the importance of establishing continuity in curriculum provision from the later stages of the primary school to S3 and beyond, the danger of fragmentation through proliferation of individual subjects, the problem of exposure of pupils to too many teachers, and the desirability and extent of mixed-ability classroom organization within the common course. On the basis of its reappraisal, the Study Group concluded that the social subjects might be represented in three different ways:

1 As a collection of more or less discrete subjects conceptually and methodologically insulated from one another.
2 As a logic and methodology of social science for interpreting and intervening in human affairs.
3 As a broad intellectual tradition in which the constituent elements overlap in contents and concerns and draw from time to time from the sciences, social sciences and arts.

The first approach was regarded as consistent with much of what is taken for granted and practised in secondary schools, subject-centred and looking towards the development in pupils of the distinctive expertise of the individual subject. The second was considered to be inquiry-based arguing for a unifying core of understanding of human affairs but it was felt that if it were interpreted too strongly it could exclude major areas of what currently constitutes teaching in the social subjects. It was believed that the third approach offered a more open yet no less forceful position looking outwards across subjects to a common concern with sound intellectual inquiry and the applications of knowledge to an understanding of behaviour and values in a democratic society. Hence the group was strongly persuaded of the value of this third representation of the purposes of the social subjects and derived certain principles that it believed should influence future policies and provision. In its report these were set out as follows:

1 All pupils should have access through the social subjects to the major ideas and attitudes of this continuing tradition and the opportunity to apply them to contemporary human affairs.
2 The social-subjects programme for all pupils should contain knowledge drawn from what, broadly speaking, constitutes historical, geographical, sociological, political and economic studies, these being the major components of the tradition.
3 The constituent areas of study within the overall programme of the social subjects should be seen as having parity of attention in the overlapping contributions they have to make to knowledge, there being no convincing grounds for arguing otherwise.
4 The subjects should be regarded as the bases of ideas and methods that provide different perspectives upon common concerns in human affairs.
5 The social-subjects curriculum should be planned co-operatively so that the elements of subject-based knowledge have the most effective force in teaching and learning, enabling pupils both to acquire sound subject knowledge and to apply the complementary perspectives in ways that both enrich their understandings of human affairs and the subjects they are progressively learning.
6 The social-subjects programme should function in S1/S2 as a

common foundation which draws upon teaching and personal experience in the primary school, developing and transforming pupils' knowledge and acting as the basis for more differentiated and selected studies in particular subjects in the following stages of schooling.

The group went on, rather more tentatively, to suggest a number of pedagogical and organizational practices that would be conducive to the kind of curriculum proposed. These were:

(a) systematic collaboration across the contributing subjects and the creation of procedures by which this can be achieved;
(b) flexibility in the development of teachers and resources within the social-subjects curriculum as a whole;
(c) development of a widely acceptable common framework of foundation concepts and skills in the social subjects, together with a range of applied themes and activities on which subject-based perspectives may have a complementary focus;
(d) development and use of an articulated set of subject-based resources for teaching and learning in the social subjects as a whole;
(e) teaching methods and classroom organization that provide for didactic, discursive, inquiry and activity modes being employed in fostering pupils' learning.

The group recognized that the preferred option was an integrated course taught collaboratively by teachers from all the subject departments but falling short of the most advanced forms of integration where existing subjects are transformed into a new unified structure of knowledge. It doubted whether such an intellectual structure could be derived from the existing social subjects without such substantial redefinition that major parts of these subjects might disappear. It might also become so abstract as to create difficulties in understanding for pupils and would also be inimical to the existing professional and organizational characteristics of schools.

So the group concluded that further development of the social subjects in S1/S2 should take place on the following basis:

1 There should be a two-year social-subjects programme that contains knowledge drawn from historical, geographical, sociological, political and economic studies.
2 The programme should arise from common planning by the staff of the relevant subject departments and should be sustained by continuing collaboration of the staff of these departments.
3 Common planning and continuing collaboration should reflect basic concerns to foster coherence of aims, awareness of the inter-relationships among the different perspectives in their ideas and

applications to the understanding of human affairs, and the appropriateness of different modes of teaching to particular topics and to pupils of differing abilities.

It recommended the preparation of a set of national advisory guidelines on the aims, scope, organization and teaching of a two-year social-subjects programme in S1/S2. The guidelines would seek:

(a) to provide a framework of reference for devising courses to be used by individual teachers and subject departments while preserving the freedom of schools to create their own courses within an acceptable framework;
(b) to provide means whereby there is a reasonable degree of common ground among courses across the country;
(c) to identify linkage between different components of the course;
(d) to allow for differentiation of curriculum material within mixed-ability groups in the common course;
(e) to provide a more effective basis of assessment for a range of purposes.

A set of draft guidelines were prepared by February 1983 and, as part of the S1/S2 Social Subjects Development Programme, issued to a small number of schools willing to pilot them in session 1983–4. On the basis of these initial trials, the guidelines will be modified and issued to a larger number of schools for a two-year period. Thus, by 1986, considerable evidence should have been assembled on the effectiveness of the approach recommended by the Study Group.

S3/S4

Curriculum Paper 15 argued that all four social subjects should have a place in certificate courses from S3 to S6, that all pupils in S3 and S4 should include at least one social subject in their O-grade course, and that in S5, wherever possible, pupils should include at least one social subject either as an examinable subject or as a minority-time study. In S6, modern studies should be equated with the other social subjects (including economics) in being offered for the Certificate in Sixth Year Studies examination.

Since 1976, however, changes have taken place in the curriculum of the 14–16 age group and also in forms of examination at 16. They result from two major reports that appeared in 1977.

The first of these, the Munn Report, *The Structure of the Curriculum in the Third and Fourth Years of the Scottish Secondary School*,[14] was essentially concerned with curriculum design. It defined four sets of aims for a balanced curriculum in secondary schools:

(a) development of knowledge and understanding, both of the self and

of the social and physical environment;
(b) development of cognitive, interpersonal and psychomotor skills;
(c) affective development of pupils;
(d) meeting the demands of society.

It used these aims as criteria for determining the scope of the curriculum, and identified eight modes of activity or fields of study that should contribute a balanced curriculum for all pupils, of which one is the mode of social studies. Finally, it offered a curriculum structure based on a core plus electives model (see Table 9.1).

Table 9.1

	Core area			Elective area
Pupils take all subjects	Pupils choose one subject	Pupils choose one subject	Pupils choose one subject	French German Spanish
English + Mathematical studies + Physical education + Religious and moral education	Economics or History or Geography or Modern studies (All to include a module or modules based on a study of contemporary society.)	Biology or Chemistry or Physics or General science or Engineering science or Food science	Art or Music or Drama or Dance or Creative craft	Latin Biology Chemistry Physics Geography History Modern studies Engineering drawing Metalwork Woodwork Catering Fabrics and fashion Food and nutrition Accounting Secretarial studies Art Physical education Religious education Integrated courses etc.

Source: The Structure of the Curriculum in the Third and Fourth Years of the Scottish Secondary School, The Munn Report (HMSO, 1977).

In this structure, all the social subjects, including economics, were given an equal place in column 2 of the core area on the understanding that whichever subject was chosen pupils must study a module or modules dealing with the political, economic, industrial and environmental aspects of life in modern society. It should be noted, however, that economics, unlike the other social subjects, was not included in the elective area.

The second report came from the Dunning Committee which was invited to consider what form or forms of examination would be most likely to meet the needs of fourth-year pupils of varying academic ability. In its report *Assessment for All*,[15] the Committee recommended three levels of award – Foundation, General and Credit – to cover the whole range of ability, and advocated over-lapping of syllabus levels to avoid premature categorization of pupils. It believed that syllabuses leading to certification should have internally and externally devised components at all levels and that the internal syllabus components should be subject to external moderation.

The appearance of these two reports in 1977 was followed by a period of intense debate on the curriculum and assessment issues that they raised. The Labour government gave its initial response to the reports shortly before it left office in 1979, but it was not until the following year that the Conservative government decided on a development programme in the form of a feasibility study in English, mathematics and science and three multidisciplinary programmes (health studies, social and vocational skills, and contemporary social studies) mainly at Foundation level (i.e. for the least academic pupils). A further and flexible element in the programme was introduced from 1981 by the CCC in the form of proposals for a series of short modular courses.

Following the appearance of *Framework for Decision: A Consultative Paper on the Government's Proposals for Implementation* (September 1982),[16] the Secretary of State gave his approval in April 1983 for the new curriculum and assessment arrangements in the third and fourth years of secondary education as set out in this Paper. Schools were asked to adopt the balanced curricular framework provided by the eight modes of study proposed by the Munn Committee and assessment would be at the three levels recommended by the Dunning Committee with all Foundation-level courses and some General-level courses being assessed by a combination of internal and external assessment, and all Credit and the remainder of General courses being externally assessed.

Joint Working Parties of the CCC and the SEB have been set up to prepare syllabuses and the examination arrangements for the new Standard Grade, which will gradually replace the existing grade. In the first phase of the programme, comprising English, mathematics, science and social and vocational skills, courses began in schools in August 1984 for certification in 1986. The other multidisciplinary courses, together with a number of single subjects, are in the second phase of the programme starting a year later, and the third phase, which includes all the single social subjects, including economics, will commence in August 1986 for certification in 1988.

It is now possible to give some preliminary indication of how the countervailing arguments relating to the disciplines and integration within the social subjects will affect the character of the courses that emerge for S3/S4 under this greatly changed system. The Joint Working Party on Social and Vocational skills reported in August 1983 and its proposals offer some opportunities for the development of economic ideas and skills, mainly in relation to business studies, but the other social subjects are not so directly affected. The report of the Joint Working Party on Contemporary Social Studies issued in April 1984 is even more relevant in showing how the social subjects might be brought together to fulfil the wish in the Munn Report that all pupils should study, perhaps on a modular basis, different facets of life in modern society paying due attention to the political, social, economic, industrial and environmental aspects.

S5/S6

Curriculum change in Scotland does not stop at the age of 16. The future of Higher Grade and the Certificate of Sixth Year Studies is being reviewed as part of *16–18s in Scotland: An Action Plan* produced in January 1983.[17] This sought to meet the need for a coherent provision of education and training for 16–18-year-olds covering all levels of attainment and motivation. It argued that at 16 young people are faced with a bewildering choice, including a large number of O- and H-grade courses, many certificates and diplomas awarded by FE examining bodies, and other possibilities, such as the Youth Training Scheme, if employment cannot be obtained. The Action Plan called on schools to adjust more quickly to changes in technology and in society and to respond to the needs of a more diverse population, especially in S5. It proposed a curricular framework for this age group based on the design of 40-hour modules that are sufficiently flexible to be built into individual programmes in a large variety of ways and by a process of negotiation. It is intended that this modular provision will be closely related to the 14–16 programme and will lead to the award of a single vocational certificate which will provide an alternative goal to the Higher Grade for those pupils who remain at school after 16 but have limited academic potential.

The whole curriculum that emerges from the Action Plan includes for the 16–18 age range a continuation of the development of literacy and numeracy, further specialist studies, experience of the world of work and the community, social studies (including moral and religious studies), industrial studies, and informal aspects such as education for leisure. It is believed that each of these experiences will contribute to an individual's preparation for life and participation in society. The modules to be devised will be based on those already in existence in certain non-advanced FE courses already developed by SCOTBEC and SCOTEC. Four curriculum areas have been identified for development – technology, science, business and administration, and inter-disciplinary.

It is already clear that the modules produced on interdisciplinary themes, not exclusively in the social sciences, will offer considerable opportunities for collaboration between departments within schools and between schools and colleges where physical proximity permits and where there is a readiness to share resources and secure their most economic use.

Implications for economics

This survey of recent changes in the secondary school curriculum in Scotland indicates some of the opportunities for provision of courses in the social subjects that exemplify both single-discipline and integrated characteristics. Education authorities and schools will be able to make choices from a diet that is potentially rich and varied but that could be indigestible if too much is attempted within a short time and with limited staffing and financial resources.

Within the past decade, as a result of a feasibility study in S1/S2, which led to the devising of a two-year course, and of important changes in examination syllabuses at S3 and above,[18] a conceptual consistency in economics courses throughout the secondary school in Scotland has been attempted. The new framework for courses brought about in 1983 by the decision of the Secretary of State to implement the Munn and Dunning programme and by the appearance of the Action Plan for the 16–18 age group provide exciting possibilities for economics both as a single subject and as a component in one or more multidisciplinary courses.

In addition, in the Final Report of the Education for the Industrial Society Project, *An Education for Life and Work*, a five-year investigation, sponsored by the CCC, into the relevance of the secondary-school curriculum in preparing pupils for life and work in an industrial society, a strong plea is made for the incorporation of economics into the curriculum of pupils at some stage during secondary education:

We believe that all pupils should learn about Economics. Some aspects of it are already present in several school subjects such as Modern Studies, Geography, History and Accounting, as well as in the school subject Economics, but we consider that these require greater emphasis so that young people become more aware of the economic basis of society. The production of wealth and its distribution; the functions of labour, land and capital; the causes of recession and unemployment: these are all vital to an understanding of our industrial society. The nature of manufacturing industry from the processing of raw materials to the completion of the final product are but little understood by our young people and insufficiently taught. It is time they occupied a more important place in the curriculum.[19]

It is significant that this recommendation recognizes alternative organizational patterns for the teaching of economics in the hope that all pupils will be able to achieve at least some economic literacy. This is in keeping with a policy of curriculum flexibility that recognizes different organizational possibilities within schools but the important proviso must be that whatever pattern is chosen the key concepts of the subject must be communicated.

Yet economics is still a relatively small subject within the secondary school curriculum in Scotland. With the commitment of an education authority and the support of individual head teachers and principal teachers, it can be a significant element in its own right in the curriculum in S1/S2, but it is more likely that its general development at this stage will depend upon the extent to which the social subjects are more collaboratively planned and taught within a coherent S1/S2 course. As with all subjects with a relatively small place in the total secondary curriculum, economics is vulnerable to falling rolls and the restriction of options that schools may have to apply as a result, and the future of economics education at S3 and above will be strongly influenced by the patterns of the new Standard and Higher grade courses, including such multidisciplinary options as social and contemporary studies, and by the achievement of the Action Plan.

Conclusion

There has been an intensive debate in Scotland in the past decade on the relative merits of discipline-based and integrated courses in the social sciences. The outcome of this debate has been a compromise – a recognition that both approaches have validity and that it would be unwise to support one to the exclusion or virtual exclusion of the other. The S1/S2 Development Programme will encourage co-ordinated modular courses that are subject-based but not subject-centred and the process of piloting will determine the acceptability of these within schools. The changing curriculum framework at S3 and beyond will offer opportunities for both approaches to be pursued so that pupils of varying abilities and inclinations will be able to make a genuine choice, and this should increase their motivation. For economists who cannot rely on their contribution to general education being made exclusively through a single-discipline course, the preservation of both approaches and the continuation and strengthening of the links between economics and multidisciplinary school subjects such as modern studies (and also, outside the social-subject area, with business studies) seems the most sensible way forward.

This case-study approach to the issue of the disciplines and integration within the social sciences has been developed in some detail to show how attempts have been made at different stages in the secondary school within one education system to translate philosophical statements into curriculum practice. Inevitably, there will be different value judgements on the philosophical arguments but experience in Scotland would suggest that to design a curriculum in the social sciences exclusively on the basis either of single disciplines or of integration will polarize attitudes among teachers and will deny to pupils the variety of courses that should improve the quality of their learning experience and provide a relevant preparation for their life in society. If this conclusion is accepted, economists, as well as other social scientists, have to face up to its implications.

Notes and references

1. Lee, N., and Entwistle, H., 'Economics education and educational theory', in Lee, N. (ed.), *Teaching Economics*, 2nd edn (Heinemann Educational Books, 1975) pp. 44–9.
2. Lawton, D., 'Economics in relation to other subjects within the curriculum', in Lee, (ed.), op. cit., pp. 85–93.
3. SCCSS, *The Social Subjects in Secondary Schools*, Curriculum Paper 15, (HMSO, 1976) p. 1.
4. Politics and sociology are not taught as separate subjects in Scottish secondary schools, but elements of these disciplines appear prominently in modern studies courses.
5. Scottish Education Department, *Geography in Secondary Schools* (HMSO, 1951) p. 12.
6. *Modern Studies for Young School Leavers*, Curriculum Paper 3, (HMSO, 1968).
7. SCCSS, *Social Subjects for Young School Leavers*, Bulletin no. 1 (HMSO, 1973) p. 4.
8. As used in Phenix, P.H., *Realms of Meaning* (McGraw-Hill, 1964).
9. As used in Hirst, P.H., 'Liberal education and the nature of knowledge', in Archambault, R.D. (ed.), *Philosophical Analysis and Education* (Routledge & Kegan Paul, 1972).
10. See SCCSS, *Economics in S1/S2: A Feasibility Study*, Bulletin no. 3 (HMSO, 1976).
11. SCCSS, *An Inquiry into the Teaching of Modern Studies in S1 and S2* (HMSO, 1980).
12. SCCSS, *Integration in the Social Subjects in S2 (3rd term)* (HMSO, 1981).
13. SCCSS, *The S1/S2 Social Subjects Curriculum* (HMSO, 1982).
14. *The Structure of the Curriculum in the Third and Fourth Years of the Scottish Secondary School*, The Munn Report (HMSO, 1977).
15. *Assessment for All*, The Dunning Report (HMSO, 1977).
16. *Framework for Decision: A Consultative Paper on the Government's Proposals for Implementation* (SED, 1982).

17. *16–18s in Scotland: An Action Plan* (SED, 1983).
18. For further details of these developments, see Robinson, T.K., 'Economics in the secondary school curriculum in Scotland', *Economics*, vol. 19, pt 4, no. 84, winter 1983.
19. *An Education for Life and Work: Final Report of Education for the Industrial Society Project* (CCC, 1983).

10 Economics Teachers and Industry
Susan Holmes

The debate about how schools should prepare their pupils for life in industrial society is not new. Mr Callaghan's speech at Ruskin College, Oxford, in October 1976 urging a 'Great Debate' about the relationship between industry and education, and about how teachers and young people could become more aware of the realities of economic life, merely served to highlight and reinvigorate a debate that began with the development of universal schooling. It is too simplistic to picture the debate as one between those who wanted all young people to have the benefits of a liberal education, and those who wished to prepare a malleable work-force; another important factor was concern about the role education could play in the economic growth of Britain. Were standards of achievement falling? Were the more-able students being discouraged from entering industry? Were schools preparing pupils for examinations at the expense of preparation for 'life'? All of these questions continue to be asked of schools and in recent years many have felt it necessary to review the curriculum and see if they could make some response.

'The Debate' has often been confusing and schools have found it difficult to frame a response to the questions being asked. They see themselves as providing education for pupils of all abilities rather than training pupils for a particular job of work. Industry has always found it extremely difficult to specify the 'needs' of its work-force in general terms, although recent studies have suggested that its general requirements match far more closely than is generally supposed to the schools' aspirations for their pupils: that school leavers should have good basic social skills and a familiarity with basic arithmetical skills. Perhaps a more significant outcome of the Debate has been a recognition that 'training' would not be provided within the confines of the traditional school system, and the Manpower Service Commission designed the New Training Initiative to take account of the training needs of school leavers. The New Training and Vocational Education Initiative (NTVEI), funded by the MSC and piloted by local education authorities, is a fascinating new departure since it is intended to investigate ways of incorporating a great deal more technical and vocational education into the secondary curriculum. Even so, the emphasis is on education in the technical and more general skills relevant to the world of work; training for specific careers is not an objective of the schemes being piloted. These new initiatives have not diminished the pressure on all schools to prepare pupils for the world of work, as this quotation from the DES's *A Framework for the School Curriculum* (1980) underlines:

The Secretaries of State consider that substantial attention should be given at the secondary stage to the relationship between school work and the preparation for working life. Pupils need to acquire an understanding of the economic basis of society and how wealth is created.

Schools–industry organizations

A unique feature of attempts to bring about curriculum changes to meet these ends is the group of organizations, with substantial funding raised from outside the education system, who offer assistance to schools who wish to make changes. They are largely staffed by people from industry and offer a wide range of services such as work-experience placements, sixth-form conferences, and materials from a wide range of firms, to schools who request their use. Figure 10.1, produced by the Industry Project (SCIP), aims to summarize the services offered by the various groups in England and Wales.

This figure is built around the proposition that it is helpful to distinguish three broad groupings within the schools–industry organizations: those who seek to introduce technology into the school curriculum led by the Science and Technology Regional Organizations (SATROs), those who are primarily concerned with the transition to employment, and those with a more general brief for improving the understanding of modern industrial society. These are represented as three overlapping sets, the areas of overlap being manufacturing industry, personal skills and competence, and specific skills that are held to be important for industry, and especially technological skills.

This chapter draws on the experience of one project, the Industry Project, funded originally by the Schools Council and now by the School Curriculum Development Committee (SCDC), whose specific remit is to help pupils understand the role of industry in industrial society.

The Industry Project is unique because it is funded by government and the local authorities and works in conjunction with the CBI and TUC. Through its network of local authority teacher co-ordinators, it aims to involve the local economic community in the curriculum review and development process and to see how pupils in individual schools can be helped to a greater understanding of the role of industry in the industrial society in which they live. It should be noted that SCDC projects cover England and Wales but there has been a broadly parallel development in Scotland called 'Education for the Industrial Society'. Although the two projects have differed in their strategies of operation,

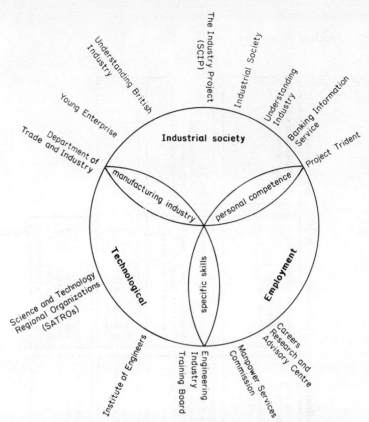

Fig. 10.1 A quick guide to some projects and organizations working with schools.

Source: The Industry Project.

differences to a large extent created by the different education systems, their findings and recommendations are broadly similar.

Fundamental to SCIP's philosophy is that pupils should understand their *own* industrial society in which goods and services are produced by private firms and public enterprise and where the country depends on its wealth creators who are, in turn, dependent on the state and the local authorities to provide essential goods and services. An understanding of industrial society thus involves awareness not only of the role of manufacturing industry but also of the service industries, and of the part played by the state in economic activity. In many areas the local authority is the major employer and to ignore its role in the local economic community is perverse, to say the least.

The concept of 'wealth creation' is one that raises needless difficulties. For the economist, value is added to raw materials as a result of each stage of production, and when the products are sold wealth is created. Thus the production and selling functions are as important as manufacturing; and the role of banking and commerce in facilitating

Fig. 10.2   The Industry Project 'grid'.

	The Individual	The Organization		The Nation	International
A working life	What is work really like? Work and life patterns Among the unemployed Leisure Earning a living	Manpower planning and career development Training Technological innovation Job satisfaction and enrichment On your own		Policies for education and training Regional patterns Unemployment	Working lives: international perspectives
Relationships	Responsibilities and rights	Unions	Employers Co-operation and conflict Industrial democracy Collective bargaining	Economies – free, mixed and planned Economic role of the state Governing Britain Nationalization and rescue	The EEC The multinationals Trade cartels Overseas and development
The environment	Qualities of life	Health and safety The firm and its environment		Energy Resource use Pollution	
Rewards and Resources	Pay and standards of living Status, skill, differentials and relativities Tax, insurance and pensions Social security	Profits and wealth creation Capital and investment Growth Job security Productivity		Incomes policy Inflation Balance of payments Public expenditure The financial institutions	

Source: The Industry Project.

wealth creation is fundamental. The nation's standard of living clearly depends on its ability to create wealth, but to say this is not to demean the role that a variety of institutions play in an interdependent economy such as ours. For example, the National Health and Education services make a direct contribution through raising the quality of the workforce; even Her Majesty's Inspector of Taxes plays a crucial role in redistributing the wealth that is created!

Curriculum change

For schools, the decisions about curriculum change to foster greater pupil understanding of industrial society can be complex and far-reaching, with many subject teachers involved. A fundamental refocusing of the curriculum is required so that we avoid the sort of anomalies that arise when, for example, the economics department is offering a general course for all fourth-year pupils on 'Living in Industrial Society' and the science department is providing examination courses that the HMI have said do not give pupils opportunities to reflect on the application of the techniques acquired to the world outside the classroom. In this process, the local economic community, industrialists and trade unionists are an infinite resource. On too many occasions pupils work through textbook descriptions of industrial processes even though there are people within a few yards of the school who can bring these processes to life. How often have we struggled through a lesson where we try to make our pupils think about 'economies of scale' when there are innumerable local workplaces where they could find their own examples?

What contribution should economics teachers be making to pupils' understanding of the industrial world? The economics department in the school has a key role to play since perhaps more than any other department it wants students to be able to relate the concepts acquired to current economic issues. In addition, economics teachers are often seen by the school staff as the 'experts' on industry or, at the very least, interested observers of the industrial scene, who could assist staff from other departments to relate subject work to the industrial world, or could lead a group of staff and industrialists in preparing a course on industrial and economic literacy for all the pupils in the school.

Let us first look at ways in which the content of economics lessons can be related to the industrial world. Whatever the level of teaching, be it examination work for the fourth and fifth year, A-level economics or the range of so-called 'vocational' examinations for the 'new sixth', economics teachers aim to help their pupils understand certain key concepts. Most teachers would agree that an understanding of these concepts is enhanced if pupils are given opportunities to apply their learning to case studies from the real world, and for many pupils this feeling that their economics lessons will offer them something relevant to their lives is a powerful motivator.

The value of the industrial link is mainly in regard to providing applications as exemplars of economic theory, particularly on the micro side. The teacher's task is to devise ways of working with industry so that pupils can see the relevance of industry for themselves and it seems that the personal experience of industrialists and trade unionists, whom SCIP call 'adults other than teachers', can be invaluable. Perhaps the greatest value of using the local economic community is to highlight the dynamic nature of the economic world, in particular the constant need to make choices and the tensions that result from the choices made. A group of students working on location theory might discuss in class how they could try out the theory on a local firm by looking at the decisions that led it to choose a particular site. Students need to discuss the questions they might ask of managers and employees and will be encouraged by their teacher to look for questions that will try to elicit how closely business people base their decisions on factors that economists consider to be important. Subsequent interviews between student and industrialist will undoubtedly highlight the unquantifiable and apparently irrational factors in the decision-making process, and the consequences of taking a particular decision.

Using the local economic community as a resource

This is just one example of the value of 'links' between teachers and pupils and the economic community. Too often 'links' are merely interpreted as involving local industrialists and trade unionists coming into school to 'lecture' on certain topics. Teachers readily testify how bored pupils are to hear local business people lecture on British industry or a trade unionist lecture on the development of trade unions. This is not at all surprising since it is local working people's expertise that needs to be harnessed for most effective learning. There is worry that these 'adults other than teachers' will make a biased presentation to the class. The issues of values and bias in economics teaching are dealt with elsewhere, but for SCIP an important strategy has been to try to introduce pupils to the plurality of views in society by bringing people with differing views of industry into the classroom and helping students to see why individuals hold such views. It is fallacious to assume that perfect balance can be achieved by teacher or adult other than teacher, and we should not underestimate the ability of pupils to draw independent conclusions.

For teachers and pupils visits to local enterprises bring a wealth of resources that can be used in class and examination work. For the teacher a visit to a firm offers the opportunity to investigate what information can be obtained. If the visit is carefully planned beforehand and ample notice given to the enterprise, it is usually possible for the teacher to interview a range of working people, such as the finance, marketing, personnel managers and the works convenor, who can provide important data. Flexibility is essential if useful material is to be acquired, since terms such as 'fixed and variable costs' and 'monopolistic competition' are commonly used by economists but not by company accountants. The nature of the case study will determine how much time needs to be spent in the organization since information about pricing or sales policies could be acquired relatively quickly, but a more detailed analysis will take at least a week since a range of people need to be interviewed and the various production processes observed.

A group of teachers can cover much more ground than one teacher, perhaps visiting several companies and bringing back ideas for development. A group of economics teachers who spent two days with the local branch of an electrical engineering firm were able to develop materials for use in class on the following:

the diverse goals of the company;
the barriers to entering the industry;
location of the firm;
economies of scale;
the labour market;
industrial relations;
union procedures;
tax incentives and work;
problems of moving from mass-production conditions to small-batch production;
costs and buying policies;
pricing strategies – 'bargaining' with monopolistic buyers;
differential pricing;
coping with inflation and exchange-rate fluctuations.

Once the material has been collected a case study needs to be prepared for classroom use. Careful thought needs to be given to the way in which it is intended that this stimulus be used. Is it to form one of a series of examples to illustrate a theme such as 'economies of scale' or is it to be a large single firm case study from which a range of exercises will be developed? Will the case study be in written form or will it be a series of slides, photographs and tape recordings? Finally, it can be helpful to ask the firm to look at the material produced so that any factual inaccuracies or important omissions are corrected. For the firm this has the added advantage of offering an 'outsider's' view of the enterprise, which can be valuable. Representatives from the firm can be involved in the classroom acting as 'consultants' to the pupils working on the case study.

In addition to the preparation of a case study, teachers, through observation at the workplace, can gain a wealth of useful information about the impact of technology, the production process and organizational structure, and pupils are much more responsive to using examples from firms they pass on the way to school or where they or their parents may seek employment, than to looking at a firm many miles away. Of course, most companies possess a wealth of documentation that can be of value for teachers of economics, business studies and commerce. Many public companies now attempt to 'demystify' the traditional balance sheet by producing an accompanying simplified document for their workers and these are more appropriate for use in class. The Bank Information Service makes available a wide range of documents and many companies will spare bills of lading, contracts of employment, invoices and statements.

An important strategy is for pupils to visit or have a work-experience placement in an enterprise. Work experience is a most powerful learning exercise for young people in their final years at school, and yet all too often the learning is diminished. Many employers, far from seeing this as an additional burden, would prefer to see how they can help students to learn as much as possible from the experience, and are relieved to see that there is teacher support for the activity.

Learning about industry is more effective if active learning strategies are used so that pupils learn as a result of a series of 'experiences' rather than as a result of reading all about it. Examination courses designed in recent years, partly to 'dignify' the teaching of industrial studies, recognize this, so that 'understanding industrial society', 'industrial studies' and 'business studies' examinations all see practical work as an integral part of the examination course. However, it is not always necessary for workplace visits to be involved since case studies, role play and simulation are all effective ways of communicating knowledge about an ever-changing industrial world. These techniques are at present used much more extensively in industrial and trade-union education than they are in school and the 'raw materials' used in industrial programmes can be a useful resource for the teacher. In addition, people from industry are invaluable consultants to teachers who want to write case studies and simulations, and to students as they start to work on them. The consultant's advice, based on experience of the workplace, can be an important facet in building understanding and it allows adults other than teachers to play to their strengths. Simulations are often devised to facilitate understanding of the division of labour and production techniques, and there are many based on the running of business where students are required to act as managers of key functions in the enterprise. More traditional business games can be used as a basis for further work, for example, a pay bargaining exercise can be developed with pupils who are members of the work-force acting with their union to frame and justify a wage demand to which managers must respond. In addition, students need to be encouraged to look at the repercussions of the management decisions they take on the labour force, the consumer and the local community, for example. The roles of banks and building societies become clearer if students frame their own submissions for financial assistance, using a small firm identified from the local newspaper as a basis for their submission to a bank. Subsequently, they are interviewed by a student 'manager' who decides whether their request for assistance meets requirements. Again, a local bank manager could play a crucial role in training the 'bank manager' and evaluating the students' work.

Strategies for change

In many schools significant changes will need to be made 'across the curriculum' if the school curriculum is going to offer sufficient opportunity for pupils to learn about the industrial world. Most pupils in their final years at school are heavily involved in examination work and fundamental changes need to be made in many courses to allow pupils to have opportunities to apply their knowledge to practical examples. In addition, many schools try to make available a timetabled 'slot' for all pupils to study important economic, social and personal issues. This might take the form of regular weekly lessons of the 'living in modern society' genre or a one- or two-week block course, perhaps involving work experience, in the students' final year at school. The economics teacher is often seen as the natural co-ordinator of such activities. Schools that have involved the industrial community in devising the syllabus from the very beginning have found that industrialists have challenged the schools' ideas about what might be covered and have made available a variety of resources that have immeasurably improved the course. Thus, trade unionists have frequently steered the school committee devising the course away from the development of trade unions to a discussion of the functions of unions at the workplace and have produced case studies for pupils to debate on issues such as the impact of technology on employment, health and safety at work, participation, authority, democracy, etc. Employers have helped to frame a course on starting a small business, the consequences of recession, and have devised simulations for use in class. The Industry Project, in consultation with the CBI and TUC, drew up a 'grid' of topics (see Fig. 10.2 on p. 182) that it was felt 'covered' the area with which the Project was concerned. It is not a syllabus, although some schools have found it useful as a map to guide them to areas of interest that might be developed in a general course.

Other schools have opted for a block of time for all pupils during the school year when the focus was on 'industry'. There are obvious drawbacks to this approach and most teachers would agree that a two-day course of 'lectures' from industrialists was more an exercise in sitting quietly for a long spell rather than learning about industry. Most evaluations of such events point to difficulties of speakers appreciating how much pupils can learn in a short spell. However, if a reasonable block of time can be secured there is an advantage in an intensive experience over a 'drip feed' approach and, once the decision to stage an event has been taken, further problems of ensuring the availability of pupils of all abilities disappear.

Pupils need to be involved in an active way if their attention is to be held over this period. One school used the local industrial community and its resources to prepare a three-day conference for its pupils. Case studies were prepared beforehand with the local economic community to look at various aspects of the industrial scene. The Borough Planning Department devised an exercise on siting a business, with plans for use of a piece of land, local objections from a planning inquiry, and alternative use proposals. Pupils had to make their own decisions about the use of the site. Later the planning officer revealed that it was a well-known local site and explained how the final decision had been made. The bank devised a small business simulation; the law centre, the women's employment group, industrialists and trade unionists prepared case studies on employment problems. For the rest of the time pupils went on visits to firms, but in addition to a tour, they were invited to work with the enterprise on one of its 'problems', such as health and safety at the paperworks, testing water samples at the Water Board, investigating the problem of shoplifting at the department store, and a variety of others. All pupils were accompanied by teachers who had the opportunity to see how they could use the pupils' experience in subsequent follow-up lessons. Another school prepared all of the year group to visit local industry and commerce with a specific theme in mind – such as 'recession'. Pupils interviewed managers and workers and their research findings became the raw material on which to build 'inputs' from a variety of 'experts'. They put together a not inconsiderable piece of work on economic change. When time is limited, it is important that the year group should have as wide a variety of experiences as possible and these should be pooled in subsequent discussion.

Perhaps the most exciting development in the use of a block of time is to organize the whole year group into a production unit of some kind. This has enormous advantages as the operation can be closely dovetailed into the timetable and curriculum structure. Pupils have to make production decisions from conception to sales and aftercare, so that individual pupils will have first-hand experience of the problems of organizing people, time, materials and space. It gives them an opportunity to exercise responsibility and develop decision-making skills. On a work-experience placement their roles tend to be limited to the more mundane tasks, but in the school production unit they can be 'marketing manager', 'shop steward' and 'production manager' as well as 'worker', and at the same time gain some insights into the routine and pressures of a work situation. Many teachers see this exercise as a way of introducing their pupils to the small business scene since they will need to identify a product and a market, find ways of financing the operation and devise a means of production. One essential element in the process is that of using the knowledge and skills of the local community. Schools have called on parents, local employers and people who are unemployed, not only to provide some of the raw materials for production, but also to act as advisers and consultants in the marketing and manufacturing process. Perhaps two examples would be useful here. In one school a one-year course for all pupils in the fourth year covering one double lesson each week was planned by a steering committee of teachers and local business people. The course covers finding a business opportunity, market research, sources of finance, internal organization, the risks of running a small business. From the very beginning pupils were encouraged to think about a product and eventually each class broke up into small groups and decided what they would market. Each group prepared a document for a bank in order to secure a loan and this document was constantly updated as business progressed. In another school all of the fourth year devoted a week to producing goods to sell at a profit in an exercise devised jointly by the craft, English and humanities departments. The craft area became a workshop, pupils made their own decisions and, through follow-up lessons with industrialists, were encouraged to learn from their triumphs and mistakes. Based on the experience of those schools who have run successful operations, the level of commitment among pupils to an operation that is essentially their own and upon whom the success of the venture lies, is very high. The economics department could have a key role to play in any such exercise, encouraging other members of staff to become involved in this important mode of learning and assisting pupils in acquiring important skills.

There is no doubt that in recent years schools have made enormous strides in looking at the relevance of the curriculum in preparing pupils for the transition to adult life. Helping pupils to acquire industrial literacy is not an easy task, particularly when this seems to require that people from industry be involved in the process. Teachers are often discouraged when their initial overtures to industry appear unwelcome, or are met with a barrage of criticism of the school system. Just as a teacher would be hesitant to talk to the shop-floor about education, people from industry are reticent to return to school; it is most helpful, therefore, to approach individuals with a specific task in mind. It is worth the effort since experience suggests that, once people from industry and the trade-union movement have seen a comprehensive school at work, they have a far clearer idea of the teaching task and can make a more informed contribution to the schools–industry debate.

One of the problems with studying industry through local institutions and the experience of local working people is that it can be too easy to ignore those who are out of work. In addition, pupils are not introduced to alternative forms of economic organization; a local study tends to 'fossilize' the pupils' perception of industry. Unemployment is a major feature of the industrial scene in many parts of Britain and many teachers would consider it important to understand the reasons for the lack of industrial activity. We would argue that the strategy of using local 'adults other than teachers' is crucially important since it helps pupils to see the relationship between the world of economics – as they find it portrayed in the media with its problems of 'downturns in the international economy' and 'international competitiveness' – and the changing fortunes of the local economic community. Pupils will gain a greater understanding if they examine the implications of recession for local employers and trade unionists and for those who are out of work; and they can begin to look at some of the alternatives to traditional employment in their own communities.

For teachers trying to enlist the assistance of the industrial community, there are certainly frustrations when, for example, firms that have been persuaded to work with a school close down completely or cut back on the time they allow their employees for involvement in such work. However, the need to help pupils understand the interdependence of the enterprises in the British economy does not diminish. Many teachers who have experience of the processes involved in learning about industry, particularly in offering pupils opportunities to work alongside a range of adults other than teachers, have pointed to the increased self-confidence and autonomy gained by pupils. These are skills needed for survival in a world with or without work. The traditional examination courses do not provide pupils with a whole range of skills needed for working life, and yet for many, until recently, they have been the passport to working life.

Perhaps one of the most difficult areas to tackle is that of attitude change. Many people see the development of industrial understanding at school as the key to bringing about fundamental changes in attitudes towards industry. The role of schooling in moulding attitudes is debatable; certainly, a large survey of pupils in Industry Project schools revealed that pupils did not regard schools as being as important in shaping their views as their families and the media. What is clear is the meagre knowledge pupils have of industry; any teacher who has asked pupils to role play an industrial scene without giving them advice will point to the enormous ignorance revealed and the desire to stereotype the participants. By providing pupils with more personal experience of and relationships with working people, pupils might have more informed, although not necessarily more positive, judgements.

Further reading

For teachers

Dale, R., *et al.*, *Schooling and the National Interest* (Falmer Press in conjunction with the Open University, 1981).

Holmes, S., and Jamieson, I.M., *Schools Industry Practice. An Approach through Key Questions* (Schools Council Industry Project, 1982).

Jamieson, I.M., and Lightfoot, M., *Schools and Industry* (Methuen Educational, 1982).

Sanday, A., and Birch, P., *Understanding Industrial Society. Teachers' Guide* (Hodder & Stoughton, 1979).

Willis, P.E., *Learning to Labour* (Saxon House, 1977).

For pupils

Baddeley, J.M., *Understanding Industry* (Butterworth, 1980).

Cambridge University Press for the Industry Project, pupil booklets:

  Industrial Relations
  Trade Unions
  Employers
  Industry and Money
  Industry and the Environment
  Work and the Individual
  Futures and Alternatives

From Education for the Industrial Society Project:

  Industrial Relations: A Depth Study by C.J. Lockyer.
  The Toy Industry: A Resource for Teachers of Business Studies and Economics by R.D. Wilson.

Sanday, A., and Birch, P., *Understanding Industrial Society* (Hodder & Stoughton, 1979).

11 Economics and Social Education
Alain G. Anderton

The contribution of economics to social education
'Social education' is an umbrella term that covers a multitude of sins.
Numerous are the Mode III CSEs that aim to teach everything from
careers education to sex education, from consumer education to personal skills. What links this amorphous mass of divergent material is
the idea that the person being educated will somehow or other be better
fitted to live in society as a result of pursuing such a course.[1] 'Better
fitted' means, for instance, being a more careful consumer, a worker
who is more aware of his or her working environment or simply a
person who is better able to deal with himself and other people.

At its worst, such courses can degenerate into 'social slops' courses.
Because the subject-matter is so diverse, everybody and anybody is
considered able to teach social education. Rather like sixth-form
general studies, social education is often used as a timetable filler. The
consequence is that it is often badly taught, not only in terms of material
being put across to the learner, but also in terms of the motivation
engendered in the pupils themselves.

As economists we ought to be concerned about this since so much of
social education is in fact economically based. The world of work, for
instance, often considered essential background knowledge for careers
education, contains important economic concepts. Consumer education equally brings up fundamental economic questions. The most
obvious economic part of social education is money management, often
with an unduly heavy concentration on financial institutions. However,
there are other areas where economics plays a part. Political literacy
requires an understanding of the main economic issues facing a locality,
a nation and indeed the world. Voting often necessitates choosing
between different economic programmes. Even computer appreciation
courses are peddling some science fiction economics proclaiming the
good news that high unemployment is here to stay for ever owing to
automation. Economics, then, can play an important role in social
education.

Economics, social education and the curriculum
In the context of social education, economics can be found in three
main areas of the curriculum: as an economics course in its own right, as

part of a general education course, or as part of another academic or vocational school subject such as home economics.

Social economics as an academic subject is offered by only one O-level examination board, the AEB. The syllabus covers three main areas. 'Individuals and the Economy' looks at the world of work, the consumer, the distribution of income and production. The second area, 'The State and the Individual', looks at the way in which the government affects the individual through its taxation and spending policies, as well as looking at broader policy, *vis à vis* inflation, employment and conservation. The third area, 'Britain and the World', considers foreign trade, and in particular our relations with the European Community and developing countries.

What distinguishes this course from a straight economics course is that 'the syllabus is designed round the individual'.[2] Thus, 'most of the syllabus is sequential, working outwards from the individual . . . to the state and then to international considerations'.[3]

Mode I and Mode III CSE courses exist to complement this course. These too have as their focus the interaction between the individual, society and the economy.

General education courses are becoming increasingly popular as curriculum designers try to find somewhere on the timetable to fit in a whole host of relatively new areas considered important enough to be part of the curriculum. The philosophies of such courses vary widely. They may be an unashamed rag-bag of topics that it is felt are sufficiently important to have in the core curriculum, but not as separate courses. Or the course might be social science-based, where social science is not interpreted as narrowly as sociology. Or the course might be part of the pastoral curriculum, where it is the personal tutor who is teacher.

Whatever the philosophy, it is rare to find such a course devoid of any economic content.[4]

Unfortunately there is a great difference between economic content and teaching pupils economics. It is all too easy at this level to reduce such courses to lists of facts without providing pupils with any theoretical framework within which they can build an understanding of the real world.

Lastly, many academic or vocational courses have a social economics component. If we consider the JMB, some courses with social economic content are:

1 'British Economic and Social History, from the Early Eighteenth Century to the Present Day – topics include trade unionism, free trade, banking and monetary policy, the welfare state.
2 'Social Science' – includes work and types of economy.

3 'Integrated Humanities' – includes work and consumer affairs.
4 'Commercial Mathematics' – includes money management calculations.
5 'Computer Studies' – includes computers and employment.

The JMB O-level home economics course contains virtually no economics. However, its A-level covers the welfare state, marketing and cost of food, family expenditure and consumer protection.

Again, it is important to remind ourselves that the presence of economic content does not mean that any economics will actually be taught. It will be argued below that a topic such as trade unions can be taught without bringing out any economic concepts at all.

Having looked at where economics as part of social education may be found in the curriculum, we will look more specifically at the economic components of social education.

Money management

Money management is often what non-economists believe economics is all about, since money is seen as synonymous with the economy. Certainly money is fundamental to our economic system. However, at the 14–16 level, money management normally has little to do with academic economics.

A possible syllabus would be:

1 Budgeting – the allocation of income to different forms of consumption, such as housing, food and fuel.
2 Methods of payment – cash, cheques, standing orders, credit cards, etc.
3 Saving – reasons for saving, including the need for pension provision, methods of saving short and long term.
4 Borrowing – reasons for borrowing, methods of borrowing such as mortgages, overdrafts, credit cards, hire purchase and loans. Advantages and disadvantages of being in debt.
5 Insurance – the need to mitigate risk, risks to be insured, levels of insurance needed.
6 Income – how an individual can gain purchasing power.

The rationale for such a course is very persuasive. It argues that every pupil will need to manage money.[5] In our modern economy, as incomes increase, money management becomes more and more complex. Pupils therefore need to be prepared so that they can manage their money wisely and be aware of problems that can arise in an always uncertain and sometimes dishonest world.

Money-management courses often degenerate into a catalogue of facts – 'the mortgage rate is 10 per cent, mortgages can be obtained from building societies, mortgage interest is subject to tax relief'. This is not particularly useful to the pupils, first, because facts are constantly changing, and second, because facts do not help provide a framework for future decision-making.

Economics as a discipline can help provide that framework. For instance, the above syllabus could be rearranged as follows:

1 Scarcity – spending for an individual can never be infinite. It is constrained by the levels of income and wealth of the individual.
2 Choice – at every point in the individual's budget he is faced by choices. Because his purchasing power is finite, he has to choose between different forms of consumption, between consumption and saving, between different methods of payment, etc. The concept of opportunity cost is particularly useful here because pupils should be aware that taking one course of action (e.g. buying a motorbike) necessarily results in the impossibility of taking other courses of action (e.g. buying a hi-fi system).
3 Economic efficiency – is the consumer spending his money such that he is obtaining the largest possible basket of goods and services? For instance, spending at hypermarkets and discount stores is likely to lead to greater efficiency of spending for the individual than shopping at local corner shops. Is the consumer allocating his purchases in such a way as to maximize his welfare? To what extent is he wasting scarce resources because he purchases goods only to find that they do not yield the anticipated utility? To what extent is this poor money management the result of advertisements and other promotions on the part of companies? Will his utility be maximized by choosing to consume now rather than at some future date (saving and borrowing)? Will reducing everyday risks through insurance be worth the premiums to be paid?
4 Rises in living standards. How could an individual secure rises in living standards? A discussion of the possibility of increasing income, making use of goods and services that are free to the individual and generally altering lifestyles to secure the availability of more goods and services within a given budget would help here.

This framework of scarcity, choice, efficiency and rising living standards could provide a sound basis for pupils to move into the complex adult world. It is good economics and avoids a concentration on a wealth of petty detail that is of little help to the learner.[6]

Consumer education

Everybody is a consumer and one of the prime aims of consumer education is to enable the individual to function more effectively in this role in the economy. However, consumer education is often also seen as providing a vehicle for considering some of the more global issues, such as pollution, the 'rat race', the over-exploitation of natural resources, the balance of power between producer and consumer and the quality of life.[7]

The tendency is for such courses to revolve around facts: 'What are your rights under the Weights and Measures Act 1963?' 'What are the functions of the Office of Fair Trading?' A more sophisticated approach is a problem-solving one: 'If you buy a pair of jeans with a tear in it, what are your rights?' 'If you decide to sue a retailer, what is the cheapest way of doing so?' Neither approach, however valid, is an economic one.

An economic approach might develop along the following lines:

1   Scarcity – the consumer lives in a finite world. On a personal level, consumption is limited by income and wealth. On a global plane, resources available for production are also finite, and will determine both present and future consumption possibilities.

2   Choice – every consumer has to make a choice. The opportunity cost of the purchase of one good is another good that is now no longer available.

3   Efficiency – if consumers are rational they will seek to maximize the basket of goods that they are able to consume. A shopping survey will easily illustrate the fact that prices for the same products differ between retail outlets. Careful shopping will enable the consumer to make his scarce income go further. A rational consumer will also wish to maximize the utility to be gained in the consumption of a good. Shoes that quickly fall apart or washing-machines that break down three months after purchase are examples of ways in which maximum utility will not be gained. Consumer rights in law can then be seen as a way of correcting economic inefficiency in the market-place. Allocative efficiency – maximizing utility through buying the right combination of goods – is also an important concept. Pupils should be made to consider how consumers' spending patterns are distorted by advertising and other sales techniques.

4   The market – a study of the market-place is needed in order to understand the interaction between producers and consumers. The concepts of consumer sovereignty and knowledge are very important in this content. Consumer sovereignty returns us to the theme of sales techniques. It also opens up the idea of the need for counter-valuing power through consumer laws and organizations. Knowledge returns us to economic efficiency, for the further away from a state of perfect knowledge is the consumer, the more he needs the help of consumer organizations such as the Consumers' Association. Oligopoly theory could be used at a more advanced

level to explain why non-homogeneity of goods exists in so many markets and to lead into a discussion of whether a proliferation of products benefits the consumer.

The world of work

Paradoxically, preparation for the world of work in schools increased in popularity in the 1970s as the chances of pupils obtaining jobs declined. More often than not, this area is covered as essential background material for careers education.

A number of arguments are put forward to justify education concerning itself with the world of work:

1 It will enable the learner to be more aware of the career possibilities open to him or her.
2 The learner will have a better appreciation of his rights in his future workplace.
3 Industry will benefit because future workers will be more aware of their responsibilities and in particular more aware of the need for private industry to make profits.

Content is likely to centre narrowly on choice of career, how to deal with teenage unemployment and conditions to be found in the workplace. Trade unionism may also get a mention. A fairly extensive coverage of this area can be found in the 'Work' unit in JMB's Integrated Humanities O-level course.[8]

The scope for the development of economic concepts in this area is enormous. Career choice, for instance, is an application of the concept of opportunity cost. Potential workers have to make a choice between a number of different occupations. The skills they have to offer are not unlimited (i.e. their human capital is scarce). Since demand is also limited, they will find that they will only have a limited choice of occupations. Potential workers therefore have to maximize the use of their scarce human capital. All too many youngsters today have insufficient human capital to obtain employment. In that case, the only choice facing that person may be unemployment or some government work scheme.

Studies of characteristics of work will involve the concept of specialization. The advantages and disadvantages of the division of labour are likely to get some mention. Highly specialized mechanized jobs, for instance, are likely to be monotonous and boring leading to worker alienation and industrial strife.

When discussing wage levels, pupils could be introduced to the concepts of demand, supply and labour markets. Trade unionism will inevitably bring up the idea of protecting workers' interests. Among these interests will be the 'protection' of wages. Strong trade unions act in such a way as to increase the scarcity of labour within their market, thus pushing up wages.

It is, of course, possible to mention wages, trade unions, assembly line work, etc. without introducing any economics. However, a school leaver equipped with some economic concepts is likely to be better able to deal with the world of work than one without these concepts.

Economics and political literacy

The concept of political literacy, the successor to 'civics' or 'citizenship', has enjoyed the same rise in educational fortunes in the 1970s and early 1980s as the concept of economic literacy. Just as pupils ought to be prepared for their future economic environment, so they should prepare for effective participation in the decision-making processes of the nation. In order to be able to participate effectively, citizens need to have an understanding of the main economic issues of the day. This is because so much of political decision-making is concerned with economics.

Again, what is considered relevant and what is left out is very much open to debate, as with all the topics in social education. However, economics components of a political literacy programme might possibly include:

1 Types of economic system – free market v. mixed v. planned economies.
2 Government spending – its size and distribution.
3 Taxation – its scope and incidence.
4 Public sector enterprises – their role in the economy, nationalization and denationalization.
5 Government economic policy – its effect on inflation, employment, growth, the balance of payments and the environment. Methods by which the government can implement policies such as fiscal policy, monetary policy, prices and incomes policy, and import controls.
6 The effect of government on the distribution of income – welfare services, national insurance, social security, taxation and government spending.

The above content would not disgrace half an O-level economics course, and it serves to show how much good economics can be dealt with in this area.

Methods of teaching in this area are little different from those used when covering these topics in a traditional economics course. However, it should be remembered that this is part of a political literacy course. As such, topics should be approached from the political standpoint. For instance, when considering the size of the public sector, pupils ought to be made aware of party division on this issue and the relationship between voting behaviour, class, income distribution and party policy deserves study.

Conclusion

It is now widely recognized that social education should form part of the core curriculum. What is less clear is exactly what social education means in practice, and where it ought to appear on a typical school curriculum. Economics can make an impressive claim to being a necessary part of a social education programme. It may well be that in the next ten years economics 14–16 will increasingly be found not in specialized economics courses but as part of a general education package. Economics teachers need to be aware of this development, so that they can make a persuasive claim for time on such courses.

Notes and references

1. See, for instance, the importance placed by head teachers, economics teachers and commerce teachers on 'personal economics' in a survey conducted for the Phase 1 of the Economics Education 14–16 Project. Summary: Holley B.J., 'The Project: A Summary of the Findings of Phase 1', *Economics*, vol. 16, pt 3, no. 71, autumn 1980.
2. AEB Economics Syllabus II, Social Economics 061, Guidance Notes.
3. Ibid.
4. One such published course is 'Active Tutorial Work' developed in Lancashire in the late 1970s and early 1980s as a pastoral curriculum programme. Fundamental to its philosophy is the idea that the pastoral curriculum can be programmed in the same way as any academic curriculum. In the last year of compulsory schooling, the course has a number of 'economic' units.
   (i)   Why do we go to work?
   (ii)   Finding out from the world of work – what is it like?
   (iii) Looking to the workaday world (terms such as gross pay, sickness benefit and giro).
   (iv)   Which job? Will I get it?
   (v)   Money in your life
   (vi)   Joining the union
   (vii) What is the difference (between school and work or unemployment)?

   As can be seen, the emphasis is mainly on the world of work, with some money management as well. Consumer education and the economic part of political literacy are not present. Published courses are not, however, prescriptive and it is up to the economist in a school to argue the case for more economic content.
5. Future money managers are 'helped' to develop the 'right' attitudes by organizations such as the Banking Education Service, the British Insurance Association, and the Life Offices' Association.
6. Regular features on money management are contained in the *Times Educational Supplement*.
7. See Maclean, R., 'A case for consumer education in schools', *Economics*,

vol. 17, pt 2, no. 74, summer 1981; and Jensen, H.R., 'Some reflections', *Economics*, summer 1981.

8. Namely:
    i. The need to work and the effects of work.
        (a) Work to obtain a livelihood and to retain self-respect: the nature, extent, and effects of unemployment.
        (b) Work to improve the standard of living: the relationship of prosperity and production, payment for imports with exports, maintenance of the balance of trade.
        (c) The need for specialization of work activities in an industrialized society compared with work patterns involved in subsistence for individuals.
    ii. The spheres of work.
        Manufacturing, services, mining, farming, fishing.
        (a) Location.
        (b) Nature of the typical work in each sphere.
        (c) Interdependence of spheres of work.
        (d) Constraints on choice of work: qualifications, opportunities, job satisfaction.
    iii. The organization of work.
        (a) Ownership: state, public, private.
        (b) Management: functions.
        (c) Workers: trade unionism.
        (d) Relationship of owner managers and workers: collective bargaining, dispute procedures, worker participation in ownership and management.
    iv. The government and work.
        (a) The distribution of work: the relocation of work, development areas.
        (b) The protection of work: subsidies and grants, import controls.
        (c) The control of work: control of wages, prices and dividends; monopoly and competition, restrictive practices, taxation.
        (d) The regulation of work: legislation concerning working conditions, product standards, fair trading consumer protection.

12 Comparative Economics
Vivian Anthony

There are many reasons for the remarkable growth in the teaching of economics in schools and colleges, but not the least of them is its relevance to the world around us. It deals with matters that are in constant debate in the media and that seem to affect our own lives in a fundamental way. A further attraction to students has stemmed from the fact that in economics there has been a stimulating process of curriculum development and a lively exchange of ideas on methodology. It is, of course, easier for a comparatively 'young' teaching subject to adopt an enterprising curriculum philosophy; one that is ready to challenge the existing credo. Moreover this is a fundamental feature of the science of economics. The dialectic approach requires the propounding of new theories to explain emerging phenomena. The new theory soon comes under challenge and alternative theories are put forward. The new established 'wisdom' will be a synthesis of these theories.

If economics is to continue to hold a major place in the curriculum of schools and colleges in an era when considerable change is likely – the emergence of newer subjects like computer studies and electronics, the development of other social subjects like politics and sociology, and the efforts of long-established subjects like modern languages and history to restore their position – then economics must continue to be vigorous in its curriculum development and determination to maintain its relevance and coherence.

The responsibility of university economists for developing and challenging the established wisdom of the subject is clearly recognized. Most of what is now taught in schools was first taught in the universities. Teachers in the secondary sector have a major responsibility for keeping up with the advances made in higher education and finding suitable teaching methods to enable the new ideas to be incorporated into the syllabus. Examiners, subject associations, lecturers in education departments and teachers themselves all have a vital part to play in this process.

Because most curriculum ideas filter *down* through the education system, they emerge first in schools and colleges at A-level, in Scottish Highers or the equivalent in colleges of further education. This chapter is concerned with the teaching of comparative economics, an area that is likely to be of growing significance in the coming decade. Comparative economics is concerned not only with the different economic systems and theories for resource allocation but also with the way in which different countries tackle their current economic problems. So the subject-matter includes a knowledge and understanding of market systems, command and mixed economies and of developed and developing economies. All the principles and tools of economics can be applied in a comparative dimension: indeed it can be argued that this is more relevant than exclusively national application. The problems of inflation, balance of payments, unemployment, economic growth and so on are faced in different degrees by all countries and each country has its own way of dealing with the problems. Furthermore, there are world economic problems that can only be tackled by co-operation between countries. Some countries co-operate in economic blocs: the relationships within and between these communities are of considerable significance. International economic institutions have been established to aid the process of international economic co-operation. Comparative economics deals with all these matters. The interaction between different economies through trade, payments, interest rates, exchange rates, etc., is a field in which university specialists have evolved sophisticated theories supported by high-level econometric analysis, but the same is true of many of the topic areas presently studied by A-level students. We do not expect students of economics at the secondary level to handle these theories and analyses.

All the current 'upper secondary' syllabuses expect students to have some knowledge of institutions in the British economy. They must be able to apply economic principles in the analysis of current problems. They will need 'a knowledge of the significant events and features of policy in recent years and . . . a broad understanding of the origins of the problems' (JMB). It is right and proper that students of economics should first and foremost have a good working knowledge of the economy of their own country. However, it would be a sadly inadequate syllabus that relied entirely on the home country for an analysis of economic problems and the methods used to deal with them. An insular attitude in economics is no more acceptable than it would be in geography or history. Britain is heavily dependent on its economic relations with other countries; in its trade, its services, its membership of international institutions and economic communities. There is no reason to believe that Britain is so successful in dealing with its problems that we have no need to study the methods used by other countries to solve those problems. A pointer to an improvement in Britain's performance might come from a study of the methods used elsewhere. Students will be quick to see the relevance and importance of such study though they will need to be aware that policies that are successful elsewhere will not always transplant readily to other countries.

Britain can be said to operate a mixed economy some way between a market economy on the one hand and the command economy on the other. It is perhaps not surprising that most teachers have concentrated their efforts on explaining the workings of the former. However, this system has been operated very differently in different countries. Even within a country, different political parties can produce substantial variations in the way the economy is managed. Judged against such criteria as growth of GNP, or industrial production, the level of unemployment or even control of inflation, Britain cannot claim to be doing well when compared with other countries operating a similar economic system and at a similar stage of development. It is important for the student to examine the reasons for the varying levels of success. If industrial relations are worse in Britain than in other industrialized countries – and that is open to argument – are there things we can learn from other countries to improve our performance? Concentration on the market and even mixed systems ignores the fact that over two-thirds of all the people in the world live in economies of a different type. Our students will find it difficult to understand the economic perspectives of these people without knowing something of their economic system and how they carry out their resource allocation. Why do the people of Poland suffer from such severe economic dislocation? Such study and analysis is a useful way of acquainting the student with the methods used by economists in the real world and it should give them an awareness of the different situations in which the economist operates. Comparative economics will thus not only extend students' knowledge and deepen the understanding but it can help them to develop the higher-order skills of synthesis, analysis and evaluation.

The basic concepts of economics are the same whether they are applied in the single or the comparative dimension. It is not necessary to extend the range of concepts but rather to show how the same concepts are applicable to a greater or lesser extent in different economies. It should not be beyond students of the upper secondary level to learn how to make sensible comparisons between countries and economies. Piaget concluded in *The Growth of Logical Thinking* that at this age students should have reached the stage of intellectual development when they can make intelligent generalizations of their own from a number of given instances. It is of course possible to introduce comparisons in several ways, not only between economic systems, countries within a system and policies of parties within a country, but also comparisons over time. The study of economic history involves an important comparative element. Obviously we should guard against making the comparative study too complicated. Professor Peston observed in his presidential address to the Economics Association in

1982 that explanations in economics need to be simple. He warned against making things too difficult for teachers to understand or, even worse, too difficult for examiners to understand!

The need for the comparative element in a social study has been recognized by teachers of other subjects for some time. It is at the heart of a study of geography. In history, papers in European or American history are not uncommon. In politics, the comparative study of the political systems of the USA and France is a valuable part of some syllabuses.

The introduction of the teaching of comparative economics

While elements of comparative economics as described above have appeared in syllabuses for many years, a significant step forward came with the report of the Economics Commissioned Group (based on the Economics Association) to the Schools Council as part of the research programme studies on the N- and F-level proposals. As the representative of the Steering Committee of the Schools Council, I was the adviser to this group, which was chaired by the late Brian Robinson.* A full report of the findings of the Working Party was published in *Economics*, volume 14, part 1, no. 61, spring 1978. We were instructed to examine the feasibility of a specific N- and F-level model. Our report recommends the use of syllabuses that are more relevant to the economic reality of the modern world. Our F-level brief required us to consider the introduction of comparative economics into the syllabus, but we consider this dimension to be of such crucial relevance that substantial elements are included at N-level. The Working Party picked out certain topics for inclusion in a syllabus suitable for these levels of examining. They included at N-level 'Pricing and planning in command economies'. 'International trade groupings', 'Comparisons of standards of living between countries and over time' and 'Economic growth in different economic systems'. F-level involved a more detailed treatment of N-level topics plus some additional topics. They advocated case studies involving comparisons of living standards, one of which must be a developing country, the second a command economy and the third the UK. The opening statement in the introduction to the F-level syllabus was that 'this syllabus seeks to achieve its aims and objectives by involving the student *throughout the course* with the study of developments in the UK economy and those of either a command economy or a developing country'. In studying government decision-making, it was suggested as an example that reference might be made to 'Soviet economic development plans and their annual modifications'. Also

---

* The other members of the group were I.R. Credland, P.M.Davis, E.S.Janes, A. Maclehose and C.L. Marsden.

included in the comparative element of the syllabus was a knowledge of the aims and functions of such international institutions as the IMF, the IBRD and the GATT. It was recognized that students could not be expected to have detailed knowledge of particular government decisions. Case studies of chosen economies were suggested as a more realistic approach. It was expected that candidates would be able to make reference where appropriate to the countries chosen for their 'on-going' study. The ultimate conclusion of the group was that 'it is possible, even within the time constraints of the N-level syllabus (three-fifths of A-level), to introduce a comparative dimension between economic systems concerning basic theory and relevant institutions'. A similar conclusion was reached by the Oxford and Cambridge Board Group, which produced an alternative syllabus for N and F economics, and described the comparative element as 'the application of fundamental concepts to alternative economic systems'.

The comparative element in existing syllabuses

Most of the syllabuses at the upper secondary level of education contain some elements that involve the study of international institutions and economies outside the UK. The Cambridge Board A-level economics syllabus requires the study of the central problem of economic societies, the IMF and international monetary arrangements and problems of comparison of national income over time and between countries. JMB refer to classification of national economies by their system of allocation; the contrast of 'developing' and 'advanced' economies; the generation of income in the international economy, problems of comparing levels and rates of growth over time and between economies. In the statement of aims and objectives of the Scottish Certificate of Education Board and O-grade examination, is the sentence 'pupils should be able to understand that there are different ways of organizing an economic system to achieve a greater production of wealth, e.g. private enterprise, planned economy, mixed economy'. Teachers are expected to develop an understanding of the need for responsible use of resources for promotion of economic welfare of our own and other societies at different stages of development. Pupils should be able to understand that different communities are at different stages of economic development, and that the economic policy of one community has effects on the production and use of resources in other communities. The syllabus for the Certificate of Sixth Year Studies for 1983 included the option 'Standards of Living in the European Economic Community'. Included in the syllabus for Higher Grade are the effects on economic policies of membership of international trading and monetary organizations, and international economic development – problems of primary producers; patterns of aid and trade; relations between developed and less-developed countries.

The Oxford Board syllabus requires study of the central problem of economic societies. At A-level, London lists 'the alternative resource allocation systems in different societies' among its objectives. London has a large overseas market and candidates are invited to illustrate their answers from the UK economy or the economy of their own country, or both. The O-level syllabus includes 'trading blocs' and their effect on international trade and the role of major international institutions. The syllabuses of the other boards include similar references. The Northern Ireland Board syllabus includes comparison of national income between countries, the problems of developing countries, customs unions and free trade areas, IMF, GATT, the World Bank. AEB include most of the above and add 'world population problems'.

Perhaps the best-developed syllabus with a comparative dimension is that of the Cambridge Board A-level 'Economic and Public Affairs', though this is a much broader syllabus than that of any A-level economics syllabus. For example, Paper 3 is concerned with World Affairs since 1945. The aim of this subject is 'to promote the understanding of international relations and evolution of present-day political systems, economic conditions and social life of other peoples'. Economic topics detailed for study include: world population and migration problems; factors influencing world economic relations; problems of low-income countries; the US economy; USSR economic planning and achievements; organization of industry and agriculture; the Middle East oil industry and its significance.

It is not surprising to find the International Baccalaureate among the front runners in developing the teaching and examining of a significant element of comparative economics. The IB was established more than twenty years ago, in an attempt to find an examinations system that would be acceptable as a qualification in all the countries of the world. The IB has gained a wide reputation but there are still relatively few candidates in Britain. Atlantic College, the first of the United World Colleges, has done some excellent work in developing suitable syllabuses. Alan Glanville, the head of economics, has a realistic view of the difficulties involved in teaching comparative economics: he has written the following advice to teachers of the IB economics syllabus:

Students need to be familiar with resource allocation in centrally planned countries, and specifically the USSR, as well as in mixed economies. They should also be aware of the particular differences and difficulties of the developing countries, including the very poorest societies. This will be one of the biggest problems facing the new IB teacher and probably one of the most rewarding. Most textbooks cover in detail the working of western industrialized nations, markets, unions, firms, etc. The student could be entirely forgiven for thinking that no one lived in any other economic system than those of the European, North American type. Teachers will find very little on large-scale poverty, development and the socialist countries in most textbooks. Much of what is available on development is either very general or too complex, being aimed at the general public or at graduates. Many of the books on planned economies are also difficult and blend history, politics and ideology with economic theory and structure. Political bias may also reduce usefulness. The study of economics in these countries is often subsumed under politics, which adds to the difficulty of study by using different terms and concepts. Sources that are available, useful and at the right level are included in the book list [see Appendix 12.2]. Nevertheless, it is in these areas that the IB differs in emphasis from most national syllabuses and it is in these areas that teachers will need to collect resources and to strengthen their own knowledge. The individual teacher will need to plan more flexibly with respect to other IB teachers than is perhaps the case within a national examination system. The economy in which the school is located is likely to be utilized extensively for applied work. Comparison with similar economies is conceptually not difficult, though more and better source material is required.

A more detailed consideration of the IB economics syllabus is to be recommended.

The study of comparative economics has been advocated for students below sixth-form age. When Brian Holley and Valerie Skelton came to write the Final Report of Phase 1 of the Economics Education 14–16 Project in 1978 they concluded:

in respect of comparative economic systems we recommend that (a) pupils' economic perspectives be broadened beyond that of their own national economy to include some appreciation of other major western-style economies (e.g. USA, Japan or other EEC countries) and economies that are not based on this model; (b) in the case of these other types of economy pupils should develop some awareness of the operation of developing economies, planned economies and traditional economies, and of the differences between these and 'western-style' economies.

A high proportion of the head teachers and economics teachers surveyed rated comparative economics as an important part of an economics course.

The Oxford and Cambridge Board syllabus

The process of syllabus revision continues almost without a pause with most examination boards. If the actual rubric is not changing then the way it is interpreted by chief examiners certainly will be. In 1978 the Oxford and Cambridge Board began a major revision of Paper II of their A-level economics, previously known as 'The British Economy'. After consultation with schools, it was decided to include four elements within an 'Applied Economics' paper, namely: the British economy, documents and commentaries, numeracy, and comparative economics. Candidates were required to answer questions from at least three of the sections. The questions were to deal with the application of basic principles and relating economic concepts to a knowledge of current institutions, structures and activities, both within the UK and in other countries. The comparative section is not compulsory, but, if the candidate opts for it, a maximum of two questions may be answered. Five questions are set, two of which relate to international institutions. One of these will be on the IMF, GATT or the World Bank, and the other on the EEC. Candidates need to study the policies of the EEC and how they affect Britain and other member countries. The three remaining questions are set on the three main types of economic system – command, developing and developed industrial. It is expected that schools will concentrate on one country from which candidates can illustrate their points. The teacher decides whether it is worth sacrificing the depth of study of one country to broaden the choice of questions by studying two or three countries more superficially.

The 'comparative' syllabus is not as broad as that for the British economy, but it does include most major topics – economic growth, national income, multinationals, industrial development, industrial relations, employment, nationalized industries, distribution of wealth and income, government policy objectives, money supply and international trade. The questions set are usually of a broad nature to give the candidate a chance to show his knowledge, understanding and power of analysis. This section of the paper is proving more and more popular; over half of the candidates attempted questions from it in 1982 and 1983. The most popular questions are those that relate to the EEC and to international institutions, but developing countries are attracting more and more attention from students. While relatively few candidates have offered answers on comparative questions involving other industrialized countries, a growing number are studying a command economy.

Comparative economics teaching in the USA

Three months visiting schools and universities in the USA in 1983 convinced me that economics education has taken very different lines of development from those in Britain. While the major growth in English schools has been at A-level and only recently has attention been turned to the earlier years of secondary education, in the USA the opposite is true. The work that has for years been at the heart of sixth-form economics is considered more appropriate to American college courses. However, in many US school districts, the teaching of economics in high schools is compulsory: a course in economics is a requirement for graduation. While there is a good deal of vagueness about the exact content of these courses, a widely agreed element is a comparative study. The excellently produced textbooks for these high-school courses contain a selection on communist, socialist, developing and free-enterprise economies. Britain is firmly placed among the 'socialist' economies. Those who are interested to see how American textbooks handle the comparative element should consult: B.S. Schiller, *The Economy Today* (Random House); Sampson, Mortenson and Marienhoff, *The American Economy: Analysis, Issues, Principles* (Houghton Mifflin; and, R.B. Carson, *Economic Issues Today* (New York, St Martin's Press).

The problems of teaching comparative economics

The working party on N & F in 1976 highlighted a major problem: 'teaching resource materials are not yet adequate enough to enable us to effectively tackle comparative economics in many areas with students of this age. There is particularly a shortage of coverage of command and developing economies in existing school textbooks.' However, there has been a considerable improvement in the position since 1976, perhaps justifying their comment that 'there is no better stimulus to the development of teaching resources than the inclusion of a new element in examination board syllabuses'. The book list that appears in Appendix 12.2 gives some indication of what is available. Not all these books are suited to the needs of the A-level student; some are too difficult, others contain too much detail and others are not entirely relevant. However, all of them contain some useful material and would, at least, be valuable as reference books for the teacher. The book by Marsden, Adams and Crewdson, *An Introduction to Comparative Economics*, was written with the A-level student in mind. Moreover, even the critics recognize that there is a considerable amount of material freely available. All four of the major clearing banks publish regular country reports, which are relatively easy to digest. For example, the Barclays ABECOR report on the USSR has paragraphs on economic policy, industry, standard of living, agriculture, foreign trade, economic indicators, the present situation and outlook. This report, which runs to less than 2,000 words, is typical of the material from the banks and provides some valuable material for illustrating lessons and examination answers. The National Westminster report on Nigeria is rather broader in scope, covering politics as well as the domestic economy, oil and gas, other sectors, development, external economy and prospects, and providing some very useful economic statistics.

Given the constraints involved in a two-year A-level syllabus, it is important that the teaching material is easily digestible. It is, of course, true that time spent on the comparative element is time not available for teaching other aspects of economics. It is important that it is seen as a vehicle for the application of economic principles and not simply the accumulation of knowledge. In this respect, *The Economist* briefs, *Europe's Economies* and *The World Economy*, set excellent examples. The bank reviews are publishing a growing number of articles in this field. *The Times* supplements are usually well written and interesting, if not always entirely relevant. The embassies are usually very helpful in providing information and speakers on their countries. Co-operation with geography departments in schools would also be useful, for, just as the historians provide a useful overlap in some aspects of our course, so the skills used by the geographers could be relevant to the comparative element.

Doubt has been expressed about the capacity of A-level students to make effective comparisons. Clearly, it requires skills that are seldom adequately tested in other parts of the syllabus. The successful application of these skills effectively distinguishes the able candidate from the rest. The weakness of the answers of the less able to the questions in the comparative section of the Oxford and Cambridge paper is not so much the lack of knowledge displayed but in the inability to apply it effectively in a comparative dimension. It will be some time before students or even teachers feel really confident in handling the analysis of other economic systems. However, there is no doubt that such analysis is worthwhile and considered relevant, interesting and challenging by the student. As confidence grows, more and more economics teachers will want to include this element in their teaching. No doubt they will be stimulated by the publication of the proceedings of the 1982 conference of the Economics Association, where comparative economics was the theme and published in *Economics*, volume 19, part 2, no. 82, summer 1983. While we must heed the advice to make haste slowly, we must not allow those who wish to take advantage of the opportunities offered by comparative economics to be frustrated by the argument that this is the preserve of economists in higher education.

Appendix 12.1

Some A-level questions in comparative economics

1. Explain what is meant by the term 'standard of living'. Discuss how living standards in countries such as the UK and India are likely to be affected by current trends in their respective rates of population growth. (*JMB*)
2. What factors are important in determining the world price of oil? Discuss how increases in oil prices may affect (a) poverty in the Middle East and (b) affluence in Western capitalist economies. (*JMB*)
3. Why did the UK experience slow growth relative to most other developed countries in the period 1962–1972? (*Southern Regional Examining Board*)
4. (a) What is the difference between a Customs Union and a Free Trade Area? Illustrate your answer with examples.
   (b) What would be the implications for the UK of the establishment of economic and monetary union in the EEC? (*SREB*)

5. Explain the distinction which economists make between wealth and income. How far is it possible to distinguish between advanced and less developed nations solely in these terms? (*JMB*)

6. What are the principal potential costs and benefits of multinational companies to the host countries in which they operate? (*SREB*)

7. Approximately 80 per cent of the exports of the less-developed countries are primary products.
   (a) Would economic theory predict that the dependence on primary products would produce instability in export earnings?
   (b) Would a scheme to stabilize the price of primary products be of benefit to the less-developed countries? (*SREB*)

8. Discuss the implications of rapid population growth and limited stocks of natural resources for rates of economic growth in all countries of the world. (*Oxford*)

9. What evidence would you use to substantiate the claim that the United Kingdom is one of the poorer countries of Western Europe? What are the difficulties in making such comparisons between countries? (*Oxford*)

10. In the UK the problem of unemployed labour has increased in recent years. Compare and contrast this with the situation in a communist country. (*Oxford and Cambridge*)

11. How has the developing nation you have been studying been affected by (a) the decline in world trade and (b) the rise in oil prices? Compare this with the situation in the UK. (*O & C*)

12. The report of GATT comments ' . . . all Governments continue to resist protectionist pressures. It is remarkable how well the international trade situation has held up in the face of current levels of unemployment.' Discuss the importance of GATT in the light of this statement. (*O & C*)

13. What difficulties are encountered in trying to compare the economic performance of different countries? (*Cambridge*)

14. Some under-developed countries set up industries whose costs of production exceed import prices. In the light of the law of comparative advantage how can such a policy be explained? (*N. Ireland*)

15. 'The EEC gives greater markets to West Germany and safeguards French farmers. And that is all.' Discuss. (*London*)

16. Evaluate the economic arguments for increasing the scale of aid from the developed countries to developing countries. (*London*)

17. Compare and contrast the principal economic characteristics of a free market with those of a planned economy. (*London*)

Appendix 12.2

A brief bibliography

Allen, G.C., *How Japan Competes* (Institute of Economic Affairs, 1978).

Allen, G.C., *The Japanese Economy* (Weidenfeld & Nicolson, 1981).

Berstein, H. (ed.), *Underdevelopment and Development* (Penguin, 1973).

Bhagwati, J., *Economies of Underdeveloped Countries* (World University Library, 1966).

Campbell, R.W., *Soviet Economic Power* (Macmillan, 1967).

Cheung, S.N.S., *Will China go 'Capitalist'?* (Institute of Economic Affairs, 1982).

Cipolla, C.M. (ed.), *Contemporary Economies* (Fontana, 1976).

Dahrendorf, R. (ed.), *Europe's Economy in Crisis* (Weidenfeld & Nicolson, 1982).

Denison, E.H., and Chung, W.K., *How Japan's Economy Grew so Fast* (Brookings Institution, 1976).

Donges, J.B., *What is Wrong with the European Countries?* (Institute of Economic Affairs, 1981).

Elkan, W., *Introduction to Development Economics* (Penguin, 1973).

Fields, G.S., *Poverty, Inequality and Development* (Cambridge University Press, 1981).

Freedman, R. (ed.), *Karl Marx: On Economics* (Penguin, 1971).

Hare, P., Radici, H., and Swain, N. (eds), *Hungary: A Decade of Economic Reform* (Allen & Unwin, 1981).

Horvat, B., *The Yugoslav Economic System* (M.E. Sharpe, 1980).

Howe, C., *China's Economy*, 2nd edn (Granada, 1980).

Lewis, D.E.S., *Britain and the European Economic Community* (Heinemann Educational Books, 1978).

Liggins, D., *National Economic Planning in France* (Saxon House, 1975).

Livingstone, J., *Britain and the World Economy* (Penguin, 1966).

Livingstone, I., and Ord, H.W., *Economics for Eastern Africa* (Heinemann Educational Books, 1968).

McQueen, M., *Britain, the EEC and the Developing World* (Heinemann Educational Books, 1977).

Marsden, C., Adams, S., and Crewdson, J., *An Introduction to Comparative Economics* (Heinemann Educational Books, 1980).

Myers, R.H., *The Chinese Economy: Past and Present* (Duxbury, 1980).

Myint, H., *S.E. Asia's Economy* (Penguin, n.d.).

Nove, A., *The Soviet Economy* (Allen & Unwin, 1969).

Nove, A., *The Soviet Economic System* (Allen & Unwin, 1981).

Schwartz, E., *Trouble in Eden: A Comparison of the British and Swedish Economies* (Praeger, 1980),

Swann, D., *The Economics of the Common Market* (Penguin, 1970).

Templeman, D.C., *The Italian Economy* (Praeger, 1981).

Thurrow, L.C., *The Zero-Sum Society* (Penguin, 1981).

Wilczynski, J., *The Economics of Socialism* (Allen & Unwin, 1977).

Part Four
Methods and Techniques

13 Approaches to Economics Teaching
Raymond Ryba

Introduction

> For fools rush in where angels fear to tread
> (Pope, *An Essay on Criticism*).

Pope's aphorism has a double edge in the context of this chapter: it is all
too true of teaching; it is equally so of writing about teaching. Let me
take up the second point first.

To write about teaching approaches, let alone to write about them at
chapter length, remains just as presumptious an undertaking as I
recognized it to be when I accepted the challenge to write equivalent
chapters for the first and second editions of *Teaching Economics*.[1] And
as I recognized then, the presumption is all the greater when, as the
editor requires, the writer addresses teachers in an enormous range of
school and college situations. So, in accepting the challenge yet again, I
do so on the same understanding as before: that no more is possible in
the space available than to offer a brief enumeration of principles, a
general survey of possible approaches, and a consideration of how these
approaches may be applied in the context of a rapidly developing range
of teaching aids and resources. As in previous editions, the reader is
referred for more detailed treatment to the succeeding chapters in this
part of the volume and to the increasingly impressive list of books[2] and
articles on economics teaching.[3]

There is a French proverb to the effect that the more things change
the more they remain the same. Certainly, since the last edition of
Teaching Economics, many things have changed in the teaching of
economics and in the world in which it is being taught. Numbers of
pupils learning economics in schools and colleges continue to grow
dramatically;[4] and whereas, ten years ago, economics was largely confined to the post-16 age group, an expansion has begun, and will
certainly continue, in the numbers studying the subject below sixth
form and college level.[5] The teaching force teaching economics has
expanded rapidly, as has the proportion of economics teachers with
degree-level qualifications in the subject and formal educational qualifications. The number of textbooks and other resources now available
for teaching economics at every level is incomparably greater than ten
years ago and the quality has also undoubtedly improved.[6] Major

changes have also occurred within economics, with questioning of Keynesian orthodoxy, a surging fashion, perhaps now waning again, in monetarism, and a growing respect both for inductive approaches to economics and modelling. Finally, the climate of national opinion is clearly turning from a position of indifference to economics in school curricula to one of support.[7]

All these changes and their consequences must undoubtedly influence and affect the individual teacher in his choice of approach to his teaching. Yet, at the same time, the fundamental features of the teacher's art remain essentially unchanged. That art, which, in the hands of an expert, looks so simple to the observer, is the complex and sensitive practical business of contributing to the educational development of others. And its central scene is still the classroom or lecture room. It is true, of course, that much preparatory and follow-up work is done outside the classroom, both by the teachers and by their pupils or students. It may also be that, as the years go by, the importance of the classroom will decrease. Certainly, the burgeoning influence of the microcomputer and the videotape recorder in education, together with new ways that are developing of using television in two-way educational interactions, may tend to that end. Yet, for the immediately foreseeable future, it will still be largely in the classroom that the essential interaction between teachers and their pupils or students will take place.

That interaction, like other human relationships, is complex. In its conduct, and in the transactions that result, short-term considerations vie with longer-term ones, cognitive considerations with affective ones, the products of reason with the intuitive, the positive with the normative. And, always, the context – in its place, time and situation – is specific and unique. No two teaching situations are ever identical. No infallible formula for teaching success exists. No teacher who sought to depend exclusively on the advice of others could reasonably hope to make the best of his or her situation. No writer who pretended otherwise would be doing a service to his readers.

The situation is further complicated because any teacher worthy of the name does not rely on any single teaching approach. Individual teaching style is usually made up of a complex amalgam of approaches that are deployed in a variety of ways from course to course and from teaching period to teaching period. Experimental evidence so far collected has little if anything conclusive to say about individual approaches, let alone about the unique combinations of these that teachers generally use. There is, moreover, increasing scepticism, among educational researchers as well as among practising teachers, about whether it could ever be otherwise. In all these circumstances there is little room for dogma.

Choosing approaches

To accept this diagnosis of the teaching situation is to accept that the question of choosing appropriate teaching approaches is ultimately one that each teacher must settle for himself or herself. But this is not to say that the choice is unconstrained. Important sets of variables that contribute to the definition of each teaching situation are those relating to:

(a) the pupils or students being taught;
(b) the nature of the teaching environment;
(c) the nature of economics; and
(d) the teachers themselves.

The pupils' or students' reasons for learning the subject and their attitudes to the teaching situation will vary. Their ages, aptitudes, abilities and interests will also influence their reactions.[8] So will their social backgrounds.[9] In terms of institutions, there is a fundamental distinction between school and college environments, and further distinctions within each of these educational sectors.[10] In terms of economics, distinct demands are made upon the teacher and his classes by different aspects of the subject – for example, as between descriptive and analytical issues, or as between micro- and macroeconomics.[11] There are also distinctions affecting teaching approach between courses with different objectives – for example, between courses for young school leavers and those for A-level students or for BTEC classes.[12] And, finally, teachers themselves, their personalities, intellectual equipment, acquired knowledge, and also special skills and particular limitations add further, and perhaps particular, variance to the teaching situation. No two teachers are exactly alike. The most suitable methods for one are unlikely to be entirely suitable for another.

The considerable art of the skilled teacher lies precisely in taking all the components of the teaching situation outlined above, reconciling the complex and often conflicting considerations that they pose, and ordering teaching approaches accordingly so as to achieve the educational aims and objectives that have been set. In practice, of course, many important teaching decisions need to be taken quickly and intuitively in the classroom situation itself. However, even where this is the case, forethought and planning augment the chances of successful decision-making and lead in turn to sounder judgement and practice.[13]

Tradition and change in teaching approaches

The traditional approach to economics teaching was of a systematic formal unidirectional kind in which the teacher aimed to structure verbal presentation of material in a way that encouraged its comprehension and either contributed to its memorization or made possible the compilation of notes and summaries from which the content could be learnt. In colleges, this traditional approach to teaching is represented by lectures. In schools it can still be found in formal teacher-dominated lessons. At its best, and in the right circumstances, such formal teaching can be remarkably successful and still has a place in the teacher's armoury of techniques. But, not infrequently, it degenerates to the dull, boring and educationally unproductive business of filling passive learners' minds by the strenuous efforts of the teacher. Fortunately, despite the pressures of examination syllabuses and the temptations that teachers feel to follow this easy course, such teaching is on the wane.

Contemporary educational opinion clearly favours the replacement of teacher-dominated teaching by newer styles in which pupils or students are more explicitly involved in their own education. In the case of economics, changes in this direction seem to have come more slowly than in many other subjects. Perhaps this is partly because the deficiencies of traditional teaching are less obvious in the classes restricted to older, more able, and more advanced pupils or students. However, it is now more than ten years since the full authority of the joint Royal Economic Society, Association of University Teachers of Economics and Economics Association Committee on the Teaching of Economics in Schools was placed behind newer approaches, and the support given to them by the Economics Association and economics teacher trainers across the country are helping to change the picture.[14] The present rapid expansion of economics education at levels below college and the sixth form has added further pressure in the same direction.[15]

The need to gain the attention and interest of the learner has always been realized intuitively by good teachers. Psychological research has underlined this. It has also led to a growing appreciation of the need to ensure the learner's active participation in the learning process and in the discovery of what is to be learnt. Responding to this view, teachers' main concerns have shifted towards a more learner-oriented and experientially based conception of their task. Lessons are more frequently planned to allow pupils and students to grapple with problem situations based on relevant resource materials carefully selected and arranged to contribute to the intended learning.[16]

As for the demands of the subject itself, whereas the traditional approach in economics frequently led to an emphasis on the passive acquisition of a knowledge of economic facts, there is now a much greater appreciation that this is not enough. There is much more to 'knowing economics' than knowing, for example, six functions of the Bank of England or five assumptions underlying a perfect market. Much more fundamental is the need to develop a thorough understanding of the subject's fundamental structure, of its key concepts and of the skills needed not only to acquire that understanding but also to act appropriately in its light.[17] Keynes's famous remark that 'Economics is a method rather than a doctrine, an apparatus of the mind, a technique of thinking'[18] relates well to what Ryle called 'knowing how' as opposed to simply 'knowing that'.[19] The importance of what 'knowing economics' means is discussed more fully in other chapters in this book. For the purposes of this chapter, what needs to be stressed is its equally important implications for teaching approaches. No amount of 'listening to the teacher' can ensure the internalization by the learner of the 'knowing how' side of what he needs to learn in economics. What is needed here, as the Joint Committee emphasized, is the structuring of learning situations that encourage the development of relevant skills by actually applying them in appropriately simplified contexts.[20]

As in the case of notions of 'knowing economics', consideration of the educational aims and objectives of economics education has important implications for the teaching of the subject as well as for its content. These aims and objectives are considered in more detail elsewhere in this volume. However, from the point of view of teaching, as opposed to course planning, two things need to be stressed. First, consideration of aims and objectives in economics education reinforces the importance, referred to above, of mastering basic concepts and skills, and forming attitudes, specific to the subject. Second, it draws attention to objectives of a more general nature that it may be important to master, both in order to benefit from an economics course and because such a course provides an appropriate vehicle for their mastery in the wider interests of the learner's education. These general objectives, as opposed to subject-specific ones, may appear of less significance in more advanced college courses. In school courses, however, and also in the more elementary courses in colleges, the position is quite different. For example, at the level of developing different facilitative learning skills, explicit attention may need to be given to the attainment of skills in the selection, ordering and evaluation of relevant information and in the formulation and expression of appropriate ideas on their basis.

The traditional teaching approach can only meet some of these general objectives, for example, developing the ability to learn by listening to an expert, and the skills of recording what the teacher has said. These are certainly important. But pupils and students need to develop a whole range of other learning skills that the traditional approach does little to encourage: study skills, for example, in extracting relevant information and meaning from other sources than the teacher; from books (and not just textbooks), statistical tables, diagrams, photographs and surveys in the field; 'economic' skills, for example, those of applying demand and supply or managerial analyses to appropriate data or situations; and general skills related to meeting everyday situations in an educated way and reading, writing, and talking about them.

For all these reasons, then, teachers are moving away from the traditional formal didactic methods towards a greater variety of approaches. Equally there is now general acceptance of the need to construct courses in which the mastery of basic concepts and techniques, the development of intellectual sk ills and the development of values and attitudes take precedence over the mere acquisition of factual knowledge. This does not mean, of course, that the knowledge of facts is no longer considered important. What is being advocated is not the abandonment of *factual knowledge* but the abandonment of *fact memorization for its own sake.*

The organization of learning time

Changes are taking place in the organization of learning time in both schools and colleges. These changes are already breaking down long-standing distinctions between their distinctive patterns of organization. They are likely to continue to do so. It would nevertheless be unrealistic not to recognize that the distinctive patterns of provision that have grown up over time still continue to exist. College economics courses, like those in universities, still largely function in terms of lectures, complemented by tutorials and seminars; and those in schools continue to be made up of lessons, supplemented for older and more-able children by homework and other forms of individual study. Obviously there is overlap. The use of 'lesson'-type organization is increasingly evident in some colleges, especially in its non-advanced further-education classes.[21] And some lecturing is still found, though decreasingly so, in schools, particularly in sixth forms.

Lecturing and the lecture

Lectures were once useful; but now, when all can read, and books are so numerous, lectures are unnecessary (Boswell, *Life of Johnson*).

Lecturing is the classic traditional form of approach to teaching. Once very prevalent in schools as well as colleges, its use as a standard form of teaching has almost disappeared in the former and is declining in the latter. For very good reasons, courses consisting *entirely* of lectures are increasingly rare. Nevertheless, opinions on the merits of lectures tend to be strongly held and frequently voiced, and they are still sufficiently important to demand some consideration.

Established facts about their merits remain hard to come by. Donald Bligh summarized such evidence as exists in a valuable book on the subject which every lecturer should read.[22] This suggests that, while in appropriate circumstances the lecture is no less effective than other approaches as a means of imparting information and transmitting knowledge, it is much less useful in promoting thought or in changing attitudes. What is more certain is that the skill of the lecturer is a vital ingredient in its effectiveness. The best lecturers can create unique learning experiences. In lesser hands, the deficiencies and limitations of the lecture approach can become all too evident.

Various benefits have been claimed for the lecture technique.[23] Some lectures give the student an initial outline of the subject that provides him with a framework for further study. Others present material that is not available in print or is only available from scattered sources. In other cases the lecture is regarded as a demonstration of the analytical technique and as a means of awakening a critical attitude on the part of the student. Strictly speaking, these potential benefits could arise from a variety of oral approaches to teaching; but the lecture can be expected to be better prepared, more profound and better thought out. It also enables more ground to be 'covered' in a given time.

These are important considerations where time is limited and syllabuses extensive. Furthermore, the lecture is economical of staff time and may enable a greater number of students to have some contact with an exceptional teacher. But feedback from students is scant and unreliable. Ground covered meticulously by the lecturer may in no sense have been 'covered' by the class. Rote learning of hurried notes may well be encouraged at the expense of reading and the exercise of a critical attitude. Opportunities for using and developing skills in debate and in verbal presentation, and of enhancing aspects of understanding achieved through discussion, are missed. Moreover, unless the lecturer is exceptionally good, the lecture is a relatively weak motivational instrument for sustained learning.

In higher-level school and college courses, the problems and possibilities of the lecture approach are essentially similar to those in universities. Motivation, level of learning skills, and level of prior knowledge on the part of the students help to make up for the deficiencies of the lecture approach. Even so, as in universities, the increased provision of alternative teaching approaches, involving the student in more active and varied learning situations, is clearly valuable.

In lower-level courses a 'lesson' approach similar to that in schools is almost certainly more efficient. Initially, some hesitancy may occur in students who see this as a return to the 'childish' methods of the schools which many of them have so recently left. However, with careful handling, this kind of early difficulty can more easily be overcome than the dumb resentment that soon develops among those at this level who are unable to keep up with an unadulterated diet of lectures.

When lectures are retained, it is necessary to consider what can be done to ensure that students derive the maximum possible benefit from them. Skill in lecturing, as Bligh points out, is acquired by practice rather than by reading books. Nevertheless, his book offers much useful advice, as do a number of others.[24] In essence, this boils down to stressing the importance, first, of aiming at objectives that the lecture approach can achieve; second, of framing lecture content in a way that helps the student to understand and remember what is being said; and third, of delivering the lecture in a way that stimulates attention and motivation. Clarity, meaning and structure in the material being delivered, and confidence and enthusiasm in its delivery, are all important ingredients. Where relevant, the use of audio-visual aids can also be valuable.

Care in seeing things from the students' point of view is important. What matters is the use that students make of what they hear. Too frequently this is left to chance. But it is possible to structure a lecture in ways that help students to make efficient notes and develop subsequent discussion and consideration.[25] Equally, the provision of duplicated hand-outs containing important factual material, reading references, and an outline of the lecture can help them to attend more usefully to what is being said. Opportunities to help in these ways should not be missed. Finally, if complementary tutorials cannot be arranged, the provision of question periods during or at the end of each lecture is particularly necessary. They are a poor substitute but better than nothing.

Knowing one's subject is an essential condition of good lecturing, but it is not enough. The fundamental importance of knowing one's subject should not be obscured; but nor should the purpose of the exercise – the transmission of learning – be forgotten.

Lessons

While the lesson continues to be the basic teaching unit in schools, recent years have seen the general acceptance by teachers of many changes in its form and content.

The lesson, like the lecture, originated as a formal means of instruction. Its traditional form, perfected in the nineteenth century, often incorporated the famous Herbartian 'steps', requiring, in sequence, revision of relevant material that had gone before, an explanation of new material, relationship to previous work, application to relevant problems and consolidation in systematic summary form.[26] The teacher's procedure included the verbal presentation of his topic, the questioning of pupils, both to ensure their understanding and to relate new material to what they already knew, and the dictation of notes. At its best, the approach 'covered' ground efficiently. At its worst, as in the case of the poor lecture, it could degenerate into monotonous note dictation.

Some teachers still stick fairly closely to methods of this kind, pinning their procedural flag to the masthead of 'sock-it-to-them' teaching.[27] But, while the ability of a really good teacher to manage without recourse to other approaches should not be lightly dismissed, the analysis in the preceding sections of this chapter helps to explain why the view of the teacher's role implied by such an approach is now generally considered to be too limited. Many teachers and educationists interested in economics teaching have understood for a long time the importance of more active student involvement, more resource-based teaching materials, more learner-centred activity, greater reliance on problem-solving situations, and the like. It is not without significance that academic economists have added their support to these approaches.[28]

In times when the blackboard and a textbook were the only teaching aids at a teacher's disposal, adherence to a traditional formal approach was understandable. Today, with a rapidly increasing variety of available aids and resources, teachers have only themselves to blame if their teaching perpetuates the belief that economics is 'the dismal science'. The value and use of teaching aids and resources is discussed more fully in subsequent chapters. Enthusiasm for their use can of course be overdone. They nevertheless offer a useful contribution to the teaching possibilities of the classroom. Carefully selected resource materials, such as statistical tables, original documents, diagrams, graphs, and case-study data, open up immeasurably the possibility of inductive, inquiry-based approaches.[29] Audio and visual aids not only enable the teacher to add variety and interest to the presentation of lessons but also provide convenient means of increasing the availability of otherwise inaccessible resources. To suggest that their use can in any way replace the teacher who knows his subject would, of course, be ridiculous. But, to condemn them, as one well-known writer on economics teaching has done, as 'at best trivial' is to misunderstand their potential.[30]

As for note dictation, although this is still a fairly common practice in some schools, it is increasingly difficult to see why this should be so. Superficially, it may appear to offer an easy way to ensure an accurate record in the pupils' or students' notebooks. Frequently it does not even produce this. Nor, as examination 'howlers' often make all too clear, does it in any way ensure meaningful understanding of what has been noted. By contrast, the skill of compiling one's own notes from what has been said or written is one that every pupil or student is likely to need. Consequently, every encouragement, including explicit guidance, should be given to its development, in relation to the pupil's or student's own reading.

The remaining sections of this chapter examine some of the main ways in which greater variety can be introduced into economics classes.

But, even where relatively formal lesson structures are retained, there is a much greater possibility of variety of approach than some teachers appear to realize. There is no reason, for example, why lessons should always begin with the teacher's exposition of content. Provided that adequate guidance is offered by the teacher, classroom analysis of the implications of appropriate data can make an equally good starting point. Nor is there any reason why homework should always be of a follow-up nature. Research or reading by the pupils or students prior to a lesson enables them to participate in the class in a way that is less dependent on the teacher's introduction than would otherwise be the case. Similarly, the organization of classwork need not always be on a whole-class or individual basis. The division of a class into several smaller groups, each with its own assigned group-learning task, offers a useful alternative.

Tutorial work

Tutorial work, whether in universities and colleges or in schools, is work in which pupils and students prepare material and discuss it with their teacher.

The organization of tutorial work can take a variety of forms, ranging from individual tuition to formal university-style seminars.[31] It may be relatively learner-centred or subject-centred. But whichever form it takes its main characteristic is that it provides good opportunities for active learner participation. Problems can be discussed arising out of what has been taught or from reading. Further reading and activities can be suggested and written work examined critically. Discussion often brings difficulties to light and allows them to be ironed out. Through discussion participants gain practice in a variety of useful skills, including the abilities to frame pertinent questions, express their thoughts more cogently, and engage in critical dialogue with others.

These methods are not without their difficulties. It is not always easy to get discussion started, particularly if a group is not used to the approach. Furthermore, while participants who are shy or self-conscious can be difficult to handle, those who are always willing to dominate a discussion, whether usefully or not, can also be a problem. For some, the creation of a free and uninhibiting atmosphere is essential. For others, firm and careful guidance is needed if aimless discussion is not to develop. The happy medium required from the teacher – a subtle and varying blend of unobtrusive guidance, direction and participation – is made easier to achieve by careful preliminary preparation of the ground to be examined. By choosing suitable themes, suggesting lines to be followed, and advising on suitable preliminary reading, teachers can fulfil a guiding role before the discussion begins. If they do this successfully, it then becomes possible to develop a less teacher-centred atmosphere during the discussion itself.

Selecting appropriate themes and guiding tutorial work are by no means easy tasks, but at least they are matters within the teacher's own control. Equally important but more difficult for the teacher is to ensure that adequate preparation is done by the pupils or students. Without this, discussion can quickly become sterile and vacuous. Much depends on the teacher's tact, leadership qualities and ability to encourage. The very least that is needed is the giving of clear instructions regarding the kind of preparation needed. With less advanced students, more specific guidance about sources, and even about the detailed points to be extracted and considered, may also be necessary.

One good way of initiating tutorial discussions is to allow them to arise from short papers or lecturettes prepared and presented by different members of the group. The titles chosen and the nature of the material expected would naturally vary with the type of class involved. Nothing very elaborate need be expected. A short paper that asks a number of questions, rather than providing a final answer, can be most useful. Considerable variation of approach is possible. Or, a single member of the class could prepare a paper on a particular topic, basing it on a textbook account or using some other source suggested by the teacher. At other times, several pupils or students might, between them, tackle a group of related topics. Alternatively, they might present information on a single topic from a number of different sources. Thus the concept of opportunity cost could be the subject of a short paper based upon a particular textbook account, and this could be followed, after discussion and analysis of the concept, by a series of illustrations contributed by other members of the class. Similarly, in studying the Bank of England, each of its functions could be the subject of a short lecturette from a different member of the group. Provided the teacher is careful in his choice of subject, in giving helpful direction for locating a suitable source, in correcting errors, and in filling important areas left uncovered by his pupils or students, many topics lend themselves to treatment of this kind.

Another useful procedure is to give each member of a class responsibility for noting and reporting on a particular industry or aspect of the economy. For example, one member of the class might be concerned with developments in the motor industry while another concentrated on the balance of payments. Each 'expert' can then make occasional reports to the class and can keep a scrapbook of newspaper cuttings on his own particular topic or contribute to an economic diary kept by the class as a whole.

Discussion approaches are more likely to succeed where the group size is limited. The ability to implement a satisfactory tutorial or seminar system is always constrained by the amount of staff time that can be made available. Moreover, there is the question of the time taken up by these methods.

Some teachers feel a sense of frustration when conducting tutorials or seminars because they consider that the same ground could be covered more quickly and in a more ordered way by direct teaching. They may also be apprehensive of the tendency, in discussion, for the thread of the argument to take unpredictably different paths from those that they themselves would have chosen if they had been dictating the route. On the other hand, such approaches evade the alternative dangers of passing too quickly and lightly over aspects of the subject that trouble the pupil or student in ways that the teacher cannot always foresee. They therefore provide an opportunity for the development of a surer and deeper understanding of the subject, and for the growth of an increased sense of involvement in the learning process. Perhaps teachers are too often prone to feel guilty when they are not *actively teaching*, rather than when their classes are not *actively learning*.

Problem-solving approaches and the use of source materials

Problem-solving requires the manipulation of data by pupils and students as part of the activity of anticipating and evaluating the likely results of taking alternative decisions. At its best, this approach simulates the kind of situation in which, at some future time, pupils and students are most likely to need to use their economic knowledge. Study of this kind can also help to indicate the concrete basis behind economic generalizations, thus making them easier to understand. Perhaps even more important, it helps to create insight into the nature of decision-making and into the limitations imposed by uncertainty and non-economic considerations.[32]

The value of the problem-solving approach is greatest where the problems tackled are based on real situations within the experience of the pupils. Every area, for example, has at least one local industry on the basis of which a problem approach to the division of labour can be worked out at an elementary level, without the usual recourse to Adam Smith's example of pin-making. Thus in a furniture-manufacturing district, an examination of the way in which a chair or table is made by hand can be followed by the pupils' or students' own attempts to devise a suitable division of labour to increase production. An examination of their solutions would then form the basis of an analysis of its advantages and disadvantages. If such a study can be related to actual visits to a local cabinet-maker and to a large-scale furniture factory, even greater benefits would accrue.[33]

Such experience-based approaches gain their strength from the relation of learning to the pupils' and students' existing knowledge and experience. But an experiential approach is not limited only to this.

Similar fruitful teaching approaches can create experiential situations in the classroom by the provision of appropriate learning resources which, through the use of pictures, recordings, and written accounts, help pupils and students to enter imaginatively into real situations from which learning can take place. At the 14–16 level of teaching, the Economics Education 14–16 Project has developed a valuable range of resource-based units that help teachers to build their lessons on exactly this basis.[34]

The use of such approaches clearly leads to better and more sophisticated learning. Pupils and students internalize what they learn rather than simply memorizing it. Moreover, their active involvement in the learning process teaches them essential skills that cannot be perfected by simply listening and reading. In addition, from the teacher's point of view, they lend themselves much better than traditional approaches to use with mixed-ability classes. Starting from a common piece of resource material, it is not difficult to devise lessons that allow pupils to increase their knowledge, skills and understanding in different ways and at different paces.

At a more advanced level, problem-solving approaches can also be used very fruitfully on a wide range of topics through which economic learning can take place. Thus they can be used in the exploration of the profit-maximizing level of production to be adopted by a manufacturer with specified costs and market conditions. Similarly, problems concerning the size of the labour force or the possibility of introducing new capital equipment are useful topics to take up in the discussion of the economics of a firm. Some successful experiments have been made along these lines with the use of business games, but while these invariably generate interest and teach useful lessons concerning appropriate strategies in dynamic business situations, their pure economics content is not always very great.

Successful problem-solving situations are predicated on the provision of suitable source materials and the adequate structuring of their use by the teacher. Sources for such materials are many. Case studies offer one such source. Statistical data, in table or graph form, are another. In one sense, use of such data is by no means new. Good teachers have always included them as examples and illustrations of topics being dealt with, and most textbooks include at least some illustrative material of this kind, for example, tables, often hypothetical, illustrating relationships between total, average and marginal revenue, and the concept of comparative costs. However, in the problem-solving approach, the process involved is really the reverse. Instead of case material being used as illustrations of an ordered study of principles, the principles themselves are examined as they arise from an ordered succession of cases. Thus principles are learned through the study of actual situations, institutions, industries, firms, and the like. The appeal of an approach of this kind has been strengthened in recent years by changes in economic research in which increased emphasis has been placed upon building up economic understanding by induction from real-world situations, as for example in behavioural theories of the firm, rather than simply through successively more elaborate developments of deductive models. Readers interested in following up this approach are referred to Peter Maunder's chapter on case studies (Chapter 14).

The use of projects

The use of projects is closely related to the problem-solving approach. The term 'project' has acquired a rather different meaning in colleges to that applied to it in schools. Essentially, however, in both settings, it involves the conducting and reporting of an inquiry carried out, with more or less guidance, by the pupils or students themselves.

In further education, the project often refers to an individual and self-contained piece of work by the student who will have been expected to select, with teacher guidance, a suitable topic for investigation. Over a period of time, which may be a term or even a year, students will have collected and analysed sources of information relevant to the topic and will finally have presented the findings in the form of a written dissertation. Provided the student does not select an over-ambitious topic for investigation, this can be a very worthwhile educational exercise. Its use is growing in further education and, in a number of instances, the quality of the project is taken into consideration in examination assessments.

The kind of project outlined above also has its uses in schools, particularly in the sixth form. In simplified and modified form, it may also play a part in CSE classes where the completion of a project may be needed for part of the examination. However, in schools, the project method is often a more complex affair, owing much to the American philosopher and educationist, John Dewey, and his followers.[35] In the first place, it usually involves more positive guidance and participation by the teacher. Second, it often implies the development of groupwork by the pupils. A typical project might consist of a sequence of several parts whose completion might take four or five weeks or even as long as a term, depending upon the theme selected. To begin with, a central topic is selected and the class is divided into groups, each of which is designated to discover appropriate information about a particular aspect of the topic chosen. Once this has been collected, each group then sets to work sorting and collating what has been discovered. In the school setting, this process requires considerable help from the teacher. Often each group then prepares material for an exhibition in which all the material collected by the class is displayed. Finally, the groups examine each other's work and, in the follow-up period, the teacher tries to bring together all that has been learned.

Several interesting examples of economics projects have been reported in past numbers of *Economics* and elsewhere, and it is clear that teachers who use the method generally find it to be most valuable.[36] On the other hand, unless a project is very carefully structured and controlled, it can easily become time-consuming and diffuse. It clearly requires considerable preparatory work by the teacher and can prove extremely demanding; it is very far from being the easy option to formal teaching that some teachers have imagined it to be. For these reasons and also because the method does not lend itself well to covering a broad curriculum, it is not easy to fit projects into the timetable of a rigid examination syllabus. Nevertheless, forms of assessment now adopted seek to test skills that learning by this approach is likely to develop.[37]

Role playing and simulation

Economic role playing enlists the pupils' or students' powers of introspection in an attempt to understand economic implications of the motives and actions of others. In simulation games, the assumed roles are harnessed to game situations that simulate actual economic situations. The intention here is that the actors develop their understanding not simply of their own individual roles but also of the interplay that takes place between them, and of the principles governing the development of the situation being simulated.

In role playing at its simplest level, the appeal of 'What would you do if you were in the Chancellor's shoes?' or of 'Imagine you were the managing director of British Leyland' is one that invariably engages the interest of a class and may help pupils or students to see that decisions made by such people are not so remote and divorced from their own experience as they had previously thought. Invitations, in their various forms, to play roles of this kind are a useful method of exploring many parts of the subject. One role that pupils and students are frequently asked to assume in developing the theory of consumer demand is that of 'themselves as consumers'. Less frequently, but equally profitably, they may be asked to take the role of producers: the invitation to 'imagine that you are about to set up a small business' can reveal remarkable reserves of potential entrepreneurial ability and can also provide an excellent starting point for such varied topics as business organization, location theory, the theory of the firm, the factor markets and the functions of joint stock banks.

With younger children, the use of a 'kit of objects' has been advocated,[38] and kits of concrete objects, representing, for example, different factors of production, have been developed. These have been found to help younger pupils to 'play' economic roles and thus to develop for themselves important economic concepts, such as the concepts of scarcity and opportunity cost. At a more sophisticated level, role playing may involve the dramatization of events, with several members of a class taking different parts. The resulting performance can then form the basis of discussion and analysis of the topic being studied. Where this is done, the use of actual statistics rather than hypothetical ones, particularly if these can be obtained from local firms and organizations, helps to add reality to the study.

Simulation games take role playing a stage further, generally creating dynamic situations that attempt to simulate real-life situations, and placing pupils or students in roles within the game. Their object is usually partly to develop an understanding of the real-life situations being simulated, partly to develop skill in participating in them. In general, games so far developed in relation to economics teaching have been based on competitive models, but there is no reason why, where appropriate, co-operative models should not be adopted.[39] Some games require relatively simple equipment. Others are more demanding and more complex, even, in some cases, requiring organization and equipment outside the capacity of individual teachers to provide. Examples of these include inter-school and -college competitions[40] and the increasing number of computer-based games and learning situations.[41]

There can be little doubt about the power of role playing and simulation games to stimulate interest, even to the point of obsession. What must remain more doubtful is the extent of the benefit, in terms of economic education, of such participation. These methods, perhaps more than any others, require particularly careful handling by the teacher. In role playing, the advantages to be derived by the pupil or student, through identifying with the person whose role is being played, can easily be destroyed by concomitant disadvantages. In most role-playing exercises, for example, simplification – sometimes considerable – of the role to be assumed is a feature. In these circumstances, it is all too easy for the novice role player to mistake for the real thing features of the played role that relate to the simplification that has taken place rather than to the actual role itself. Thus, to take one of the examples mentioned above, the parameters of decision-taking that actually affect the Chancellor of the Exchequer are really quite different from those bounding the experience of the novice assuming that role. Sensitive handling of the situation by the teacher may be needed to bring this out. Similar dangers attend the use of simulation games, and for similar reasons. Thus, for example, making stock exchange investment decisions with simulated money, and under simulated conditions of uncertainty, entails quite different penalties from the real thing and is quite different from it for that reason alone. Equally, 'discovering' and 'playing to' the rules and assumptions built in to the programme of a computer-based economy-management game may all too easily lead to misconceptions about the management of the economy itself. In both these cases, the very success and excitement attendant on the games being played add to, rather than detract from, the risk of these misconceptions being developed.

On the other hand, provided due caution is exercised, there are also great potential gains in the development of life and social skills as well as of economic learning. Listening, talking, discussing, persuading, analysing under pressure and making judgements are all involved. And, perhaps above all, decision-making is practised.

Individualized learning

Where the teaching approach involves the creation of a shared class experience, problems of content, method and pace require nice judgements by the teacher. Even in streamed and setted classes, the pace set rarely fits exactly the needs of any individual pupil or student. As long as teachers remain the only source of knowledge for their classes, little can be done to avoid this state of affairs completely. Where other resources are used, however, the possibility exists of creating more individualized learning situations. —

Attempts to do this are by no means new. For example, the Dalton and Winnetka plans of the 1920s are well known and widely copied examples.[42] Nevertheless, the expanding impact on the classroom of educational technology has led to a considerable recent renewal of interest. Striking schemes for individualized instruction have been created in several countries. In Sweden, for example, individualized instruction systems, based on the conversion of classrooms into resource centres, and utilizing teaching machines, programmed instruction, a whole range of audio-visual aids, and individual study booths, have been introduced into all schools.[43] The proliferation of microcomputers in schools has given new impetus to the development of individualized learning. Indeed, it is particularly suited to it. The development of appropriate economic programmes is proceeding rapidly and may be expected to extend much further and to increase in sophistication.

The essence of individualization of instruction lies in the provision of self-tuition schemes that can be followed, largely unaided, by each individual pupil or student. These liberate the teacher from his traditional front-of-the-classroom role, and allow him to attend to individual needs and learning problems. Successful individualized instruction depends on the availability of adequate source material for study. At the most sophisticated levels, where individualized instruction largely replaces other teaching approaches, the demands for source material can be very extensive, and the provision of adequate storage and retrieval facilities becomes crucial. At less all-embracing levels, however, successful individual assignments can be built round textbook material, especially where this can be supplemented by topical newspaper cuttings, bank review material and the like, and access to a reasonable school or college economics library.

The provision of carefully prepared worksheets or assignments is particularly important in this approach. Successful worksheets are by no means easy to devise, but they have the advantage that, once produced, they can often be used, with only minor alterations, for several years. Explicit and unambiguous guide questions need to be formulated to aid fact finding, to guide pertinent problem-solving, and to shape a satisfactory record of the pupil's or student's work. As in oral teaching, questions that seem clear enough to the teacher may prove very puzzling to the pupil or student. Often, therefore, considerable revision of a first attempt is needed in the light of experience of its use. Some teachers find it most useful to relate worksheets to a particular textbook in use in their classes. In this context, the publication, in recent years, of carefully constructed companion workbooks to several popular textbooks has been a particularly welcome development.[44] Nevertheless, there are many teachers of economics who prefer to frame their own worksheets containing exercises devised to suit the needs of their own particular pupils.

Teachers who employ individualized instruction often swear by it. Yet it is by no means a soft option for the teacher. Less expository teaching is involved; but this is replaced by more time devoted to preparation, to the discovery of suitable source material and to personal attention to the pupil's or student's needs. Various devices have been adopted from time to time to try to increase its effectiveness. One example is the development of a contract-learning approach.[45] Another is the production of the student's own economics journal.[46] However, these are little more than surface glosses on an approach to teaching whose essential features remain the provision of adequate resource material and careful teacher-guidance to its use. In the past, only a minority of teachers have committed themselves entirely to an individualized approach to learning. Perhaps, despite its advantages, this is just as well. Yet there can be little doubt that its employment as part of a mix of teaching approaches that also include group learning situations can add an important dimension to economics lessons and a valuable preparation for future autonomous learning on the part of our present pupils and students.[47]

Reconciling the demands made by teaching

This chapter has been directed largely at the novice teacher. It contains little that is not already known, understood and practised by good economics teachers in all kinds of schools and colleges. Its aim is restricted to providing a basis from which the interested reader can begin to widen the range of his or her approaches to the problems of teaching. It offers through its references a route to further useful reading about how to proceed. Its major premise is that by being able to call upon a wider range of approaches, the teacher can make the classroom or lecture room a more interesting and effective environment for the student.

It can of course be argued that what is being offered is a counsel of perfection, far divorced from the current realities in the schools. Teaching, even for the teacher who restricts him/herself to traditional approaches, is a complex matter. The adoption of newer approaches further complicates things. So does the need to master the ever-increasing range of available audio-visual aids and other teaching resources.[48] Taken together, the amount of preparatory work that is required of the teacher is increased considerably, particularly when newer approaches are used for the first time. In these circumstances, advocating variety of approach may appear to represent an unreasonable and unrealistic demand on the teacher's time and effort.

To some extent, such a view misses the point. Different approaches should be considered less as theoretical desiderata that complicate the teacher's life, and more as an armoury of possibilities from which appropriate alternatives can be selected as required. Even so, their use does place irreducible additional demands upon teachers. It also involves a by no means easy reassessment of their classroom roles, with less weight being placed on the traditional view of teachers as sources of expert knowledge and directors of mental training, and more on their functions as managers of learning environments and consultants on knowledge-acquisition and learning problems.

Different kinds of complication are created by external constraints. Of these, by far the greatest is the pressure of external examinations. Many teachers, while favouring in principle the newer teaching approaches and the objectives that they serve, nevertheless feel bound by this pressure to teach more factual material, and in more prosaic ways, than they would like. Despite recent revisions in many public examination syllabuses, in which superfluous content has been axed, it is by no means evident that constraints on the teacher imposed by the demands of the boards on their pupils and students are in any way diminishing. Nor is it likely that the restructuring of public examinations now being proposed will do much to ease the teacher's task.

No easy solution exists for problems of these kinds. In general, it is true that the teacher using the newer approaches cannot 'cover ground' as quickly as in lecturing or formal teaching. On the other hand, as has been pointed out, there are compensating gains that should not be overlooked. The increasing popularity of economics as a school and college subject leads to larger classes in which discussion and pupil involvement are harder to arrange. Yet the same trend is leading increasingly to economics departments with two or more specialists, thus making possible the introduction of a team-teaching approach.[49] Equally, rising numbers in economics classes enhance the claims of the economics teachers to specialist rooms of their own. Such economics rooms offer perhaps the greatest single contribution to easing teaching problems. Inevitably, some compromise must take place between what any economics teacher might like to do and what is in practice possible. Whatever that may be, some understanding of the variety of approaches available should help teachers to present their subject in a rich, interesting and illuminating manner, thus guiding their pupils or students to levels of understanding that would not have been so easily attainable in the past.

Notes and references

1. Lee, N. (ed.), *Teaching Economics* (1st edn, Economics Association, 1967) (2nd edn, Heinemann Educational Books, 1975).
2. They include: Knopf, K.A., and Stauss, J.H. (eds), *The Teaching of Elementary Economics* (New, York, Holt, Rinehart & Winston, 1960); Fenton, E. (ed.), *Teaching the New Social Studies in Secondary Schools* (Holt, Rinehart & Winston, 1966); Calderwood, J.D., Lawrence, J.D. and Maher, J.E., *Economics in the Curriculum* (John Wiley, 1970); Assistant Masters Association, *The Teaching of Economics in Secondary Schools* (Cambridge University Press, 1971); Lawton, D., and Dufour, B., *The New Social Studies* (Heinemann Educational Books, 1973); Oliver, J.M., *The Principles of Teaching Economics* (Heinemann Educational Books, 1973); Helburn, S., *et al.*, *Economics in Society. Strategies and Methods* (Addison-Wesley, 1974); Wentworth, D., Wentworth, D.R., *et al.* (eds), *Perspectives in Economics Education* (New York, Joint Council for Economics Education, 1977); Henderson, W., *Teaching Economics in African Secondary Schools* (Heinemann Educational Books, 1980). See also Whitehead, D., 'Learning processes and teaching strategies in economics education', *Economics*, vol. 19, pt 4, no. 84, winter 1983. For practical examples of successful teaching approaches, see also Whitehead, D.J., *Handbook for Economics Teachers* (Heinemann Educational Books, 1979).
3. The main journals in which these are found are: *Economics*, journal of the Economics Association, Economics Association, Temple Lodge, South Street, Ditchling, Surrey BN6 8UQ, and *Journal of Economic Education*, Joint Council on Economic Education, 1212 Avenue of the Americas, New York, New York 10036, USA.
4. See the Introduction.
5. For details, see Chapter 6.
6. See *Annotated Bibliography of Pupil Books* (Economics Education 14–16 Project/Economics Association, 1982).
7. See Chapter 6 for details of changes in official thinking regarding

economics in the curriculum.
8. See, for example, Stones, E., *An Introduction to Educational Psychology* (Methuen, 1966); Childs, D., *Psychology and the Teacher* (Holt Education, 1981).
9. See, for example, Banks, O., *The Sociology of Education*, 3rd edn (Batsford, 1976) chs 3 and 4. Also, Meighan, R., *The Sociology of Educating* (Holt, Rinehart & Winston, 1981).
10. See the Introduction.
11. See Chapter 1.
12. See Chapters 7 and 8.
13. For more elaborated discussion of these questions, see Roe, E., *Some Dilemmas in Teaching* (Oxford University Press, 1971), Fenton (ed.), op. cit., and Whitehead, D. (ed.), *Curriculum Development in Economics* (Heinemann Educational Books, 1974). See also Joyce, B., and Weill, M., *Models of Teaching*, 2nd edn (Prentice-Hall, 1980).
14. Joint Committee of the Royal Economic Society, the Association of University Teachers of Economics, and the Economics Association, *The Teaching of Economics in Schools* (Macmillan, 1973) pp. 16ff.
15. See Chapter 6.
16. See, for example, Gagné, R.M., *The Conditions of Learning*, 2nd edn (Holt Rinehart & Winston, 1970).
17. See Ryba, R., and Drake, K., 'Towards a taxonomy of educational objectives for economics', in Whitehead, D. (ed.), *Curriculum Development in Economics* (Heinemann Educational Books, 1974).
18. Taken from original Editorial Introduction to the Cambridge Economic Handbooks, written by J.M. Keynes, and quoted by C.W. Guillebaud in his revised introduction to the second edition of the series.
19. Ryle, G., *The Concept of Mind* (Penguin, 1963).
20. Joint Committee of the Royal Economic Society, the Association of University Teachers of Economics and the Economics Association, op. cit., pp. 18–19.
21. See, for example, Lowes, B., and Sparkes, J.R., 'Teaching business economics: course objectives and planning problems', *Economics*, vol.10, pt 3, no. 45, winter 1973–74.
22. Bligh, D.A., *What's the Use of Lectures?* (Penguin, 1972).
23. See Ibid.; also, Roe, E., *Some Dilemmas in Teaching* (Oxford University Press, 1971), Beard, R., *Teaching and Learning in Higher Education* (Penguin, 1970), and Wiedemann, P., and Dorward, N., 'An evaluation of the mass lecture technique in first-year economics', *Economics*, vol. 13, pt 4, no. 60, winter 1977.
24. See, for example, Bligh, op. cit., and Beard, op. cit.
25. See Fenton (ed.), op. cit., ch. 13: 'Teaching students to take good reading notes'.
26. See, for example, Dodd, C.I., *Introduction to the Herbartian Principles of Teaching* (London, 1898).
27. Oliver, op. cit., p. 61: 'When I come right down to it, I hope to live and die an old-fashioned "sock-it-to-them" teacher.'
28. Joint Committee of the Royal Economic Society, the Association of University Teachers and the Economics Association, op. cit., p. 18.
29. See Fenton (ed.), op. cit., ch. 16, and the publications of the Economics Education 14–16 Project.

30. Oliver, op. cit., p. 54.
31. University Grants Committee, *Report of Committee on University Teaching Methods* (Chairman: Sir E. Hale) (HMSO, 1964). The Hale Report distinguished between 'tutorials' consisting of four or less students and 'seminars' which were larger groups.
32. See Gregory, A., 'Using a source materials approach in economics', *Economics*, vol. 18, pt 1, no. 77, spring 1982. For an American viewpoint, see Eikenberry, A. *et al.*, *The Problem-solving Approach to Economic Education in Senior High School* (Joint Council for Economic Education, n.d.), and Senesh, L., 'Teaching economics through the problem-solving approach', and Knopf, K.A., 'An experiment in economics at Grinnell College', in Knopf and Stauss, op. cit., pp. 26ff., and pp. 62ff. See also Oliver, op. cit., pp. 75ff., and the Joint Committee of the Royal Economic Society, the Association of University Teachers of Economics and the Economics Association, op. cit., pp. 19ff.
33. See Chapter 15.
34. See Ryba, R., Hodkinson, S., *et al.*, *Understanding Economics* (Economics Education 14–16 Project, Economics Association, 1983), also, the Project's Exemplar Materials Pack; and Whitehead (ed.), *Handbook for Economics Teachers*, op. cit.
35. In its most complete form, as conceived by W.H. Kilpatrick, an associate of Dewey and his followers, the project method involved a problem-oriented approach divorced from traditional subject boundaries and drawing, in an integrated matter, on whatever traditional fields were relevant. However, a project approach can be applied just as well within a subject area.
36. See, for example, Johnson, M.K., 'Aspects of the balance of payments: a sixth form project', *Economics*, pt 1, no. 21, spring 1966; Cox, P.G., 'Economics field studies in schools (III)', *Economics*, pt 1, no. 24, spring 1967; Knights, M., 'Further food for thought: a sixth form project', *Economics*, vol. 9, pt 6, no. 45, winter 1973; Lesser, B., 'A comment on the case study approach to teaching economics', *Economics*, vol. 14, pt 1, no. 61, spring 1978. See also Sandford, C. T., and Bradbury, M. S., *Projects and Role Playing in Teaching Economics*, Case Studies in Economics Series (Macmillan, 1971).
37. For example, Paper 1, Part 2, in the JMB A-level economics examination.
38. Christie, D., 'Economics in the early stages of the secondary school', in Whitehead, *Curriculum Development in Economics*, op. cit., ch. 8.
39. See Lewis, D.R., and Wentworth, D., *Educational Games and Simulations in Economics* (New York, Joint Council for Economic Education, 1974).
40. Noble, P., and Barker, R., 'The Stock Exchange game', *Economics*, vol. 9, pt 4, no. 40, summer 1972. See also Noble, P., 'Role playing opportunities and educational games in sixth form economics', *Economics*, vol. 9, pt 5, no. 41, autumn 1972; Jennings, W., ' "Survival" – a game for introducing economics', *Economics*, vol. 13, pt 1, no. 49, spring 1975; and Murphy, T., and Edwards, V., 'Using game theory in introductory microeconomic courses', *Economics*, vol. 17, pt 4, no. 76, winter 1981; Ryba, R., 'The Eurecom game in the United Kingdom', in Ryba, R., and Wilson, R. (eds), *Teaching the Economics of the EEC* (Economics Association, 1982).
41. See Chapter 17, and also Cotterell, A., 'Computer programmes for teaching economics', *Economics*, vol. 19, pt 1, no. 81, spring 1983.

42. See, for example, Knox, H.M., *Introduction to Educational Methods* (Oldbourne Press, 1961).
43. For a brief description, see Stenholm, B., *Education in Sweden* (Swedish Institute, 1970).
44. These include, for example, Samuelson, P.A., *Study Guide and Workbook* (McGraw-Hill, 1979); Stilwell, J.R., Lipsey, R.G., and Clarke, R., *Workbook to Accompany the Sixth Edition of 'Positive Economics'* (Weidenfeld & Nicolson, 1983); Lipsey, R.G., and Harbury, C., *An Introduction to the UK Economy* (Pitman, 1983); Harbury, C.D., *Workbook in Introductory Economics* (Pergamon, 1974); Harvey, J., and Johnson, M., *Workbook to Accompany Modern Economics* (Macmillan, 1983); Harvey, J., *Elementary Economics Workbook*, 2nd edn (Macmillan, 1983). Other workbooks include: Marshall, H.A., and Mould, J.R., *Economic Analysis – A Workbook* (Butterworth, 1971); Oliver, J., *The Economist: Data Response Questions in 'A' Level Economics* (Collins, 1983).
45. See Noad, B.M., 'Student contract learning: an Australian experiment', *Economics*, vol. 10, pt 3, no. 45, winter 1973–4. See also, 'Behavioural objectives and student learning contracts in the teaching of economics', *Journal of Economic Education*, 1972.
46. See Rock, J.M., and Weaver, R., 'The economics journal as an educational device', *Journal of Economic Education*, spring 1972, pp. 134–6.
47. See Negus, P., 'How to organise individualised learning at "A" level in colleges of further education', in Whitehead, *Handbook for Economics Teachers*, op. cit.
48. See Chapter 16.
49. See Nuttall, T., and Torevell, A., 'Team teaching in economics: an experiment and its implications', *Economics*, vol. 17, pt 4, no. 28, spring 1968; and Trainor, D., 'Team teaching at Leeds Grammar School', *Economics*, vol. 10, pt 1, no. 43, summer 1973.

14 Case Studies in Economics*
Peter Maunder

What are case studies?

The words 'case studies' are capable of quite different meanings depending on the branch of science in which we are interested. It is therefore appropriate to make clear at the start of this chapter what these two words mean to an economist and, in particular, to one in a *teaching* situation. Before doing so it is pertinent to note that the case-study approach of doing *research* appears no longer to be 'a method of last resort' and one leading 'to unconfirmable conclusions'.[1] As a full-blown research strategy, case studies seem to have won increased favour applicable to all phases of scientific inquiry.

We may define a case study in economics as involving the consideration and detailed examination of something specific concerning the course of economic activity. As in other areas of social science, case studies in economics tend to focus on a plurality of interests – firms, organizations and the government – rather than on a single individual, as is usually typical of study (for example, medicine and psychology). There needs of course to be some sharpness of focus on some aspect of, say, business behaviour or government policy for there to be a genuine case study. Specifics concerning when and where and context necessarily point to microeconomics being much richer in case material than macroeconomics. The 'traditional' use of case studies in economics has been to show the applicability of economics principles. As Professor C.T. Sandford and M.S. Bradbury pointed out in the previous edition of *Teaching Economics*, 'ever since Adam Smith illustrated the principle of division of labour by the famous case study of a pin factory, economists have attempted to give concrete illustrations to principles by referring to particular cases'.[2] Appropriate illustrative material should bring realism to the learning process and help the student feel that he or she is dealing with the real world. It may be the real world but that very much of the past, such as Radford's description of life in a PoW camp in Germany,[3] or the current problems of a country depend-

---

* In preparing this chapter, the author has drawn on an earlier paper, 'The case study approach in bridging actuality with theory', in Ryba, R., and Robinson, B. (eds), *Aspects of Upper Secondary Economics Education in EEC Countries*, published by The Economics Association of Great Britain on behalf of the EEC Working Committee on Economics Education (1977), pp. 107–20.

ent on one commodity as in the case of Zambia.[4] The 'vividness derived from realism'[5] in case studies is shown in, for example, Westaway's illustration of the impact of inflation on individuals in very different economic circumstances.[6] Radford's case study first appeared in an academic journal whereas the other two case studies just cited form part of a collection of case material in particular branches of economics. Shorter straightforward illustrations of economic principles can also be found in newspaper articles. For example, *The Financial Times* for 7 April 1981 included a chart showing the sudden jump in demand for electricity when programmes on two television networks ended simultaneously. The switching on of electric kettles, lights and blankets at the end of *That's Life* on BBC1 and part one of *Ben Hur* provided the essence of the problems facing management in the electricity industry. From this vivid example it is a short step to an appreciation of the basic supply and demand problems of the electricity industry. (See Figures 14.1 and 14.2.)

In pursuit of the relevance of economic principles there has been during the past decade a change in the style of many basic economics textbooks published in the UK. The gap between economic theory and the real world has increasingly been bridged by the incorporation of material so as to colour some of the seemingly 'arid' areas of the discipline. This increased emphasis on real-life extended examples has none the less lagged behind the trend apparent in the USA. There, for many years introductory and intermediate textbooks have incorporated a self-contained teaching programme. Thus successive editions of Paul Samuelson's *Economics* have been expanded to include up-to-date empirical material in support of basic theoretical analysis. Indeed, so large have these basic texts become that they have been open to criticism on the grounds of overloading the student! Relatively few true casebooks have appeared, the most notable of which is by Fels and his associates. The casebook by Rendigs Fels and his colleagues at Vanderbilt University was prepared in the belief that 'in principle a person with a liberal education might take a lively interest for the rest of his life in economic theory rather than policy: but in practice a person with one year of economics will promptly forget the theory unless he has developed an interest in applying it to what he reads in newspapers and magazines. For purposes of a liberal education, theory and application must go hand in hand.'[7] Accordingly, Fels and his associates compiled material to which students could apply their understanding of supply and demand, allocative efficiency, national accounting and macro income determination. By 1979 they had prepared four editions of the casebook within a decade.

Kieffer and Spector's textbook collection of articles from recent American newspapers and periodicals is another casebook.[8] In Canada,

Fig. 14.1

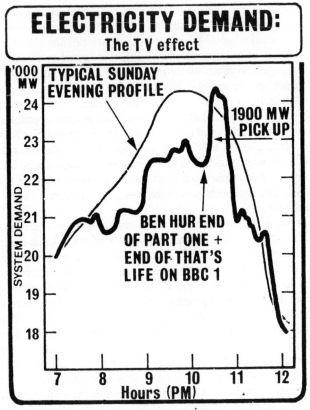

Source: The Financial Times, 7 April 1981.

Issues in the Canadian Economy offers a similar approach, itself in a newspaper format.[9] There is no obvious British parallel to these publications but the case approach is perceptible in various comprehension-type texts.[10]

Why has there been this growing interest by publishers for texts to become more empirically oriented? At root, the answer is that teachers have become uneasy concerning over-reliance on the deductive approach to economics teaching. John Maynard Keynes's favourite dictum that 'the theory of economics is a method rather than a doctrine, an apparatus of the mind, a technique of thinking which helps its possessor to draw correct conclusions'[11] emphasized deductive skills. However, how many students when first introduced to economics, at school, college or university, find the definition of concepts unappeal-

Fig. 14.2

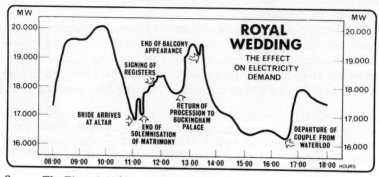

Source: *The Financial Times*, 31 July 1981.

ing and wonder where is the relationship with the real world? As the late Professor Alan Coddington put it, this 'technique-oriented' approach convinces 'most students that economics is just a game, and a rather tedious game at that. Whatever interest or enthusiasm they arrive with is gradually replaced by the conviction that economic analysis cannot, in principle, be relevant to anything they would ever be concerned with.'[12] The view that getting principles of economics understood first before turning to see how they stand up to real-world testing has fewer supporters these days. Professor Walter Elkan has argued that at undergraduate level it is misguided to teach theory one year in order to prepare students for its application in the following year. 'They must be taught in harness and that theory which has no applications in the solution or elucidation of real economic problems is not worth teaching at the undergraduate level.'[13]

It is with these reservations about deductive approaches that we turn to examine the alternative of teaching economics from looking at a specific problem before moving on to the general situation.

The inductive approach

Through the use of case studies, as the initial teaching vehicle, a start is made with the specific before moving to the general. Students have to grapple with a particular problem before attempting to perceive it in its broader theoretical context. Thus the need for theory is created and the theory becomes relevant. As Lesser has argued,[14] a student will, typically, more readily understand 'price elasticity of demand', say, if he is first put in the position of store owner setting prices for an after-Christmas sale or a car owner reacting to the increasing price of petrol. This, he suggested, is in keeping with people like Bruner[15] who consider that it is important for the student to have immediate experience prior to being asked to visualize or to build a mental picture of the abstract, so that ultimately he may manipulate words and symbols with confidence.

Teachers of marketing and management have for many years used case studies in order to promote the process of deriving basic principles, that is, to evolve generalizations from a series of particular company situations from 'learning by doing'. At the Harvard Business School where they have long been popular, a 'teaching case' is seen as:

a record of a business issue which actually has been faced by business executives, together with the surrounding facts, opinions and prejudices upon which executive decisions had to depend. These real and particularized cases are presented to students for considered analysis, open discussion and final decision as to the type of action which should be taken.[16]

The use of case studies in the teaching of business studies typically draws on the recent experience of a real company even though identities of personnel and products are often disguised. In other words, the case study is of a past event and is more properly described as a case *history*.

Hayward has stated neatly that: 'the essential purpose of a case is to enable students to take part in a real decision-making process without the costs (other than to personal esteem) of making mistakes'.[17]

One American writer of case material for the training of students of business administration has put it that 'instruction by the case method is participative and the main responsibility is on the student. . . . The student's benefit from the case method will be approximately proportional to the effort he puts into his analysis of the case.'[18] Greer is here emphasizing that the case study is a means to an end. 'The use of the case method is not primarily to help the student to accumulate a store of knowledge or to acquaint him with current business practices. These may come as side benefits. The primary purpose is to develop and sharpen the student's skills in working through a complex problem.'[19]

Space does not permit detailed critical consideration of the case method so intensively adopted at the Harvard Business School. In recent years some have come to doubt whether innumerable hypothetical business situations leave students with an undigested mass of impressions and only a slight grasp of principles.[20] Such doubts have even been expressed within Harvard itself. In his 1979 report on the Graduate Business School, Derek Bok, the President of Harvard University, argued that 'by concentrating on detailed factual situations, the case study method actually limits the time available for students to master analytical techniques and conceptual materials'.[21] Certainly there appears to be a trend at Harvard and elsewhere in the USA towards using shorter cases to avoid them becoming 'long and rather tortuous, testing the patience of teachers and participants alike'.[22] Duly noting this criticism, we can none the less note that in the UK the popularity of using business case material on many vocational courses appears unquestioned and has reached a point where clear guidance on their presentation and use is now widely available. Practical guides have been written by, for example, Easton[23] and Reynolds[24] while the Case Clearing House of Great Britain and Ireland continues to make available a wide range of materials concerning financial and marketing management.[25]

Now no teacher or lecturer of economics, even in higher education, will expect to rely *solely* on case studies à la Harvard. Sandford and Bradbury could trace only one economics course based *entirely* on case studies when writing in 1975. Even then they noted that this course was for mature students who had previously followed an introductory course taught by more traditional methods. But if we accept that an unrestricted diet of case material is improbable for teaching economics, what does examination of the case material in the business-studies area indicate about the merits of a more inductive approach to the teaching of economics?

The case for case studies

In essence, the enthusiasts of the case-study approach have emphasized steps in the learning process that should not lack support from teachers of economics. The teaching approach is to stress the understanding of given information – before the diagnosis of problem areas. Only then can consideration be given to specifying alternative courses of action and anticipating their possible outcome. Evaluation of these options and making a selection from among them then follows. Although the focus is typically on one firm, the emphasis on study skills has much relevance to teachers of economics. The need to develop inductive skills – plausible arguments from given facts – has now received powerful support from the incorporation of data-response questions in A-level examinations. It was in 1973 that the then two chief examiners in A-level economics for the London University Board argued that the existing range of examining modes needed to be extended. They stressed that sixth-form texts greatly overemphasized deductive reasoning and how difficult it was to frame questions in the essay paper that adequately tested inductive reasoning. The proposal for a data-response paper was not seen as innovative given that in other disciplines A-level candidates had to do more than recall conventional wisdom in essays. Their argument for an additional form of examination was, and is, in tune with the view that case material can help to develop a student's powers of interpretation, and that such an approach forces the student to grasp the essentials of the situation – to develop the need to recognize key points and explain them tersely. They need to recognize the really relevant as distinct from the less essential and peripheral. As Paul Tedesco has put it, 'Students learn (a) to sift and evaluate specific factual information; (b) to relate these facts to alternative situations and to become familiar with the tools of conceptual analysis; (c) to move cautiously toward value judgements while recognizing the need for careful analysis of conflicting legal and ethical values in the light of facts, the conceptual generalizations and the alternatives.'[26]

The following example from a recent London University A-level examination paper illustrates the arguments very well:

'Pan Am has formerly been the unchallenged leader of the airline industry. Last week it announced price cuts on an unprecedented scale. Is that the long-awaited death-rattle or the first sign of a new aggressive Pan Am?

Pan Am is axing its fares on all transatlantic routes by up to 60%. These cuts take their prices right down to Laker's own cut price preserve. (Laker had pioneered low price transatlantic air travel.) There is scarcely an airline left unharmed. British Airways and TWA are reluctantly following suit; British Caledonian face new, cheaper competition on the economy fare to Houston. Sir Freddie Laker has complained to the Department of Trade about Pan Am's 'predatory' attack.

Pan Am's move reverses the industry's drive to get fares up and goes against what British Airways thought was a consensus. Hope of boosting fare yields as part of the latter's salvation plan now look slim – the industry is locked into the cylce of price cut feeding on price cut.

The North Atlantic has always been a heartbreaking route for airlines: in and out of the red but too important to ignore. The total cost to the average airline of operating a wide-bodied 747 between London and New York is between $75,000 and $90,000 for the one-way trip. Breakeven occurs with about half the 402 seats filled on a 747. In the depth of winter this is difficult to achieve and traff.c is down this year.

What has stung Laker most is that they were about to launch a Regency Class, replacing 82 economy seats with 46 generously sized and spaced armchairs. With free champagne and menus this was aimed at businessmen, just about the only substantial winter market on the North Atlantic.'

With reference to costs, capacity and competition, what economic rationale can you offer for the situation described in the above passage?

Question 2, Paper 3, University of London GCE A-level, June 1983.

A good response to this extract would have included analysis of the types of competition to be found in an oligopolistic market with due attention paid to the seasonality of demand for air travel. Prior knowledge of the economics of international air travel was not the objective of the examiners. Now the purist might argue that this case study hardly required from the student a commitment to a case *solution*. None the less, it did require the student to recognize the existence of a few salient facts and, as Schnelle succinctly put it many years ago, to 'determine their meaning'.[27] Consideration of what is involved 'on the spot' sharpens the need to think critically. Appraisal of the situation minimizes the room for memory recall!

What further arguments can be cited for incorporating a more empirical content into teaching economics?

Apart from the realism brought to learning and the promotion of logical argument, a third argument in support of the case-study approach is that real-world illustrations of their very nature indicate the need for care in using pure tools of economic analysis. In practice, there may well be difficulties of measurement or of definition that circumscribe our theoretical tools. For a firm making consumer goods the nature of the price and income elasticity of demand is obviously of crucial importance: but how firms try to discover the relevant coefficients is something given scant attention in purely theoretical texts. Case material does tend to be incomplete but it does indicate the problems faced by decision-makers in possessing typically inadequate information.[28] We cannot always echo the thoughts of Sherlock Holmes who, on hearing Miss Morstan's story of the mysterious disappearance of her father, remarked 'a singular case'.[29]

A fourth argument in favour of actual industry examples is that they can highlight issues that otherwise tend to be rarely mentioned in the traditional approach. For example, a study of the glass bottle industry necessarily touches on the externalities problem given the increasing use of the one-trip bottle. Another key aspect of business life is the decision of firms to diversify into new areas of activity and the reasons for such a strategy. Of course, our basic theory of the firm radically simplifies the real world and can easily be criticized for its restrictive assumptions. What is argued for here is that we are candid about these assumptions. Firms typically make several products, a situation that arises from product development in conditions of risk and *uncertainty*. Too often the traditional approach to economics assumes a one-product firm with costless omniscience. Students are unaware of the uncertainties of the 'ordinary business of life'. The essential dynamic nature of the economy often fails to come through to students and, as a result, the crucial role of *decision-making*, so emphasized in business studies courses.

Using case studies

Case studies can be used in a variety of ways. Kemp[30] has suggested that some are essentially *exercises*, as in the pioneering text by Duesenberry and Preston;[31] others involve *problems* requiring imagination to see beyond the immediate effects to the long-term results; and yet other case studies can involve students in *role playing*.

There is considerable variety in the length and degree of difficulty of case material. Case studies are not standard in form. They do not typically result in a definite answer to questions but rather a series of alternative possibilities. (Anyone who has used 'The price of sin', the case written by Rendig Fels based on his own experience as a price controller concerned with the comfort of American troops stationed in Japan in 1945, can testify to that!)[32] Thus they offer a potentially very fruitful way of involving students with differing outlooks and prejudices. Some students are well motivated by being obliged to concentrate on something specific and can appreciate both the weaknesses of real-world data and the partiality of viewpoints of vested interest groups. Yet others find themselves uncomfortable in making something out of what appears meagre details! Enthusiasts of the case-study approach stress the importance of feedback both from student to student and also from student to teacher. The case method encourages interaction with other students: differing approaches enrich the learning process.

The problem in using case studies

The dangers in using poor, biased or unrepresentative extended examples should be obvious enough. The major weakness of the case-study approach is, however, that so many by their very nature are micro-oriented. Macroeconomics tends to be less specific in either temporal or spatial dimension, such that it offers few obvious case studies. It is something of a moot point whether, for example, 'Incomes policy since 1964 in Britain' is really a case study. This is a *topic* that is an inherent part of an A-level course. Some case studies cover issues in the micro area that are *not* explicitly part of the A-level syllabi. It has to be recognized that computer simulation games need to provide something to fill the weakness of the case-study approach in the macro area.

A second problem alleged to arise with case studies is their time-consuming nature, which is a serious issue given the limited time to cover a wide syllabus. Thus, as Sandford and Bradbury succinctly put it, 'realism in depth may be purchased at the price of realism in breadth'.[33] We have the economist's familiar trade-off of the costs and benefits of using a particular case. Of course, the teacher has to be prudent over the extent of case studies but in fact he is facing an issue with which the whole subject concerns itself – the allocation of scarce resources. J. Oliver has stressed the danger that case studies 'can easily become anecdotal rather than analytic'.[34]

It has been fairly pointed out that case material 'needs constant revision and renewal'.[35] However, this does not conflict with the interests of publishers of such material who are increasingly lowering their first-print runs and favour reprinting *amended* copy rather than tying up capital in large stocks for a lengthy period. The report, *The Teaching of Economics in Schools*, by the joint committee in Britain of the Royal Economic Society, the Association of University Teachers of

Economics and the Economics Association, which referred to this problem of dating, also considered that 'good microeconomic case studies, if they are to excite the interest of boys and girls, should relate to current and *local* problems. They will differ from region to region of the country and from rural to urban areas.'[36] Here the report emphasized that case material with a local orientation is rarely available and its preparation must be the responsibility of the keen teacher.

Conclusion

The arguments above are put forward in the belief that in the teaching of economics the use of case studies can contribute to the building of a good foundation of economics understanding. But not every teacher will find them easy to use. Even at Vanderbilt University where Rendigs Fels has striven for a more empirical approach to economics teaching, the case approach has not found general support. Professor W.O. Thwealt abandoned the case-study approach, claiming, 'I felt like Leonard Bernstein with no orchestra. I was the only one doing anything . . . Rendigs is a master of the Socratic method – the ability to ask questions, get things out of students, but keep it orderly, not let it get too diffuse. The case method requires that. I tried and failed miserably.'[37] However, others have found that at least some students have enjoyed using case studies and of course enthusiasm is a valuable ally for the teacher. Attiyeh *et al.* have claimed that 'cases are both fun and intellectually satisfying and students learn most when they enjoy what they are doing'.[38]

In the UK there has, as yet, not been much research made of the value of case studies in teaching economics. This is really not very surprising given the predictable problems involved – What is one testing? With whom does one make the comparison? But one recent piece of research can be cited. Using a case study(!) based upon the subscription rates, revenue and financial strategy of the Amateur Fencing Association, Carr tried to measure whether this enhanced the understanding of the concept of elasticity. He found a group taught using this case had no statistically superior score compared with a second matched group taught in the 'traditional textbook way'. Evidence of how students were stimulated by the case study was necessarily very subjective but Carr appeared to believe that case-study appraisal had encouraged participation by those students usually backward in contributing to class discussion.[39] More such research is needed to substantiate this proposition.

Notes and references

1. Yin, R.K., 'The case study as a serious research strategy', *Knowledge: Creation, Diffusion, Utilization*, vol. 3, no. 1, September 1981, p. 97. See

also Casley, D.J., and Lury, D.A., *Data Collection in Developing Countries* (Oxford University Press, 1981) ch. 5: 'The case study', for a review of the case approach in a particular geographical context.

2. Sandford, C.T., and Bradbury, M.S., 'The use of case studies in economics', in Lee, N. (ed.), *Teaching Economics*, 2nd edn (Heinemann Educational Books, 1975) p. 244.

3. Radford, R.A., 'The economic organization of a PoW camp', *Economica*, vol. 2, 1945, pp. 189–201.

4. Potts, L., 'Zambia – the development of a one-product mineral economy', in Maunder, P. (ed.), *Case Studies in Development Economics* (Heinemann Educational Books, 1982) pp. 113–38.

5. Sandford and Bradbury, op. cit., p. 245.

6. Westaway, A.J., 'The British tax system and the effect of inflation', in Maunder, P. (ed.), *Case Studies in Public Sector Economics* (Heinemann Educational Books, 1982) pp. 88–114.

7. Fels, R., Buckles, S., Johnson, W.L., *Casebook of Economic Problems and Policies: Practice in Thinking* (St Paul, Minnesota, West Publishing, 1979) p. v.

8. Kieffer, R.J., and Spector, L.C., *Applying Microeconomic Principles: A Student Guide to Analyzing News* (New York, Harper & Row, 1979).

9. Published by the Canadian Foundation for Economic Education, 252 Bloor Street, Toronto, Ontario, Canada.

10. For an Australian perspective, see also Gregory, A., 'Using a source materials approach in economics', *Economics*, vol. 18, pt 1, no. 77, spring 1982, pp. 27–9.

11. Keynes, J.M., General Editorial Introduction to all texts in the Cambridge Economic Handbooks series which he founded in 1922. Books in the series include Bauer, P.T., and Yames, B.S., *The Economics of Under-developed Countries* (Nisbet & Co., and Cambridge University Press, 1970). One might also note Lord Robbins's well-known pronouncement that 'The nature of economic analysis . . . consists of deductions from a series of postulates', in *Nature and Significance of Economic Science*, 2nd edn (Macmillan, 1952) p. 99.

12. Coddington, A., 'Teaching economics', *Universities Quarterly*, vol. 26, autumn 1972, pp. 467–8.

13. Elkan, W., 'Bringing economics back to earth', *The Times Higher Education Supplement*, 13 December 1974, p. 13. Also published as 'How one might teach Economics to undergraduates', *Economics*, vol. 11, pt 4, no. 52, winter 1975, p. 214.

14. Lesser, B., 'A comment on the case study approach to teaching economics', *Economics*, vol. 14, pt 1, no. 61, spring 1978, p. 9.

15. Bruner, J.S., *Toward a Theory of Instruction* (Cambridge Mass., Harvard University Press, 1963).

16. Gragg, C.I., 'Because wisdom can't be told', in McNair, M.P. (ed.), *The Case Method at the Harvard Business School* (London and New York, McGraw-Hill, 1954) p. 6.

17. Hayward, C., 'Case study developments in the UK', *Industrial and Commercial Training*, vol. 6, no. 10, October 1974, p. 480.

18. Greer, T.V., *Cases in Marketing: Orientation, Analysis and Problems*, 2nd edn (New York, Macmillan, 1979) p. 2.

19. Ibid., p. 2.
20. This danger has long been recognized by enthusiasts of case studies. For example, Willings, writing in 1968, stated that:

> As a training method it must also be said that the case study is often notoriously unsuccessful. This is because too much is expected of it. The term case study *method* is an unfortunate one. The case study can never be a method in itself. It is a training aid. . . . The failure of the case study to achieve what is expected of it is often not due to the case itself. It is due to the fact that either too much was expected of it, or that the person using it had not a sufficiently clear idea himself of what could be expected of it. It is important to know what the case study can do. It is of equal importance to know what the case study cannot do (Willings, D.R., *How to Use the Case Study in Training for Decision Making* (Business Publications, 1968) p. 6).

21. Dafter, R., 'Harvard's sacred cow in dispute', *The Financial Times*, 13 June 1979, p. 15. See also Kiechel III, W., 'Harvard Business School restudies itself', *Fortune*, 18 June 1979, pp. 48–58. For a Harvard student's experiences, see Cohen, P., *The Gospel according to the Harvard Business School* (Penguin, 1974).
22. Binsted, D., Stuart, R., Long, G., 'Promoting useful management learning problems of translating and transfer', in Beck, J., and Cox, C. (eds), *Advances in Management Education* (*John Wiley*, 1980) p. 344.
23. Easton, G., *Learning From Case Studies* (Prentice-Hall, 1982).
24. Reynolds, J.I., *Case Method in Management Education: Guide for Effective Use* (Geneva, International Labour Office, 1980).
25. The Case Clearing House of Great Britain and Ireland is based at Cranfield Institute of Technology, Cranfield, Bedford.
26. Tedesco, P., 'Using case studies to teach economics', *Rapport*, no. 5, winter 1976, published by the Canadian Foundation for Economic Education, Toronto, Canada.
27. Schnelle, K.E., *Case Analysis and Business Problem Solving* (McGraw-Hill, 1967) p. 15.
28. As a professor of business management noted in the preface of his book of cases, one is always looking for 'perfect material for an excellent case'. He noted this hesitancy could be used as an excuse to put off indefinitely his intention of assembling a collection of cases for an Indian audience! Murty, V.S., *Case Problems in Business Management* (London, Asia Publishing House, 1962) p. xii.
29. Conan Doyle, Sir A., 'The sign of four', in *Sherlock Holmes: Selected Stories* (Oxford University Press, 1951) p. 79.
30. Kemp, B., 'The housing market – a case for supply and demand analysis', *Economics*, vol. 13, pt 2, no. 58, summer 1977, pp. 40–5. This flexibility has been noted in other social science disciplines. See Cohen, A.R., 'The teaching of organizational behaviour', in Freeman, R.D., Cooper, C.L., Stumpf, S.A. (eds), *Management Education: Issues in Theory, Research and Practice* (New York, John Wiley, 1982) p. 142.
31. Duesenberry, J.S., and Preston, L.E., *Cases and Problems in Economics* (Prentice-Hall, 1960).
32. Fels, R., 'The price of sin', in Fels, Buckles, and Johnson, op. cit.

33. Sandford and Bradbury, op. cit., p. 251.
34. Oliver, J.M., 'The educational value of economics: some practical implications', in Whitehead, D. (ed.), *Curriculum Development in Economics* (Heinemann Educational Books, 1974) p. 146.
35. *The Teaching of Economics in Schools*, Report of a Joint Committee of the Royal Economic Society, the Association of University Teachers of Economics and the Economics Association (Macmillan, 1973) p. 19.
36. Ibid., p. 20.
37. Jenkins, E., 'Should Cincinnatti Bell charge extra? A case study approach to economics', in *Report on Teaching 3* issued by Educational Change Inc. (New York) with *Change: The Magazine of Higher Learning*, vol. 9, no. 1, January 1977, p.9.
38. Attiyeh, R., Bach, G.L., Lumsden, K., *Basic Economics: Theory and Cases* (Englewood Cliffs, Prentice-Hall, 1973) preface.
39. Carr, N.J., 'An evaluation of the use of case studies in economics at Advanced Level in schools', *Research Papers in Economics Education no. 2* (University of London Institute of Education, 1982).

Economics teachers have long recognized that field-work has gre~~
value, but it was only in the 1960s and 1970s, at least in the UK, that the
activity came to be seen as an integral part of the well-balanced
economics curriculum.

Yet it is a technique that sometimes causes anxiety. New teachers,
having for the first time arranged a visit to a factory, will be nervously
hoping that the right firm has been chosen, and that the pupils will
co-operate. The more experienced teacher, though perhaps used to
arranging visits to establishments near the school, may find that it takes
more confidence to extend their field-study to include survey and
observation work in the locality or to a residential course in another
region.

Therefore this chapter has a dual task. On the one hand, it must
provide practical advice to teachers so that they can arrange field
activities with confidence. On the other hand, it must first show how
field-study can be the most productive and rewarding of learning
experiences, and how it can involve a much wider variety of approaches
than might be supposed.

The range of field-work opportunities

All field-work requires pupils to use their eyes, ears or mouths (perhaps
aided by pens, cameras or tape-recorders) in some kind of inquiry using
the people and the environment beyond the school gates.

Field-study often focuses on a programmed visit to an institution,
'programmed' in the sense that the visit will involve carefully
sequenced activities for the participants. For the economics teacher
the dominant example of this will probably always be the 'factory visit',
typically lasting perhaps one or two hours, and consisting of an introduction of some sort (such as the company film), followed by a works
tour, and ending with a question and answer or forum session with the
firm's personnel.

Yet the term 'factory visit' is to be regretted, since it implies an
unnecessarily restricted view of the opportunities available. Many
goods are produced in establishments other than factories. (There is,
for example, much to be observed on a farm or at the premises of a
newspaper.) More particularly, there are valuable lessons to be learned

from seeing the operations of the service sector, which of course ranges from financial institutions and retail outlets to transport depots and markets of all kinds.

Even those economic undertakings that consist primarily of offices may have much to observe, particularly with the introduction of new technology. Even if they do not, it is common for teachers to realize the benefits of meeting decision-makers in the context of their usual working environment rather than requiring them to visit the school environment where they may be ill at ease and have less of an impact on the pupils. This applies as much to trade-union officials and local authority or planning staff, as to management or managers of Job Centres. Visits to more specialist institutions may even allow pupils to hear real-life discussion and debate in progress, particularly in Parliament or local council meetings, legal bodies or public inquiries.

If the desire is to find visual stimulus rather than to meet decision-makers, then the economics teacher should not neglect the wide range of specialist museums. Some of these are designated as 'industrial museums', covering a wide range of the economic activity in the area served (Kirkcaldy, Manchester, Birmingham, Bristol and Cardiff, for example), while others focus on one local industry (pottery at Stoke, brewing at Burton, cider at Hereford, shipbuilding and sewing-machines at Clydebank, coal-mining at Blaenavon, Stoke and Retford, textiles in various North of England towns, and so on). Many museums are explicitly historical in emphasis (the Black Country Museum at Dudley, the Ironbridge museum at Telford, or the National Museum of Labour History in London), whereas others are at pains to emphasize recent innovations (the London Telecom Technology Showcase, for example). Though most of these museums are geared to school visits with a scientific or historical orientation, they can be used by the economics teacher too, at the very least to provide the background understanding necessary for subsequent visits to firms.

The institutions that can be visited, therefore, range from factories to offices and service establishments to museums. However, field-study need not focus on an institution at all, and a second category of activity might usefully be designated 'outdoor inquiry work'. This often involves survey and observation work either at one location (the archetypal case is the 'traffic count') or travelling from place to place (on foot in a town trail, or on wheels in a coach trail). Some activities additionally involve inquiring of individual people, either formally through questionnaires, or in a less structured way by talking to shopkeepers or people at bus-stops or the receptionists of firms on an industrial estate.

The focus of any of these examples of 'outdoor inquiry work' might be a particular topic or issue (supply and demand in the housing market, relative prices in different shops, seasonal employment irregularities, and so on). Alternatively, the focus might be on the area itself and the interaction of all the economic forces within it (for example, an 'economic planning study' might look at recent economic change in an area).

These different kinds of field-study, under the two broad headings 'visits to institutions' and 'outdoor inquiry work', are not mutually exclusive, indeed they are likely to reinforce each other. Thus many economics teachers arrange a block of field-work, usually of between three and seven days. This can be a residential experience in a region that contrasts with that of the school or college.

Such a field-course can incorporate the whole range of techniques described above: a typical day might include a visit to a large and a small firm, a discussion with a trade-union official or newspaper editor, an hour's survey work on foot, with coach travel in between for observation work, and perhaps even with the evening used to record the day's findings (though some relaxation time is advised!). Field-courses may take the form of a straightforward study of the area or region, but there are advantages of coherence in following a particular line of inquiry (such as economic policy in the inner city), or to follow a chain of decision-making (such as the impact of monetary policy and banking-sector decisions on industrial investment).

The range of field-work possibilities, whether integrated with the school timetable or in block field-courses, is extensive. The teacher will choose between these depending on the purpose of the field-work and the demands which she or he wishes to make on the youngsters involved.

The aims and objectives of field-work

Teachers who have used field-work over a period of time are often amazed at how much knowledge and understanding their pupils seem to gain. Some of this concerns information that it is difficult to acquire in the classroom, such as facts about economic activity in a lesser known area or firm, or it involves expertise that the teacher may not have – such as the field of industrial relations.

However, the improvement is not confined to new knowledge; field-study seems also to reinforce past learning and to facilitate subsequent learning. For example, it seems easier to grasp the essential ideas about investment after seeing new machines alongside old. In particular, subsequent learning of concepts and theories is made easier if the learner has a wealth of experience on which these can be based.

Indeed, field-work provides a substantial opportunity for pupils to develop higher-order abilities, such as learning to generalize from particular concrete situations, and the ability to synthesize information, ideas or viewpoints. Moreover, whatever their academic ability, economics pupils will have some acquaintance with concepts and theories that they can apply to the real world, and so the locality can be used as a laboratory to test theories by comparing their predictions with reality.

The pupils may of course discover that reality does sometimes diverge from the consensus of the textbook; the role of the teacher is then to show that both the textbook analysis and the actual observations have legitimacy. The results of direct observation may of course supplement textbook learning in examinations, provided that the pupils do not distort the questions to accommodate their enthusiasm to report on their own findings!

Indeed, for many teachers the main benefit of field-study is this generation of enthusiasm about economics. This may arise simply because the pupils are escaping the confines of a classroom whose activities all too often fail to tap their full ability, but in the main the gain in interest arises because direct acquaintance with a situation kindles an interest in it. Any demonstration of a subject's relevance is bound to enhance motivation. It should be added that the teacher may have wider affective objectives than these: for example, experience of the sights and sounds of a factory may change youngsters' feelings about industrial bargaining, and meeting people may make it easier to instil in pupils the concern for humanity that is the proper basis for all social science.

As these last comments have suggested, the economics teacher's aims and objectives should not relate too narrowly to the subject of economics. Visiting people at work or who are unemployed may help youngsters to consider their own options for later life, working in groups in a non-competitive situation may help them to learn to co-operate with others and to exercise leadership and organization. The pupils may acquire skills of observation or data collection and analysis that are transferable to other subjects and situations. Being exposed to various views may help them to develop a critical faculty and the ability to form their own judgements in all subjects, not just in economics. Pupils engaged in open-ended interrogation may be developing language and listening skills, and field-work will demand the confidence to relate to adults who are not in a position of authority over them.

Perhaps above all the pupils' relationship with the teacher will be changed, not least because in field-work the youngsters learn without the teachers teaching, and in subsequent sessions they may have experience to offer that matches or even exceeds that of the teacher.

The place of field-work in the syllabus

The realization that field-study arranged by the economics teacher may have benefits beyond the economics component of the curriculum prompts the question whether it is sensible for field-work to aim at the outset to build links with other subjects. There are various possibilities – from visits focusing on employment arranged jointly with the careers teacher, to visits centring on industrial processes arranged with the science or home economics department. There is probably most potential, however, in linking with history, geography or social science subjects. The pupils will see how the separate contributions of these humanities disciplines need to be integrated in understanding reality; economics students will learn to see problems in human as well as economic terms.

In the main, however, field-work tends to focus initially at least on one teaching subject. In economics, almost any syllabus topic can be illuminated by a visit or inquiry outside the classroom. For example, visits to firms are useful not only for microeconomic topics such as industrial location, monopolies and mergers policy, or costs and pricing, but also to inquire into the impact on the firm of the recession or macroeconomic policy or exchange rate changes or links with the Third World.

Of course, certain kinds of firm may best illustrate particular topics: perhaps smaller firms for finance, bakeries for economies of scale, farms for EEC policy, or the coal industry for wage systems. Some topics lend themselves to field-study but require a wider variety of field-work methods: to examine a labour market (including aspects such as labour mobility, or the local employment multiplier) it would be necessary not only to visit employers, but also perhaps to use a questionnaire in the street or from door to door, to examine advertisements for jobs, and to meet trade union representatives. However, it has to be admitted that some topics can only be examined in the field once good contacts have been developed: for example, studies show that subtle sex discrimination is still a feature in keeping women's wages low, but casual inquiries of employers will hardly illuminate the matter. Indeed, one must beware of bias resulting from selecting out topics that focus on distribution simply because ones relating to economic efficiency are easier to study on the ground.

If, however, the time allowed for field-work is restricted, perhaps to one or two visits to firms in a teaching programme, then the teacher may want to use such opportunities to examine a wide span of the syllabus. This raises the question of whether such visits should be used at the end of an economics course so that students can apply as much as possible of their learning in an integrated way, or at the start when the pupils have an urgent need for experience of the concrete.

Which pupils can benefit from field-work?

This chapter has argued that economics field-work can take a wide variety of forms, with a diversity of aims, and can be used to teach many topics including some that draw together a number of subject disciplines. The implication of this reasoning is that it is wrong to see field-study as suited only to older or more academically inclined students.

It has been shown in a number of schools that quite young children, even those in primary schools, can make good use of survey work or visits to firms (where this is legally and practically possible). Indeed, the younger the pupil, the more important are activities of this kind: without it they lack the experience of the real world that older students have begun to acquire (through part-time jobs, etc.); with it, economics lessons are less likely to avoid the danger of overconcentration on abstract material. Similarly, older but less academic pupils need experience of the concrete in order to stimulate them, and through which to develop skills that teachers have a tendency to leave dormant – such as the collection and organization of information, or the ability to generalize from experience.

Clearly, the emphasis in field-work must differ according to the pupils' ages and abilities; the important principle is that it must stretch the youngsters involved, and (for the less academic) lift their horizons beyond visits to firms concentrating solely on the jobs open to them in later life.

Sometimes, however, teachers are less willing to arrange field-study for younger or less academic pupils because they fear that the numbers involved may be too great to provide for. This is partly a practical question. For extensive work outside the school, teacher unions recommend that there are never less than two teachers involved, and that there should be one teacher for every ten pupils (the LEA may have different rules). If transport is necessary, the school minibus may take only twelve or fifteen at a time. Therefore, field-work for a class of twenty-five or thirty would certainly require co-operation from colleagues either to join the party or to supervise the section of the class whose turn it is to work on their own in the classroom. Fortunately, staff are usually willing to do this since they have much to gain too.

Even without such constraints, group size is an important consideration for the success of the field-work activities themselves. Large firms will sometimes accept a visit for a full class of thirty, but teachers should steel themselves to insist that this is only worthwhile if the works tour component of a visit takes place in groups small enough to hear the guide and to ask questions (which normally means no more than six to eight in a group). Fortunately, firms can often manage this using apprentices or retired members; however, if not, the visit is often enhanced not diminished if groups have to be split into two to go to different establishments with the onus of reporting back to each other.

Activities for the pupils

Finding ways of ensuring that pupils participate fully in the field-work is the key to the success or failure of the enterprise.

Fortunately, 'outdoor inquiry work', such as town trails or area surveys, almost inevitably involves activity by the pupils. Unless the aim is to take photographs or tape-record interviews, it is usually essential for them to have clipboards (which can be made from bulldog clips and stout card, enclosed in a transparent plastic bag in case of rain). Even coach tours can involve stops in lay-bys to allow information to be recorded.

The activity can involve plotting information on a map, such as classifying buildings according to whether they involve primary, secondary or tertiary economic activity. The inquiry can be precisely defined or can be open-ended: the younger pupil might be told to look at a particular building and discover its history from the plaque on the wall (a sequence of instructions of this sort forms the basis for many town trails), whereas older students might simply be told to go to a designated area and look for evidence of buildings having changed their economic use. Inquiry work is particularly successful if each pupil has to bring back different information – this is a necessity in a cross-section analysis such as a price survey. Such outdoor inquiry work requires that the pupils be carefully prepared in observation techniques (such as ways of dating buildings) and ways of eliciting and recording information.

During a visit to an institution, however, there is a danger that some of the potential benefits will be lost if the pupils are expected merely to be passive listeners and watchers rather than to take an active part in the discovery process. There are many pupil activities that the institution or firm involved might agree to if the purpose is explained to them. In a factory visit, it is not completely unknown for youngsters to be able to try their hand at a small part of the production process (fitting components, etc.), but more usually their role is that of observing and asking questions of their guides and perhaps the production workers. During the visit itself, it is possible for them to complete a worksheet or questionnaire. This can be useful if the objective of the visit is to elicit particular information such as the firm's payment system and workers' response to it, but in many cases open-ended questions are less restrictive – the pupils could be told to look for examples of the division of labour, or of differing capital : labour ratios, or to find evidence explaining the firm's location.

The recording of verbal information can be time-consuming (unless tape-recorders are available) but other forms of information could be considered. For reasons of commercial security many firms ban cameras, but the pupils may still make sketches or draw diagrams of the production process. The visit itself may culminate in a discussion session involving management, workers and trade unions, but the end result of the visit using follow-up periods in class or homework may be more ambitious: a debate, an essay, a wallchart, a case study or a printed report, for example.

In many instances visits can generate sustained links with the firms. This may be stimulated if the pupils mount a report-back session in front of representatives of the firm, of if A-level students (particularly following in-depth visits to smaller firms) produce a report containing ideas of use to the firm concerned.

Whatever form the visit takes, it is essential that the pupils know why they are going and what they are supposed to be doing. The firm may be able to supply marketing literature for use beforehand. However, the onus is on the teacher to structure the preparation carefully in order that the pupils do ask questions in the limited time available. Giving each pupil responsibility for obtaining information on a particular aspect of the topic gives each one some responsibility to speak up during the visit; alternatively, perhaps the pupils could decide the questions to be included on the questionnaire they will fill in.

Arranging visits to firms

If the pupils are to engage in any of the more productive activities outlined in the previous section, visits to firms have to be organized with that goal in mind. Ideally, the teacher should visit the firm in advance to meet the staff and see the works where the tour will take place, and the firm should be involved with the teacher in drawing up the programme. A sheet summarizing the purpose of the visit could usefully be given to all employees involved in the visit. This is the only certain way to avoid the danger that the emphasis on economics in the visit will be misunderstood and to prevent the guides orientating their tour towards careers or the details of the technical process.

It should be possible to find firms that are prepared to commit themselves to this extent; after all, they may be dealing with people who are not only potential employees, but local inhabitants, future voters and potential customers. Ironically, the recession has sometimes made it easier rather than more difficult for firms to work with schools, since they sometimes have underemployed staff, or at least feel that public relations are more important at a time when the future is uncertain. None the less, during the recession, and because of the growth of requests from schools (for example, those connected with the Technical and Vocational Education Initiative), the economics teacher must be prepared to come across rather more firms who are unable to help, and must therefore adopt a more professional approach to convince the others that field-work is worthwhile.

The teacher's first organizational task is to choose which firms to approach. The school (perhaps through its careers teacher) may have long-standing contacts. If not, advice may come from the local chamber of commerce, the local authority's industrial development officer, or the local schools industry liaison officer (who may have issued a schools' directory of firms); the TUC has regional liaison officers who can help with trade-union contacts. Otherwise it is a matter of using publicly available information: for example, most public libraries have a large directory of firms called *Kompass*.

Using small firms may have advantages, such as proximity to the school and the likelihood of speaking directly to the owner, though there are also drawbacks such as the limit to the size of the party. A teacher should certainly give preference to a firm that will accommodate particular requests – such as the inclusion of a woman manager in the staff involved to avoid giving the impression that industry is not relevant to girls, or the opportunity to speak to the firm's shop stewards.

Whichever firm is selected, the first approach will normally be by letter (to the managing director or personnel manager), giving details of the pupils and the course, the proposed content of the visit, suggested dates and times, the offer of a preliminary visit, and a proposal that the teacher will follow up the letter with a phone call. Subsequent letters or phone calls can explore restrictions related to the visit itself (such as the suitability of various kinds of clothing and footwear).

How far in advance this initial contact needs to be made depends on how intensively the establishment is used by schools: one month may be sufficient for a small local firm, whereas in peak periods up to nine months may be needed for a national newspaper or the Bank of England. Thus, full field-courses need to be prepared well in advance, with accommodation, and any popular firms being given six to nine months' notice.

Most teachers can probably draw heavily on experience within the school for guidance on practical arrangements. Accommodation during a course is usually in youth hostels or even cheap guest houses, but the LEA may own a field centre. Transport for short trips can often be provided by school mini-bus, though for longer trips the organizer should look into coach hire or rail travel (which has reduced rates for parties of schoolchildren). On longer trips the teacher must ensure that the pupils understand the arrangements for refreshments. Parents must have given consent for the trip (many LEAs have a standard indemnity form for them to sign), but even so the teacher must make arrangements that will apply when things do go wrong, such as what happens when pupils get lost.

If the cost of the trip looks prohibitive to the school or to the pupils, then the teacher may even be able to raise some money, perhaps through a fund-raising enterprise by pupils (which can teach them some economics at the same time).

Extended field-work courses

Some teachers who run block field-study courses use them to substitute for field-work that would otherwise be integrated with school work. In these cases the motive for running a field-work course may be to avoid the practical difficulties involved in getting the school timetable to accommodate outside trips. In practice, however, there are other ways round timetable problems, such as using breaks or lunchtimes to extend lesson time, doing inter-subject field-work involving adjacent lessons, or convincing the head and fellow staff of its merits sufficiently to allow you to eat into other teaching periods. Moreover, the extended field-courses themselves cannot always be arranged to coincide with half-term or Easter holidays, and some teachers have to use a period of term-time such as Sunday–Thursday in the autumn or spring (carefully timed to avoid clashes with Saturday jobs, or with the summer term's overbooked hostels and end-of-year lethargy).

Therefore, in practice blocks of field-work should usually be justified not in terms of their practical advantages but because of the scope they offer. Students can get to know a region very different from their own – perhaps the 'M4 belt' with its new technology, or the Scottish lowlands and the north of England with their declining heavy industry, or the capital itself, or the mixture of agriculture and industry found in north-west Wales, Cumbria and the Thames Valley. These longer courses permit the extended lines of inquiry referred to earlier, perhaps with a visit to a firm being followed by contact with its suppliers, and then a local study of its impact. During the course, each day's experience builds on the cumulative experience of the preceding days, and the group enthusiasm that is generated allows day and evening work to capitalize on this opportunity. There are of course equivalent advantages to field-work that is integrated into the normal timetable: it can be timed at just the right moment in the syllabus when outside experience is most needed, and it enables youngsters to know their own locality. But clearly, the extended course of field-work need not replace school-based field-work (at least not in every year of a teaching programme) and therefore it has much to commend it.

In recent years, economics teachers have begun to experiment with field-work abroad. The increased cost can sometimes be partly offset by sponsorship – by the EEC, by the British Council, or by local firms whose sister companies will be visited overseas. Such money-raising allowed one teacher, for example, to arrange a study tour in India, though more usually visits are to the Continent. Initial contacts can be made through the embassy of the country concerned, or the target city's chamber of commerce, with youth hostels as the accommodation. If the visit is to countries such as West Germany or the Benelux group, the visits are often conducted entirely in English – although the possibility of joint field-courses with the modern languages department could be considered.

Conclusion

Some field-work is ambitious, some is more limited in scope. But the willingness of teachers to put effort into arranging it is testimony enough to its potential. The message of this chapter is that this potential will only be fully utilized if teachers adopt a purposeful and professional approach to the organization involved and take great care to plan tasks for the pupils that make full use of their abilities.

Appendix 15.1

Annotated bibliography on field-study in economics teaching

*   sources that give examples of field-study courses;
†   sources dealing with overseas field-study courses;
‡   sources giving practical hints on organizing visits to institutions;
§   sources dealing with outdoor inquiry work and town trails;
●   sources that discuss the use of field-study in economics education.

†‡   Assistant Masters and Mistresses Association, *Out of School – A Practical Guide to the Responsibilities of Teachers in Charge of Pupils on School Journeys* (1982).

†‡   Central Bureau for Educational Visits and Exchanges, *School Travel and Exchange*; *Help*.

*‡§●   Davidson, D., and Robinson, B., 'Visits and field studies – non-classroom teaching methods for the younger secondary pupil', in Robinson, K., and Wilson, R., *Extending Economics Within the Curriculum* (Routledge & Kegan Paul, 1977).

§   Hough, J., 'An economics trail', *Economics*, vol. 13, pt 1, no. 57, spring 1977, pp. 19–21. (This article is also reproduced in Whitehead, 1979; see below.)

*‡●   Houser, M., 'Close encounters of the first kind – experience programmes in economics education', *Economics*, vol. 18, pt 3, no. 79, autumn 1982, pp. 108–13.

*†●   McDougall, D., 'A trip to Europe', *Economics*, vol. 13, pt 1, no. 57, spring 1977, pp. 16–18.

*●   Ord, T., 'Voluntary residential economics course for part-time students', *Economics*, vol. 13, pt 3, no. 59, autumn 1977, pp. 78–80.

*†‡§●   Robinson, B., *Field Studies in Teaching Economics* (Economics Association, 1975).

‡●   Robinson, B., *Guidelines for Industrial Visits in Teaching Economics – The Small Firm, The Farm as a Firm, The Retail Store; The Education and Industry Centre* (Worcester College of Higher Education (free)).

*‡§●   Robinson B., 'Visits and field studies', in Lee, N., *Teaching Economics* (Heinemann Educational Books, 1975).

*†‡●   Robinson, B., 'The use of factory and farm visits', in Ryba, R., and Wilson, R. (eds), *Teaching the Economics of the EEC*, vol. 2 (Economics Association, 1983).

†‡   Schools Council, *Out and About – A Teachers' Guide to Safety on Educational Visits* (Evans/Methuen, 1972).

‡§●   Whitehead, D. (ed.), *Handbook for Economics Teachers* (Heinemann Educational Books, 1979) chs 8,9,25,26.

Appendix 15.2

A selection of museums with industrial themes

Birmingham   Museum of Science and Industry, Newhall Street, Birmingham B3 1RZ. Tel: 021 236 1022.

Blackburn   Lewis Textile Museum, Exchange Street, Blackburn. Tel: 0254 667130.

Blaenafon (Gwent)   Big Pit Museum of Coalmining. Tel: 0495 790311.

Bolton   Tonge Moor Textile Museum, The Library, Tonge Moor Road, Bolton. Tel: 0204 21394/22311 Ext. 383.

Bradford   Bradford Industrial Museum, Moorside Road, Eccleshill. Tel: 0274 631756.

Burton-on-Trent (Staffs)   The Bass Museum of Brewing, Horninglow Street, Burton-on-Trent. Tel: 0283 42031/45301.

Cardiff   Welsh Industrial and Maritime Museum. Tel: 0222 371805.

Dublin   Guinness Museum, Watling Street, Dublin.

Dudley   The Black Country Museum, Tipton Road. Tel: 021 557 9643.

Hereford   Museum of Cider, Grimmer Road, Hereford HR4 0LW. Tel: 0432 54207.

Kirkcaldy   Industrial and Social History Museum, Rectory Lane, Dysart.

Liverpool   Prescot Museum of Clock and Watch Making, 34 Church Street, Prescot L34 3LA. Tel: 051 430 7787.

London   Museum of Labour History, Limehouse, Town Hall, Commercial Road, London E14. Tel: 01 515 3229.

    Science Museum, Exhibition Road, South Kensington, London SW7. Tel: 01 589 3456.

    Telecom Technology Showcase, 135 Queen Victoria Street, London EC4V 4AT. Tel: 01 248 7444.

Manchester   North Western Museum of Science and Industry, and National Paper Museum, 97 Grosvenor Street, Manchester. Tel: 061 273 6636.

Newcastle upon Tyne Museum of Science and Engineering, Blandford House, Blandford Street, Newcastle upon Tyne. Tel: 0632 326789.

Northwich (Cheshire)   Salt Museum, London Road, Northwich.

Nottingham   Industrial Museum, Wallaton Park, Nottingham. Tel: 0602 284602.

Retford (Nottingham)   National Mining Museum, Lound Hall, Retford. Tel: Mansfield 860728.

St Helens (Merseyside)   Pilkington Glass Museum. Tel: 0744 28882 Ext. 2492.

Salford (Manchester)   Museum of Mining, Buile Hill Park, Eccles Old Road, Salford. Tel: 061 736 1832.

Sheffield   Kelham Island Industrial Museum, Alma Street, Sheffield. Tel: 0742 22106.

Stamford (Lincolnshire)   Stamford Brewery Museum, All Saint's Street, Stamford.

Stoke Bruerne (Northampton)   The Waterways Museum, Stoke Bruerne, Nr Towcaster. Tel: 0604 862229.

Stoke-on-Trent   Chatterley Whitfield Mining Museum, Chatterley Whitfield Colliery, Tunstall ST6 8UN. Tel: 0782 813337.

Stoke-on-Trent   Gladstone Pottery Museum, Uttoxeter Road, Longton. Tel: 0782 319232 or 311378.

Street (Somerset)   The Shoe Museum, C. & J. Clarke, High Street, Street, Somerset. Tel: 0458 43131.

Swansea   Maritime and Industrial Museum, South Dock. Tel: 0792 55006.

Telford (Shropshire)   Ironbridge Gorge Museum, Shropshire TF8 7AW. Tel: 095 245 3522.

See also: *Museums and Galleries in Great Britain and Northern Ireland* (ABC Publications, annual).

16 Audio-visual Aids in the Study of Economics
Robert Wilson

'The teacher presents the learning task. . . . The manner of presentation depends on the sort of outcome expected. . . . Presentations are more or less abstract. The more verbal, the more technical, the more theoretical they are, the greater their demand on the abstractive potential of the pupil. Visual aids, examples, diagrams and demonstrations concretize presentation. Invoking the familiar is another way of lowering the cognitive stress or the abstract demand on the learner.'[1]

'No reception without reaction, no impression without correlative expression – this is the great maxim which the teacher ought never to forget. An impression which simply flows in at the pupil's eyes or ears, and in no way modifies his active life, is an impression gone to waste. It is physiologically incomplete. It leaves no fruits behind it in the way of capacity acquired. . . . The most durable impressions are those on account of which we speak or act, or else are inwardly convulsed.'[2]

Audio-visual aids have no automatic, self-evident virtues. Any case for introducing them into a learning process stands or falls on their ability to make learning easier or quicker. The capacity of audio-visual aids to contribute to learning lies not so much in the intrinsic merits of the particular aid but in the skill of the practitioner, the user of the aid. In this chapter, the reader is introduced to the main aids available, and suggestions are made with regard to ways and means of maximizing the potential benefit of audio-visual aids in the teaching of economics.

For the teacher working in an institution that is to be equipped, re-equipped or rationalized in terms of its audio-visual resources, financial stringency is likely to dictate for the foreseeable future that no item is available as a matter of course, and a case must be made for each in turn. All parties to the discussion will have their own idea as to what constitutes an acceptable minimum level of provision, and the enthusiastic advocate of audio-visual aids should not be surprised, alarmed or offended when confronted by scepticism on the part of officialdom.

Surfaces for notes and diagrams
There was a time when it could safely be assumed that a *chalkboard* would be a standard fitting in all teaching rooms, but such is no longer

the case; for some authorities blackboards requiring the use of chalk are *passé*, and newly built educational institutions may well be equipped instead with mobile whiteboards offering surfaces designed to make use of fibre-tipped pens. Whatever the style and composition of the display board, the eonomics teacher will require a large surface area because it is frequently the case that fairly complex diagrams, graphs or tables need to coexist with supporting explanatory notes, and clarity of exposition dictates the need for salient features to be distanced from each other, as in the teaching of the theory of pure monopoly, for example. The need for a sizeable surface area suggests that a permanent fitting is desirable. A mobile, smaller writing surface will prove valuable for use in group activity work. For example, a group of four or five students can be assigned the task of constructing key diagrams relating to the theory of value or demonstrating the impact of a falling exchange rate on export and import prices. Students can take turns to tackle a diagram, table, etc. and their efforts will be sufficiently large to permit group discussion and evaluation. Provided that the tasks assigned are worthwhile, the display-board corner need not appear any less attractive to students than, say, the games and simulations corner in a room set up for group activity. Frequently, a teacher may wish to retain a piece of boardwork for use in a subsequent lesson. Given that few teachers have exclusive use of a classroom, it is well nigh essential for display boards to be sectioned if a plaintive 'please leave' is to be acknowledged and respected by other users.

The display board's ubiquity is a source of both strength and weakness. A chalkboard is sufficiently uninteresting intrinsically to prevent the medium diverting attention from the message, but its barrenness implies that its ability to excite interest or to promote understanding depends wholly on the skills of the user. The practical skills of speed allied to neatness and accuracy can be acquired by most trainee teachers fairly rapidly. Less certain is the extent to which individual teachers can be persuaded that regard for techniques of layout and display greatly enhances the efficacy of boardwork in economics teaching. For example, systematic colour-coding can be a useful aid to learning (the use of red when referring to costs, blue for revenues, green for demand curves, yellow for supply curves, etc.), the more so if allied to a similar scheme for differentiating between various concepts depicted on graphs (thick lines, thin lines, broken lines, dotted lines to represent total, average, marginal, etc.). Relative importance can be suggested in a variety of ways: by altering the size and style of print, by underlining, by spacing, or by using colours meaningfully. Careful regard to layout, spacing and use of colour combinations and/or style of print can also highlight key relationships, for example, symmetry, asymmetry, causality, affinity. It is all too easy to overestimate the legibility of routine boardwork. Certain colours perform extremely poorly, being either virtually indistinguishable from some other colour or invisible at a distance; purple and brown are best avoided altogether and orange should not be used in close proximity to yellow. All boardwork should be appraised at a distance and tested for clarity and legibility, particularly from the rear of a room, where it is not unknown for the least well-motivated students to congregate. Reference has been made to 'colour-coding' and to a systematic approach, but all too often teachers assume that the codes and systems that they use are self-evident to students. They are not, and need to be made explicit, the more so because in economics there is not an established code of practice among teachers, lecturers and broadcasters. Teachers who take the time and care to maximize the potential of display boards as teaching aids do more than their students a good turn – they may also promote themselves in the queue to gain access to an overhead projector on which similar skills can be demonstrated; and possibly to greater effect.

Projected images

An *overhead projector* (*OHP*) is widely regarded as superior to a display board as a provider of visual stimuli. Any visual aid that can be produced using a board is capable of being reconstituted for use with an OHP without loss of quality. The greatest single gain resulting from the change of medium is the ability to store and retrieve visual aids intended for regular use, and herein lies the strength of any claim for access to an OHP. For the economics teacher there are aspects of the subject that change little from one year to the next. For example, a pack of visual aids built up on OHP transparencies to assist in the teaching of the theory of value, the theory of the firm, national income accounting, etc. may well be used for many years with only minor amendment. Since an OHP not only projects an image but also magnifies it, storage of transparencies presents less of a space problem than is experienced with posters and wallcharts. Being easily portable, transparencies can be prepared away from the classroom in time other than class-contact time, so that teachers' time is more gainfully allocated between competing claims upon it. Moreover, creating an OHP visual aid demands not so much the time-consuming learning of new skills but the transference of old ones first developed in primary school. For most people, OHP pens prove to be no more unwieldy or uncontrollable than other pens and pencils, and acetate is, if anything, more homogeneous and predictable to work on than a paper surface. Errors are easily eradicated by the application of water or, in the case of 'permanent' inks, by applying spirit duplicating fluid or plastic rubber. For the person who continues to find working with inks on acetate difficult, alternative methods of transparency creation are available. Transparencies can be made by means of a thermal copier using masters prepared on paper with a pencil having a high carbon content. By this method, coloured transparencies can be produced from monochrome originals. Many modern photocopiers will produce transparencies from originals prepared using paper and any form of black ink. Transparencies can also be created using coloured adhesive film cut to the shape required, and titles can be added by making use of proprietary brands of self-adhesive letters and numbers. Shapes cut out of coloured paper can also be deployed in the construction of monochrome transparencies; they will show up as black on the screen. By these means, the limitations resulting from a poor standard of personal calligraphy can largely be overcome. A word of caution is required on producing transparencies from typed material. Almost without exception, the end-product will be too full, too condensed and the legibility too restricted for general classroom use, irrespective of the tabulation and display skills of the typist. As a general guide, seven lines of writing should be seen as the maximum desirable on any one transparency, and even within this constraint a policy of key words and phrases rather than complete sentences is to be preferred: the OHP is 'a source of visual stimuli' and not a substitute for a textbook or activity sheet.

Reference was made earlier to building up diagrams on blackboards. Visual synthesis is a satisfying and effective way to teach and to learn. For the blackboard operator, the build-up takes place, of necessity, in front of the class in real time, and can be achieved only as fast as the teacher's blackboard skills allow. This pace may be slower than either the material deserves or the students require, putting a premium on the quality of supporting patter and increasing the risk of class irritation and boredom. The OHP has made the process of building-up diagrams, etc. easier and quicker. Two different techniques are available. The first involves overlay. Being transparent, acetate sheets can be laid on top of each other with little loss of illumination, thereby allowing a complex diagram, chart, graph or table to be compiled progressively at a pace that can be tightly controlled and, if necessary, rapidly accelerated. Using complete sheets of acetate within some form of rigid frame allows exact positioning to be achieved each time, but this method is expensive and may seem profligate in so far as not one of perhaps four or five sheets deployed may have more than 10 per cent of its surface area actively used. A cheaper overlay method is to attach items to be projected to a blank acetate sheet by means of strips of transparent sticky tape which are long enough to allow the material to be stored out of range of the projected image and steered to its appointed place only as and when required. Since the diagram's components have been compiled originally in clusters on an acetate sheet, and then cut to size, acetate is conserved; but the resulting visual aid is more fiddly to use and less pleasing to look at. Overlay techniques allow visual aids not only to be built up but also to be taken apart quickly and accurately. Areas of economics for which overlays are particularly useful include basic models of economic systems (allowing the terms production, consumption, saving, investment, taxation, public expenditure, imports, exports, etc. to be introduced in turn), categories of production (primary, secondary, tertiary), types of business integration, changes in conditions of demand and supply, location of industry, etc.

The second OHP build-up technique involves masking; material remains concealed until it is unmasked. Masking is most appropriate for items that are capable of being presented in a tight vertical format, revelation taking place little by little. It is a device frequently used in expository teaching linked to a 'key word' approach, for example, the asset structure of a commercial bank, the canons of taxation, the functions of money, the factors influencing demand for a good, etc. Its attraction lies in the ability to pre-prepare visual aids to a desired standard and to become familiar with the content in advance of use; these attributes enhance the user's confidence. An anxious teacher using pre-prepared material needs only to control an opaque masking sheet rather than face the hazard of mislaid pens and pen tops, erratic pen movements, or incorrect spellings in the course of 'live' transparency creation. Masking also gives the opportunity to inject pace into presentation, and pace can help sustain interest. Sophisticated masking techniques incorporate the use of templates which enable partial revelation to be sustained throughout the presentation with a view to concentrating attention only on the item under consideration, but leaving an overview facility available. Masking takes time to prepare, but conserves acetate. Masked OHPs can also come in handy for group work involving revision, since a task can be assigned in the form of a written instruction, and a possible solution remains hidden until required, but this is an area of learning in which computers already offer a superior service and, with graphics provision on mini-computers improving all the time, the superiority of computers for revision purposes is likely to become more marked as time progresses.

Sequential presentation techniques outlined above instil a sense of dynamism and forward momentum into visual aids which are in essence static. Such an illusion is much easier to create and sustain with an OHP than with a blackboard. A further advantage of OHPs is that commercially produced material is available, complete with teachers' notes. At its best, such software sets standards of visual presentation that are hard for individual teachers to match, but to justify the expense of purchase, regular and sustained use is necessary. In addition, OHP transparencies can be used to reproduce items from a printed page, but it is essential to avoid infringing copyright. Much printed material is unsuitable for direct conversion into OHP transparencies, being too small, too dense or too cluttered. A process camera enables enlargements or reductions to be made of original material either in whole or in part, and OHP transparencies can be prepared from the resulting paste-ups.

Finally, an OHP can function merely as a blackboard substitute. When equipped to accommodate an acetate roll, the OHP can match the blackboard for expansiveness, but if an OHP is to be used solely or mainly for the extemporary creation of unretained visual aids, then the wisdom of acquiring an OHP in place of a blackboard is questionable since OHPs also have comparative disadvantages. Unlike blackboards, they generate noise and heat in operation, require the use of comparatively expensive materials, and can be rendered ineffective by poorly fitted screens, unsuitable lighting conditions, inadequately maintained focusing mechanisms and 'blown' projector lamps. Even if used only as a blackboard substitute, however, an OHP has the advantage of allowing the user to remain facing others in the group. For the teacher, the challenge of the OHP is to rescue it from a preponderance of low-grade use for which it is no more effective than a display board. Since many economics courses have a high theory content, and since visual aids relating to theory may well prove usable for many years, there are many areas of economics in which the time devoted to preparation of attractive OHP transparencies is amply rewarded. Transparencies can be used not only for class teaching, but, in conjunction with printed notes, for self-instruction and for revision purposes on an individual or group basis.

Photography

If teachers want to bring pictures of the real world into a classroom, an OHP needs to be supplemented with a *slide projector*. For most uses, a hand-operated push-pull slide projector is quite adequate, and lack of an autochange facility is seldom a plausible reason for sustained non-use. To increase longevity and flexibility in use, filmstrips should be cut up and mounted, thereby also eliminating the need to acquire a dual-purpose machine. Storage and retrieval of slides is far less space-consuming than either OHP transparencies or charts, so for diagrams that are intended for use always *in toto*, conversion into slide form makes good practical sense. If copyright precludes direct photography of commercially produced posters, etc., 'cultivation' of an art teacher can prove rewarding! Fixed and variable costs, the cheque-clearing system and the capital market are among many topics amenable to this type of rationalization process. The unique contribution of slides lies in their ability to encapsulate real-life scenes. Photographs taken on oil rigs or inside car factories, chemical works, poultry sheds, etc. do more to convey the meaning of 'large-scale production' than can any diagram or form of words, and for relatively little cost. Slides remain silent and static, however, and require skilled teachers to give them vitality, meaning and relevance. As a teaching aid in economics, slides remain generally under-used, despite a marked reduction in the cost of high-quality cameras requiring little skill on the part of the operator and despite a wealth of appropriate photogenic material being available locally. A major cause of neglect appears to be inadequate provision of viewing facilities. To be used successfully, slides require a darker environment than do OHP transparencies, but back-projection techniques have reduced the need for total blackout, and with an older type of slide projector using forward projection, the use of a more powerful lens (e.g. 60 mm instead of 100 mm) allows the projector to be sited at the front of a room no more than, say, 3 metres from the screen. In these circumstances, a source of light at the rear of the room allows students both to see the pictures adequately and also at the same time to have access to enough light to read and to write. Given such viewing conditions, the type of activity that can be undertaken using slides is transformed. It becomes possible to test students' powers of observation and to produce worksheets, the successful completion of which is dependent on accurate use and interpretation of the slides being projected. For example, a junior class might be asked to look at a picture and list the capital goods, consumer durables and consumer single-use goods to be seen. Using the same picture, a more senior class might be expected to list the taxes associated with the economic activity seen in the picture and be required to explain their findings. Portable projectors and screens allow work stations to be set up at which the task is always rather more than merely viewing the slides. For poor readers, written materials in support of slides may be inappropriate, in which case another piece of equipment is required: a cassette or tape-recorder.

Sound and vision

Work with slides or OHP transparencies can be supported by making use of tape-recordings. For successful activity, high-quality sound reproduction is essential, so it is generally better to borrow a dearer *tape-cassette-player/recorder* from a central pool than make do with the inferior products that might be purchased using a departmental budget. Much of the material for use with slide projectors and cassette-recorders is available in the form of tape/slide presentation. Unimaginatively used, such presentations reduce students to a level of passivity normally associated with indiscriminate unsupervised viewing of television programmes. There is much to be said in a classroom situation for a teacher mastering the material on the tape and presenting the slides together with his own commentary. In large gatherings, there are not many occasions on which a disembodied voice trapped in the language and syntax of a prerecorded script can legitimately claim superiority over the animated utterings of a well-motivated and visible human being, provided he/she is properly prepared and sensitive to class response. Good tape/slide programmes provide a disciplined and logical order of presentation for teachers to emulate but, by and large, sound tapes and tape-recorders earn their keep in individualized learning activities in libraries or at home, preferably with the aid of headphones. They can also prove their worth when learning is organized on a workshop basis; a tape/slide programme together with a set of notes and a series of tasks allied to it can make a useful station in a room where students move from one task to another. Even if teachers are reluctant to produce their own slides, production of activity sheets or tapes to support commercially produced slides should not prove too difficult or demanding. A common fault to be guarded against is the over-provision of tasks that do not depend for their successful completion on careful viewing of the slides provided. This deficiency in tasks set is not hard to identify, for example, an instruction to 'establish the link between this picture and the concept of occupational mobility of factors of production' makes demands that are absent from a request merely to 'give a definition of occupational mobility'. The former needs the picture, the latter does not.

One step further on from tapes and slides is the use of *films*. Here the teacher's freedom of action is constrained in so far as soundtrack and moving pictures are integrated. For maximum benefit to be derived from the use of films, previewing by the teacher is essential. During a preview, the teacher can identify the film's strengths and weaknesses. Strengths are usually visual, and weaknesses are often in the commentary: unsuitable pace, inappropriate vocabulary, convolution or elision of ideas. Forewarned, the teacher can anticipate the areas of difficulty and produce additional material to overcome them – for example, if a film describes credit creation verbally, charts and diagrams can be prepared and used in advance of showing the films. If lighting conditions permit, students can make brief notes about key points in the film as the film progresses, using a specially prepared sheet to guide them. Any subsequent discussion can be shaped around a predetermined framework of reference. Questions can be set for all levels of age and ability; for example, 'How many different jobbers were approached and asked for a quotation?' requires no interpretation skill, whereas 'Why was more than one jobber approached and asked for a quotation?' is more demanding, and 'What factors were determining the prices quoted by jobbers?' is more demanding still in the case of a film about the Stock Exchange.

In the teaching of economics, *television* has so many advantages over the aids mentioned to date that its relatively low level of use borders on the scandalous. Whereas OUP transparencies and photographic slides are static, film and television pictures are dynamic. Since economics postulates a dynamic world in which constituent elements are continually reacting and interacting, moving pictures offer the possibility of providing convincing visual demonstrations of concepts and relationships that previously had to be explained either verbally or by recourse to a series of static diagrams presented sequentially. An examination of the range of possible effects on the UK balance of payments of a reduction in the basic rate of income tax is but one example of a topic well suited to teaching by means of television, provided that adequate support material (an informed commentary, an accompanying text and teachers' notes) is made available. It is ironic that in the 1970s a marked increase in the output of commercially produced didactic television material with an economics content aimed at the general public coincided with a decrease in the absolute amount of commercially produced television material available for extended use by economics teachers within educational institutions. The abject failure of interested parties to resolve copyright problems satisfactorily has continued to mean that economics teachers who seek to maximize the educational potential of television programmes produced for general viewing usually place themselves on the wrong side of the law. The result is that a wealth of expensively produced material remains underutilized (being transmitted perhaps twice at the most), while the few economics programmes produced under the aegis of educational television continue to bear the hallmarks of tight budgets, namely, a preponderance of 'talking heads' in studio locations. In a stimulating article written as long ago as 1967, F.J. Bayliss wrote, 'The main point about the use of television in teaching is that . . . it must be used for what it can do better than other media'.[3] Since that time there has been ample opportunity for television to demonstrate its capabilities, and in recent years the advent of computerized graphics has further enhanced the medium's attractiveness. As a result, economics teachers frequently recommend students to watch specific programmes scheduled for general viewing, for example, analyses of the problems of a particular industry, evaluations of the efficacy of government economic policy, studies of the impact of a particular industry on aspects of the economy, etc. Treated to the full panoply of television wizardry (dramatic moving pictures of technical processes, high-resolution graphics, interviews with top people, visual access to the sanctum sanctorum, flips across the world to allow international comparison, etc.), viewers are almost certain to be impressed, to be entertained and to have their interest aroused. But are they left permanently better informed? A single viewing of a programme unsupported by additional material is of limited educational value. With television, 'the immediate visual impact is powerful . . . yet the lasting impression is weak. The impact, though sharp, has little depth.'[4] The viewer may be dazzled rather than illuminated. In an interesting review of a major television series replete with economic content for which a supporting text was produced, Chris Dunkley wrote that the author's programmes represented 'quite unusually high television journalism. Yet having said that, the most striking fact about his programmes was how much less they managed to convey than his book of the same title. Contrary to the idea that every picture is worth a thousand words, what these two versions show is that a book can leap from one idea, century or example to another without any trouble, whereas television needs ten minutes of film to convey an essentially simple notion.'[5] If books of the same title as a television educational series manage to survive into the age of mass ownership of video-recorders, then further evidence will be available to support the view that television programmes, however excellent, are enhanced in their usefulness if accompanied by supporting text. This suggests that for television material to serve its purpose in classrooms, it must be possible for the teacher to preview it and to ensure that adequate supportive literature is available, either by purchase or by dint of his own effort. Such effort is more likely to be forthcoming if the teacher sees the programme as potentially useful and actually usable legally over a number of years. One of the teacher's main tasks will be to identify and illuminate the programme's 'message'. Professionally produced television programmes are normally tightly scripted, meticulously photographed and carefully edited. There is not, however, any legal or moral obligation on the part of producers and directors to go for 'balance' in the coverage of controversial socio-economic topics: indeed, it is often said that balanced programmes make for dull viewing. Much television material (e.g. on trade unions, unemployment, inflation, protectionism, monetarism) arrests attention by taking up a particular stance. It is usually highly successful at captivating interest, but the difficulties of promoting understanding may be underestimated. The introduction of video libraries and portable VCRs into schools and colleges has enabled repetitive partial viewing of a programme to become an everyday possibility and, with forethought, using a television programme can become an activity involving a great deal of student participation rather than simply an occasion for passive viewing.

Reprographics

With regard to *reprographic facilities*, provision has generally improved. Economics teachers might reasonably lay claim to acquisition or retention of a spirit duplicator for as long as they remain available commercially. A hand-operated machine is not only cheaper than a fixed-speed electric model but also gives better quality control of the final product and permits marginally longer production runs. Spirit duplication remains appropriate for limited runs of transient material, being comparatively cheap and simple to use. Of all teachers, economics teachers probably have most cause to jettison in whole or part a previous year's notes and diagrams, particularly in the case of applied economics, so low-cost production is attractive. The humble spirit duplicator should not be scorned. As an unfussy feeder and a mechanically simple regurgitator of multi-coloured material, it comes into its own towards the end of a financial year when parsimony is the order of the day. With luck, ink duplication using stencils will not survive much longer in educational institutions; the introduction of offset-litho machines has made much superior finished products available at a moderate material cost. Capital outlay, though much higher, can be spread over high-volume output, particularly where teaching departments and administration share time on the same machine. Paper plates keep down the cost of short-runs, and back-to-back reproduction conserves paper with little detriment to product users. Anybody able to wield an appropriate type of pen can produce original master materials capable of high-quality reproduction. Non-copyright items extracted from a file of fugitive materials can also be reproduced. The extra expense of investing in a machine capable of reproducing in A3 format allows teachers to produce A4 booklets which can be neatly and cheaply 'stitched' using a hand-operated long-arm stapler. This type of technology gives every economics teacher the opportunity to develop course materials of a high standard of presentation. It is cheering to witness the extent to which teachers are taking advantage of this opening, and becoming authors and originators. It is ironic that interest in producing the printed page should be stimulated at a time when rapid developments are taking place in alternative communication systems involving the use of television satellites, information networks and computers, which are allegedly preparing the way for a paperless society. The high level of teacher participation in the preparation of written materials can be explained with reference to the accessibility of the medium; that is, little training or practice is required to produce acceptable input and the cost of making and distributing high-quality output is relatively low. Neither television nor computers can claim a similar profile, and fewer teachers are practising *aficionados* as a result.

Do audio-visual aids achieve anything?

Evaluating the *efficacy of audio-visual aids* in the teaching of economics is an activity still in its infancy, and not a great deal appears to have happened to justify a reassessment of a view expressed in 1975 that there remains 'ample scope to explore the role of audio visual resources in the introductory phases of the subject at various levels'.[6] More disturbing, perhaps, than teachers' reluctance or inability to requisition audio-visual equipment and materials is the low-level utilization once both are acquired. Reasons for this phenomenon vary, and among the more plausible explanations offered are: shortage of ancillary staff to offer support services (maintenance, repair, porterage etc.), deficiencies in overall coverage of audio-visual packages resulting in too high a level of teacher-input in relation to the perceived benefit, inadequate time for planning and preparation, and the vicissitudes of teacher vagrancy resulting from the relaxation or abandonment of the practice of allocating rooms to specific teachers of specialized subjects. Should this last trend continue, economics teachers may no longer enjoy the experience of working from the sort of 'base' that a previous generation tended to take for granted. If a teaching base is available, the economics teacher might try to acquire two roller blackboards wall-mounted side by side, with retractable screens attached to each at an angle designed to eliminate picture distortion. One screen is for use with the OHP, the other screen for use with a slide projector. With this arrangement, neither machine need be moved, and several combinations and permutations of visual presentation become readily available.

If, however, teachers lose access to a teaching base and if the process of contraction and rationalization of educational institutions continues, departmental allocation of audio-visual equipment may well be abandoned altogether in favour of centralized pools to which claimants gain priority access by demonstrating need, not on protestations of good intent but on hard evidence of established use and previous good practice. It is hoped that this chapter will encourage economics teachers to ensure that as each day passes they will have less cause for anxiety in the face of such scrutiny.

Notes and references

1. Broudy, H.S., in Vandenberg, D. (ed.), *Teaching and Learning* (Chicago, University of Illinois Press, 1969) p. 55.
2. James, W., in ibid., p. 134.
3. Bayliss, F.J., in *Teaching Economics*, 1st edn (Economics Association, 1967) p. 169.
4. Ibid., p. 165.
5. Dunkley, C., 'Stranger than fiction', *The Financial Times*, 12 January 1983, p. 19.
6. Noble, P., in *Teaching Economics*, 2nd edn (Heinemann Educational Books, 1975) p. 237.

17 Microcomputers and Economics Education
Steve Hurd

The modern micro provides low-cost, portable computing power, and is no more difficult to use than the standard tape-recorder or 16 mm projector. It performs complex calculations speedily, enables data to be stored and retrieved at a later date for analysis, and can generate colourful graphic and pictorial displays. These features give rise to a variety of educational applications and, in particular, enable the microcomputer to contribute to the two main preoccupations of modern economics – exploring economic models, and handling economic data. The microcomputer is a uniquely flexible resource. It can support both formal instruction and more active styles of learning. Whether as a stimulus and vehicle for discovery in new areas of work, or for the reinforcement and review of previous work, the micro provides enormous opportunities which have led to some remarkable claims being made in its favour:

The modern digital computer is the most versatile information processing machine ever invented . . . the range of educational applications to which it is suited is limited only by the imagination of those who intend to use it.[1]

The growth of interest in the use of computers in teaching economics coincides with changes taking place in the economics curriculum. The gradual shift towards the adoption of more conceptual and analytical approaches to the subject, with their greater reliance on the use of models and real data, marks a growing desire to reflect the methods employed by professional economists in the teaching of the subject at school and college level. Unlike teachers of physics and biology, economics teachers are unable to replicate experimental conditions in the school classroom. The 'world' is our laboratory, and direct experimentation is out of the question. Despite the difficulties, however, teachers are becoming increasingly skilled in creating contexts for investigative activity. The use of case studies and role-play games bears witness to this. Computers can reinforce this trend by reproducing laboratory conditions and creating opportunities, through experimentation, for students to 'discover' key economic relationships for themselves.

Fig. 17.1 Results page from the Heriot-Watt 'Running the British Economy' game.

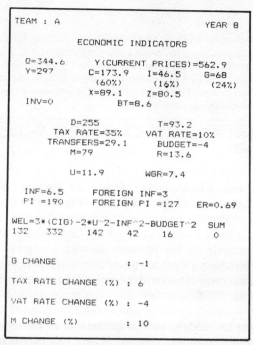

```
TEAM : A                              YEAR 8

              ECONOMIC INDICATORS

   Q=344.6        Y(CURRENT PRICES)=562.9
   Y=297        C=173.9    I=46.5      G=68
                 (60%)      (16%)      (24%)
                X=89.1      Z=80.5
   INV=0          BT=8.6

        D=255               T=93.2
     TAX RATE=35%      VAT RATE=10%
    TRANSFERS=29.1        BUDGET=-4
        M=79               R=13.6

       U=11.9           WGR=7.4

   INF=6.5       FOREIGN INF=3
   PI =190       FOREIGN PI =127    ER=0.69

WEL=3*(CIG)-2*U^2-INF^2-BUDGET^2   SUM
132     332    142    42    16      0

G CHANGE              : -1

TAX RATE CHANGE (%) : 6

VAT RATE CHANGE (%) : -4

M CHANGE (%)         : 10
```

Source: Lumsden, K. G., and Scott, A., *Running the British Economy, 1983* (Longman, 1983).

Development work in Computer Assisted Learning (CAL) in the UK has emphasized those applications where the student is active in the learning process. Foremost among these has been the use of games and simulations, and the embryonic but fast-growing field of data retrieval. These receive the major attention in this chapter, with instructional and teacher-centred applications of computers given rather less prominence.

Games and simulations

Business and macroeconomic games are among the success stories of CAL in economics. In business games[2] alternative management teams grapple with the day-to-day problems facing a dynamic enterprise. Profits are traded off against growth and other behavioural objectives to achieve success. In macroeconomic games,[3] rival Cabinets devise alternative Budget packages to stabilize their economies in the face of successive challenges and conflicting policy goals. The more involved

Fig. 17.2   Example of an exogenous shock

> **TEAM : t**   **YEAR : 12**
>
> A new programme of investment credits to energy industries causes
> investment expenditures in certain sectors to increase by 10 this year and
> to remain at that level. However, the behaviour of investment expendi-
> tures in other industries will depend on factors such as the state of the
> economy and the rate of interest. Hence total investment expenditures
> will not necessarily increase by 10.

Source: Lumsden, K. G., and Scott, A., *Running the British Economy, 1983*
(Longman, 1983).

games incorporate a large number of variables (Figure 17.1) and highly
plausible sequences of exogenous shocks (Figure 17.2).

The benefits that accrue from well-constructed games are considerable, and have been explored at length by Taylor and Walford.[4] They
provide a valuable bridge between abstract concepts and reality,
and often introduce a broader interdisciplinary perspective. Games
develop an awareness of the need to trade-off the various priorities, and
help to counter the simple view that each problem has a unique and
independent solution. Students gain an intuitive grasp of the workings
of quite complex models, and an impression of the dynamic forces
operating within economic systems. Where role play is involved, an
empathetic appreciation of the goals and constraints facing the various
actors on the economic stage can be acquired. Broader benefits arise as
students become aware of the need to develop appropriate procedures
and forms of interaction within their teams. Tasks have to be allocated,
relevant data identified, organized and evaluated; strategies devised,
appraised and modified in the light of events. Students learn to communicate their own ideas to the rest of the group, and practise the arts of
negotiation and compromise. Good team games generate considerable
enthusiasm, and even the normally more reserved members of a class
are able to play an active part in the small group decision-making that
results.

A major constraint on the use of games is the time required both to
play them and to follow up the ideas exposed. As a consequence,
paper-based games are frequently relegated to the status of an end-of-
term activity. By taking care of the game mechanics, the computer can
streamline the process of game playing and leave students free to
concentrate on the essential principles. Group games are particularly
useful in situations where the teacher has access to just a single microcomputer. With the micro acting as game manager, and decisions being

Fig. 17.3 Team game using a single micro. Groups make decisions away from the computer.

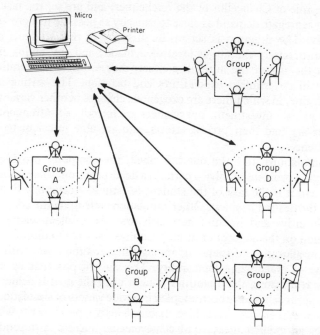

made in groups away from the computer, economical use is made of a limited supply of hardware (Figure 17.3).

In providing immediate feedback on decisions, the computer promotes continuity, and maintains the level of motivation. Where the results are transferred to a printer students receive a 'hard-copy' on paper, which acts as a reference source for group decision-making, and a permanent record for follow-up work. When a printer is not used the results need to be transcribed from the screen to record sheets. Some computer games store the team results from each round on disc files. This allows a game to be continued over several lessons without having to start from the beginning each time. The more sophisticated programs include analysis options that enable the performance of each team to be analysed in a subsequent lesson, thus ensuring that the key relationships of a game are exposed for general discussion.[5]

The full-blown game with its complex interrelationships and chance elements, and for all its merits, is probably not the best place to learn the fundamental principles of economics. If we want students to 'discover' the significance of specific concepts and relationships, such as the MC=MR equality, or the nature of the multiplier effect, a more controlled environment has to be created – one where the *ceteris paribus* assumption can be maintained. A typical example from macroeconomics is a simulation designed to investigate the multiplier effect.[6] Students play the role of Chancellor of the Exchequer, and are set the task of keeping aggregate demand as close to capacity as possible in a growing economy. The program is set up in such a way that students can calculate precisely the target level of demand, and, by taking into account the size of the multiplier effect, they estimate the required changes in government expenditure and taxation. The setting is a dynamic one, in which there are exogenous changes in other variables, such as private investment, but changes are introduced infrequently, students are told their precise effects, and are able to calculate the consequences.

In simulations, like the one described, the computer provides a challenging problem to solve – perhaps a departure from some optimal state – and it is the task of the student to estimate accurately how to restore the desired position. Other simulations rely upon the adoption of an intuitive and iterative approach towards problem-solving. A simulation on the concept of utility[7] requires students to discover the optimum allocation of spending among three commodities, with the objective of maximizing total utility. The student proceeds by continually readjusting the quantities bought until the goal is achieved. Similar approaches have been adopted in a wide variety of simulations.[8] In each case, there is a clearly identifiable objective, proximity to which provides an explicit measure of achievement. Success is dependent upon the adoption of a logical and systematic method of working. The student is encouraged to keep a careful record of each decision and its consequences, and to explain any relationships observed. The computer simulation provides the nearest thing to the experimental approach we can probably achieve in economics.

In both simulations and games the computer calculates the effects of changes and provides an immediate response to decisions – so enabling the student to cover more ground, and to concentrate on the underlying principles. Despite the fact that the computer performs some of the more tedious arithmetic, simulations often call for higher levels of numerical competence than is customarily asked of economics students. The very fact, however, that students are pitting their wits against the computer often appears to stimulate higher levels of performance.

When developing computer simulations for the pre-16 age group, the possibility of generating graphic or pictorial displays is particularly important. Simulations on siting an industrial plant,[9] or allocating labour in an industrial production line,[10] rely heavily upon the visual representation that micros can provide (Figure 17.4). At this level a rigorous, theoretical approach is rarely called for, and the computer

Fig. 17.4   Workers and machines. This production simulation is enhanced by the use of graphic displays.

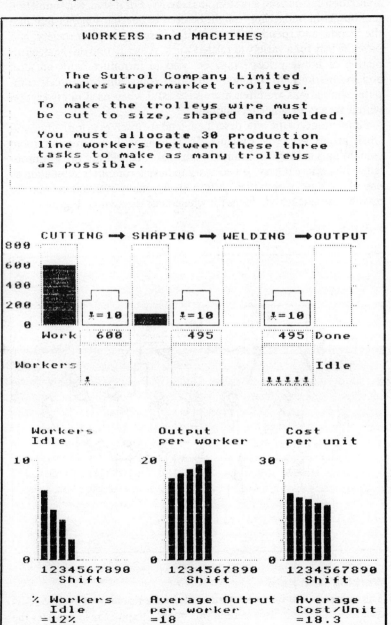

Source: Murley, A., and Greenwood, A., *Workers and Machines* (Longman, 1984).

simulation can be used as a stimulus activity. For instance, a simulation on household budgeting[11] might be used to develop some insight into the income and spending patterns of different groups in society, and pave the way for a variety of related work. A simulation on the determination of house prices[12] may be used to introduce work on local housing markets. In common with other educational resources, computer simulations are often more successful when used in association with a variety of other techniques.

Simulations, of the type described, lend themselves to individual and small group work by students. In schools with a computer room containing a substantial number of micros, this will not present problems. Elsewhere it may be necessary to have a computer simulation as one of a circus of activities. Alternatively, many simulations may be used by the teacher as a focus for whole-class discussion (Figure 17.5).

Fig. 17.5   Use of one micro as focus for class discussion.

Working with data

The value of data interpretation work in the teaching of economics is discussed at length elsewhere in this book. Despite the increase in the use of data-response questions in examinations, the level of analysis called for in the interpretation of statistical data is superficial, even in comparison with that required of, say, geography students at a similar level. The principal requirements are that students be able to estimate rough proportions, and identify trends and turning points in data. Opportunity cost appears to provide the main objection to going further than this. More time spent on data interpretation means less time for other aspects of economics. This is reinforced by a widespread view that students find numerical work unpalatable, and take an inordinately long time coming to grips with quite elementary operations in arithmetic and graphing. As these are the main strengths of the computer, it is conceivable that this is an area where the micro will make a great impact on the teaching of economics.

In data analysis there is scope for combining the main attributes of the microcomputer – data storage and retrieval, sorting and calculation, and tabular and graphical presentation of results. Selected data from the commonly used sources, such as the *Annual Abstract of Statistics*, and *Economic, Regional and Social Trends*, can be stored on computer disc for retrieval as required. A data retrieval and display package based on the CSO abstract *Regional Trends* brings together a variety of comparative regional data on such things as population, occupations, income levels, housing tenure and the ownership of consumer durables.[13] Students are able to recall data for their own region and make comparisons with others over different periods of time. The comparisons can be made on the basis of either raw data, or bar graphs for easier visual comparison. This type of program can stimulate and support a wide range of studies by students, and provides a valuable adjunct to local survey work.

There is an enormous range of data that could be usefully made available on computer. This includes time-series data for the important macroeconomic variables, household expenditure survey data, and comparative country data. A macroeconomic data base[14] can be used by students to examine the movements of inflation and unemployment over time, and their relationship to possible explanatory variables, such as money supply and wages. The computer enables data to be lagged, line graphed, and scatter graphed, as well as subjected to various statistical operations. Lines of inquiry can be pursued quickly, and the computer can switch between data and displays as required. Updating data bases is much less of a problem than hitherto. Many statistical data are available on magnetic media, or through Prestel and teletext services. Given the expense of the annual abstracts, and the difficulties that many teachers face in gaining access to photocopying, it could well be that disc-based data sets will become the principal source of current data.

Both the amount and the quality of data interpretation work undertaken by economics students can be enhanced considerably. With ready access to computers, students can practise inductive skills by observing and identifying relationships first-hand. They can examine the ways in which different economic variables relate to each other and attempt the construction of simple hypotheses to explain any links they find. It is important in all data work to alert students to the dangers of what professional economists call casual empiricism, the practice of drawing inferences in a theoretical vacuum. As students spend more time working with data they inevitably begin to appreciate some of the pitfalls for themselves. Exposing students to data reveals that the real world is messier, and more complex, than that of conventional theory. Few relationships are as stable and predictable as economics textbooks are inclined to suggest. Computers, if used on occasions in this unbridled way, could make an enormous impact on current practice, and serve the emancipatory role that CAL practitioners have advocated for some time.[15]

The computer as calculator

Once the microcomputer has been accepted as a standard piece of equipment in every economics classroom, it can be used for a host of things that would not, in themselves, justify the purchase of a computer. The Stock Market game is a popular activity with sixth-formers, and yet few teachers consider that it is worth the effort with younger students, who may find great difficulty calculating the week-to-week transactions. When the computer takes on the bookkeeping side, it becomes a more realistic proposition for a wider range of students.

One way for students to develop an understanding of the limitations of the index of retail prices as an indicator of inflation, is to construct their own local index. The consistent accuracy that is required in calculation, however, is likely to defeat the operation. A computer-based index, where students enter their own price data, having first decided the appropriate weights, can overcome this sort of problem.

Computers can also assist with local survey work. Apart from the well-known logistical problems involved in taking classes out during school time, or of drawing together sufficient local source material for use in the classroom, there are the problems involved in satisfactorily processing any information collected. Questionnaire and survey analysis programs, which enable students to enter their own findings, can do much to lighten the burden. At the simplest level the computer can be used to calculate straightforward averages, and proportional breakdowns of data. The improved presentation of results in computer print-out form is also likely to give students a greater feeling of pride in the work. When computers are employed students can gain the benefits of generating and analysing their own data, without being daunted by the task of collating and processing the results.

Other applications
This section deals briefly with instruction and teacher-centred applications of microcomputers, and with program writing.

Programmed Instruction (PI)
In contrast to the CAL applications described so far in this chapter, PI involves using the computer as a teacher substitute. In PI the student works through a sequence of carefully structured questions, to which he is expected to select appropriate responses. The system works on the principles of stimulus, response and reward. The student is provided with a piece of information, and then asked a related question. The computer provides immediate feedback and positive reinforcement to correct responses (this constitutes the reward), and provides some guidance on incorrect ones. The more sophisticated programs have complex branching structures, where the route through is tailored to the responses of each student.

The drill and practice approach of PI, while popular in the USA, has not found favour in the UK. This is despite the fact that a number of major studies have demonstrated large gains from the approach. A study by Attiyeh, Bach and Lumsden, for instance, demonstrated that, 'programmed instruction can accomplish almost as much in three weeks as conventional instruction in seven'.[16] The programmed approach could well play a part with topics that need to be taught in a systematic, step-by-step way. National income accounting is an obvious example. It may also provide a useful vehicle for students wishing to review areas of past work.

Computer Managed Learning (CML)
CML is a management tool. It is designed to enable teachers to monitor closely the performance of individual students, as well as to provide a type of tutorial supervision to students. Students complete a series of computer-based diagnostic tests, any gaps in understanding are identified, and students are guided to appropriate reading. The approach has been tried successfully with undergraduate students, the main benefit being that the computer can provide the close supervision that is difficult to maintain on courses with large numbers of students. It is unlikely that CML will be employed in the typical school. It may, however, be useful in larger sixth-form and tertiary colleges.[17]

Electronic blackboard
A microcomputer connected to a large monitor can be used to supplement the blackboard and overhead projector when dynamic displays are called for. Circular flow of income, and national income/expenditure diagrams presented in this way can be used by the teacher

to step through various numerical examples of income and expenditure flows. Most of the topics requiring a diagrammatic treatment, such as demand and supply analysis, can be usefully presented in this way.

The approach has to be used with care. On microcomputer systems where the graphics resolution is low, the results will be disappointing, and blackboard diagrams using coloured chalks, or coloured overlays on an overhead projector, may well show up more clearly. Micro-computer-generated diagrams are also likely to lack the immediacy and the flexibility of the blackboard-drawn article. On the other hand, they can provide very convincing demonstrations of graphic relationships, when precise values are required. Such programs, when supplemented by suitable worksheets, also lend themselves to small group work around the computer, and for use in checking paper based exercises.

Worksheet production
The advent of easy-to-use word processing packages on a departmental microcomputer are likely to have a significant impact on the day-to-day running of an economics department.

With access to a good-quality printer, teachers can produce their own worksheets and test material to a consistently high standard of presentation. Printed material can be stored on floppy disc, and amended at a later date to include recent statistics and other current material.

Program writing
It should be evident from what has been written already that perfectly satisfactory use can be made of a computer without needing to write a single program. CAL materials in general are designed with the non-specialist user in mind. Having said this, however, an increasing number of both teachers and students are learning to program computers, and using the computer to program economic models has featured in a number of undergraduate courses for some years.[18] After a few hours' instruction, students can learn sufficient to be able to design short programs to investigate the properties of the multiplier, or the variations in total revenue along a demand curve.

Incorporating a similar element of computer modelling into the A-level course is feasible, though clearly not costless. On the benefit side, students are likely to become more conscious of the nature of assumptions, and of model building in general. An appreciation of the quantitative dimensions of modelling could provide a much needed insight into the limitations of economic forecasts, and the problems faced by policy-makers. A similar insight could, however, be gained through carefully designed simulations, where students are free to determine the values of key parameters.

Discussion

Technological innovations are worthwhile when the increase in the value of output, adjusted for quality improvements, outweighs the additional costs. We can obtain reasonably reliable estimates on the cost side of CAL, but the benefit side of the equation is more problematical. Hardware costs have fallen to the extent that they are beginning to come within the bounds of departmental budgets. Furthermore, once installed, the marginal cost of additional use is effectively zero – at least until there is competition for computer time. Software is now the major element in total costs, though once purchased it can be used repeatedly – at least until obsolete! Less tangible costs include the time and organizational disruption involved in gaining access and setting up the computer, and necessary monitors. There are also the inevitable risks that are taken when using any sophisticated educational technology. Although computer hardware and software are becoming more robust, they remain less reliable than audio-tapes, video and projected aids, so teachers always need to be prepared with alternative activities in the event of failure.

Research evidence on the effectiveness of CAL in economics, and of computer games and simulations in particular, is scanty. Siegfried and Fels[19] surveyed US research at college level up to the late 1970s. US studies confirm anecdotal reports from the UK that computer games generate considerable enthusiasm on the part of students. Although CAL appears to be helpful in motivating students towards the subject, this does not, however, necessarily guarantee that specific economic concepts are successfully learned. A small-scale study in the UK by Wood,[20] involving students using the multiplier program mentioned earlier,[21] evinced a significant improvement in test scores based on past A-level multiple-choice questions on the concept. The US studies, however, reveal no conclusive evidence that game-playing is superior to other, perhaps less costly, strategies for advancing knowledge of economic concepts. This should not be too surprising, nor disappointing, as the proponents of games and simulations tend to justify them on the basis of generating higher-order abilities. Tentative support for this is provided in a study by Emery and Enger[22] which demonstrated 'higher achievement on questions requiring analysis and policy decisions' on the part of students who had been given greater exposure to computer games. It is unlikely that standard test instruments would identify some of the other expected outcomes from the use of CAL. The methodological and data-interpretation skills that students acquire when using simulations for investigative work, and the discussion and decision-making skills associated with group games, while attested to by individual teachers, are difficult to quantify.

There is mounting evidence from a number of disciplines that both the style of use and pattern of organization have an important bearing on the effectiveness of CAL. Hassell,[23] working with two parallel 12–13-year-old lower-ability geography sets, used the same program for teacher-led discussion with one set, and for small group work by students at the computer with the other. The student-centred style produced higher test scores, a greater ability to explain the underlying concepts in a detailed manner, more worthwhile interaction, as well as more interest and involvement. In the teacher-centred style, 'many children found it frustrating not being able to use the computer themselves'. Care must, however, be exercised when organizing group work. If groups are too large, much above four or five students, it becomes more difficult for everyone to participate. Wood[24] noted that a smaller improvement occurred in one group of students dominated by a particularly bright individual. Robinson,[25] using the same CAL unit with three streamed classes in geography, observed that while 'the upper and middle ability groups enjoyed the active learning situation . . . the lowest ability pupils clearly disliked the problem solving approach'. The lower-ability pupils also appeared less comfortable when placed in a competitive situation. Wetzel *et al.*[26] advise that we should expect to find differences in student characteristics at all ability levels. Some students are at their best in collaborative group work, others perform better when left to work independently, and many are highly dependent upon the teacher and prefer formal instruction. It must follow that it is advisable to organize computer use in a variety of ways, to suit the needs of different students.

CAL, in common with other forms of resource-based learning, has implications for the role of the teacher in the classroom. With the computer acting as problem setter and judge of performance, the teacher moves from the centre of the stage and becomes a helper and guide rather than sole authority. The teacher must ensure that intended learning takes place, that new leads are explored, and that CAL is integrated into the overall framework of classroom activity.

When programs are selected the teacher will need to check that they are appropriate to the conceptual and language development of the students. Program developers will often design for flexibility, by providing a range of options to suit different circumstances. The teacher must be willing to restrict students to using only those parts of a program that are suited to the objectives in mind. As Payne[27] *et al.* pointed out, 'The teacher has to decide just how much the computer should do for the students. In the interests of creating an active role this may be less than that which it is capable of.'

The computational power of the computer may be counter-productive in more ways than one. Joseph[28] expressed the following concern:

'there is some danger that the complexity permitted by the computer will obscure the learning objectives of the simulation'. This is evident, perhaps, in some of the more complex macroeconomic games that contain numerous variables, multiple objectives and instruments of policy, with random events thrown in for good measure. Herein lies a very real dilemma for CAL design. It is the realism of many games that generates so much enthusiasm on the part of students, and yet the dangers that they fail to dissociate the simplifying abstractions from reality are substantial.[29] Another rather ironic consequence of making theory more accessible to students by setting it within the simulated realism of the computer game, is that it may entrench the more abstract approach to economics, and detach the subject still further from the issues and complexities of the 'real' world. In order to obviate this possibility, it is crucially important to see that 'students are led back to the real world'[30] by thorough debriefing, and by supplementing CAL with case-study and data-response materials that are firmly rooted in realism.

A final aspect of both computer- and paper-based games and simulations that is apt to cause concern, is their tendency, on occasions, to obscure value questions. Many macroeconomic games pre-empt discussion of the relative importance of unemployment and inflation as policy goals, by incorporating them in a composite welfare function, over which neither the teacher nor the student has any control. Similarly, business games often leave it to be inferred that profit maximization is the goal, when students may exhibit a preference for some quite different behavioural objective, such as satisficing or sales maximization. Where explicit criteria for success are incorporated into a program, it behoves the teacher to discuss their wider implications.

CAL must be seen as the application of new technology to existing teaching approaches. Only rarely does the computer enable us to do things that we could not do in some other way. As pointed out in the previous edition of this book, 'research suggests that the design of resources is more important than the "delivery systems" by which they are presented'.[31] The computer makes a number of valuable but time-consuming activities more manageable. In facilitating investigative work on both economic models and data, the computer can help to support the move towards a position where students learn economics by adopting the methods employed by economists.

Notes and references

1. Shepherd, I.D.H., Cooper, Z.A., and Walker, D.R.F., *Computer Assisted Learning in Geography* (Council for Educational Technology, 1980).
2. *The Paraffin File* (BP Educational Service, 1983); Carter, H., and Greenwood, A., *Teddytronic – The Story of a Firm* (Longman, 1984).

3. Lumsden, K.G., and Scott, A., *Running the British Economy, 1983* (Longman, 1983). Updated and reissued for 1984.
4. Taylor, J., and Walford, R., *Learning and the Simulation Game* (Open University Press, 1978).
5. See *The Paraffin File*, op. cit.
6. Randall, K.V., 'The multiplier', in Killbery, I., and Randall, K.V., *Computers in the Economics Curriculum* (Longman, 1980).
7. Yates, I., *Equi-marginal Utility* (Longman, 1983).
8. See, for example, Green, J.R., 'Elasticity of demand', in Killbery and Randall, op. cit.; Young, G., and Killbery, I., *Wages* (Longman, 1983); Hornby, W.B., Holley, B.J., and Still, D., 'Theory of the firm', in Killbery and Randall, op. cit.
9. Proctor, B., and Greenwood, A., *Location – Iron and Steel* (Longman, 1984).
10. Murley, A., and Greenwood, A., *Workers and Machines* (Longman, 1984).
11. Reynolds, D., and Waterworth, G., *Family Budgeting* (Computers in the Curriculum Project, 1984).
12. Davies, P., and Waterworth, G., *Estate Agent* (Longman, 1984).
13. Hurd, S.J., Banks, B., and Greenwood, A., *Regional Statistics* (Computers in the Curriculum Project, 1984).
14. Lumsden, K.G., and Scott, A., *Macro-economic Data Base* (Longman, 1984).
15. Hooper, R., *National Development Programme in Computer Assisted Learning – Final Report of the Director* (Council for Educational Technology, 1977).
16. Attiyeh, R., Bach, G.L., and Lumsden, K.G., 'The efficiency of programmed learning in teaching economics: the results of a nationwide experiment', *American Economic Review*, May 1969; Siegfried, J.J., and Fels, R., 'Research on teaching college economics: a survey', *Journal of Economic Literature*, September 1979.
17. The CML literature is surveyed in Siegfried and Fels, op. cit. An account of a UK investigation is reported in Lumsden, K.G., Attiyeh, R., and Scott, A., *Economics Education in the UK* (Heinemann Educational Books, 1980).
18. For instance, in the economics degree at North Staffordshire Polytechnic.
19. Siegfried and Fels, op. cit.
20. Wood, K.R.J. 'A case study of computer assisted instruction in economics', University of London Institute of Education Working Paper, 1983.
21. Randall, in Killbery and Randall, op. cit.
22. Emery, E.D., and Enger, T.P., 'Computer gaming and learning in an introductory economics course', *Journal of Economic Education*, spring 1972.
23. Hassell, D., 'Teaching style and CAL in geography', in Kent, A. (ed.), *Geography Teaching and the Micro* (Longman, 1983).
24. Wood, op. cit.
25. Robinson, C., 'An evaluation of pupil attitudes towards CAL in geography', in Kent (ed.), op. cit.
26. Wetzel, J.N., Potter, W.J., and O'Toole, D.M., 'The influence of learning and teaching styles on student attitudes and achievement in the introductory economics course: a case study', *Journal of Economic Education*, winter, 1982.

27. Payne, A., Hutchings, B., and Ayre, P., *Computer Software for Schools* (Pitman, 1980).
28. Joseph, M.L., 'Game and simulation experiments', *Journal of Economic Education*, spring 1970.
29. Ryba, R., 'Approaches to economics teaching', in Lee, N. (ed.), *Teaching Economics*, 2nd edn (Heinemann Educational Books, 1975).
30. Lewis, R., in McKenzie, J., Elton, L., and Lewis, R., *Interactive Computer Graphics in Science Teaching* (Ellis Horwood, 1978) ch.2.
31. Noble, P., 'Audio-visual resources in the study of economics', in Lee, op. cit.

18 Data and Data Response in Economics Teaching
Richard A. Powell

Introduction
In the Report of a Joint Committee of the Royal Economic Society, the Association of University Teachers of Economics and the Economics Association on the *Teaching of Economics in Schools*,[1] three essential elements of economics as a school subject were identified. These three elements, which 'should be instilled as far as may be practicable', were stated as:

1 A capacity to understand both in terms of theory and in application the principles upon which an economy such as that of the United Kingdom operates.
2 A general understanding of the more important economic institutions within which the national economy operates.
3 A capacity to handle, interpret and present the statistical evidence on which economic decisions are reached.

The report was concerned wholly with the teaching of economics at the sixth-form level and with the content and objectives of the syllabus of economics at A-level. Since the publication of that report, considerable developments have taken place with regard to the third of the 'essential elements' identified, that of the capacity to handle and interpret quantitative evidence. It is those developments in the use of data and data-response questions that are discussed here.

Data and A-level economics
The A-level syllabus of the JMB in economics states that the purpose of the syllabus is 'to enable centres to devise courses which will provide candidates with an adequate knowledge and understanding of the tools of economic analysis and of the problems to which these tools are applied'.[2]

The syllabus considers more specifically in its statements of aims and objectives the importance of the candidate's capacity and ability to handle and interpret quantitative data. For example, the syllabus refers to the student's development of 'an appreciation of the method of study used by the economist and of the most effective ways in which economic data may be analysed, correlated, discussed and presented'.[3] It is, therefore, clear in this instance of the JMB A-level syllabus that the development of skills and abilities in the use of data by candidates is an important part of the course and furthermore is one of the abilities tested in the examination. The syllabus also emphasizes the need for candidates to have 'the ability to understand and interpret economic information presented in verbal, numerical and graphical form and to translate such information from one form to another', 'to make valid inferences from material presented', 'to evaluate the reliability of material', 'to check that conclusions drawn are consistent with given information and to discriminate between alternative explanations'.

The JMB is not alone in its requirement that students should have these skills. The other examination boards also refer specifically to the use of data and the understanding of quantitative evidence. Examination papers now include data-response questions of various types deliberately designed to test and assess the interpretation and understanding of data and statistical evidence.

The case for using data in economics teaching does not depend solely on the requirements of examination boards. The attention given to handling, interpretation and analysis of data in the classroom provides many opportunities to develop economic ways of thinking. Economics is concerned with decision-making and problem-solving, and if one of the aims of teaching economics is to provide the student with the means to understand and evaluate economic policy decisions then it is necessary for the student to be aware of and understand the quantitative basis upon which such decisions are very often made.

Moreover, it is apparent that there has been an 'information revolution' in recent years. This 'revolution' has been both in the quantity and quality of information – national statistics, facts and figures, detailed and accurate breakdown and analyses of all manner of economic data. As a result it is now possible to be much better informed as to how the economy works, but this will only be the case if the introduction of data, the teaching of statistical skills and the development of the abilities to interpret data and identify trends also takes place with sufficient pace and depth.

According to some critics, such as Jackson, economics teachers still make too little reference to the real world.[4] These views can be seen in the wider light of more general criticism that has been made of the A-level syllabus and how it is taught and examined. These criticisms were illustrated by Livesey[5] in *Economics*, where he quoted comments from respondents to a questionnaire and the following points were made that are applicable here: 'There is a case to be made for relating the theoretical aspects of the subject to their practical applications – all too often theory is divorced from reality. This reflects poor teaching.'

Another comment was as follows: 'I believe that the GCE syllabus should be made relevant to an understanding of the problems and possible solutions of current economic events. The more relevant the syllabus, the more interest will be aroused.' Finally: 'The basic problem seems to be the overemphasis on theory. My students are constantly complaining about the unreality of theory, especially perfect competition and parts of the theory of the firm.'[6]

These criticisms suggest that all too often economics teaching appears to have a lack of realism and relevance to the real world. Appropriate use of data can change the situation.

Data and data-response in teaching and examinations

It is important to consider exactly what is meant by 'data', since the term is used in different ways. A look at a variety of questions that have appeared on examination papers as 'data-response' items will confirm that the data can be of different types or forms. Wilkinson comments: 'It is usual to use the word data to refer to numerical information. To be precise, however, data can be of any type of information, quantitative or non-quantitative. . . . Quantitative data can be of two types, viz. real statistical information or simple sets of numbers constructed to illustrate a point.'[7] This distinction in types of data between non-quantitative and 'real' and 'constructed' statistics will be used below. Data in an examination context occurs in many forms and in different types of questions. The multiple-choice items and the essay questions very often use data, whether quantitative or non-quantitative in type, and may test a variety of skills, such as comprehension, knowledge, evaluation and analysis. However, the data-response or stimulus-material type of question can test more directly certain kinds of skill.

The case for the use of data in teaching is a very strong one. It allows learning to become an active and not merely a passive process and may create new opportunities for the student to become more interested and aware as well as more participant. Data provides a means by which the application of theory to the real world may be undertaken. The data may be in the form of illustration of a principle or concept, or may be introduced in the context of a problem-solving exercise. Exercises can also be introduced in different ways such as simulations, games, role play and projects. Whichever approach is used should result in increased interest, relevance and participation and give positive gains in the teacher–student relationship: 'Thoughts are provoked and the relevance of ideas and concepts passively acquired are challenged by confronting the students with data.'[8]

The distinction has been made between active and passive learning and it has been claimed that by the use of data it is possible to introduce a greater element of inductive learning into the teaching of economics. By doing so the criticisms of lack of relevance in economics courses can be partly answered.

The case for data-response exercises in examinations has been made very strongly in relation to the role of such questions in achieving the declared aims and objectives of economics courses and syllabuses. It is argued that the use of data and related data-response questions helps to develop skills, analytical ability, reasoning and understanding. An article by Livesey on the nature of examinations in economics develops this point as follows: ' . . . since deductive models tend to abstract from reality while inductive models relate to actual events, data response questions allow one to introduce a greater element of reality in the examination. This is a very important consideration in view of the feeling that appears to be growing at all stages of the educational system, that Economics as it should be taught is becoming increasingly divorced from the real world.'[9]

The position of data-response questions in relation to other types of examination questions has been described by Wilkinson in the following comment: 'From the view of examinations it is possible to provide a genuine test of understanding and reasoning and give some chance to avoid the danger of regurgitation of half digested ideas "mugged up" especially for the examination. Where the question is a genuine test of skill not depending on intrinsic knowledge of the data and its context, it gives a genuine chance to the candidate who has not been drilled on how to answer typical questions.'[10]

'Real' or 'constructed' data

The distinction in terms of quantitative data as either 'real' or 'constructed' raises pertinent questions as to the suitability and relative advantages and disadvantages of the type of data used. 'Constructed' data is quite common in some data-response questions and simulations. It is also often found in textbook examples of theory, such as hypothetical opportunity cost ratios in explanations of the principle of comparative advantage in international trade, indifference curve analysis and the theory of the firm. These areas are often seen by the student to belong solely to the world of theory and seem remote from actuality in spite of the efforts taken to demonstrate and apply the principles in a wider context. Exercises based on constructed data such as mathematical calculations and applications may also appear less important and valid as they become more and more abstracted from the student's own experience. For the teacher there are problems here in that real world data may be difficult to find and collate to illustrate a particular concept or theoretical principle. The textbook example is more accessible and it is less time-consuming to use the example than to find suitable appropriate real data. It is also possible that students will gain more confidence in handling data if the data are easy to deal with and produce the desired results. It is also the case that techniques and skills in handling information and in interpretation may be gradually acquired through using 'constructed' data. These skills and techniques can then be used at a later date to tackle more complex situations and exercises involving real data. Textbooks also include 'real' data as well as 'constructed' data but often the data is out of date. There are opportunities here for students to research more recent figures and statistics if this is the case. Where this research is practicable and can be encouraged, then students become used to direct sources of information and this may help counteract the tendency of students to separate the world of theory from the 'real' world.

Data-response exercises

The selection and use of data-response material for classroom use in economics courses is not without its problems. The major difficulty, as with any teaching method or approach, occurs when conditions are not ideal and where current practice does not use the material to its fullest advantage. Misapplication of, and overemphasis on, data may lead to problems of confusion, oversimplification, superficiality in argument and poor analysis by students. Any teacher faced with the task of collecting and assembling data for data-response and stimulus-material questions will appreciate the difficulties involved in selecting suitable material and constructing appropriate exercises. Simply choosing a paragraph or two from a newspaper, journal or bank review, etc. or an appropriate table or two of statistics and tacking a few questions on the end as exercises prove of little benefit and may be counter-productive if they result in superficiality and misdirection. Inadequate preparation and lack of care in producing data-response material may result in questions where the actual data is largely superfluous and/or irrelevant. One way of seeing this in relation to a data-response exercise is to consider the questions set in isolation from the data given; if the questions still stand on their own then clearly the exercise is not a genuine data-response. It is relatively easy to avoid this in the teacher's own attempts to produce data-response material by simply taking the time to apply this 'rule of thumb' and considering whether or not the questions do depend on the data. There is little point in providing detailed statistics for the balance of payments, for example, simply to ask the question, 'How are deficits on the balance of payments financed?' However, such data may be used in a more valid exercise by structuring the questions and exercises to lead from the identification of a balance of payments problem from given statistics towards a consideration of the problems of financing.

Selecting data-response material and setting appropriate accompanying exercises involves a number of steps. It might be suggested as good practice first to establish exactly what skills and abilities the exercise is intended to develop or, in the case of material used as a means of assessment, which skills and abilities are to be tested. This puts the emphasis on the purpose of the question rather than the data themselves, so that the addition of tasks and exercises to be completed can be considered in a structured way. Depending on the nature of the data, different initial approaches to setting questions can be adopted. A given text can be set for a precis or investigated for information relevant to a particular line of argument. Numerical data, for example, a set of statistics, can be investigated for particular trends and significance and also considered as relevant or important to demonstrate a case. Prose extracts can be examined to identify arguments for and against a proposition. The principle, concept or aspect of theory illustrated by the data should be clearly brought out by the tasks and exercises set. The knowledge and understanding of the concepts or theories can then be assessed. As an additional task leading from the stimulus material, the student can be asked to consider alternative applications or contexts for the data.

Collecting suitable data for data-response exercises is perhaps best tackled by keeping a file of cuttings, extracts and articles culled from the obvious sources of newspapers, such as *The Financial Times* and the *Business News Supplement, The Economist*, the various bank reviews, Economic Progress Reports and other material distributed by the Central Office of Information. For statistical data, the *Annual Abstract of Statistics* is a very useful general source with more detailed breakdowns available in the *National Income Blue Book*, *Economic Trends*, the *UK Balance of Payments*, *Social Trends*, the *Monthly Digest of Statistics*, etc. These are the more readily available sources but there are many other more specialized published statistics. The *Department of Employment Gazette*, for example, contains articles, comments and statistics on all aspects of the labour market and labour supply. Once the data are obtained, then editing is the next important step. Irrelevant material should be discarded and the data made readily digestible for the particular students' needs and capacities. Using 'home-produced' stimulus material and data-response exercises does allow the teacher to introduce more variety into lessons. There are quite a number of published books of data-response exercises and workbooks available as an alternative to the production of the teacher's own materials.

Data-response exercises provide a means of introducing inductive analysis into teaching. Provided that suitable raw data can be made available and in sufficiently easily digestible form, students can be presented with information from which principles can be derived.

Thus, students would be able to learn part of their economics from source data. With modern technology and the increasing numbers of microcomputers and associated software available in educational establishments, the possibility of introducing a greater range of data and data bases into the classroom is becoming a reality. With appropriate guidance, the economics student in particular has much to gain from the information revolution.

Notes and references

1. Joint Committee of the Royal Economic Society, the Association of University Teachers in Economics and the Economics Association, *The Teaching of Economics in Schools* (Macmillan, 1973) p. 11.
2. Joint Matriculation Board, *General Certificate of Education Regulations and Syllabuses* (JMB, annually).
3. Joint Matriculation Board, A-level economics syllabus.
4. Jackson, D., 'Economics education and the real world', *Lloyds Bank Review*, no. 138, October 1980.
5. Livesey, F., 'The relevance of GCE economics to industry and the professions', *Economics*, vol. 15, pt 4, no. 68, winter 1979, pp. 110–17.
6. Ibid., p. 111.
7. Wilkinson, R.K., 'The use of "data-response" material in teaching and examinations', *Economics*, vol. 16, pt 3, no. 71, autumn 1980, pp. 70–6.
8. Ibid., p. 70.
9. Livesey, F., 'Examining economics', *Economics*, vol. 13, pt 1, no. 57, spring 1977, p. 11.
10. Wilkinson, op. cit., p.70.

Part Five
Assessment

Assessment and the Economics Teacher
K.P. Brookes

Clarification of terms

In this chapter *assessment* describes the process of gathering information about achievement. It follows, therefore, that pupils and teachers are assessed. By *evaluation* is meant the process of stating the value or worth of that under consideration, and involves the making of judgements, that is, courses are evaluated. The terms are inextricably linked in that assessment, which by itself does not refer to the making of judgements, is an inevitable part of evaluation because it supplies information that can be considered in decision-making. The relationship between assessment and evaluation is further continued because assessment makes available information concerning the purposes or *objectives* of a course, and such information is used in the methods of evaluation.

Assessment necessitates testing, which involves measures used during a course of study. As *testing* occurs at regular intervals throughout the course, it differs from *examination* – a term reserved for a form of assessment that is less frequently in use. The word examination frequently refers to large-scale testing.

The case for assessment

The collecting of information on pupil achievement inevitably demands the attention of all teachers. It is safe to predict that the assessment of past attainment and future potential, of pupils' strengths and weaknesses, will remain topics germane to the professional development of the teacher because assessment and evaluation are inescapable features of classroom life. Sometimes they are viewed as unpleasant aspects of social life, but this position does not recognize the essential duty of gathering evidence about performance. Mager[1] sets out the dilemma facing a teacher who views assessment with resentment by posing a critical question: 'How will I know when I have arrived?' The practice of assessment is part of the answer to this question.

Three main justifications for assessment can be advanced:

First, assessment in education is required by the public at large in order that the school can show publicly how it has organized itself to meet the perceived needs of society. A subject of the curriculum that can demonstrate its efforts to come to terms with some of the most critical needs of society will construct adequate assessment procedures to support its case and will do this willingly.

Second, assessment accompanied by evaluation strengthens the professionalism of teachers. Results of pupil performance supply information central to the analysis of teachers' intentions and the effectiveness of classroom practices. These results will lead to a questioning of intentions (aims and objectives) and almost certainly initiate variation of them if it can be seen that a more successful approach needs to be employed. In addition, the role of the teacher requires a diagnosis of the needs of individuals, and subsequent remedial action may be called for if particular needs are not being satisfied.

Third, assessment wisely used by the teacher induces pupils to recognize and appreciate what is required of them. They are thus provided with an opportunity to react to a clear operational target. Much of this response will be evident to the teacher *during* the course of study and will thus be an aid to *formative evaluation*, providing signals to the teacher who, after consideration of results, will make necessary adjustments to his or her instruction. In addition, information collected from assessment will be available *after* a course has been completed, and will be in the nature of *summative evaluation* when again judgements are made on the effectiveness of learning and teaching.

Accountability and the teacher of economics

The topic of assessment makes particularly keen demands upon the teacher of economics – principally because economics has entered the secondary-school curriculum and consolidated its position at a time when the debate for accountability has been at its most vociferous. Economics has gained for itself a somewhat individual position in the curriculum, not so much at the expense of other subjects, but because it has grown more rapidly than others.

An initial inspection of the curriculum documents that flowed from the DES during the period of this growth, and particularly those that emerged after the 1976 'Great Debate', seems to provide comfort for economics education and to reinforce the role that it currently enjoys. *Education in Schools*[2] itemizes eight aims against which schools should judge the effectiveness of their work. Among these aims is the following: 'to help children to appreciate how the nation earns and maintains its standard of living and properly to esteem the essential role of industry and commerce in this process'.

The 1980 document *A Framework for the School Curriculum*[3] gives six aims of desirable school curricular activity, of which at least three are associated with economics:

To help pupils acquire knowledge and skills relevant to adult life and employment in a fast-changing world.

To help pupils understand the world in which they live, and the interdependence of individual groups and nations.

To help pupils appreciate human achievement and aspirations.

It continues by stating that, 'pupils need to acquire an understanding of the economic basis of poverty and how wealth is created'. It would, however, be a fatal error for the teacher of economics to grasp at the reassurance contained in these documents, and to anticipate that economics education will inevitably continue to grow. The movement for accountability contains warning signs for all subjects of the curriculum, and not least for economics which claims a station somewhat different from others. The indications are that economics will need to fight to maintain this position at a time when all curricular contributions are under review. Circular 14/77, *Local Authority Arrangements for the School Curriculum*,[4] discusses the responsibilities of both schools and local authorities for curriculum policy, and proposes the introduction of local authority measures to ensure that schools meet their responsibilities to the community by framing curricula appropriate to their needs. Circular 6/81[5] calls upon each local authority:

to review its policy for the school curriculum in its area, and its arrangements for making that policy known to all concerned;

to review the extent to which current provision in the schools is consistent with that policy;

to plan future development accordingly, within the resources available.

These portents have been accompanied by the establishment of the Assessment of Performance Unit with a brief to monitor standards in schools, and the long-running, vitally important debate about the structure of 16+ and 18+ examinations. The recent spread of economics education, no matter how logical it might appear to the rational mind, will not protect it from a national movement to make education more accountable. Teachers of economics cannot stand aside from this debate but must, with full confidence, accept that it is necessary and proper that they be held accountable for their successes and failures; and above all they must, if required, be able to defend their choice of assessment procedures used in the classroom. Assessment must be viewed not so much as a tool of economics, but more as a weapon to defend the subject. Sound and varied assessment measures are required. For how else will teachers know when they have arrived?

The justification advanced for the use of measurers gathering information leads on to a further question equated with assessment. What is to be assessed? It is suggested that the answer is 'the objectives', but the explanation behind the answer covers a wide and contentious body of material that necessitates discussion.

Naturally, the diverse views on this topic did not arise because teachers were not planning their performance. Classroom observation would have disclosed the consistent presentation of invigorating material, but in the past some of this practice has been carried out without an obvious association with the intentions of the teacher. Increasingly, and not least because of the pressure for accountability, the practice of stating these intentions, drafting them in advance of a course, and thus making them available to scrutiny, has come to be recognized as an essential duty. Indeed, the seeming detachment that involves the acceptance of the intentions of others, for example, examination bodies, has been replaced by a movement encouraging teachers to draft the purposes of their courses. Inevitably they will then shed any previous hesitation in defending their practice, and this can only be to the benefit of economics education.

Curriculum design

The design of a course, and the terminology used therein, involves a complex process. Whether planning the curriculum of a school, a course, parts of a course or even a lesson, certain elements are of necessity present.

Ralph Tyler,[6] proposing national curriculum planning, viewed the curriculum as consisting of four elements: objectives, content, methods and evaluation. Wheeler[7] built upon an influential model for curriculum design by laying emphasis upon the prerequisite position of aims and objectives (see Figure 19.1).

Another model (Figure 19.2) can be studied with profit.

These variations in construction are a recognition that teachers need to acknowledge their intentions, consider the material and practices that will be employed in achieving these intentions, and at some stage identify the strengths and weaknesses of the course, for example, formative/summative evaluation.

Aims and objectives

This evaluation inevitably involves assessment and is bound up with aims and objectives. These words deal with intention and spell out educational ends but differ by virtue of their generality and specificity. By *aim* is meant a statement of intent or purpose that can be (i) *general*, for example, 'to develop an understanding of the more important British economic institutions', which is long term in intent, or (ii)

Fig. 19.1

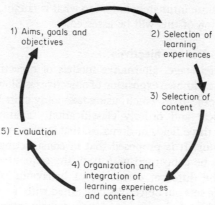

Source: Wheeler, D.K., *Curriculum Process* (Hodder & Stoughton, 1967).

Fig. 19.2

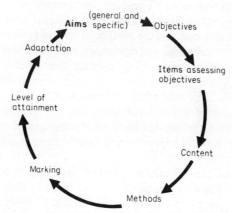

Source: Southern Regional Examinations Board, CEE: Humanities Pilot Scheme, 1982–3.

specific, for example, 'to develop a foundation of economic numeracy and literacy accompanied by the ability to use elementary data'. Specific aims are more short term in intention, more precise and can be seen as starting points for the construction of schemes of work or individual lessons.

By the nature of this definition, then, it can be seen that aims are statements of what it is hoped will be achieved. It follows, therefore, that they lack that specificity that opens them up to assessment. *Objectives* are more precise, are capable of various degrees of specificity and are technically amenable to assessment. Their use ensures that assessment is more intimately linked to what is taught, accepting that only a proportion of this will be assessed.

Alternative models of objectives

As in the design stage, alternative models of objectives are found. Probably the best-known exposition of objectives is Bloom's[8] taxonomy of educational objectives which, using taxonomy in its biological sense as a hierarchical and orderly classification, separates educational objectives into three fields or domains, that is, the cognitive, affective and psychomotor. It is proposed that in constructing objectives the teacher should be concerned with both the sequential nature of the activity and the different categories of behaviour that apply. The *cognitive domain* sets out objectives concerned with 'knowing, thinking and problem solving', the *affective domain* contains objectives related to attitudes and values; the *psychomotor* with practical skills. The taxonomies can be moulded to the development of what are known as 'behavioural objectives'. These are performance objectives referring to pupil *action*, which also indicate the conditions under which the performance will occur, and the minimum level of performance desired. If this approach were followed rigorously, each objective would describe a measurable piece of learning because the nature, conditions and standards would be given in accurate and recognizable terms. Serious and weighty criticisms of this approach have been brought.[9] Other classifications of educational objectives are proposed by Gagné,[10] whose hierarchy is founded on types of learning and not outcomes, and Ebel,[11] who favours a specification derived from groups of examination questions.

The above classifications have had little appeal for the classroom teacher because they appear to be too precise in their specification for use in the classroom on a day-to-day basis. Consequently, they have seemed remote from everyday activities.

Objectives used by teachers of economics

The intenseness of the debate concerning objectives, and the differing views of them, must not, however, deter the teacher of economics. What is called for is a realization that objectives concerned with knowledge, abilities and skills, if set, can be tested and will produce information for use by the teacher. General and specific aims are for guidance and cannot be subject to assessment. Stated objectives for assessment must detail the action, the conditions governing performance, and the level required. A variety of approaches to this matter follows:

An *AEB economics (A-level)*[12] *syllabus* indicates the aim as 'to give candidates an understanding of the basic principles of economics' – and continues with a list of four objectives that the candidate is expected to achieve at the end of the course ('a competence in organizing, interpreting and presenting economic information). The examination structure linked to these objectives is then given, that is, three papers, and guidance is provided on the main focus of each paper ('fifty objective test items testing mainly factual recall, comprehension, analysis and application'). The syllabus follows, accompanied by detailed guidance notes on the topics.

A *JMB economics (A-level)*[13] *syllabus* gives the general aims of the syllabus (e.g. 'to provide the basis for a broad understanding of economics'), and then the specific aims (e.g. 'to provide a basis of factual knowledge of economics'). It follows this section with a lengthy identification of the objectives of the examination, providing an indication of the abilities that the examination is constructed to test in association with a listing of subject material. The objectives component picks out the knowledge and abilities to be tested under the headings of 'knowledge, comprehension, application, analysis and synthesis, evaluation and expression'. The form of the examination is also described with notes of explanation.

The approaches visible in syllabuses for 14–16-year-old pupils will now be considered:

AEB social economics (O-level)[14] sets out at the onset three aims (e.g. 'to stimulate a critical awareness of current social and economic processes as they affect the individual'), and continues with an examination structure noting the intentions of each paper (e.g. Paper I: 'designed to test factual recall, comprehension, application and analysis'). The syllabus and full guidance notes follow.

A *GCE/CSE* discussion paper laying down draft criteria for *16+ economics*[15] is shaped by a statement on general aims (e.g. 'to enable students to participate more fully in decision-making processes as consumers, producers and citizens') and specific aims (e.g. 'to understand the basic economic problem of allocating scarce resources and ways in which it can be resolved'). Assessment objectives come next. Five objectives are given, to be assessed in all syllabuses of economics (e.g. 'Candidates will be expected to demonstrate recall of knowledge in relation to a specified syllabus content'). Further sections of the paper deal with, among other matters, content, the relationship between assessment objectives and content, and techniques of assessment.

A report of a pilot scheme dealing with *CEE humanities*, published by the Southern Regional Examinations Board,[16] provides an illustration of an interesting design feature. Each module dealing with humanities lists its aims and a set of objectives geared towards the production of assessable evidence. The objectives are subdivided into 'inform-

ation; methods, techniques and skills; concepts and principles; application and evaluation'. A paragraph on assessment serves notice of a minimum requirement of the pieces of work to be submitted for moderation. A praiseworthy feature of the design is that suggestions are made for course content as opposed to providing a detailed syllabus.
Structuring the assessment. The above examples are recommended for further study and decision by the economics teacher when the drafting of objectives for assessment is embarked upon. Such a study will in addition reveal the critical aspect of *weighting*, which needs to be taken into account in the drafting of procedures to assess the objectives.

It is vital that a scheme of assessment identifies the relative values allotted to different aspects of the objectives (e.g. 'the recall of knowledge, the ability to use this knowledge, skill in applying it'). Structuring or weighting may quite easily be applied to a question set in an examination for it is then a fairly simple matter to indicate the total marks and the distribution of them.

The *JMB economics (A-level)*[17] syllabus discussed above gives guidance on how to weight for a complete examination structure. An estimation of how marks allocated will be divided is shown as follows:

Knowledge	30%
Comprehension	25%
Application	15%
Analysis and synthesis	15%
Evaluation	15%

The rubric notes that questions may overlap these objectives, and no marks are given for expression, although candidates are penalized for faulty performance in this aspect. An allocation of marks between papers and parts of papers follows.

The weighting allocated to parts of an examination is shown in Table 19.1.

Table 19.1

Work for assessment	Objectives					
	A	B	C	D	E	
1	10	5	5	5		25
2		15	5	5		25
3	5	5	5		10	25
4	5		5	10	5	25
Weighting %	20	25	20	20	15	

This table reveals that more than one of the five objectives is assessed by the four items of work required, shows how each item is weighted, and illustrates that each objective counts for at least 15 per cent of the total marks available. It is recommended that when weighting is being considered, that a substantial proportion of total marks, for example, 50 per cent, should be given over to the emphasis of abilities other than factual recall.

And now a comment designed to encourage an answer to the question 'What is assessed?'

The terminological argument concerning objectives may justifiably make the teacher of economics wary in setting out objectives relating these to modes of assessment. But this has to be overcome for the conclusion to be drawn is stark. Assessment is required, and assessment demands that objectives be drafted that are technically capable of assessment, and the confident teacher must set about the task.

Techniques of assessment

Having decided what is to be assessed, the teacher of economics is, as a consequence, faced with identifying appropriate techniques of assessment from the wide variety of measures available.

General principles of test construction

It is essential to bear in mind that the value of assessment rests upon the degree to which it meets a number of criteria. The most important of these are:

Validity, that is, the extent to which a test measures what it is intended to measure. Ebel[18] draws a distinction between two basic kinds of validity. *Direct, primary validity* is found where the work set 'represents faithfully and in due proportion the kinds of tasks that provide an operational definition'. *Derived, secondary validity* means that marks rendered by a test 'correlate with the criterion scores which possess direct, primary validity'. The following example is offered for clarification. A test may require pupils to demonstrate recall of knowledge. If the results show that recall is associated with content specified in a syllabus, then the test would be directly valid. However, if the results indicated that the age of the pupils perfectly predicted recall of economic knowledge, then the test is not necessary. As a perfect predictor, a record of age would have derived validity. Clearly, then, tests of direct validity rather than derived validity are required because in this way, knowledge, ability and skills are identified as a consequence of the test.

Reliability. Another attribute that the teacher must be conscious of is *reliability*, that is, the consistency of the results produced by a test. A test in economics is reliable if the results produced are replicable in similar conditions. Reliability is a precept of testing that must be applied to the test itself, the performance of the pupils who sit the test, and the performance of the teacher who marks it. The fact that a test is set at different times, for example, should not produce radically different results.

Efficiency. The search among the techniques of assessment is intended to reveal measures that are efficient in their use of resources such as time and cost. When formative evaluation (i.e. ongoing) is used throughout a course, the teacher has to be constantly questioning the efficiency of measures used because they are so demanding of time in construction and administration. This factor provides one of the main justifications for the use of such objective tests as multiple-choice rather than essays.

Norm and criterion-referenced tests

The choice of whether to select norm or criterion-referenced tests is bound up with the purposes of the testing, in that each has characteristics that makes it suitable for particular circumstances.

A *norm reference test* is the conventional, single-score test identifying, for example, the quantity of knowledge of a topic that an individual pupil has retained. This kind of test helps the teacher to note questions that were answered correctly, and to recognize how one pupil has performed in relation to the rest who sat the test.

A *criterion-referenced test* has as its focus not individual scores, but those objectives that have, or have not, been realized. The merit of a performance is thus judged not by an indication that one pupil knows more than another, but by noting the proportion of the prescribed objectives that have been achieved by a pupil.

Because norm and criterion referenced tests have different purposes, uses and emphases, the teacher of economics needs to consider carefully the advantages of each before deciding which of these forms will be used at any given time. The choice perhaps centres around whether the purpose of testing is aimed at seeing what general level of understanding has been reached – in which case norm-referenced is appropriate – or whether decisions need to be made on information dealing with specific tasks or competencies – in which case, criterion-referenced tests will be chosen.

Approaches to assessment

Rowntree[19] provides a categorization of varying approaches to assessment that is worthy of study by the teacher before a final decision is made about techniques. The list that follows sets out practices as opposites, but his discussion of them makes it clear that he sees them not so much as alternatives but rather as labels illustrating contemporary school activities. He acknowledges that considerable overlap exists between the labels, and appreciates that a teacher would employ a judicious mix of them:

formal versus informal
formative versus summative
continuous versus terminal (or final)
course work versus examination
process versus product
internal versus external
convergent versus divergent
idiographic versus nomothetic

The alternative approaches to assessment are given here with the intention of making the teacher of economics aware of what is available and not to recommend one at the expense of another. The emphasis that is given to one of the modes, the mix of approaches that is utilized, has naturally enough to be made on the basis of informed decisions on what is most appropriate for a school's circumstances.

The following techniques of assessment are considered to be of high value to the teacher in the search for information concerning student response to courses of economics. Three types of methods of assessment are distinguished: (i) essay-type questions, (ii) objective questions, and (iii) data-response questions.

A discussion and illustration of these will be followed by some comments on projects, oral and aural work. Computer-based assessment is not discussed because this is covered elsewhere in this book. In the interests of consistency, the techniques in practice are mainly chosen from University of London GCE A-level papers in economics.

(i) Essay-type questions

This has in the past been the most popular type of item used in assessment, and has been particularly extensively used in O-level examinations. The essay gives pupils useful practice in the arrangement and effective expression of ideas, and enables them to report information and argument. However, its deficiencies include the typical unreliability of the scores, because it is a most subjective form of test item, and its relative inefficiency in the use of pupil and teacher time. If the intention is to discover to what extent pupils can recall knowledge then objective test items will normally prove more satisfactory.

The essay should only be employed when it is considered to be the most valid and efficient technique available to assess an objective. Such a decision should then be followed by a scrutiny of the title to ensure that it meets the demands set by an objective. A popular use of the essay has been to pose a question:

What are the economic implications of subsidizing the theatre? (University of London GCE A-level, June 1979.)

The traditional response to this question, suggesting a conventional introduction, analytical paragraphs and conclusion, could not so easily be applied where two questions are set, or a question and an instruction are made available:

What is meant by the equilibrium level of National Income?
Explain its significance for the level of employment and foreign trade. (University of London GCE A-level, June 1980.)

The *structured essay question* has much to offer to the teacher who wishes the pupil to give a continuous writing response and yet seeks to offer guidance in the form that this response should take; for example:

Explain what is meant by 'the terms of trade'. What might cause these to move in a country's favour? Illustrate your answer by reference to world experience during the last ten years. (University of London GCE A-level, June 1981.)

Additional guidance is made available when the framing of an essay-type question informs pupils of the way in which marks can be gained, because candidates may assume that an essay question set in two parts has 50 per cent of the marks given over to each part.

(ii) Objective questions

Objective questions come in various forms, some of which will be discussed below, but a quality common to these forms is that the mark scored is not responsive to the views of the marker. Criteria of performance is settled when questions are drawn up, and markers use the criteria consistently. Objective questions lend themselves to the assessment of a range of abilities, and the most successful of them necessitates interpretation of data, the ability to handle generalizations in the exploration and prediction of outcomes, and calls for a variety of procedures in order to arrive at answers. They demand precision of language because the marker has no leeway in determining the response of a candidate. This lack of flexibility means that pre-testing of objective questions is essential and that the methods of item analysis are utilized. Item analysis reveals how well each item has performed in terms of discrimination, difficulty and validity.[20]

The main forms of objective questions recommended for use by economics teachers are multiple-choice, assertion/reason, and short answer. Matching exercises, true/false items, and multiple completion are not discussed in this chapter.

Multiple-choice questions

A multiple-choice item is made up of a stem and one or more alternatives, one of which matches the requirement demanded by the stem.

The multiple-choice question is highly recommended for use in assessment of economics because of its high reliability. The use of several alternatives reduces the possibility of a correct guess and consequently increases its reliability. In addition, multiple-choice items can be designed so that they assess a greater range of abilities than other items and are amenable to the identification of the ability to discriminate, for example, by asking pupils to select 'the most important reason'.

Because the defects of a badly designed multiple-choice test are more obvious than those of a badly designed essay, for example, it is important that teachers who wish to construct their own tests read widely in this area[21] and practise item writing. The construction of effective multiple-choice items demands grasp of material, technical skill and a high level of creative ability – but above all, it needs time. This is not a job to be rushed because there is a lack of flexibility in marking. Consideration also needs to be given to the major and minor priorities of the course, objectives and the major themes in respect of importance and time. The forms that effective multiple-choice items may take is almost unlimited; two examples are:

(a) The item stem may be an incomplete statement with the alternative responses supplying possible endings, for example:

'A progressive income tax can best be defined as one which
  A imposes a greater burden on the rich than on the poor
  B imposes a greater burden on the poor than on the rich
  C increases proportionately with income
  D increases more than proportionately with income
  E redistributes income by taking from the rich and giving to the poor.'
  (University of London GCE A-level, June 1981.)

(b) Another form in frequent use gives a stem as a question from which the candidate is to select the correct answer:

'Which of the following measures of fiscal policy would be likely to reduce aggregate demand?
  A reduce existing charges made for drugs supplied under the National Health Service
  B increase transfer incomes without raising taxation
  C raise total government spending and taxation by equal amounts
  D reduce indirect taxes and raise direct taxes on higher income level to maintain the same revenue
  E reduce unemployment benefits without lowering National Insurance contribution.' (University of London GCE A-level, June 1981.)

Assertion/reason tests

These test items comprise an assertion and a reason, which may or may not be true. A decision has to be made by the pupil on whether the assertion is true, whether the reason is true, and whether the assertion is supported by the reason.

The value of these items lies in their ability to assess factual knowledge and, at the same time, allow pupils to make reasoned judgements that can be communicated in a logical manner.

It will be noted that the illustration that follows requires the pupil to consider five possible responses:

Assertion/reason questions
In each of Questions 46 to 50 you are given an assertion followed by a reason. Consider the assertion and decide whether, on its own, it is a true statement. Consider the reason and decide whether that is a true statement. If, and only if, you decide that *both* the assertion and the reason are true, consider whether the reason is a valid or true explanation of the assertion. Choose your answers as follows and indicate your choice on the answer-sheet.

A if both the assertion and the reason are true statements and the reason is a correct explanation of the assertion

B if both the assertion and the reason are true statements and the reason is not a correct explanation of the assertion

C if the assertion is true but the reason is a false statement

D if the assertion is false but the reason is a true statement

E if both assertion and reason are false statements.

Summarized directions for recording responses to assertion/reason questions

	Assertion	Reason	Argument
A	True	True	Reason is a *correct* explanation of assertion
B	True	True	Reason is *not* a *correct* explanation of assertion
C	True	False	Not applicable
D	False	True	Not applicable
E	False	True	Not applicable

---

46 The retail price index measures changes in the standard of living   because changes in prices affect the standard of living.

47 The most efficient way to reduce aggregate effective demand is to increase investment   because increases in investment automatically require a reduction in consumption expenditure.

48 The Labour Government in 1976 decided to curtail the growth of public expenditure programmes up to 1980   because public expenditure is entirely 'non-productive' in its character.

49	A large increase in the rate of interest will increase the amount of investment in an economy	because	savings in building societies are increased when the interest paid to depositors is significantly increased.
50	Consumption of any free good will be pushed to the point at which marginal utility is zero	because	if marginal utilities are positive then further consumption of a good will increase total utility.

(JMB GCE A-level Economics, June 1977)

Short-answer questions

As the title indicates, these questions require an answer to be given in a few lines. They are valuable for use with younger pupils, and are helpful with a wider range of ability than is normally found in GCE classes. At the same time they have the facility of testing for knowledge and understanding. They are not so demanding in construction as multiple-choice questions, and take less time to mark than essay-type questions.

A test that consisted of twenty questions, each worth one mark, might contain the following questions:

'1 What is another term for the division of labour?
2 Name *one* advantage of the division of labour.'

(iii) Data-response questions

These questions present numerical and descriptive data as a stimulus calling for an analytical reaction. They usually take the form of extracts from articles, newspaper reports, trade figures or balance sheets followed by a series of short questions calling for comment on, or interpretation of, aspects of the data, or demanding calculation before a conclusion is reached. Their intention is to test comprehension and to stimulate the use of the deductive process in arriving at this conclusion.

Data-response questions can serve as a stimulating introduction to a theme, be used as reinforcement for a series of economic concepts, or can act as a method of revision. They can have norm-referenced value showing how much overall knowledge a particular pupil has gained and criterion-referenced value determining which of the specified objectives an individual has achieved. Undoubtedly, they aid the teacher in providing information upon the ability of pupils to tease out the economic principles from a particular set of data. Their use is highly recommended to the classroom teacher at all levels, not least because they lend themselves so readily to the study of highly topical material easily assembled by both teacher and pupils.

Three different illustrations of their use follow, all taken from University of London GCE A-level examination, June 1983.

(i)   (a) Explain and interpret the diagram below.

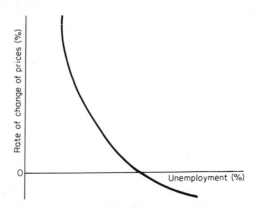

(b) In the light of the following figures, comment on the Phillips curve and
the British experience during the period 1971–76.

	Rate of change of	
Year	*Retail Price Index* (%)	*Unemployment* (%)
1971	9·5	3·4
1972	6·8	3·7
1973	8·3	2·6
1974	15·9	2·6
1975	24·2	4·0
1976	15·7	5·4

(ii)   'The optimal policy for the government on arriving in office is to deflate in
order to bring inflation down, then around mid-term to stimulate the
economy to bring unemployment down and raise real incomes in time for
the election, leaving their successors (or themselves) to cope with the rise in
inflation that is the lagged result of the policy. Such models then imply that
we observe a Boom–Election–Slump–Boom–Election cycle.'

(Source: P. Minford and D. Peel, 'Is the government's strategy on
course?', *Lloyds Bank Review*, April 1981.)

(a) Explain the meaning of 'deflate in order to bring inflation down'.
(b) Why might stimulating the economy cause a 'rise in inflation that is the
lagged result of the policy'?

(iii)   You are given the following information:

Cost per tonne of fertiliser = £140
Fixed cost of land = £3000
(Assume that no further costs are incurred.)
Selling price of wheat = £2 per unit.

Tonnes of fertiliser applied to a fixed area of land	Total production (units)
0	1000
1	1100
2	1250
3	1500
4	1900
5	2150
6	2275
7	2350
8	2380
9	2330

(a) With reference to the above data, comment on the relationship between the application of fertiliser and the production of wheat.

(b) What level of fertiliser would a profit maximising farmer choose to apply? Show the amount of wheat produced and the profit earned. Justify your answer.

Project work

'Project' is used here to describe an extensive exercise by pupils who, freed from the time limitations of an examination, are encouraged to carry out research making use of resources available locally. The word 'research' is contained within this definition so that a project can be seen as more than the gathering and recording of information. Emphasis is laid upon exploration of a question or problem, and might involve the collection and analysis of data, the stating of a problem and the consequent approaches to a solution, and inquiry into the association of an issue and economic concepts. Projects dealing with, for example, reasons why citizens borrow and save, an investigation into competitive interest rates, a study of product prices, can be of immense value to pupils struggling to establish a mastery of relevant skills.

If such an approach makes demands upon the pupil in terms of quantity and quality of work, it also requires the teacher to act as a 'research–facilitator' in encouraging and supporting pupils, and providing adequate reference material. Moreover, the emphasis upon problem-solving calls for a careful structuring of assessment criteria with due weight being given to the process rather than the product of projects.[22]

Project work can, most profitably, be linked to two 'underemployed' approaches to the assessment of economics, that is, *oral* and *aural* work. It is recommended that, recognizing the limitations imposed by oral and aural assessment in terms of validity, reliability and efficiency, they should none the less be coupled to project work. In particular, well-structured oral assessment can provide an opportunity for pupils to demonstrate their understanding of an issue and to some extent their zest for it. Pressure is placed upon the teacher who has to read the material and then administer a judicious mix of open-ended, structured and highly structured questions, but an oral approach can draw out pupil responses that are not possible in written tests. Because oral and aural work are routine classroom activities, their use directly involves the classroom teacher in examination assessment.

Self-assessment and the teacher

Techniques of assessment by their very nature produce information for the perusal of the teacher who will use this information in the process of decision-making. Whatever the design of the curriculum model, assessment provides raw material for curriculum evaluation no matter which emphasis this adopts, for example, objectives model; responsive/illuminative model. The procedures of assessment discussed up to this juncture have, naturally enough, been shaped to pupil performance. However, an equally important focal point for assessment procedures must not be neglected. An underemphasized aspect of assessment, but one that is gaining in importance because of the clamour for accountability, is the teacher. If assessment of pupils leads to diagnosis, and value judgements on classroom operations, then assessment of the person who has a key role in curriculum evaluation, that is, the classroom teacher, is capable of producing a like effect. This need not be a matter for concern if it is recognized that the activities of a classroom are highly complex and do not lend themselves to a rough and ready estimation of the qualities of a teacher. What is required is not assessment of the teacher, but self-assessment leading to self-evaluation.

The DES documents referred to in the earlier discussion of the call for accountability[23] required local authorities to accumulate information on the operation of the curriculum in schools. The reaction of many local authorities was to issue self-assessment and self-evaluation schemes to *schools*. In this way local authorities recognized that schools must evaluate curricula at regular intervals, and located decisions concerning this evaluation within the schools. Elliott[24] in his collection and discussion of twenty-one schemes of self-evaluation discovers a hesitation on whether the focal point of the schemes is the schools, the head teacher or individual teachers. Certainly, though, schools are being required to state their objectives, indicate the reasoning and choices behind these objectives and describe their working life. The document sent out by Birmingham Local Authority in 1980[25] in giving reasons for self-assessment notes that:

2.2 Individual teachers and schools as a whole need to clarify their aims and objectives, and a regular evaluation of progress towards them should be undertaken.

2.3 Schools should ensure that acceptable standards are being attained by pupils, and that resources are not only being used but used effectively.

2.6 The balance and structure of the curriculum and its organization require periodic reviews.

2.8 Because of professional commitments, teachers may too easily overlook the necessity to evaluate their work.

It would be a mistake to suppose that the school rather than the individual teacher is the target for self-assessment. The teacher of economics and the contribution that economics makes to the curriculum are under investigation. As assessment procedures for pupils must be readily welcomed, a similar position must exist for the self-assessment of the teacher. It is not the task of this chapter to construct instruments needed by teachers of economics to assess the strengths and weaknesses of classroom practice. As the professionalism of the teacher demands not requests self-assessment, so teachers must gather data on their own circumstances, perhaps make use of modern technology in observation, and accept without reservation the systematic observing of everyday teaching by colleagues. Assessment in the classroom for pupils and teachers alike will make available information for renewal, and hopefully lead to the strengthening of economics within the curriculum.

Notes and references

1. Mager, R.F., *Developing Attitudes towards Learning* (Belmont, California, Lear Siegler/Fearar, 1968).
2. DES, *Education in Schools*, Cmnd. 6869 (HMSO, 1977).
3. DES, *A Framework for the School Curriculum* (HMSO, 1980).
4. DES, *Local Authority Arrangements for the School Curriculum*, report on the Circular 14/77 Review (HMSO, 1979).
5. DES, *The School Curriculum*, Circular 6/81 (HMSO, 1981).
6. Tyler, R.W., *Basic Principles of Curriculum and Instruction* (Chicago, University of Chicago Press, 1949).
7. Wheeler, D.K., *Curriculum Process* (University of London Press, 1967).
8. Bloom, B.S. *et al.*, *Taxonomy of Educational Objectives: The Cognitive Domain* (Longman, 1956); Bloom, B.S. *et al.*, *Handbook on Formative and Summative Evaluation* (McGraw-Hill, 1971).
9. See Kelly, A.V., *The Curriculum: Theory and Practice* (Harper & Row, 1977) pp. 29–33.
10. Gagné, R.M., *The Conditions of Learning* (Holt, Rinehart & Winston, 1970).
11. Ebel, R., *Essentials of Educational Measurement* (Prentice-Hall, 1972).
12. AEB (618), *Economics – Advanced Level* (1983).
13. JMB GCE, *Regulations and Syllabuses* (1981).
14. AEB (061), *Economics Syllabus II Social Economics* (1982).
15. Joint Council for 16+ Criteria, GCE/CSE, *Draft Criteria for Economics* (1983).
16. Southern Regional Examinations Board, *CEE: Humanities Pilot Scheme 1982–3* (1983).
17. JMB, op. cit.
18. Ebel, op. cit., p. 381.

19. Rowntree, D.R., *Assessing Students: How Shall We Know Them?* (Harper & Row, 1977) p. 119.
20. See Satterly, D., *Assessment in Schools* (Basil Blackwell, 1981) pp. 103–11.
21. Ibid., pp. 90–6.
22. Rowntree, op. cit., pp. 137–41.
23. DES (1979), DES (1981), op. cit.
24. Elliott, G.G., *Self-evaluation and the Teacher: Part 4* (University of Hull, 1981).
25. Birmingham Local Authority, 'Within the school: a way of self-assessment for schools', in Elliott, op. cit., pp. 9–10.

Further reading

Ebel, R., *Essentials of Educational Measurement* (Prentice-Hall, 1972).
Macintosh, H., *Assessment and the Secondary School Teacher* (Routledge & Kegan Paul, 1976).
Satterly, D., *Assessment in Schools* (Basil Blackwell, 1981).

20 Examining Economics at 16+
Simon Smith

Introduction

Public examinations in economics for pupils aged 16 have in recent years become more sophisticated, and in many cases more interesting, for the candidates. Where previously an examination consisted of a rather haphazard collection of free-response essays where if a candidate had 'done' particular topics in depth and was sensible enough to select the appropriate questions then there was a strong probability that s/he would achieve good results, recent CSE and GCE assessments have adopted a more rigorous analysis of what a 'pass' represents in terms of knowledge, understanding and skills. Indeed it is now common practice to use a battery of different kinds of tests – written essays, short-answer questions, data-response and multiple-choice items, together with, in some instances, projects and course work – designed to measure the extent to which pupils have mastered the course. Simultaneously there has been a conscious effort on the part of examining boards to allow, and in some cases to encourage, teachers to participate actively in the business of syllabus construction and setting examination papers, particularly as evidenced in the proliferation of Mode III schemes where choice of syllabus content and examination format are determined by the teacher in consultation with the board. These changes are now well documented.

Several other important developments in assessment are taking shape. Where teachers and others have perceived gaps in the existing methods of examining and reporting, new techniques are being tried – such as graded tests and performance profiles. Above all, a whole new system of examining at 16+ has been designed, with the express purpose of replacing separate CSE and GCE examinations with a single nationally validated system. The Joint Council for 16+ National Criteria set up Joint Subject Committees whose function was to establish, after taking into account the views of teachers and other specialists, the validity of sets of criteria for each of the subjects in the school curriculum and, subject to the approval of the DES, these will be adopted to form the basis of a national system of examinations.

Fitness for purpose

Despite a categorical statement by the Schools Council[1] in 1971 that 'the common system of examining at 16+ should be designed to assess attainment', it must be understood that examinations may have many purposes: diagnostic, selective, predictive, or testing of achievement (attainment). Clearly, CSE and GCE are tests of attainment. The trouble is that these examinations are often thought to have predictive power: that they foretell how a boy or girl will, for example, perform at university, while working as a laboratory technician with ICI, or as a trainee accountant. Of course, they do not always do this job of predicting future success: they were not designed to do so, yet have become widely accepted as such by employers, professional bodies and the universities, though they often make their offer conditional on the attainment of certain A-level grades. Alex Scott[2] has shown conclusively that GCE examinations in economics are unreliable predictors of success in economics at university, yet in the past examinations at 16 had almost entirely as their purpose the selection of those thought to have attained the necessary standard to begin advanced courses in preparation for university. The target population of 16+ examinations warrants more careful consideration: it is asking for the unattainable – to use the same examination as the summit of preparation for the A-level course, and as a course for those about to leave school. Both the content and whole approach to the subject matter of economics will be different according to the nature of the target population, and the purposes for which the reporting of examination results are used. More recently, the need to equip school leavers with a basic knowledge of those aspects of the subject that would help to make sense of the economic environment they would find themselves in when they left school, has been more clearly recognized as an important purpose, and this has led inevitably to the reshaping of traditional syllabuses and examinations in economics for pupils up to the age of 16. It is not difficult to think back to a time when the vast majority of pupils left school without any formal acquaintance with the subject, even at the most elementary level, but for those who leave school at 16, the relevance of economics will now be judged in terms of its practical application to the world in which we live and the acid test 'does it work in the real world?' As an early CSE Mode I economics syllabus put it:

It is believed that the teaching of economic principles isolated from everyday life is of little value to the pupils who are likely to follow the course, and that one justification for this subject in a general curriculum is the extent to which it adequately prepares pupils for entry into the adult world of living and earning.[3]

At the same time it is necessary to guard against an oversimplified 'applied economics'; pupils must realize that there are often no 'right answers' and that many decisions in the economy are made on the basis of political judgements about the relative weight to be attached to the benefits and costs of a particular line of action. In practice, economic decisions and their consequences are likely to be extremely complex, typically depending on an array of assumptions about which it is possible to take a variety of positions.

The task of the syllabus-maker must therefore be to come to a reasonable compromise between an oversimplified mechanistic view of the economy on the one hand, and, on the other, one so rarefied in its abstraction that the study of economics becomes unintelligible and unilluminating for the average teenager. Much the same position can with profit be taken with regard to the assessment of economics. While accepting the Schools Council's dictum[4] that it is the syllabus that should determine the examination and not the reverse, examinations do need to be challenging and intellectually stimulating for the candidates, and perhaps for the teachers too. On these grounds alone, though there are of course other advantages too, one should welcome the development of the variety of test forms mentioned earlier, and the attempt to breathe life into economic syllabuses and examinations by relating them more closely to the activities and intellectual behaviour of economists, a point more fully examined below.

It has now become *de rigueur* for any self-respecting examination system to state the aims and objectives of the course. This has culminated in the detailed, complex and extremely lengthy statements of 'operational' objectives which appear in the publications of examining boards such as RSA, City and Guilds and the Business & Technician Education Council. There is a growing literature on behalf of a body of influential educational opinion[5] that such precise statements of objectives may be undesirable for their cramping effects on the curriculum, the subject syllabus and the pupil since they tend to confine attention only to that which is observable and measurable. The conflict is essentially between a desire to achieve the utmost precision and to avoid the artificiality that can result, and clearly calls for compromise.

Less attention has been paid to the equally important requirement of making sure that the assessment adequately reflects the course objectives. Unless appropriate methods of assessment are used, for example, pupils will not be able to demonstrate their mastery of the relevant insights and skills. A prime prerequisite for any examination, then, is fitness for purpose, and failure to achieve this in some public examinations is perhaps a significant cause of the proliferation of Mode III schemes in some subjects of the curriculum and also constitutes a major reason for retaining this feature in any new examination system at 16. The syllabus and its operational objectives provide a specification for what is expected of the candidate at the end of the course, and the examination should constitute a measure of the extent to which the desired objectives have been achieved by the individual candidate. The validity of the examination exists in a precise description of what the examination is to contain, a blueprint that gives the examiner no excuse for:

(a) asking the wrong kinds of questions;
(b) asking questions that are outside the scope of the syllabus;
(c) putting the emphasis in the wrong place, as between, say items in the syllabus, or the different skills of the economist.

Frequently, however, the syllabus aims are couched in such terms as to make it difficult to see how some of the purposes stated are to be achieved. Such key phrases as, for instance, 'to encourage a lasting interest in the subject' or 'to relate the subject to everyday life', appear in the statements of the various examining boards, yet if one looks at the examination papers it is not at all clear how or where these intentions are upheld. What has gone wrong? The answer would seem to be either that the aims of the syllabus are over-ambitious or too elaborate, or because 'the papers are pedestrian and unimaginative, failing to carry out the intentions of the syllabus makers'.[6] Where teachers perceive such weaknesses there is a strong case for exerting influence on the boards to obtain satisfactory and efficient examination papers. The regional method of organizing CSE boards, with its system of local advisory bodies, makes this possible, and we may see a similar organization carried over into the new 16+ examining system.

Of course, the style and mode of examining will also affect the teaching style adopted in the classroom, whatever the formal claims of the syllabus happen to be. Even with an approach that claims to allow the teacher plenty of opportunity to develop teaching content to suit the pupils and the school environment, in practice the subject-matter is so wide-ranging that the teacher relies largely on past examination questions in the belief that pupils might otherwise omit some vital aspect required for a written answer. Thus in the past there was often great reliance in the classroom on rote learning, dictated notes, emphasis on question spotting and the development of examination-passing techniques. The introduction of a variety of methods of examining (particularly multiple-choice and data-response questions), though bringing unique problems of their own, has probably encouraged both teachers and pupils to try and achieve a deeper understanding of the principles of the subject.

Other, more sinister 'backwash' effects have been noted by Rowntree[7] and, in view of climbing unemployment rates among school leavers, would appear to have taken on greater importance in recent times. In the quest to secure a job or a place at university, getting good grades becomes the exclusive aim of pupils and may well persuade teachers to take a more instrumental view of education. Pupils may be encourged to disregard an interest in the learning itself and strive only to achieve some sort of marketable qualification, while the teacher's reputation will come to depend primarily on the number of examination passes that his pupils achieve. Furthermore, friendly co-operation between teacher and teacher and pupil and pupil, may well disappear because all are competing for what they may believe to be a limited supply of 'passes'. The teacher motivated by a future improvement in job prospects, and the pupil who feels that he might have something to gain from the poor performance of others, may well refrain from the worthwhile activity of sharing knowledge and ideas in class or staff-room discussions.

An economics vocabulary

How often do examiners' reports complain about candidates' inability to write clear and logical answers? Yet it would seem that economics teachers, like other teachers, tend to disclaim responsibility for their pupils' language skills and powers of expression. Undoubtedly one of the important factors in helping to establish multiple-choice and data-response questions in the examination of economics at O-level and CSE has been the belief that these sorts of examinations would ensure that what is being tested is not so much language facility as skill in recognizing economic relationships and making inferences with the help of appropriate economic principles. It is still important, however, to bear in mind for any system of examining at 16, that the examination papers must be designed, in part at least, so as to require from candidates the use of language skills appropriate to the age and ability group concerned.[8] Thus it behoves the teacher to spend time encouraging students not only to develop a basic economics vocabulary or literacy, but to acquire a reasonable competence in English composition; and the examiner to set questions and use stimulus material that are within the competence of those in the target range of the examination, and to take steps to indicate as far as possible the kind and level of answer required for a particular question. Perhaps, therefore, we shall see an end to a situation where candidates, faced with the instruction: 'Write short notes on . . . ', are left to wonder whether simply to recall some relevant facts, or to apply some economic principle or else to make some evaluation of the specified topic. Any guidance afforded to the candidate about precisely what the examiner is looking for is bound to be helpful and, who knows, perhaps we shall find fewer examiners claiming that candidates 'didn't seem to understand the question'. We must all have undergone the experience of sitting in an examination room wondering not so much what a particular question meant (though this too sometimes!) but what kind of approach was expected.

Klausmeier[9] stresses the need to encourage pupils to understand the processes of economics (the intellectual behaviour of economists referred to earlier), and identifies the following list: observing, classifying, inferring, interpreting data, controlling variables, deducing. It is not at all clear that the conventional written essay paper ensures that these skills will be tested systematically: a well-accepted reason for the inclusion in any overall assessment schemes of additional appropriate techniques. Klausmeier goes on, mistakenly in my view, to develop a hierarchical order in which pupils are to learn concepts, processes and skills, proposing that the level of difficulty in assessment will be a matter of:

(a)   the intrinsic difficulty of the concept or principle; and
(b)   the skills, etc. needed to answer the precise question – whether it be 'straightforward' synthesis or 'high-order' evaluation. (The contention that synthesis is 'easy' while evaluation is 'hard', is a popular but indefensible belief for one can quite easily think of examples of exercises requiring evaluation or synthesis that are simple or difficult.)

Nevertheless, the important point is that it is necessary to use a battery of methods of examining in order to test adequately the extent to which candidates have mastered the range of economic 'skills' intended by the syllabus, and reference to Klausmeier's list indicates that in addition to economic literacy, pupils would need some degree of economic numeracy, in particular some competence in the interpretation of numerical data of an elementary kind.

Assessment components

The case for retaining both essay questions and multiple-choice items in the overall assessment of economics appears to be supported by evidence provided in 1977 by the Test Development and Research Unit, Cambridge.[10] The study confirmed that ability to do well in a multiple-choice paper is not very highly related to the ability to do well in an essay paper, thus, it was held, there would appear to be a continuing need for both types of examination. While the essay paper seemed to provide a measure of candidates' ability to organize material and develop an argument within a number of chosen topics, the multiple-choice paper tested knowledge over the whole syllabus, ability to deal with quantitative as well as qualitative information, and aptitude in solving short novel problems requiring interpretative and analytical skills. As one would expect, the objective test was also found to be slightly more reliable and valid[11] and, as such, the report suggests, its results should be given greater weight than those of the essay paper.

The whole question of the correlation between different components in the same subject examination, and of the relative weights given to each of the components – essay, multiple-choice, course work, project – has received little consideration for a topic so important, when one takes into account the number of examination schemes of this nature operated by individual economics teachers under Mode III, and the probable continuation of such practice in the new 16+ arrangements. The area is one of considerable complexity and some confusion.

Having first determined what we are trying to achieve in any particular assessment scheme – generally expressed as a set of objectives – there are many reasons for thinking that it might be desirable for an economics examination to include several components. The objective test is probably the most efficient means of, for example, testing factual knowledge over the whole range of the syllabus (though of course it is capable of fulfilling other purposes too), while the essay paper would seem to provide an appropriate assessment of candidates' ability to select and organize relevant information in their own words. Projects and course work are other variants, and some boards even include an optional oral test in their economics examination.[12] Another reason, already mentioned, for including an objective test in the examination is that it is usually rather more reliable than the other forms of tests. However, the overriding principle in deciding which technique to use is that it should be the most appropriate for the particular purpose for which it is intended. Thus, in order to test knowledge of a particular economic term an objective question such as the following may be asked: 'The type of integration illustrated by a merger of two brewing companies is known as . . .?', and to examine the extent to which a candidate can use his evaluative powers, the following can be posed: 'How successful have been the measures adopted by the government to keep inflation in check?'

The situation is complicated by the fact that every test will, to some extent, measure general ability, 'G', as well as, it is hoped, whatever individual ability it is concerned with. For example, all essay-type examinations, whatever the subject-matter, inevitably assess performance in English, and this is unavoidable; that is to say, an economics essay paper samples not only attainments in the subject but also the extent to which an individual is able to comprehend and use the English language. The trick, of course, is to devise examinations in such a way as to test also whatever is required in the way of particular areas of performance or ability in economics.

Some little attempt has been made to correlate scores obtained for the different components. Matten[13] in his study for AEB A-level economics held that the 'ideal' correlation was one of + 0.5 (correlations are measured on a scale of −1 to +1, with +1 having the highest positive correlation), in that if the correlation were 'too high' there would be no gain from having an objective test as well as an essay paper. The prime purpose of having an objective test was seen as providing an examination that tested different abilities from those in the essay paper, 'and a correlation of +0.5 indicates that this is being done'. The problem is that it is surely not possible simply on the evidence of correlation figures to determine whether or not what is being tested is economics attainment. Correlations of between +0.5 and +0.8 have been found in similar studies carried out for other subjects,[14] but we cannot be at all sure that what we are testing is some ability in the subject, or whether the high correlation is due to a third factor, 'G', or some 'general examination passing ability' having not all that much to do with attainment in economics. Given a sufficient number of variables it may be possible through the use of more sophisticated statistical techniques such as factor analysis, to produce sufficient evidence to be able to conclude with rather more certainty what it is that is being measured; but correlation figures alone provide little help other than to indicate that some relationship exists between the scores on one component and those on another.

A further important difficulty exists when an examination consists of more than one component, and this is related to the possibly unintended consequences of differential weighting of the components of the assessment. Two cases will serve to illustrate the difficulty. It is often assumed that if two papers are marked out of the same total they will have the same weighting when they are added, but this is in fact not true. Consider Table 20.1 which shows the results of candidates who have taken two papers and whose marks have been added.

Table 20.1

	PAPER 1 (Essay)	Rank	PAPER 2 (Project)	Rank	Total mark	Rank
Arthur	76	1	76	2	152	2
Beverley	74		60	6	134	6
Colin	74	2=	68	4	142	3
Doreen	74		88	1	162	1
Edith	72		64	5	136	5
Fay	72	5=	40	11	112	11
George	72		44	10	116	10
Harry	70		48	9	118	9
Ian	70	8=	52	8	122	8
Jill	70		56	7	126	7
Ken	68	11	72	3	140	4
Mean	72		60.8		132.8	
Standard deviation	1.1		7.0		7.5	

Of the two sets of marks, it is those for Paper 2 which have the greater influence on the final ranking of candidates. This is because the marks for Paper 2 are much more dispersed (standard deviation of 7.0 compared with 1.1) than those for Paper 1. There will also be some important discrepancies in the way that individual candidates have fared: for example, Ken is bottom in Paper 1 and third in Paper 2 yet manages to come fourth overall, while Fay, who is fifth on Paper 1 but bottom on Paper 2, is bottom overall.

Even where two components are marked out of different totals supposedly in an attempt to give them different weights according to their relative importance, for example, Paper 1 being marked from 100 while Paper 2, regarded as being of less importance, is marked from 50, the desired result may not be achieved. Consider Table 20.2.

Table 20.2

PAPER 1 (max. 100)	PAPER 2 (max. 50)	Combined mark
55	5	60
54	10	64
53	15	68
52	20	72
51	25	76
50	30	80
49	35	84
48	40	88
47	45	92
46	50	96

The final rank order of candidates is entirely determined by the marks awarded for the second paper, again for the same reason, that is, the wider dispersion of marks on Paper 2.

In each of the above cases and wherever the marks of two or more components are combined to give a single final mark, to achieve the desired weighting the dispersions should be standardized. If it is felt necessary to add two or more sets of marks then they must be converted to a standard scale, with the same standard deviation.[15] Subsequently, any desired weighting can be applied. On the whole, examination boards do not follow such a procedure, and this is strange considering that one of the most important features of our examination process is that the results should provide a unique and consistent rank ordering of candidates – 'unique, that is, in that the order of the ranking reflects their underlying level of achievement in the subject under consideration'.[16]

Earlier in this chapter some of the more cogent reasons were given for the retention of essay questions and objective tests in any assessment of economics. Other kinds of test items in current use in economics examinations at 16 include data-response questions, projects and oral tests, and course work.

Some of these variants have been discussed fairly exhaustively elsewhere, for example by Hudson[17] Smith,[18] and Holley,[19] but again the decision regarding their inclusion will be determined according to the general principle of 'fitness for purpose'. It is essential to identify and analyse as precisely as possible the skills, knowledge and other qualities required for the production of examinable material in the form of course work and projects in order to decide what contribution each can make to the overall information about a candidate's ability in economics. Even if it is found that these components provide significant educational benefits, it must be remembered that they are particularly time-consuming and costly to operate and assess on a large scale. Special efforts are needed to provide clear and detailed criteria for their assessment, so that the reliability of the examination is maintained.

Projects and course work are particularly useful components of internal assessment where it is felt that teacher assessment of such personal qualities as perseverance, initiative, enthusiasm and originality is thought to be an important adjunct to more formal examinations. Other skills, such as those required in the location, retrieval, organization, evaluation and communication of relevant material, may be similarly tested. Again it might be contended that the preparation of this kind of material might be a more 'natural' activity where the candidate is given time to reflect on the subject-matter in a less stressful situation than the hot-house atmosphere of the unseen examination, and where the nature of the work more closely coincides with the actual nature of the work done by professional economists. There is no doubt too that such work can have positive backwash effects in providing incentive and opportunity for the teacher to use methods of teaching and encouragement not available in the more constricting conditions imposed by preparation for written examinations.

A compromise solution that retains some of the advantages of project work yet goes some of the way towards achieving a greater degree of reliability is provided by the LREB's 'Applied Economic Study' whereby the board, though expecting candidates to adopt their own particular approach to the subject chosen, nevertheless gives a general framework to assist candidates (and, of course, provides the examiner with valuable assessment criteria). Each candidate is required to submit an individual study relating *either* to an aspect of London's economy *or* to one major British industry. It must be a record of individual and/or group investigation, approximately 1,500 words in length, and including diagrams, maps and statistical tables as appropriate.

An aspect of London's economy
1. Definition. General description of the subject chosen.
2. Geographical boundaries – reasons for location.
3. Scope of productive activities.
4. Sources and determination of income.
5. Main channels of expenditure.
6. Pattern of labour employment.
7. Organization and control.
8. Development. Recent changes in the area of activity described above.

A major British industry

1. Size:	Economies and diseconomies of scale.
	Reasons for the survival of the small firm.
	Its contribution to GNP.
2. Location:	Economic factors.
	Government policy.
3. Ownership and control:	Type of firm.
	The question of power – is public or private ownership desirable?
4. Labour:	Division of labour and specialization.
	Training.
	Mobility/immobility of labour geographically and occupationally.
	Automation and unemployment.
	Trade unions and working conditions.
5. Wages:	Determination of wages: supply and demand, marginal productivity, bilateral monopoly or negotiated bargaining
	Non-monetary advantages.
6. Prices:	Determination of prices: perfect competition.
	Monopoly, some form of imperfect competition.
7. Finance:	How is the necessary finance obtained? How much money is spent on advertising, on the development of research, technology and efficiency?
8. Critique or appraisal:	Recent developments.
	Criticisms.
	Problems and possible resolutions.

The assessment of oral tests is notoriously difficult to standardize. The result depends to a certain extent on the interaction of judge and judged: different examiners may evoke different samples of behaviour, they may differ on what characteristics they are looking for and on their relative importance; they may indeed draw different inferences from the same samples of behaviour. On the other hand, the oral examination of a written economics project can provide the examiner with much useful additional information about the candidate's level of understanding of the topic that is not otherwise available. Another important reason for including an oral test is that much of our teaching is oral, and for many of our candidates this will represent the major mode of communicating knowledge to others in connection with their jobs. Oral examining (apart from languages) has always been given greater weight elsewhere in Europe, though some does of course take place in the UK. The Middlesex (now London) Regional Examining Board includes it as an option in its Mode I economics, while more recently an oral element has been introduced in AEB A-level geography, also in combination with a project.

A single examination system for children aged 16

The desirability of a national examination has been debated for well over a decade, but it was in 1980 that the Secretary of State for Education made the announcement that the present dual system would be replaced by a unified system of examinations. It was proposed that the GCE and CSE boards would work together in five groups in England and Wales to administer the new examination. In England, four new groups would be based on existing boards in the North, Midlands, South and London. The proposal did not cover the whole of the ability range in the schools but applied only, as at present, to the top 60 per cent of pupils, though it recognized that a wider range of candidates may be entered. Results in the new examination would be graded on a seven-point scale, of which the top three would be equivalent to A, B and C at O-level and the remainder correspond with CSE grades 2, 3, 4 and 5. The new grade 6 (formerly CSE grade 4) would, therefore, represent the average standard at age 16.

For some years we have been moving towards a consensus of educational opinion that the binary system of GCE and CSE is socially divisive, psychologically disabling and administratively wasteful. What is surprising about any major piece of educational reform is that it didn't occur earlier. It is hard to believe that just over twenty years ago, 80 per cent of the school population left school without any kind of qualification. Like the changes that took place in examining style and administration in the 1960s, the new single system may have profound effects on examining structures and assessment techniques. Judging by past experience reforms will be accompanied by a considerable amount of discussion, research and development by teachers, local authorities, inspectors and examining boards, and much that is educationally beneficial is likely to emerge, whether or not a national system comes into operation. Perhaps the most radical point of departure has been the requirement that examination consortia produce national criteria for syllabuses and assessment procedures in the various subjects or groups of subjects, to ensure that all syllabuses have sufficient content in common, and that all boards apply the same performance standards to grades. Consequently, much of the critical comment about differences in standards between boards may be silenced.

What were the reasons for proposing a common system of examining at 16? A Schools Council report of 1975[20] could hardly have answered the questions more aggressively: 'It is hardly conceivable that if a school examination system were now to be set up from scratch anyone would devise a structure resembling that which exists at present.' There were strong educational and economic arguments for change. Harmonization of the dual system should save on resources, the complicated administration of dealing with two or more boards would be avoided, and relief given to a large number of examination candidates – especially those in the middle-ability range who were often entered for GCE and CSE. Teachers would be relieved of the burden of having to select pupils (sometimes in the third and fourth year) for different examination groups. In a common system it is the examination that will grade children rather than the teacher, particularly where it is composed of undifferentiated papers. The new system would seem to recognize that there is a continuous distribution of capacity for attainment among the school population, whereas present GCE and CSE examinations overlap in such a way as to make it impossible to be confident about the allocation of border zone pupils to one group or the other. The confusing difference between the two examinations should also be clarified for the general public, parents and employers.

Some see more sinister reasons for the proposed merger. MacIntosh[21] suspects that devising a new examination system is part of a government attempt to control what is taught in the schools and how it is being done, since 'the government clearly sees the examination tail which it *can* control, wagging the curriculum dog over which control is much more tenuous and difficult to exercise'. He further contends that the new developments are potentially divisive – not as between GCE and CSE, but between the 60 per cent who can, and the 40 per cent who cannot, enter the 16+ examinations. Thirdly, MacIntosh sees the government's decision to make national criteria the fulcrum for its approval of the examination again in terms of increased central control, improved reliability and easier comparability – 'good things in themselves' – but also requiring traditional forms of examination. He thus draws the conclusion that the possibility of internal examinations, through, for example, course work and projects, and teacher assessment of their own pupils, would be excluded in favour of purely external examinations that are considerably easier to operate, but that may therefore: 'never match the curriculum needs of a comprehensive school system'. There may be some truth in MacIntosh's remarks but one cannot avoid the observation that they are all built upon an initial assumption, which may well be mistaken, that it was the government, and not the Schools Council, that first sowed the seeds of the idea of a national examination system.

There is no doubt that the CSE examination has suffered by comparison with the more prestigious GCE. How different are they? CSE Mode I is essentially an external examination and very little different from GCE in that the same questions are answered by the pupils of a number of different schools and results are issued in such a manner that the relative performance of the pupils of different schools can be directly compared. On the other hand, Mode 3 (of which CSE makes far greater use than GCE) is essentially an internal examination, and there are serious problems in trying to equate Mode III with Mode I or GCE. Though the boards, chiefly through their moderators, seek to exercise control, the syllabus, forms of examination and mark schemes offer no common factor on which comparisons can be based. Nor are there usually a sufficient number of candidates for statistical comparisons to be of any help. The implications for any examination that has a Mode III need to be carefully considered. Though this form of assessment allows schools to tailor their courses to meet the needs of the pupils and their environment, it is doubtful that much confidence can be placed in an examination that is largely internal to individual schools.

The difficulties of combining GCE and CSE are very real ones. GCE would appear to have two main aims:[22]

1.   To give teachers and pupils a goal or standard at which to aim.
2.   To provide a qualification for further education, particularly university entry, and a yardstick for the use of employers.

It was the latter that determined the character of the examination. It was essential for it to be scrupulously honest and impartial, to be as reliable as possible, and comparability between boards and the maintenance of standards from one year to the next were important. CSE was designed by the Beloe Committee with other considerations in mind. It was the educational role that the examination could serve in the school that was considered paramount, its purpose as a provider of qualifications less important, the requirement of paper qualifications for its target group being recognized as of minor significance. The committee went so far as to advise employers not to attach too much importance to examination results, but to take account also of teachers' reports, school records, personal interviews and so on; it actively discouraged too much preoccupation with comparability between regions on the grounds that it might inhibit local experiment with new methods of assessment.

Any system that attempts to harmonize these two rather different examinations must therefore ensure that it meets the needs of less-able pupils, avoids restrictions on schools that the use of examinations as a qualification imposes, yet provides qualifications acceptable to pupils, teachers and the public alike – some sort of hybrid examination which perhaps contains elements both of external and internal assessment, and a regional structure, yet demonstrates a national validity: a tall order indeed! Before the merger, a good deal of thought is being given to the range of understanding and of tested technical possibilities that will contribute to whatever long-term solution the boards eventually recommend. For the time being, separate GCE and CSE examinations will be offered for an unspecified period after 1986 alongside common 16+ examination papers in economics offered by the consortia.

The Joint Subject Committee has formulated national criteria for economic syllabuses together with some of the grade definitions, for an examination expected to come into operation in June 1987.[23] The criteria establish a body of subject content and range of skills and activities that will form part of the assessment, and which all pupils following a course in economics are normally expected to have covered; thus they will be specified by an individual examining consortium for all the syllabuses that it certifies under the title of economics. Within the framework of these criteria, working parties composed of economics teachers, examiners and officials of the examining boards (in consultation with locally held meetings with teachers) have constructed syllabuses and specimen examination papers. A shortened version of the draft material presented by one of the consortia, London and East Anglia, follows:

East Anglian Examinations Board
London Regional Examining Board
University of London Entrance and School Examinations Council

Draft Proposals for
Joint O-Level/CSE Examination in Economics
Syllabus

Aims
Economics is seen both as an academic discipline and as a subject contributing towards an understanding of economic decision-making in contemporary society. It follows that candidates should:

(a) acquire the basic economic knowledge, skills and concepts necessary to understand the society in which they live;

(b) develop an understanding of the main economic institutions and of the interdependence of economic activities;
(c) be able to communicate through the effective use of economic terminology and data.

The examination

There will be one paper of 2½ hours. The paper will be divided into three sections as detailed below. All of the questions in Sections A and B will be compulsory. A choice of questions will be offered in Section C.

Section A will carry 15 per cent of the total subject marks, Section B 25 per cent and Section C 60 per cent.

Section A will consist of a range of short-answer questions, some of which may be subdivided. Concise and precise answers will be required to these questions.

Section B will consist of a series of questions which will be based on stimulus material. This material may be a short prose passage on economics, e.g. taken from a newspaper, or simple economic data, which may be hypothetical. Candidates will be required to evaluate and interpret the stimulus material, and the use of simple arithmetic may be required. The questions in this section will increase in difficulty; some of the questions will test the ability of candidates to understand what they have read, but other questions will require knowledge drawn from a wider study of the syllabus.

Section C will consist of seven questions of which candidates will be required to answer three. Generally, these questions will be structured and will consist of two or more parts. The majority of the questions, or part questions, in this section will require extended answers written in continuous prose.

Candidates are recommended to spend the first ten minutes of the examination reading the question paper.

In the examination candidates are encouraged to make use of recent examples, where relevant and appropriate, to illustrate their answers.

General objectives

At the end of the course candidates should:

1 understand the fundamental economic problem of scarcity and choice;
2 understand the operation of the price system in terms of demand and supply;
3 know the different forms of enterprise and understand the reasons for the differences in their scale and organization in a mixed economy;
4 know the location of some major contemporary industries and understand the reasons for industrial location;
5 understand the role of financial institutions and their importance for the economy;
6 understand the structure of, and the reasons for, public revenue and expenditure;
7 appreciate the forces, including government, which influence the price level, employment, income, output and economic growth;
8 appreciate the importance of internal and international trade, and have a knowledge of relevant organizations;
9 be aware of the influences at work in the markets for factors of production, including the major institutions in the labour market;

10 know and understand the importance of the structure and distribution of population and of changes in these.

(*Note*: The general objectives do not presuppose either a rank order or an explicit teaching order. Each general objective should not be regarded as a discrete section of the syllabus.)

The statement of general objectives is then broken down into detailed sets of operational objectives under each of the ten main headings. In the notes of guidance to accompany the syllabus the consortium informs teachers of the broad philosophy underlying the syllabus. It is based on three assumptions:

1 That an economics course at 16 can and should provide basic economic understanding for candidates who may not continue their studies in the subject beyond the examination.
2 That it will provide a stimulating introduction to the further study of economics, and
3 That it will provide a detailed and systematic guide to teachers and candidates.

It is clearly intended that the syllabus, and examination if it is to consist of undifferentiated papers, should serve the dual purpose of preparing candidates for leaving school and for going on to an A-level course, something which, it has been argued in this chapter, is unattainable. Certainly the specific objectives are framed in rather more abstract and theoretical terms than can be useful for school leavers, and teachers will need to deploy a variety of teaching strategies in order to make the subject matter relevant and stimulating for these groups. There must be some doubt that the terms in which the syllabus is expressed are consistent with the general assumptions outlined above. Some teachers might feel regret too that the opportunity was not taken to introduce some material on comparative economic systems.

Some sample questions from the specimen paper offered by the consortium follow:

Section A

Answer ALL questions in this section

(You are advised to spend between 15 and 20 minutes on this section.)

This section would include about fifteen questions, such as:

1. A local council decides to build a leisure centre and as a result cannot afford to build a library. What economic principle does this illustrate?

....

2. Name *two* sources of revenue which are available to local authorities.

   1. ....   2. ....

3. Name *two* goods which are complementary to each other.

   1. ....   2. ....

4. (a) Name *two* types of share.

   1. ....   2. ....

   (b) Which one of the shares you have named carries the higher risk to the shareholder?

   ....

5. Define 'production'.

   ....

   ....

   ....

6. Complete the following two sentences by inserting the missing words.

   (a) A decline in the UK shipbuilding industry is likely to lead to a form of unemployment known as .... unemployment.

   (b) Due to the fall in demand for its goods a firm can no longer employ all of its existing staff; the decrease in jobs is known as .... unemployment.

   Total mark for   ——————
   Section A   ——————

Section B

Answer ALL questions in this section

(You are advised to spend between 30 and 35 minutes on this section.)

Study the fictitious balance of payments account and the accompanying description, and then answer each of the Questions 16–25. (You will be asked to calculate the figures which have been omitted from the account.)

UK Balance of Payments, 1988

Current account

Debits	£m	Credits	£m
Visible imports	75,000	Visible exports	65,000
Invisible imports	30,000	Invisible exports	35,000
Total debits	105,000	Total credits	100,000
		Current Account deficit	

Investment transactions	£m
Government and private investment abroad (net)	−1,500
Balance on current account	
Total currency flow	

Official financing account	
Borrowing from International Monetary Fund	+2,000
Drawing on currency reserves	
Total official financing	

In 1988 the value of visible imports exceeded the value of visible exports, and there was a balance of trade deficit. On invisible trade the UK had a favourable balance though this was not enough to avoid an overall deficit on the current account.

The continued development of UK North Sea oil was advantageous, as was the recent decision by GATT (General Agreement on Tariffs and Trade) to allow the UK to limit imports of cheap clothing from the Far East. However, inflation in the UK continued to make it more difficult to sell our exports.

There would be ten questions, such as:

16. (a) Name *two* goods generally imported by the United Kingdom.

    1. ....
    2. ....

    (b) Name *two* goods generally exported by the United Kingdom.

1. ....

2. ....

17. (a) What is meant by 'invisible trade'?

     ....

     ....

   (b) Write 'export' or 'import' against each of the following
       items to indicate whether it is an export or an
       import for the United Kingdom.

       1. A German ship owner insures his
          vessels with Lloyds in London   ....

       2. Shareholders in France are paid
          dividends by British Car Auctions   ....

       3. An American farmer sends a gift to
          a relative living in Scotland   ....

18. (a) Calculate the balance of trade deficit for
        the United Kingdom in 1988.   £.............m.

   (b) Calculate the current account deficit
       in 1988.   £.............m.

19. Why might inflation in the United Kingdom make it more
    difficult to export our goods?

    ....

    ....

    ....

    ....

20. Why is a deficit on current account more serious than a
    deficit on the balance of trade?

    ....

    ....

    ....

    ....

    ....

                                  Total mark for   ——————————
                                  Section B   ——————————

Section C

Answer THREE questions from this section

(You are advised to spend at least 1½ hours on this section.)

This section would normally consist of about seven essay and data-response questions, such as:

26. (a) Distinguish between (i) capital goods and (ii) consumer goods. Give *one* example of each kind of good.   (5 marks)

    (b) Why does an economy seek to acquire capital goods?   (5 marks)

    (c) Examine the difficulties which developing countries face in acquiring capital goods.   (10 marks)

27. (a) Study the table below which gives information about the demand for and the supply of grommets, and then answer questions (i) to (iii)

Price of grommets (pence per unit)	Quantity of grommets demanded per week (units)	Quantity of grommets supplied per week (units)
15	1	12
5	3	7
3	5	5
1	15	2

    (i) *On the graph paper* provided, plot and draw the demand and supply curves. Label each axis clearly.   (2 marks)

    (ii) State the equilibrium price.   (1 mark)

    (iii) Calculate the elasticity of demand when price increases from 3p to 5p per unit.   (5 marks)

    (b) Examine the main factors which affect (i) the demand for and (ii) the supply of video recorders in the United Kingdom.   (12 marks)

28. (a) Name *three* clearing banks.   (3 marks)

    (b) What are the advantages which a small business may gain from being a bank customer?   (5 marks)

    (c) How do banks attempt to reconcile profitability with liquidity?   (12 marks)

The paper, as an undifferentiated examination (the controversy regarding differentiated and undifferentiated papers is discussed below) clearly uses a variety of tests: short-answer, data-response and structured essays, which are carefully graded in difficulty to assess the economic understanding of candidates of a wide range of ability. Taking for example Section B, the questions appear to increase in difficulty as one moves from Question 16 to Question 20. If it were considered desirable to do so, further discrimination between candidates could be achieved by awarding proportionately higher marks to difficult than easier questions. Clearly also, candidates are called upon by the paper to demonstrate those skills of numeracy and literacy that are given prominence in the national criteria.

It seems highly probable that Joint Subject Committees will be pressed to provide examinations that are entirely externally assessed. Certainly the Economics Committee of the consortium has embraced this principle, mainly on the grounds that there will be staff in many schools and colleges who do not wish to assess the work of their own students, and that provision will have to be made for private (external) candidates, many of whom will be unable to present authenticated course work. There will also be formidable costs and administrative difficulties involved for any national schemes that include forms of teacher assessment. Nevertheless, many teachers will be saddened that the advantages of other modes of preparation and assessment will seemingly be lost.

Differentiated and undifferentiated papers

A question that will undoubtedly provoke much debate is whether or not the examination should consist of differentiated or undifferentiated papers. The former occur where alternative examination papers are made available to different groups of candidates and they are usually of different levels of difficulty. An example of an undifferentiated paper is the specimen paper illustrated earlier: it attempts to examine the whole ability range in one and the same paper. On the other hand, a differentiated examination in economics would present, say, two separate papers, the first deemed appropriate for lower-ability candidates containing questions such as that given in Section A questions 2 and 4, Section B questions 16 and 17 and Section C question 28 (a) and (b). The second paper, appropriate to higher-ability candidates, would contain questions such as Section A question 1, Section B question 20 and Section C question 27. The Secretary of State for Education[24] has made his position clear:

The examinations will have to provide alternative papers at different levels of difficulty but on closely linked syllabuses. The higher grades will only be available to candidates taking the harder alternatives, but most grades will be available to candidates taking either alternative depending on quality of performance.

The arguments in favour of differentiated papers may be briefly rehearsed.[25] The importance of determining the purpose of an examination has already been mentioned in this chapter, and it would seem easier to comply with this decision by providing separate examinations for those about to leave school as against those who intend to go on to further study of economics at university. One must also take into account the possible backwash effect: tough examination papers provide a challenge and a motivation to pupils, while properly prepared candidates are entitled to be confronted with questions that adequately evaluate the full extent of their attainment. The public too has confidence that where high grades are awarded, they represent a just measurement of the ability of candidates. Again there are many who believe that it is an impossible task to examine a very wide range of ability in a single examination paper.

Some of the counter-arguments run as follows. Teachers will still have to grapple with the problem of how to divide pupils into groups according to their ability to cope with papers of different levels of difficulty: it is the delaying or removal of the need for such choices that is one of the major advantages to be expected from the proposed common system of examinations at 16. When candidates sit differentiated papers there are severe technical difficulties in attempting to produce a single overall rank order of merit (and therefore grades) for a large number of candidates irrespective of the options for which they were entered. For example, how could a good performance on an easy paper be compared with a poor performance on a difficult paper? There appears to be no satisfactory method, statistical or otherwise, of resolving this difficulty.[26] Again, it is likely that if there were to be alternative papers, then syllabuses would have to contain differentiated material. There is a danger here, already mentioned, that the hierarchical nature of the objectives listed in any taxonomy might be misinterpreted as a scale of difficulty: for instance, questions set on 'higher' objectives (e.g. analysis) might be thought to be outside the range for low-ability pupils, whereas in fact analytical questions can vary in difficulty. Altogether, there is a danger that the 'common' system might deteriorate into a muddled one of differentiated syllabuses and differentiated examinations. One way out of the problem perhaps might be the reintroduction of course work and projects on the grounds that in both, candidates would be setting their own standards, and the level of difficulty (and hence grades) could be judged by examiners.

Graded tests

Connected to the foregoing discussion but worthy also of separate treatment as a method of dealing with multi-ability groups, is the idea of graded tests, such as those already in use in some quarters for

English, mathematics, music, sport and modern languages. Instead of following a five-year course leading to a single examination at 16, pupils would be allowed to progress at their own pace, taking relatively limited tests in economics as and when they are able. Up to now these kinds of tests have generally been used only for lower-ability children, but they could perhaps provide an objective, accepted measure of a pupil's mastery of economics, while simultaneously obviating the need to decide which of several alternative 16+ papers s/he should sit. Such tests might also contribute much more detailed information than conventional examinations can do about pupils' attainment in a wide range of skills and competences in the subject.

The new system at 16+ leaves unresolved the task (still be to be performed by the teacher) of dividing the sheep from the goats – of choosing the notional 60 per cent who are to enter for the examination and the 40 per cent who are not. In contrast, graded tests can be taken by pupils of all ages and ability. Highly motivated, and the more-able pupils, would move faster through the series of tests, and all pupils would have something to strive for. Teachers and pupils alike might benefit from the regular feedback as well as the stimulus of successful achievement. The great danger of such a system lies in schools forsaking sound educational practices in order to concentrate entirely on the achievement of 'good grades' for their pupils. It may well restrict study to test material, and encourage pupils to conform on tests and in the classroom to the teachers' views and opinions.[27]

Pupil profiles
Another closely related development is the idea of reporting results of examinations (and, incidentally, of providing measures of interest and attitudes) as sets of grades relating to separate elements within the area of study, in this case economics, which will provide more information about candidates to teachers, employers and others.[28] A recent start has been made in modern languages and physical sciences where examples include separate grades for oral tests or practical work as well as in written papers. Of course the former 11+ tests and also present UCCA applications to university are backed up by similar supplementary information.

Final profiles can be the result of both in-course and end-of-course assessment, and it may in the future be possible for each pupil to leave school with a record of achievement during school life.

As an example, part of a profile in economics might consist of the following:

Economics: numeracy skill	Can, with guidance, make use of basic graphs, charts, tables of economic data	Can interpret and use basic graphs, etc. unaided	Can construct graphs, etc. and extract information to support arguments

One of the advantages of academic profiles of this kind is that they report only on those components of assessment that are judged to be measuring skills and attainments – whereas up to the present, parts of an examination have been differentiated not by skill but by method of assessment, such as course work, objective test and so on. An alternative style of economics profile might be the following, which gives a more general representation of skills:

	Grade
Skill in reasoning	B
Problem-solving	C
Ability to communicate knowledge	B

and so on.

It might be sensible for schools to issue pupils with certificates that record a combination of examination marks or grades, and a profile along the lines of one of those given above.

It is probably too early yet to introduce a national system of profiles, since the problems of maintaining internal consistency and comparability between profile schemes are considerable, and teachers would require careful training in their operation. It may even be questioned whether it is desirable to attempt to define too precisely the various qualities of our pupils. Human qualities depend to a certain extent on the environment in which the individual finds himself. Academic gradings are suspected of being self-perpetuating, so that pupils have a tendency to live up or down to their teachers' expectations of them; it may be that the pace or level of difficulty of lessons are inappropriately slow so that a teacher describing a pupil as being lazy or bored may be making an unsound subjective judgement. Finally, users of profiles, such as employers, may find the profile too complicated since in most cases they need only a rough indication of ability at 16. In spite of these reservations, profiles are capable of providing much more useful supplementary information about the characteristics of pupils than a simple list of examination grades.

Conclusion

There is undoubtedly room for improvement in examining and reporting at age 16, and the introduction of a new system might be the catalyst for further changes in practice. Public confidence is an overriding requirement of an examination system, and this necessitates continuous monitoring of the characteristics, standards and techniques of examining. Checks on the validity and reliability of examinations in economics, and on comparability of standards between examiners, between boards and between one year and another, have, until now, been sporadic and uncoordinated: they need to be regularized. If ideally assessment contains a variety of elements (essay, course work, objective test) then the specific requirements and contributions of each need to be more clearly defined and made explicit.

While it is true that boards take steps to counteract undue generosity or severity of marking through moderating processes, insufficient attention is paid to the problem of standardizing results of examinations that consist of several components having different weightings, and here it is especially important that the overall work of a candidate, where the total score brings him near to an important borderline, should be reviewed by a senior examiner. Statistical techniques are now available to test the more subjective judgements of examiners responsible for setting question papers. Thus, for example, it is possible to minimize variations in question difficulty to tolerable limits by calculating facility values, and this procedure is invaluable, firstly where candidates are offered a choice of questions as in most essay-type papers, and secondly, in types of data-response questions, such as the specimen 16+ paper given above, where marks for individual questions are distributed according to a subjective estimate of difficulty. Between now and 1987, the proposed date for the first national 16+ examination in economics, the scope for teacher initiative and involvement, and the balance between internal and external assessment, will have to be discussed. One of the requirements in this connection will be the establishment of a framework for staff development and training in assessment techniques and moderating procedures.

Perhaps the most crucial question of all will be to decide whether the economics examinations of the future are going to consist of undifferentiated or differentiated papers. Some of the arguments have been discussed earlier, but there are many others for which space could not be found. The debate will no doubt continue for some time.

Notes and references

1. Schools Council, *Examination Bulletin no. 23*, 1971.
2. Scott, A., 'Advanced level economics as predictor of class of degree', in Lumsden, K., Attiyeh, R., and Scott, A., *Economics Education in the UK* (Heinemann Educational Books, 1980).
3. Middlesex Regional Examining Board, *Elements of Economics*, CSE Mode 1 Statement of Aims.
4. Schools Council, op. cit.

5. Stenhouse, L., *An Introduction to Curriculum Research and Development* (Heinemann Educational Books, 1975).
6. Threadgold, R., 'Examination language: language examined', *Journal of Applied Educational Studies*, vol. 11, no. 2, winter 1982.
7. Rowntree, D., *Assessing Students: How Shall We Know Them* (Harper & Row, 1977).
8. Threadgold, op. cit.
9. Klausmeier, H.J., *Learning and Teaching Concepts* (Academic Press, 1980).
10. Hamilton, J.S. (ed.), *Interboard Multiple Choice Economics* (Test Development and Research Unit, Cambridge, 1977).
11. For an explanation of these terms, see Lewis, D., *Assessment in Education* (University of London Press, 1974).
12. London REB CSE Economics Mode I.
13. Matten, A.E., 'Multiple choice in Advanced level economics', Paper for Economics Association Conference 1972.
14. Nuttall, D.L., and Willmott, A.S., *British Examination: Techniques of Analysis* (NFER, 1972).
15. See, for example, Hudson, B., *Assessment Techniques* (Methuen, 1973).
16. Nuttall and Willmott, op. cit.
17. Hudson, op. cit.
18. Smith, F.S., 'Terminal economics: the experience of CSE', in Whitehead, D.J., *Curriculum Development in Economics* (Heinemann Educational Books, 1974).
19. Holley, B.J., in Lee, N., *Teaching Economics*, 2nd edn (Heinemann Educational Books, 1975).
20. *Examinations at 16+: Proposals for the Future* (Schools Council, 1975).
21. MacIntosh, H.G., 'The prospects for public examinations in England and Wales', *Educational Analysis*, vol. 4, no. 3, 1982.
22. University of Cambridge Local Examinations Syndicate, *School Examinations and Their Functions*, December 1976.
23. 16+ GCE and CSE Boards' Joint Council for 16+ National Criteria, *Recommended 16+ National Criteria for Economics*, September 1983.
24. Reported statement by Sir Keith Joseph in the *Times Educational Supplement*, 18 March 1983.
25. For more detailed discussion, see *London 16+ Joint Subject Committee Information Paper no. 1*, June 1982; and Tattersall, K., 'Differentiated examinations: a strategy for assessment at 16+?' *Schools Council Examination Bulletin no. 42*, 1983.
26. See Wood, R., 'Placing candidates who take different papers on the same mark scale', *Educational Research*, vol. 20, no. 3, 1978.
27. Klug, B., *The Grading Game* (National Union of Students Publications, 1977).
28. Only a brief summary is included here. See, for example, Francis, J.C., 'Profile reporting in external examinations', *Educational Research*, vol. 24, no. 1, November 1981.

External Examinations in Economics at 18+
R.K. Wilkinson

Introduction

It is highly likely that a survey of the 16–19-year-old age group in Britain would reveal a consensus for the proposition that examinations are one of the curses of Western civilization. The examination system inflicts all kinds of suffering on its victims who include teachers and parents as well as the candidates themselves. There are some who manage to keep examinations in proper perspective and a fortunate few who positively revel in the opportunity to compete and to demonstrate their abilities. For the majority, however, examinations are things to which one has to become resigned, are psychologically as well as physically stressful, involving as they must the confrontation with the possibility of failure in at least a relative – or, worse, an absolute – sense. Every year O- and A-level results bring depression as well as elation, complaints and recriminations against teachers and examiners, and even rumours that the system is rigged to ensure that government policy is not embarrassed by a surfeit of good results.[1]

Considerable dissatisfaction with the O- and A-level system is expressed from time to time but alternative schemes do not get away from some sort of external examination. It is in fact the externality of the system that gives it greater credibility than a system of internal assessment. So many of the general problems to be considered below apply whatever the system.

Significant changes have taken place in recent years in 16+ and 18+ examining. In what follows I shall review some of these developments concentrating on the A-level examination.[2] I shall attempt to set them in the context of an optimal examination system, and in so doing discuss the general problems of external assessment as well as the specific problems concerned with setting and marking an examination.

Social aspects of examinations

Society's attitude to examinations is ambivalent. Public examinations are frequently criticized for their irrelevance, especially to the measurement of the type of personal qualities that may lead to material success. On the other hand, examinations form an important part of the socioeconomic sifting process, the ladder up which most of us have to progress. Success at examinations can become an end in itself, a sort of pot-hunting exercise in which the successful display their badges of success like trophies and expect (and often get) the sort of public admiration reserved for athletes and games players. Wittingly or unwittingly, many seem to subscribe to what has been called the bucket theory of knowledge where the object is to acquire 'qualifications' starting with O-levels and perhaps filling the 'bucket' by proceeding to a doctorate.

Examinations are a test of educational achievement but society makes more general use of them. In fact, examinations form an important part of society's mechanism for allocating labour among professions and jobs. For example, from the candidate's point of view, A-level grades constitute a price that they must pay to gain entrance to various types of higher education or professions. Like other prices, the required A-level grades will vary according to the relative desirability of the job or institution and the supply and demand for places.

A-level grades are therefore part of a 'screening process' and the examination system is a 'screening device'.[3] There are obvious private and social costs and benefits to screening – such as the effect it will have on income distribution by diverting people to jobs with different rates of pay. It is possible to show, moreover, that where information on the qualities of individuals is imperfect the resource allocation produced will be Pareto inferior to one with perfect information. The Pareto-inferior allocation may arise from too little screening, or too much, or from inaccurate or inappropriate screening.[4]

It is beyond the scope of this chapter to explore the market analogy further or to pursue this application of the theory of screening. Two important points emerge from this discussion, however. The first is that the examination system constitutes part of the information flow that helps to determine the allocation of human resources. It is important, therefore, that the screens that are applied (i.e. the examinations) are relevant to society's needs and give accurate information. The second is that the examination system is like any other system of economic organization and therefore it may be appraised in terms of its equity and efficiency in producing this information. It follows that an accurate and relevant grading system, apart from its intrinsic desirability, has economic significance and is necessary for the maximization of society's economic welfare.

The components of the examination system

In its simplest form the examination system can be thought of as comprising four groups of people related by a syllabus and set of rules. The groups are the teachers, the candidates, the examiners and the rest of society – who in a sense consume the output of the system. The structure is represented schematically in Figure 21.1.

Fig. 21.1

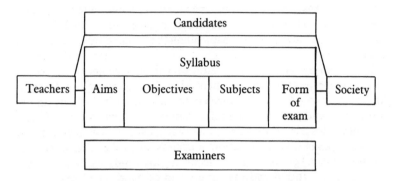

Various connections between the constituent parts could be explored but we shall not do so here except to make the point that crudely the teachers and candidates are at one side and examiners and the rest of society are at the other. If we take the connecting lines to indicate flows of information, then ideally there would be a two-way flow between any pair of components. In my view such an interchange of information is essential to the efficient operation of the system. There is in fact considerable ignorance and misunderstanding as to the nature and operation of examinations, some of which is a consequence of the examination boards being reluctant to reveal, or poor at publicizing, what they do and how they do it. It is still not the general practice to produce a fully comprehensive annual report on the performance of candidates in the examination. In my view this is an essential part of any examination system. The examination boards that preside over the operation of the system amount to a minor industry. Millions of pounds are spent annually on examinations and it is the boards, manned by a bureaucracy whose *raison d'être* is examinations, that are responsible for its use. This is an aspect of efficiency which, although important, is beyond the scope of this chapter. The focus of the system and of our appraisal is the syllabus which comprises a formal statement of the educational value of the subject and how it can be assessed as seen by the examiners.

One of the most significant changes in recent times, which started in the early 1970s and which has gathered momentum since, has occurred in the specification of economics syllabuses. Traditionally the syllabus has simply been a statement of the subject-matter to be covered; the recently agreed common core syllabus covers the aims of teaching, the objectives of examining, the abilities to be examined, as well as the subject-matter. Teachers, candidates (and even some examiners) tend to undervalue statements of aims and objectives, regarding them, at most, as a recognition of the latest educational fad. In my view this is misguided. A well-prepared syllabus is a means of making quite clear what sort of examination is to be expected and therefore what approach(es) to teaching is (are) worth adopting.

Aims of the syllabus and subject-matter to be examined

Although a statement of subject areas to be examined is essential, it is not in my view the most important part of the syllabus. The best guide to a syllabus, and to subject-matter in particular, is usually the contents of the examination papers. The examiner has to bear in mind that, however precise and detailed the statement of subject-matter may be, no two schools will have followed the identical course. Teachers differ in their outlook, and in their ability and willingness to teach the subject. Schools differ in the time and financial resources devoted to the teaching of economics from pupil–staff ratios, video equipment, computers on the one hand to textbooks, and photocopying paper on the other. Even if a precise statement can be arrived at (and I can vouch from experience that syllabus committees find great difficulty in this), it is not necessarily desirable from an educational viewpoint. It is akin to the recommendation of a particular textbook and as such it is soon likely to be in need of modification as well as possibly imposing unnecessary constraints on teachers. Precise syllabuses do not necessarily lead to identical courses, and in any case it does not follow that courses covering identical subject-matter are necessarily comparable in standard.

Comparability is much more likely to be achieved from a commonality of aims and approaches to teaching. The specification of aims adopted in the common core requires that the examiner takes a view of the subject, why it is studied at the 16+ stage, and what it is possible to achieve in approximately five terms of study. Whether or not the A-level candidate intends to study the subject further, it is important that he or she acquires a feel for what economics is about and how economists pursue their trade. This, then, involves an approach that encourages in students an ability to use statistics and diagrams, to read critically, to take an interest in current affairs and to develop a certain independence of spirit in thinking about and analysing problems. This then emphasizes *how* things are done rather than *what* subjects are covered. As such it will not necessarily produce bias in favour of candidates who are favoured with, for example, textbook resources, and to this extent it will lead to a more equitable system.

The objectives and the form of the examination

The specification of what it is desirable (and to some extent what it is possible) to test follows directly from the aims outlined above. The common core syllabus agreed for A-level in 1982 by all the GCE boards, adopts modified Bloomian categories of knowledge, comprehension, application, analysis and synthesis, evaluation and expression. Without going into the detailed definitions of these abilities,[5] we can say that they are listed in order of increasing difficulty so that their occurrence in or accessibility to candidates can be modelled roughly in terms of a triangle (Figure 21.2) where knowledge forms the basis (shaded), comprehension is the dotted area and the 'higher skills' make up the next area. This helps to emphasize that the higher skills in economics cannot be tested independently of the 'lower skills' of knowledge and comprehension. The figure automatically depicts the nature of the examination when the areas represent the weighting of abilities. A weighting like that used by the Joint Matriculation Board (JMB), where knowledge and comprehension are intended to account for 55 per cent of the mark allocation, suggests very approximately that the average candidate should be able to accumulate over half marks in the examination without having to display more than a minimal endowment of higher skills.

What weighting is most appropriate is a matter for debate. It would be foolish to suggest that examiners can control their specified weightings in any detailed way. Apart from the fact that it would be an impossible task to detail the skill content of all questions and to relate these to an examination structure, it is also true that questions that to one candidate may demand powers of independent reasoning, to others

Fig. 21.2

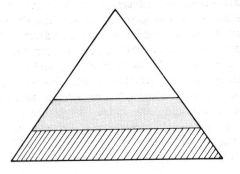

are simply a question of knowledge because they have been rigorously trained. All that an explicit weighting of skills shows is the examiner's attitude to the general standard of the examination. Obviously the statement of aims and objectives is likely to put a minimum to the weight accorded to certain skills but a variety of emphasis is still possible. Pitching the standard too low or too high will make the job of the examiner of discriminating fairly among candidates impossible. It is also a matter of equity. When so much rests on the results of the A-level examination, the examiners have a social as well as an educational responsibility to get the demands of the examination right. There is no simple formula for this; it is partly a matter of experience and partly something that must ultimately be justified by measures of the statistical reliability of the examination.

The form of the examination follows directly from the statement of aims and objectives. Decisions on the best form of assessment raise issues that affect both equity and efficiency. While there may be agreement on aims and objectives, opinions seem to differ on how best to assess knowledge and other abilities. All boards use the traditional 'free-response', three-hour essay paper though the amount of choice differs. Similarly, all boards now use an objective test paper though there are variations in the time allowed, and the number and style of question. The main distinction lies between those boards that use the objective test to examine 'economic principles' alone, and those like the JMB that use it in a broader context. A further significant change in recent years has been the introduction by all boards of some form of 'data-response' question. I have written at length on this topic elsewhere[6] and will therefore confine the discussion here to one or two key issues.

The use of data-response material follows directly from the statement of aims and objectives discussed above and represents at least a degree of consensus on how to assess the sort of abilities it is thought worthwhile to teach. These sorts of skills, such as using statistical sources and reference material, working independently on a topic, have been developed by some teachers via projects and case studies. The problems with assessing projects and case studies are those of deciding how much of the work represents the students' unaided efforts, how far the topic selected has constrained the skills displayed and how far different topics are comparable. In short, the examiner has less control over the method of assessment and many other factors can therefore potentially influence the candidate's performance. In addition, this is a less efficient way of assessing achievements. Apart from the fact that students invariably devote more time to projects than the marks available would justify, the task facing examiners when the number of candidates is measured in thousands is insurmountable. The data-response question therefore represents a way of examining these worthwhile skills with the minimum inconvenience to both candidates and examiners.

Since the purpose is to test skills rather than subject-matter, the approach I have developed in the JMB examination is to use a single set of data on which a three-part question is set. Giving the candidates a choice only introduces a further unnecessary source of variability into the test. An incidental advantage of this approach is that it does not demand any specific preparation by the candidate. Where the questions are not of the same type (e.g. some are based on real data, some on constructed or stylized data), different candidates may avoid a test of certain skills and therefore they may not do a comparable test. In the JMB examination the candidates are allowed one hour to complete the question but are encouraged (via the rubric) to spend not less than fifteen minutes in absorbing the material. The first part of the question tests the candidates' understanding by asking them to reproduce the argument in their own words or to outline the 'message' contained in one or more statistical tables. The next question seeks to discover whether they can recognize the applicability of a concept or piece of economic theory to analysing the topic under consideration, and finally, the candidates are given the opportunity to show their ability to think around the topic, to explore connections, suggest other relevant material and so on. No mark distribution is shown on the question paper, first, because the candidates should be left to judge the relative importance of the parts of the question and, second, they should also decide which parts they can answer most impressively and concentrate on those. The third and perhaps most important reason is that a declared mark distribution would not only indicate how candidates should allocate their time but it would place an unnecessary constraint on the examiners. When, for example, a question does not work as expected (e.g. if most candidates seem to find one part more difficult than expected) then the examiners should be free to vary the allocation of marks so that they fairly represent the candidates' efforts and abilities. This freedom would be lost if the mark allocation were shown on the paper. On the whole, this approach has worked very successfully.[7]

The main strength of the objective test paper from the examiner's point of view is that it provides a very reliable test of knowledge and comprehension. Questions that test the higher abilities are a lot more difficult to come by, especially when a pre-testing system is used because such questions tend not to obtain the required statistics. This simply confirms that the 'higher abilities' are in fact less accessible to the average candidate. The more difficult the question, the smaller the proportion of candidates who get it right. If this proportion is less than, say, 30 per cent, the normal cut-off point for measures of facility, then such questions will be unacceptable for an A-level examination. Questions that candidates find difficult tend to lead them to guess at the answer. In such cases, therefore, the measure of the discrimination of the question tends to be unacceptable.[8] Objective test papers provide a very reliable guide to the abilities of candidates over the range of abilities tested and, on the whole, they tend to be liked by the candidates requiring, as they do, less effort to answer. The inclusion of a multiple-choice paper in an examination, together with a data-response paper, allows the essay paper to be used to test those abilities that it is most fitted to test, namely, the higher abilities of analysis and synthesis, evaluation and expression.

Perhaps because it is the most familiar form of examination, the essay paper tends to be taken for granted. The problem for examiners with essay questions is to make them equally demanding, stimulating to the candidates, and last, but by no means least, easy for assistant examiners to mark, a subject that will be dealt with below. In an attempt to deal with these problems and to recognize explicitly the types of skill to be tested, the JMB essay paper mostly comprises questions set in two parts. The first part tests the candidate's knowledge and understanding of a concept, theory, area of policy, etc., the second asks the candidate to argue a point or defend a view on a related topic. For example, What is meant by economic efficiency? Will privatization of the public sector lead to greater economic efficiency? As for most interesting economic questions, there are usually at least two plausible lines of argument to adopt on the second part of a question. The examiners are less interested in the conclusion reached than the abilities to argue, to evaluate and express an argument displayed by the candidate. When teachers and candidates either do not understand or do not believe the examiners' intentions, then their uncertainty tends to express itself in the reproduction of 'model answers' prepared for questions on similar topics. Candidates also resort to the 'blunderbus technique' and pepper the examiner with any bits of information they may feel could be relevant to the question. These techniques are well known to all examiners on more conventional papers and merely testify to the need to *inform* teachers and candidates more precisely about what is expected of them in order for the examination to operate efficiently. The assumption behind the two-part question is that it is pointless to ask candidates in effect to reproduce parts of textbooks as essays, when this type of knowledge and analysis is more efficiently tested in other ways. Moreover, it is misleading to suggest, as many conventional 'straightforward' essay questions do, that there are precise and agreed answers to some quite complicated issues, especially if, at the same time, one is expecting students to use their eyes and minds critically in observing events in the world economy and in the UK. Essays are fundamentally concerned with the selection and evaluation of evidence and its coherent expression in the form of a logical argument. It therefore makes sense to concentrate on these skills in an examination.

The analysis of essays into two distinct parts also contributes to the accuracy of assessment, because in most cases the examiner can analyse the total mark awarded into two component parts. In preparing a marking scheme, the type of material and arguments to be expected on each part of the question can be itemized, though at the JMB we discourage examiners from deducting marks for omitting material. What we try to assess is the general quality of the answer, taking *everything* into account, and the marking scheme is there only as a statement of expectations and to establish comparability among examiners. The examiners are instructed first to decide whether an answer is 'good', 'bad' or 'indifferent' (in fact, we use six specific categories defined by a mark-range) then to arrive at a mark that can be (and is) justified in terms of the marking scheme. One of the features of the scheme is that up to fifteen marks can be awarded for either part of a two-part question, though the total mark for the question is 25. This allows candidates to deploy their knowledge and abilities as best they can. Those with determination but *perhaps* less flair can gain the majority of their mark on the first part of the question. The most able will be able to impress with their answer to the second part, and demonstrate their grasp of knowledge on the first part implicitly perhaps rather than explicitly. The main points about this approach are that it corresponds in fact to the way most people assess proper essay work (i.e. as opposed to the reproduction of notes) and it permits a degree of flexibility that is desirable with essay work. The marking scheme is the servant of the assessment process rather than the master and, as such, examiners are instructed to discard it when they come across an approach that is different. I would obviously not wish to claim that this is the only way to set and assess an essay paper, or necessarily the best. I can say, however, that to judge by the stability of the mark distribution from year to year, this scheme works reasonably well, and it should perhaps be pointed out that it takes forty examiners to mark the JMB entry. This is simply offered as an illustration of one way of coping with some of the problems of external assessment of 'free-response' questions.

Some implications

The general implications of the discussion are that in choosing between alternative examination schemes we should ask, given the desired educational standard, which imposes the least cost on candidates and examiners and whether or not there is any possibility of either reducing (or increasing) the opportunity of some candidates to succeed compared with others. The assumption of maintaining fairness raises the wider issue of comparability among the candidates of different examination boards.

It is sometimes suggested that in order to achieve comparability of standards, a standardization of examination syllabuses is necessary. I hope that I have shown above this is not necessarily the case. Identical syllabuses do not necessarily lead to identical examinations. Moreover, the adoption of identical syllabuses would be potentially inequitable to the candidates of at least some boards, if not all. Where there is an established level of expectation about what constitutes an examination, then there is a limit to the speed at which change can be introduced, governed by the type of candidate and school who form the clientele of individual boards. Examiners have a responsibility to their clients to 'make haste slowly' in any direction. Moreover, the adoption of common syllabuses can have a stultifying effect on progress since inevitably the general syllabus becomes the lowest common denominator of the group and any change desired by a member of the group has to be approved by the rest. This could exert an inhibiting effect on the development of economics teaching in schools.

It is apparent from the experience of recent years referred to above, that innovations in teaching and examining do ultimately manage to spread themselves throughout the national system. It follows also from the argument advanced above that the way to achieve comparability is to achieve some sort of commonality of aims and objectives among the examiners of the individual boards. It is the practices and expectations of examiners that ultimately determine standards and the degree of comparability among the grades awarded by individual boards. To achieve greater comparability, therefore, the information flow among boards should be improved and especially the contacts between those who set and mark the papers.

Thus while all the examination boards agreed to a common set of elements to their syllabuses in 1982, it makes sense for them to weight the examination of those elements in a way appropriate to their current practices and candidates. Standardization imposed from outside could have disastrous effects in the short term.

A further implication of this is that little progress is likely with establishing common grade criteria. One might query the possibility of this in any case with the present system of five A-level grades. As recently pointed out,[9] the distinction between the top of the D range and the bottom of the B is more apparent than real. The practice and meaning of dividing about 70 per cent of the candidates in any year into five grades implies that examiners can operate with a degree of precision that their techniques of examining just do not permit. At this age candidates are developing rapidly intellectually, as in other ways. The present system of assessment takes no account of progress but simply concentrates on attainment. It is not surprising that in many subjects performance at A-level is an unreliable predictor of future performance.

Finally, what are the implications of all this for teachers (and candidates)? The first, and perhaps most important, point is that examinations and examiners do differ in their aims and objectives and it is vitally important to find out what they are in order that candidates are prepared correctly. Thus teachers should not only read the detail of syllabuses but they should try to relate the style of questions and papers to the declared aims and objectives in the syllabus. They should also pay special attention to examiners' reports and generally they should press for information from the examination boards, which will help to clarify examiners' expectations.

Secondly, they should attempt to match the style of and approach to teaching with the aims of the syllabus. This means that objective test questions and 'data-response' material need to be part of the teaching process rather than things that are added on to a course presented in the traditional didactic way. It is common to find teachers complaining of the lack of time to give their pupils practice in answering multiple-choice and data-response questions when what is required is a little less direct instruction and more variety in the presentation of material.

Thirdly, they should practise the candidates in the techniques of writing essays. Paradoxically, although the skills that are required to write a good essay (namely, analytical ability, the ability to evaluate material and, most difficult of all, the ability to express an idea or an argument) are understood and beyond dispute, essay work in schools tends to be preoccupied with *knowledge* and *understanding*. All A-level examinations in economics give at least 50 per cent of the marks on the strength of essay work and therefore it makes sense to take essay writing seriously and not treat the essay as merely a vehicle for the communication of 'knowledge'.

These are simple measures that obviously cannot guarantee success for every candidate because the present system assumes that the results will be normally distributed with the pass mark around the value of the lower quartile. They should, however, contribute to the improvement of the fairness and the efficiency of the examination by ensuring that the candidates achieve their maximum performance.

Notes and references

1. *The Sunday Times*, 5 September 1982.
2. These changes have taken place since I contributed a chapter to *Teaching Economics* in 1974. The fact that this chapter is now revised should not be taken to indicate any change of view on my part. The previous essay still represents my general stance. The present chapter adds and expands certain topics.
3. For a discussion of this topic see Stiglitz, J., 'The theory of "screening", education and the distribution of income', *American Economic Review*, vol. 65, no. 2, 1975.
4. Ibid.
5. The logic of this taxonomy can best be illustrated by an example. Many candidates can define the price elasticity of demand (knowledge) but some would find difficulty in using elementary data to make a numerical estimate (comprehension). Fewer are likely to be able to recognize, say in a newspaper article, when the concept is relevant to understanding the writer's argument (application). The ability to draw an inference about the behaviour of total revenue or of market behaviour (analysis and synthesis) demands a higher ability, as does an appreciation of the use and value of the concept in making market forecasts (evaluation).

   Finally, the ability to express in one's own words an argument involving elasticity is the most difficult of all because it must depend on a thorough grasp of the concept, which is achieved only when the other skills have been mastered.
6. See Wilkinson, R.K., 'The use of data response material in teaching and examining', *Economics*, vol. 16, pt 3, no. 71, autumn 1980, pp. 69–74; Wilkinson, R.K., and Wilkinson, M., *Exercises in Economic Analysis: A Textbook of Data Response Questions* (Macmillan, forthcoming 1985) chs 1 and 2.
7. See Wilkinson, 'The use of data response material', op. cit.
8. The statistical criteria for accepting objective test items are the measure of 'facility' (i.e. the proportion of candidates obtaining the correct answer) and 'discrimination' (i.e. a measure of the degree of correlation between the score of candidates on an individual question and their overall score on the test, the expectation being that those who do best on the test will do best on any single question, and those who do worst on the test will tend to be worst on any individual question).
9. JMB, *Problems of the GCE Advanced Level Grading System*, 1983.

Further Reading

JMB Examinations Council, *General Certificate of Education Regulations and Syllabuses 1983, 1984. Social Studies.*

JMB, *Problems of the GCE Advanced Level Grading System*, 1983.

Stiglitz, J., 'The theory of "screening", education and the distribution of income', *American Economic Review*, vol. 65, no. 2, 1975.

Wilkinson, R.K., 'Problems of external assessment in economics', in Lee, N. (ed.), *Teaching Economics*, 2nd edn (Heinemann Educational Books, 1975).

—— 'N and F proposals for economics: a comment', *Economics*, vol. 15, pt 1, no. 65, spring 1979, pp. 20–22.

—— 'Comparative economics in examinations', *Economics*, vol. 19, pt 2, no. 82, summer 1983, pp. 60–63.

—— and Wilkinson, M., and Archer, C.A., *Exercises in Economic Analysis: A Textbook of Objective Test Questions* (Macmillan, 1984) chs 1–3.

Yates, J., 'An approach to economic education', in Cramer, J.S., *et al.*, *Relevance and Precision* (Samson/North Holland, 1976).

—— 'Research in economic education: are our horizons too narrow?' *The Journal of Economic Education*, vol. 10, no. 1, 1976.

Index

Topics and authors from the text have been indexed with the prime intention of assisting teachers, those engaged in teacher education or in research into education. As far as possible, issues relating to economics as an academic study have been indexed alphabetically under 'Economics knowledge', topics related to curriculum under 'Economics education' or 'Assessment' and issues related to methodologies of teaching under 'Teaching economics'. Where possible, entries include reference to key bibliographic notes and sources given at the end of each chapter.

The Editor would welcome comments on the index as, with access to microcomputer facilities, the Economics Association can make a particular effort to meet the needs of its readers.